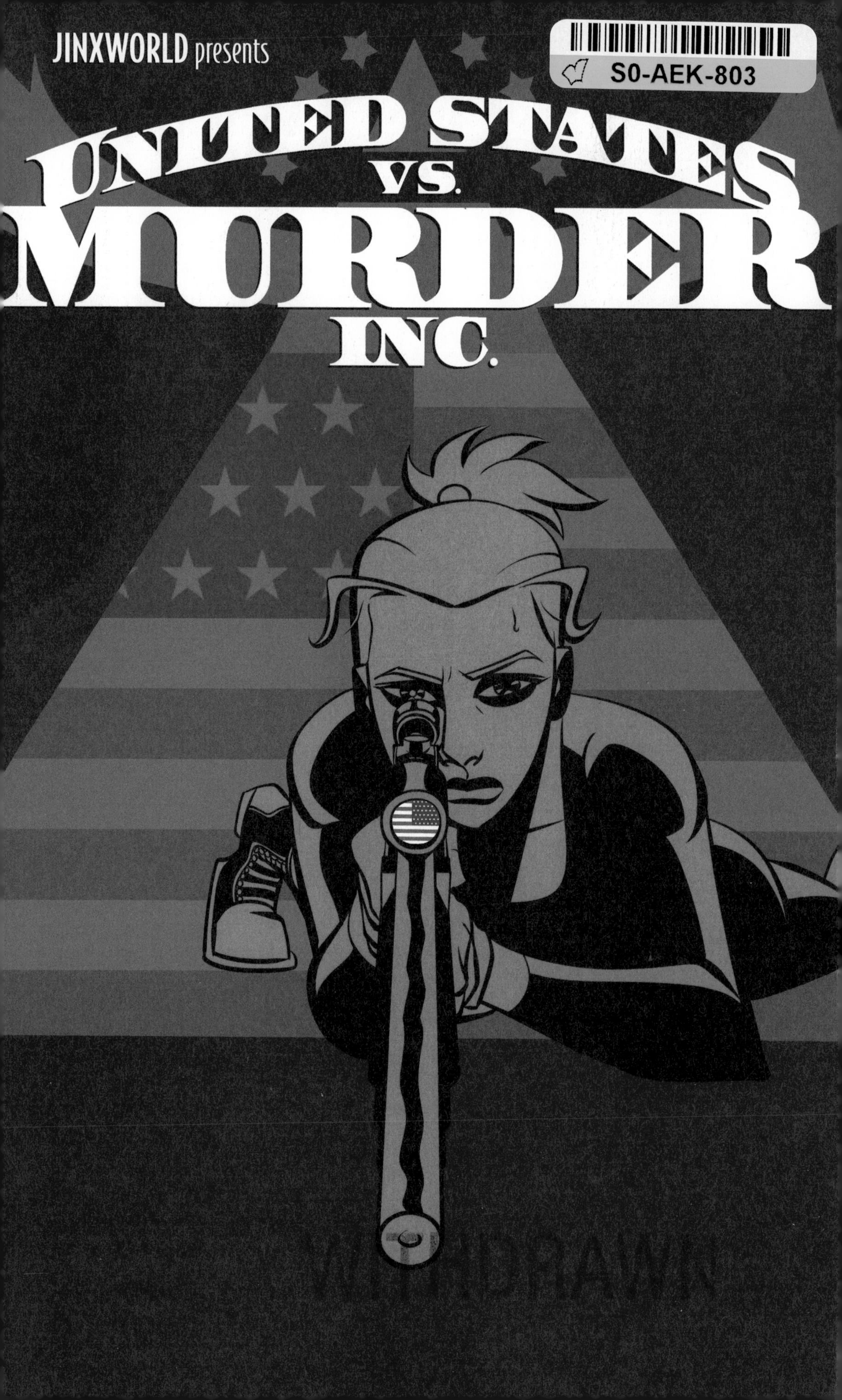
JINXWORLD presents
UNITED STATES VS. MURDER INC.

UNITED STATES VS. MURDER INC.

Created by
BRIAN MICHAEL BENDIS
& MICHAEL AVON OEMING

Colors:
TAKI SOMA

Letters:
CARLOS M. MANGUAL

Series and collection cover art:
MICHAEL AVON OEMING

Design:
CURTIS KING JR.

Editor:
MICHAEL McCALISTER

Publisher:
ALISA BENDIS

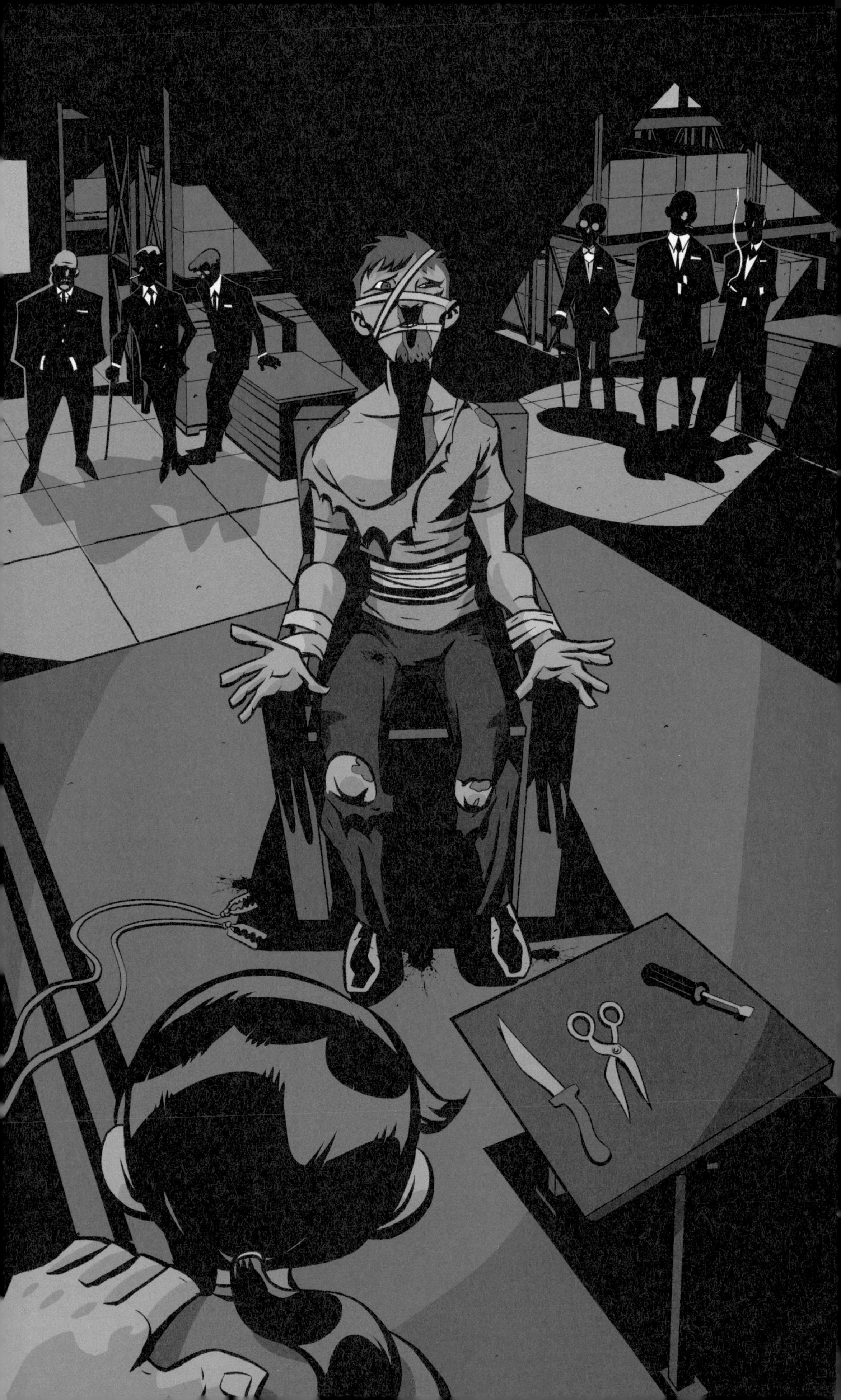

UNITED STATES VS. MURDER, INC. VOL. 1

Published by DC Comics. Compilation and all new material Copyright © 2019 Jinxworld, Inc. All Rights Reserved.

Originally published in single magazine form in UNITED STATES VS. MURDER, INC. 1-6. Copyright © 2018, 2019 Jinxworld, Inc. All Rights Reserved. United States vs. Murder, Inc., its logo design, the Jinxworld logo, all characters, their distinctive likenesses and related elements featured in this publication are trademarks of Jinxworld, Inc. The stories, characters and incidents featured in this publication are entirely fictional. DC Comics does not read or accept unsolicited submissions of ideas, stories or artwork.

PEFC Certified

This product is from sustainably managed forests and controlled sources

PEFC/29-31-337   www.pefc.org

DC Comics, 2900 West Alameda Ave., Burbank, CA 91505

Printed by LSC Communications, Owensville, MO, USA. 5/10/19.
First Printing. ISBN: 978-1-4012-9150-1
Library of Congress Cataloging-in-Publication Data is available.

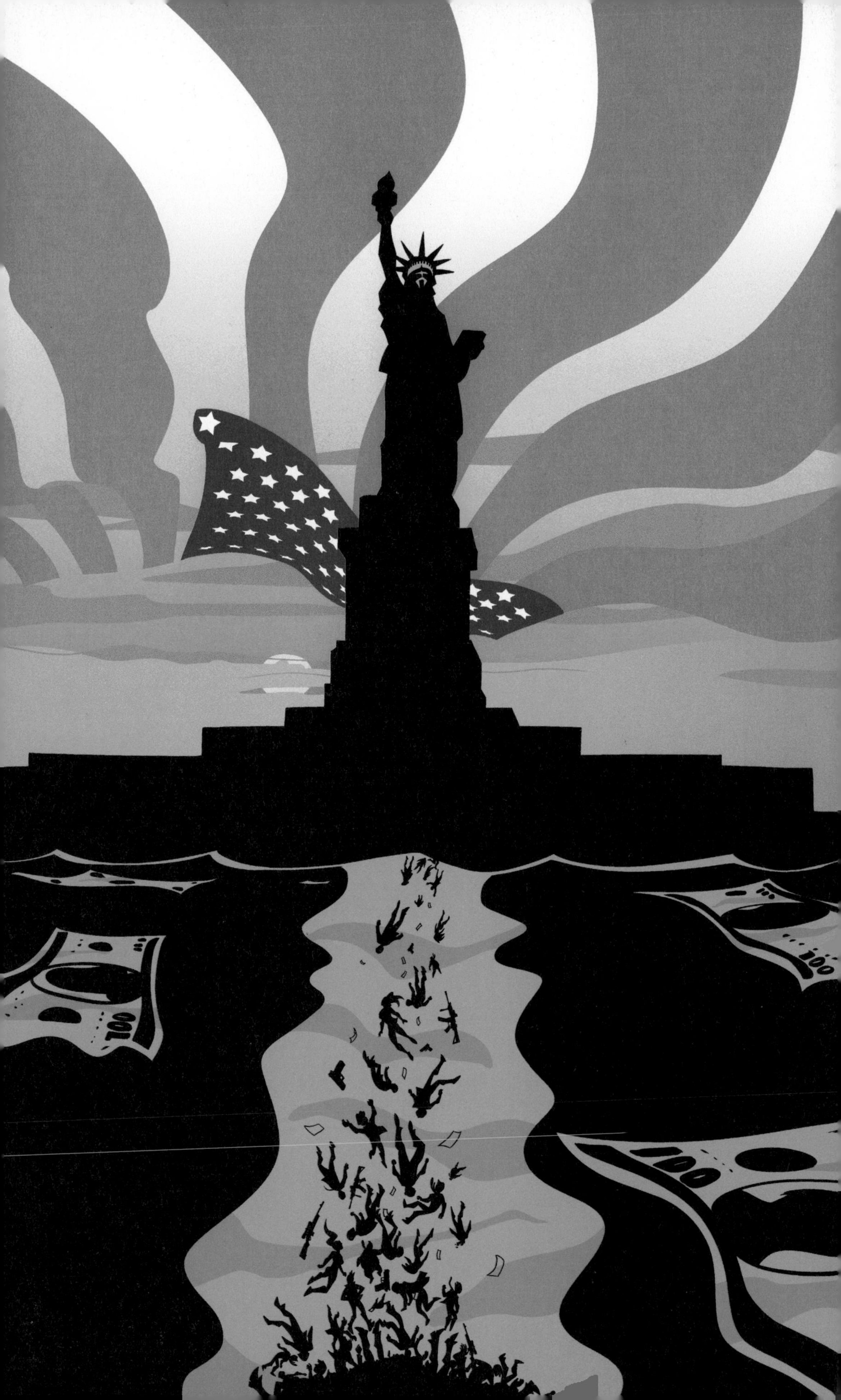

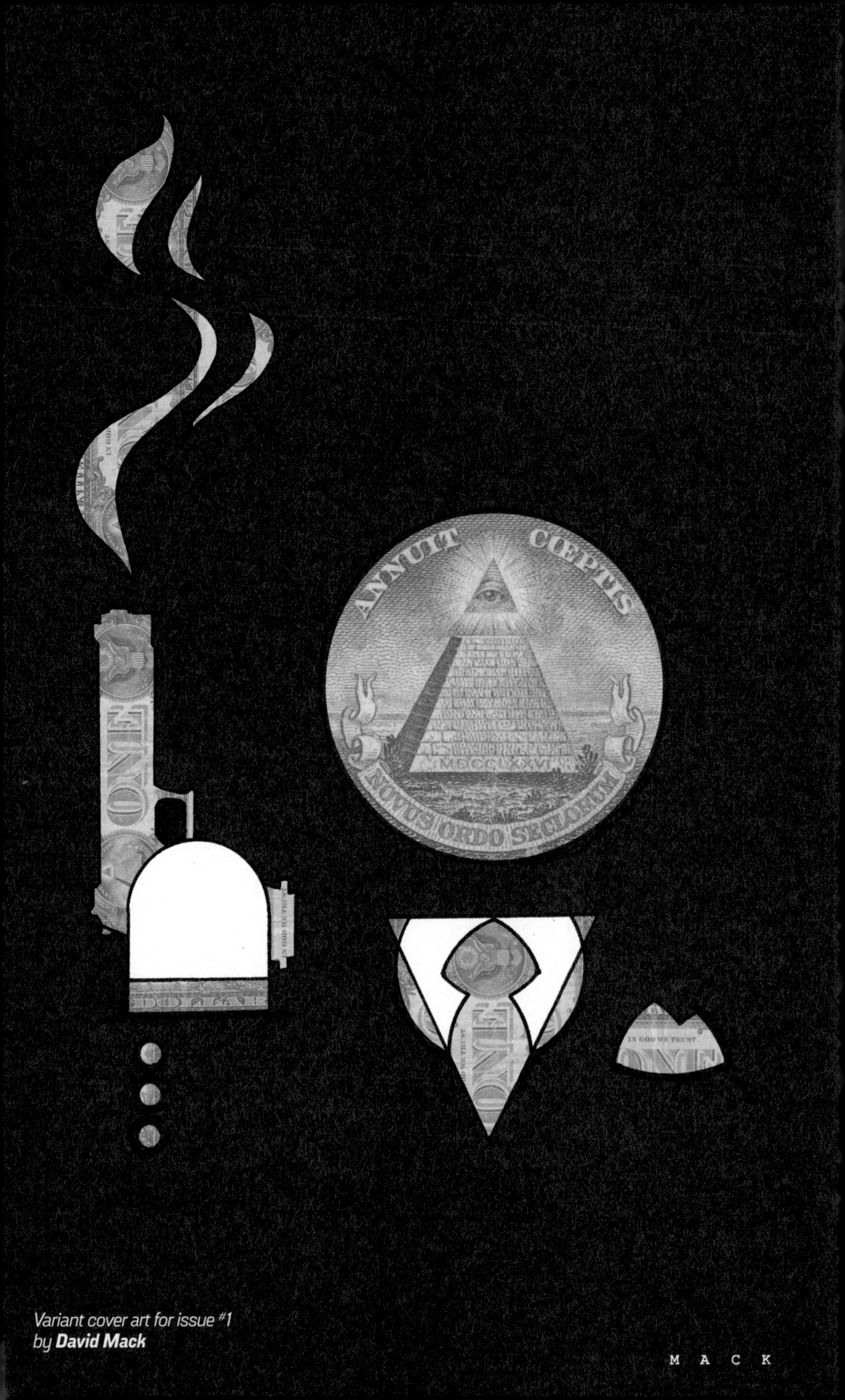
ANNUIT COEPTIS
MDCCLXXVI
NOVUS ORDO SECLORUM
IN GOD WE TRUST
ONE
DOLLAR
MACK

Variant cover art for issue #1
by ***David Mack***

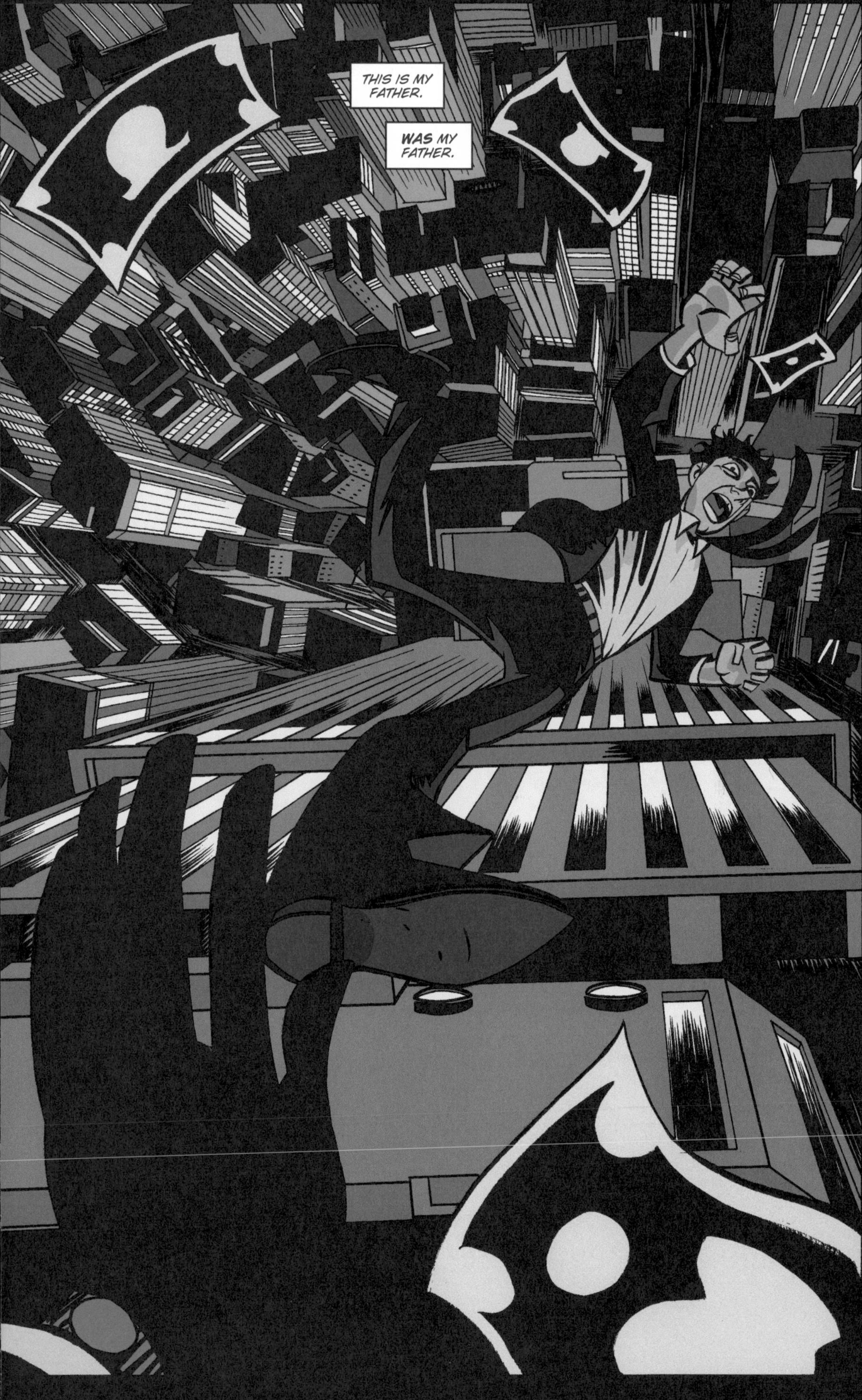
THIS IS MY FATHER.
WAS MY FATHER.

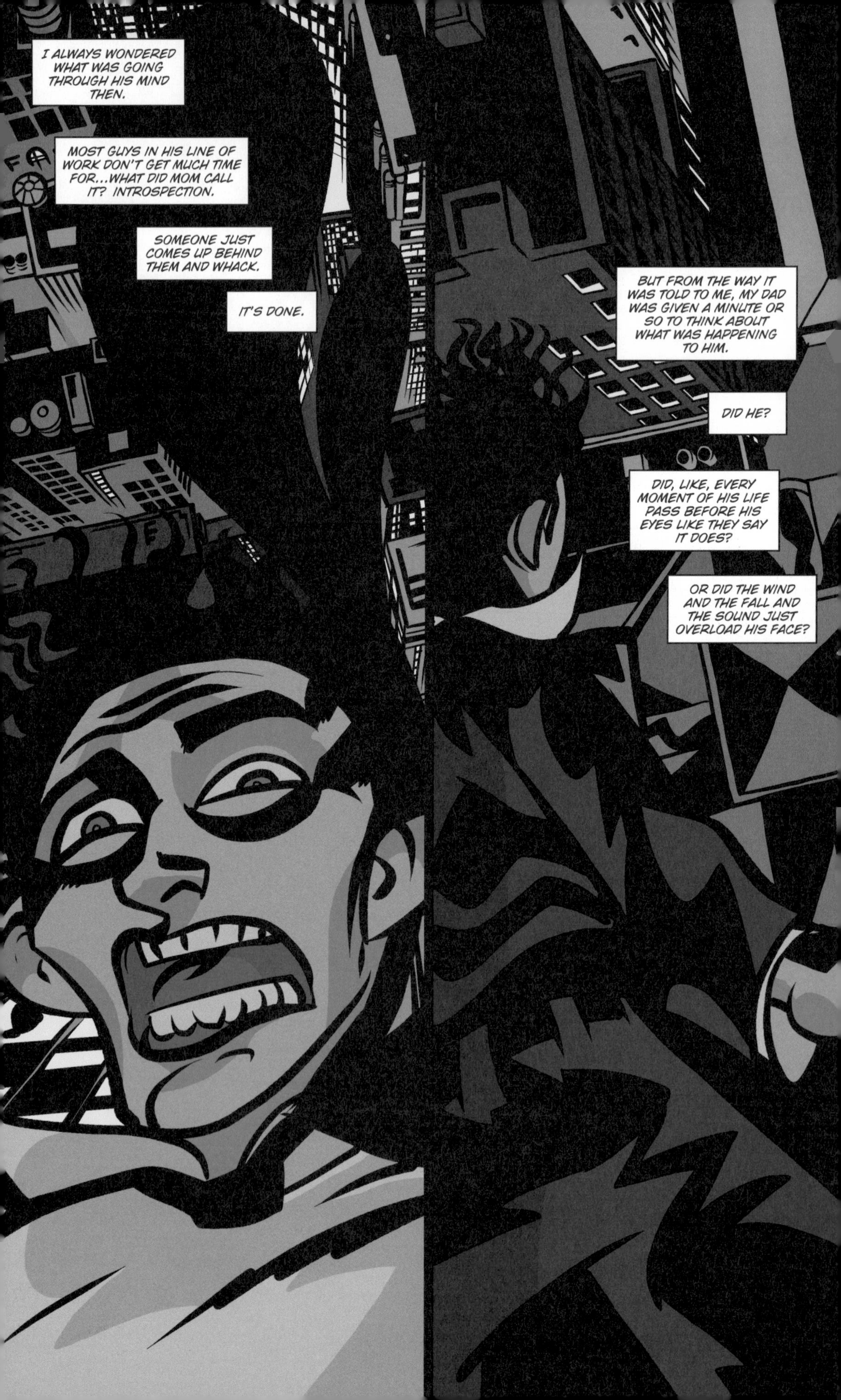
I ALWAYS WONDERED WHAT WAS GOING THROUGH HIS MIND THEN.
MOST GUYS IN HIS LINE OF WORK DON'T GET MUCH TIME FOR...WHAT DID MOM CALL IT? INTROSPECTION.
SOMEONE JUST COMES UP BEHIND THEM AND WHACK.
IT'S DONE.
BUT FROM THE WAY IT WAS TOLD TO ME, MY DAD WAS GIVEN A MINUTE OR SO TO THINK ABOUT WHAT WAS HAPPENING TO HIM.
DID HE?
DID, LIKE, EVERY MOMENT OF HIS LIFE PASS BEFORE HIS EYES LIKE THEY SAY IT DOES?
OR DID THE WIND AND THE FALL AND THE SOUND JUST OVERLOAD HIS FACE?

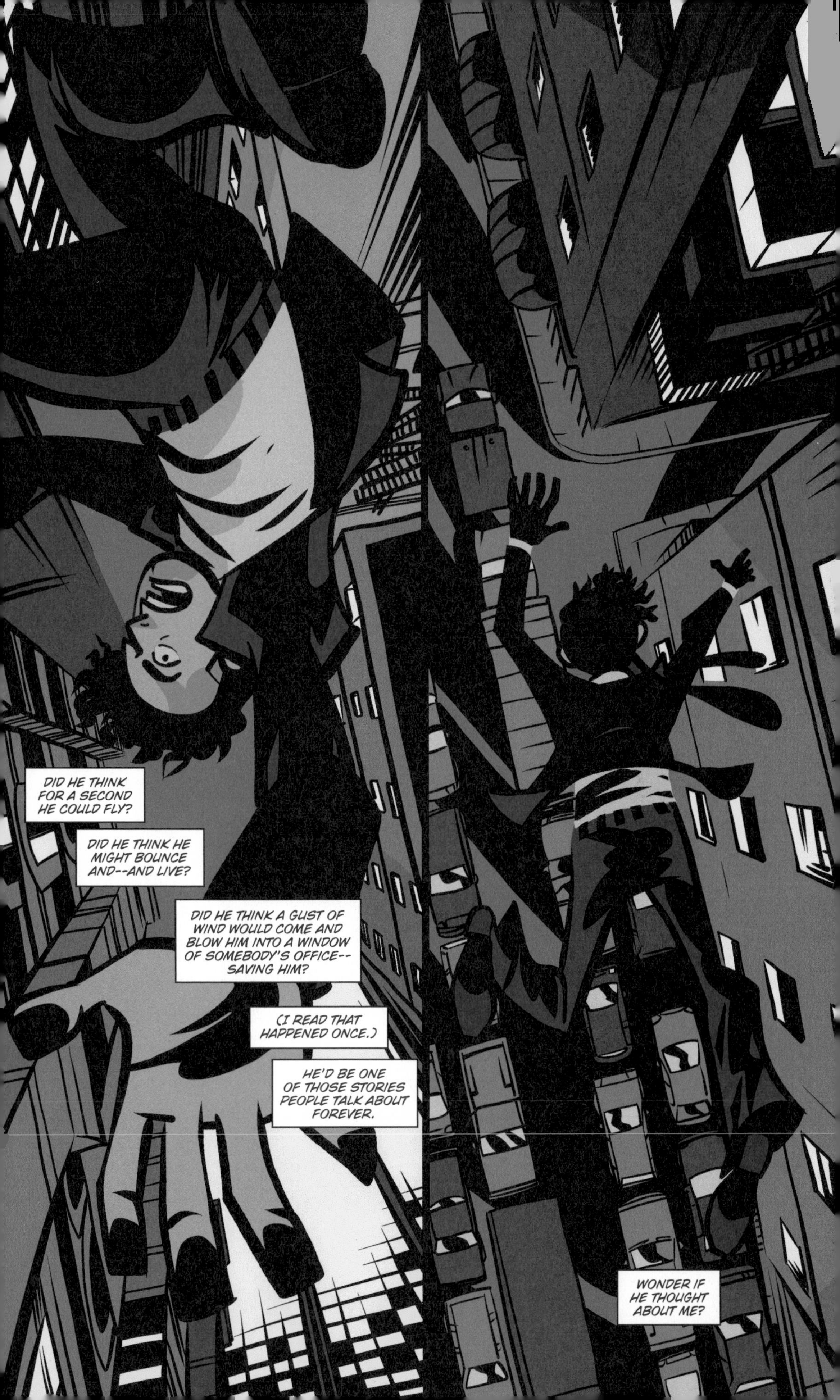
DID HE THINK FOR A SECOND HE COULD FLY?
DID HE THINK HE MIGHT BOUNCE AND--AND LIVE?
DID HE THINK A GUST OF WIND WOULD COME AND BLOW HIM INTO A WINDOW OF SOMEBODY'S OFFICE-- SAVING HIM?
(I READ THAT HAPPENED ONCE.)
HE'D BE ONE OF THOSE STORIES PEOPLE TALK ABOUT FOREVER.
WONDER IF HE THOUGHT ABOUT ME?

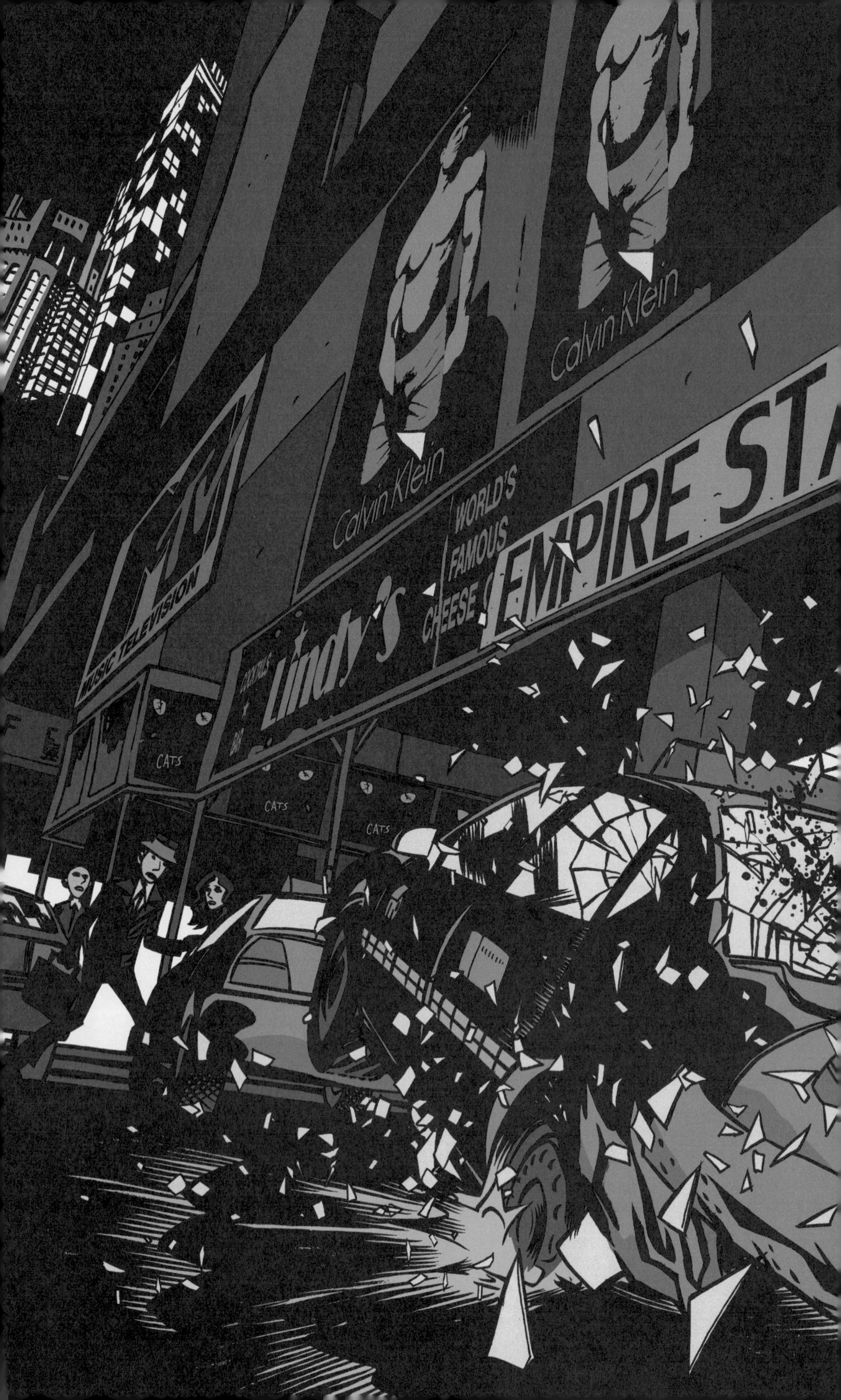

Calvin Klein
Calvin Klein
MUSIC TELEVISION
Lindy's
WORLD'S FAMOUS CHEESE
EMPIRE STA
CATS
CATS
CATS

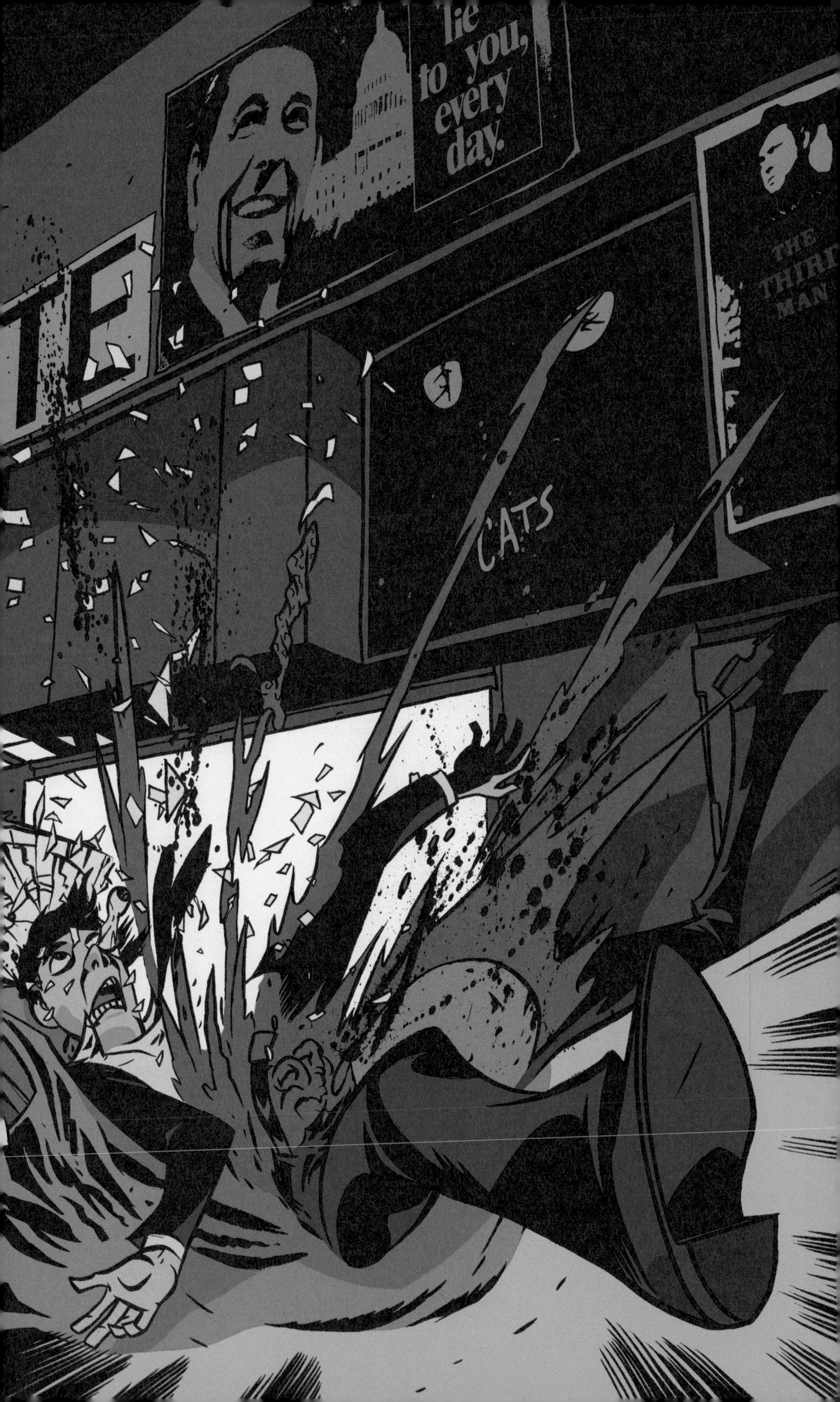

lie
to you,
every
day.
TE
CATS
THE
THIRD
MAN

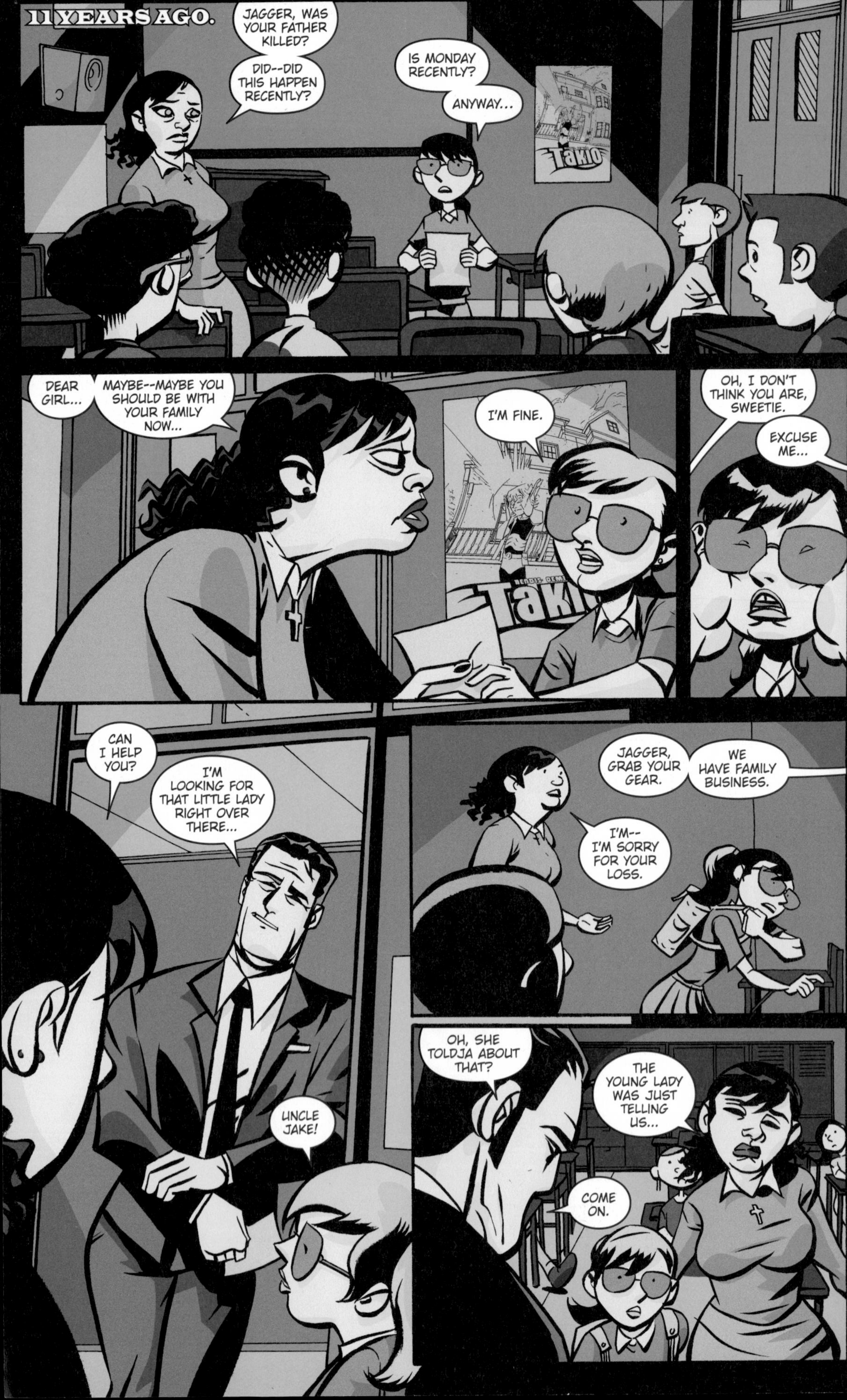
11 YEARS AGO.
JAGGER, WAS YOUR FATHER KILLED?
DID--DID THIS HAPPEN RECENTLY?
IS MONDAY RECENTLY?
ANYWAY...
DEAR GIRL...
MAYBE--MAYBE YOU SHOULD BE WITH YOUR FAMILY NOW...
I'M FINE.
OH, I DON'T THINK YOU ARE, SWEETIE.
EXCUSE ME...
CAN I HELP YOU?
I'M LOOKING FOR THAT LITTLE LADY RIGHT OVER THERE...
UNCLE JAKE!
JAGGER, GRAB YOUR GEAR.
WE HAVE FAMILY BUSINESS.
I'M-- I'M SORRY FOR YOUR LOSS.
OH, SHE TOLDJA ABOUT THAT?
THE YOUNG LADY WAS JUST TELLING US...
COME ON.

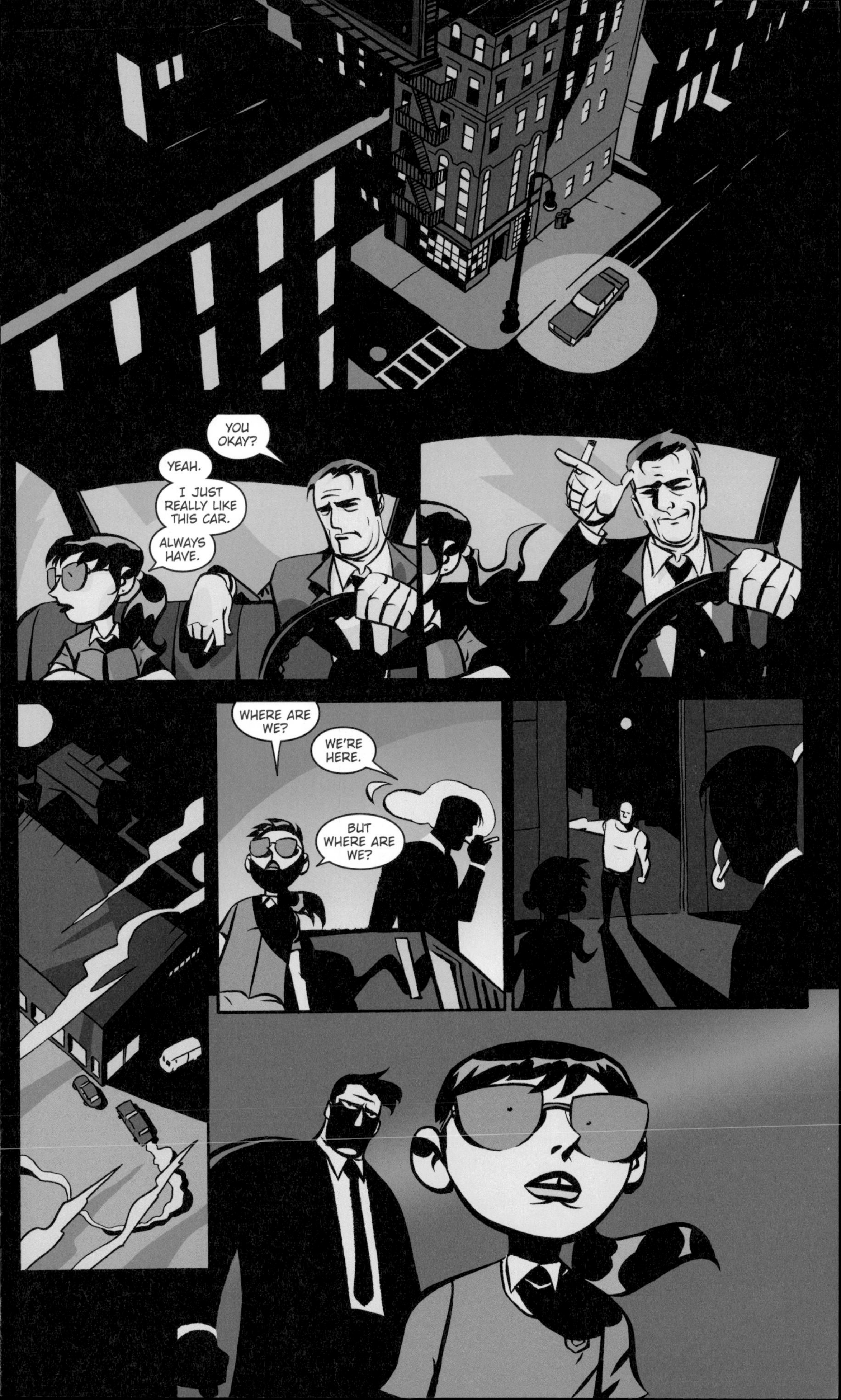

YOU OKAY?
YEAH.
I JUST REALLY LIKE THIS CAR.
ALWAYS HAVE.
WHERE ARE WE?
WE'RE HERE.
BUT WHERE ARE WE?

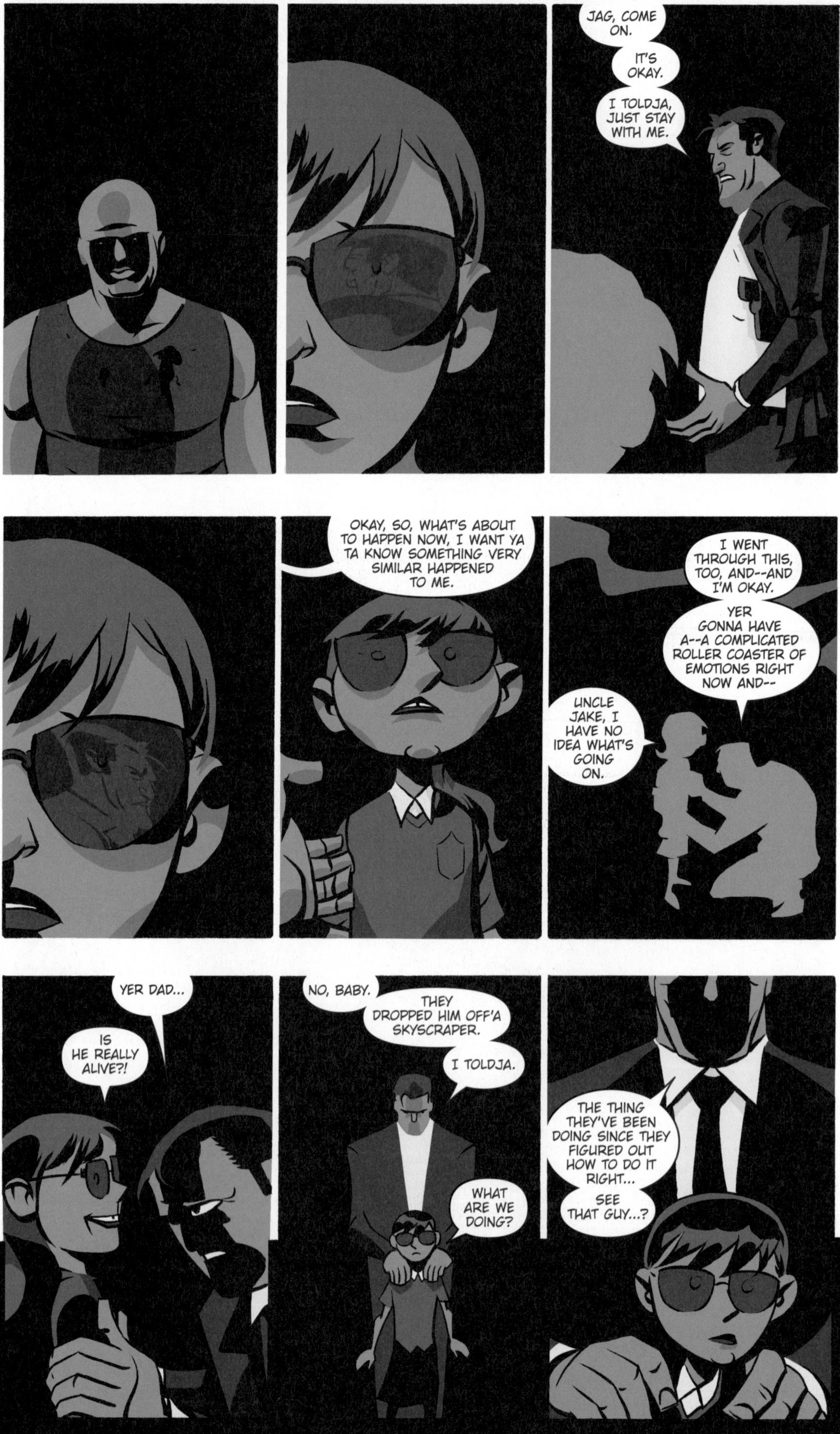
JAG, COME ON.
IT'S OKAY.
I TOLDJA, JUST STAY WITH ME.
OKAY, SO, WHAT'S ABOUT TO HAPPEN NOW, I WANT YA TA KNOW SOMETHING VERY SIMILAR HAPPENED TO ME.
I WENT THROUGH THIS, TOO, AND--AND I'M OKAY.
YER GONNA HAVE A--A COMPLICATED ROLLER COASTER OF EMOTIONS RIGHT NOW AND--
UNCLE JAKE, I HAVE NO IDEA WHAT'S GOING ON.
YER DAD...
IS HE REALLY ALIVE?!
NO, BABY.
THEY DROPPED HIM OFF'A SKYSCRAPER.
I TOLDJA.
WHAT ARE WE DOING?
THE THING THEY'VE BEEN DOING SINCE THEY FIGURED OUT HOW TO DO IT RIGHT...
SEE THAT GUY...?

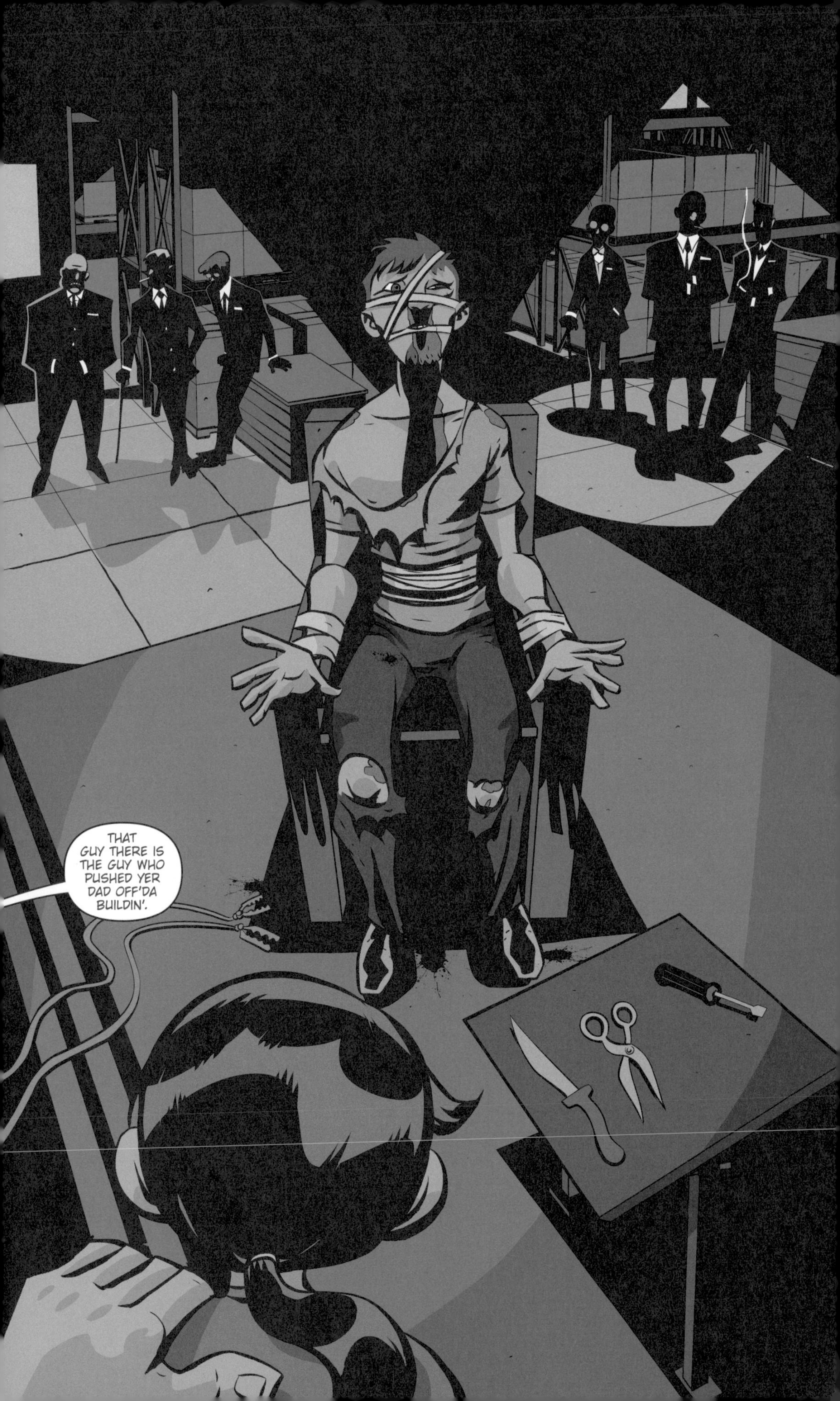
THAT GUY THERE IS THE GUY WHO PUSHED YER DAD OFF'DA BUILDIN'.

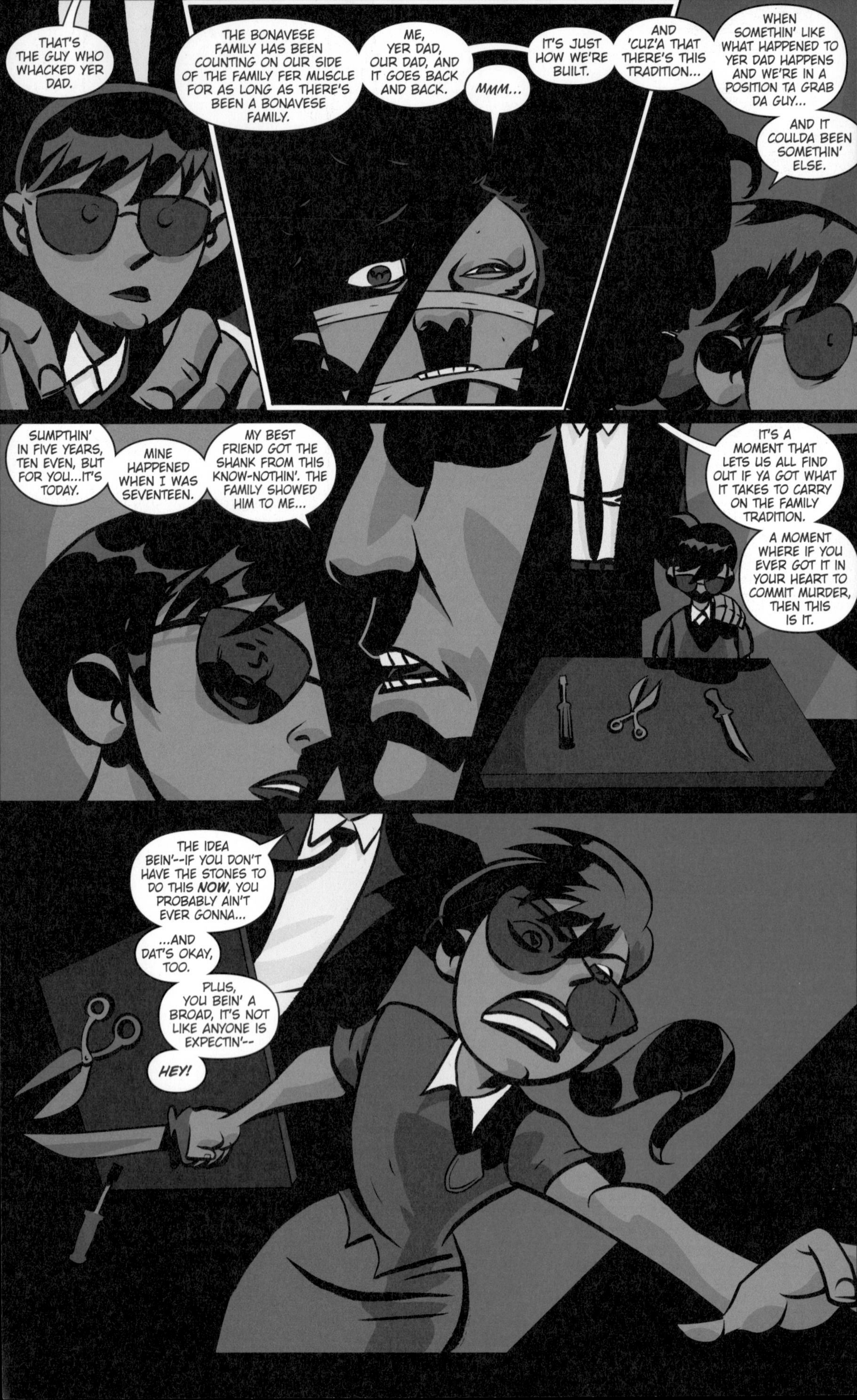
THAT'S THE GUY WHO WHACKED YER DAD.
THE BONAVESE FAMILY HAS BEEN COUNTING ON OUR SIDE OF THE FAMILY FER MUSCLE FOR AS LONG AS THERE'S BEEN A BONAVESE FAMILY.
ME, YER DAD, OUR DAD, AND IT GOES BACK AND BACK.
MMM...
IT'S JUST HOW WE'RE BUILT.
AND 'CUZ'A THAT THERE'S THIS TRADITION...
WHEN SOMETHIN' LIKE WHAT HAPPENED TO YER DAD HAPPENS AND WE'RE IN A POSITION TA GRAB DA GUY...
AND IT COULDA BEEN SOMETHIN' ELSE.
SUMPTHIN' IN FIVE YEARS, TEN EVEN, BUT FOR YOU...IT'S TODAY.
MINE HAPPENED WHEN I WAS SEVENTEEN.
MY BEST FRIEND GOT THE SHANK FROM THIS KNOW-NOTHIN'. THE FAMILY SHOWED HIM TO ME...
IT'S A MOMENT THAT LETS US ALL FIND OUT IF YA GOT WHAT IT TAKES TO CARRY ON THE FAMILY TRADITION.
A MOMENT WHERE IF YOU EVER GOT IT IN YOUR HEART TO COMMIT MURDER, THEN THIS IS IT.
THE IDEA BEIN'--IF YOU DON'T HAVE THE STONES TO DO THIS NOW, YOU PROBABLY AIN'T EVER GONNA...
...AND DAT'S OKAY, TOO.
PLUS, YOU BEIN' A BROAD, IT'S NOT LIKE ANYONE IS EXPECTIN'--
HEY!

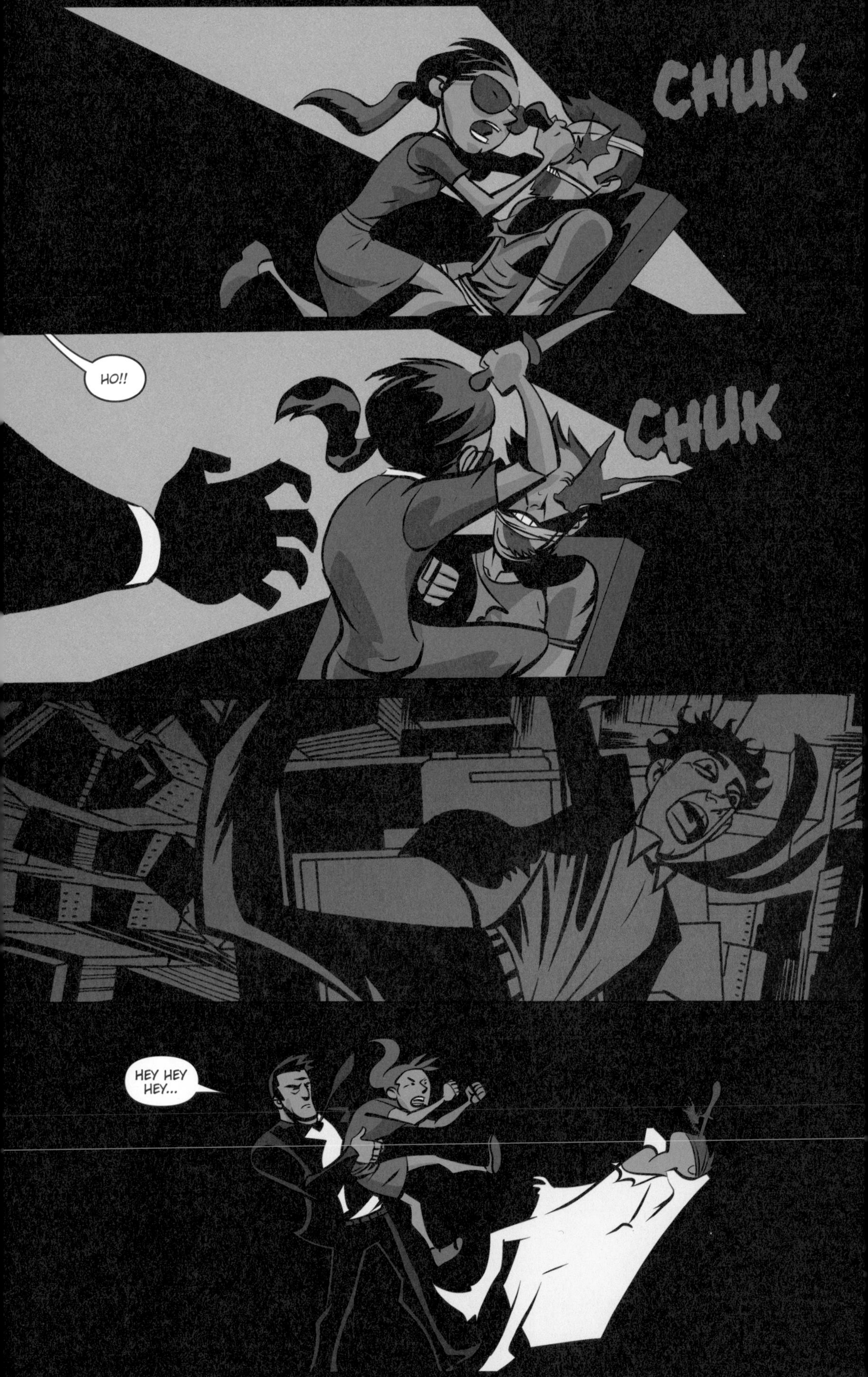
CHUK
HO!!
CHUK
HEY HEY HEY...

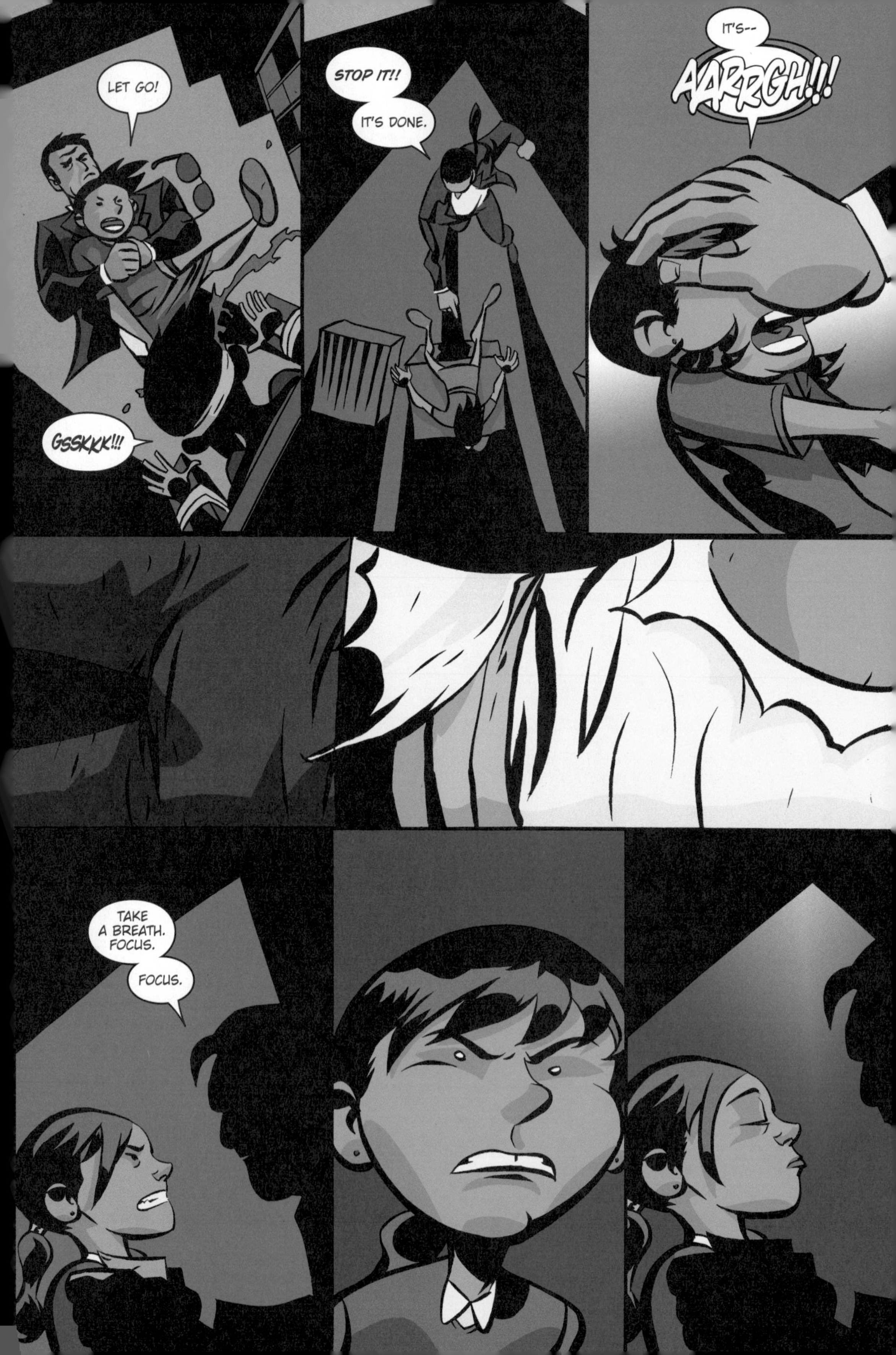
LET GO!
GSSKKK!!!
STOP IT!!
IT'S DONE.
IT'S--
AARRGH!!!
TAKE A BREATH. FOCUS.
FOCUS.

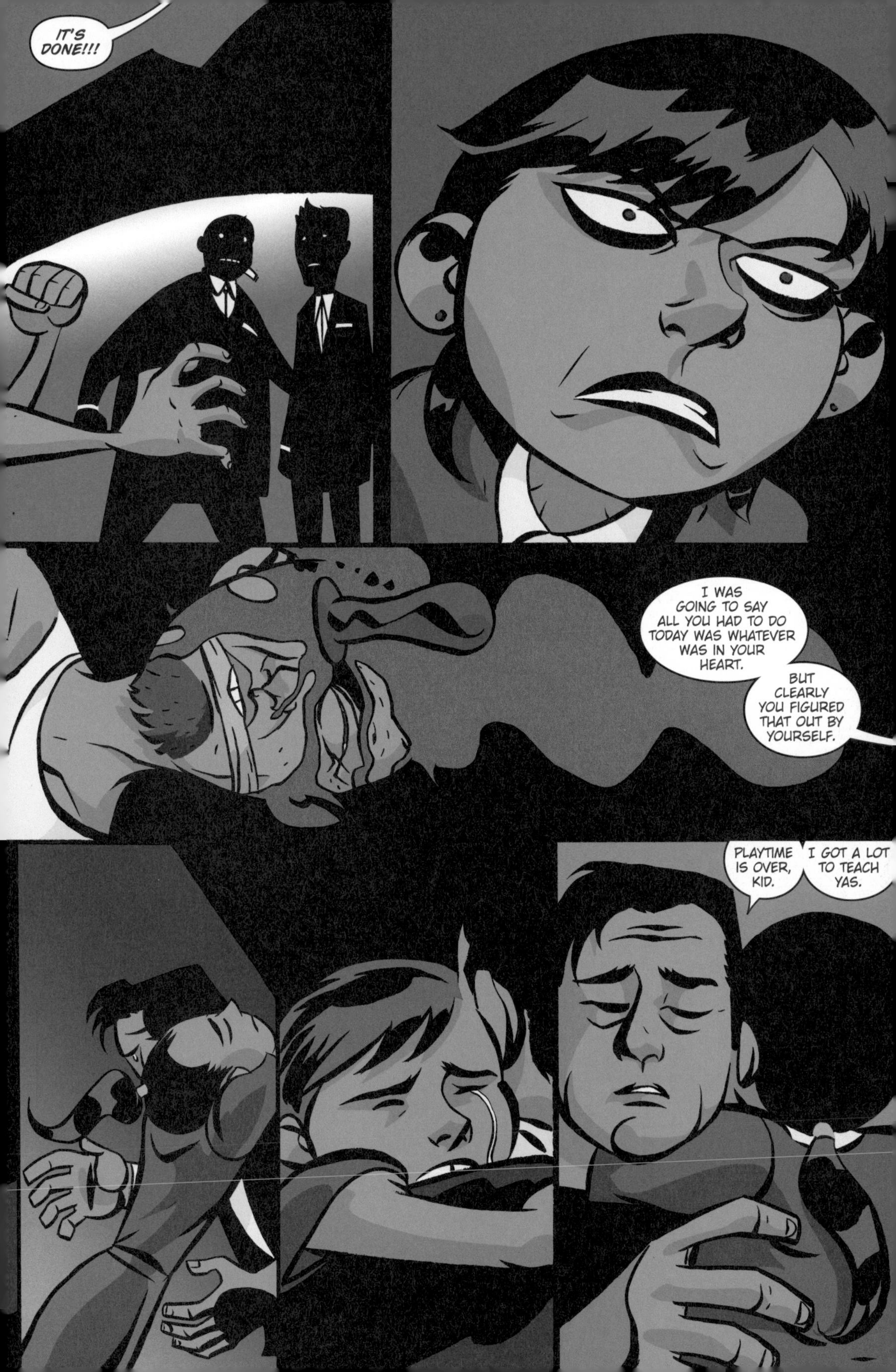
IT'S DONE!!!
I WAS GOING TO SAY ALL YOU HAD TO DO TODAY WAS WHATEVER WAS IN YOUR HEART.
BUT CLEARLY YOU FIGURED THAT OUT BY YOURSELF.
PLAYTIME IS OVER, KID.
I GOT A LOT TO TEACH YAS.

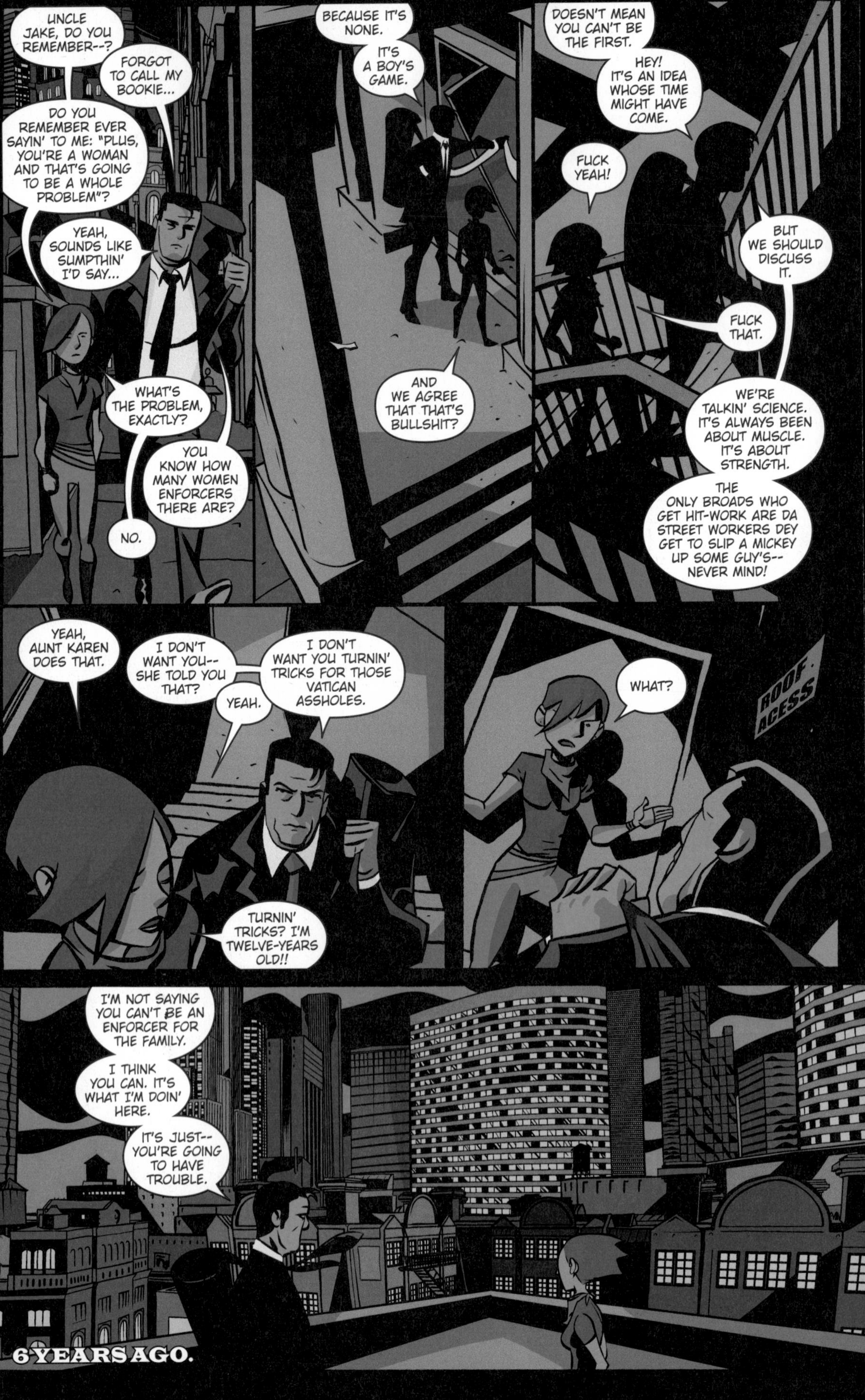
UNCLE JAKE, DO YOU REMEMBER--?
FORGOT TO CALL MY BOOKIE...
DO YOU REMEMBER EVER SAYIN' TO ME: "PLUS, YOU'RE A WOMAN AND THAT'S GOING TO BE A WHOLE PROBLEM"?
YEAH, SOUNDS LIKE SUMPTHIN' I'D SAY...
WHAT'S THE PROBLEM, EXACTLY?
YOU KNOW HOW MANY WOMEN ENFORCERS THERE ARE?
NO.
BECAUSE IT'S NONE.
IT'S A BOY'S GAME.
AND WE AGREE THAT THAT'S BULLSHIT?
DOESN'T MEAN YOU CAN'T BE THE FIRST.
HEY! IT'S AN IDEA WHOSE TIME MIGHT HAVE COME.
FUCK YEAH!
BUT WE SHOULD DISCUSS IT.
FUCK THAT.
WE'RE TALKIN' SCIENCE. IT'S ALWAYS BEEN ABOUT MUSCLE. IT'S ABOUT STRENGTH.
THE ONLY BROADS WHO GET HIT-WORK ARE DA STREET WORKERS DEY GET TO SLIP A MICKEY UP SOME GUY'S-- NEVER MIND!
YEAH, AUNT KAREN DOES THAT.
I DON'T WANT YOU-- SHE TOLD YOU THAT?
YEAH.
I DON'T WANT YOU TURNIN' TRICKS FOR THOSE VATICAN ASSHOLES.
TURNIN' TRICKS? I'M TWELVE-YEARS OLD!!
WHAT?
ROOF ACESS
I'M NOT SAYING YOU CAN'T BE AN ENFORCER FOR THE FAMILY.
I THINK YOU CAN. IT'S WHAT I'M DOIN' HERE.
IT'S JUST-- YOU'RE GOING TO HAVE TROUBLE.
6 YEARS AGO.

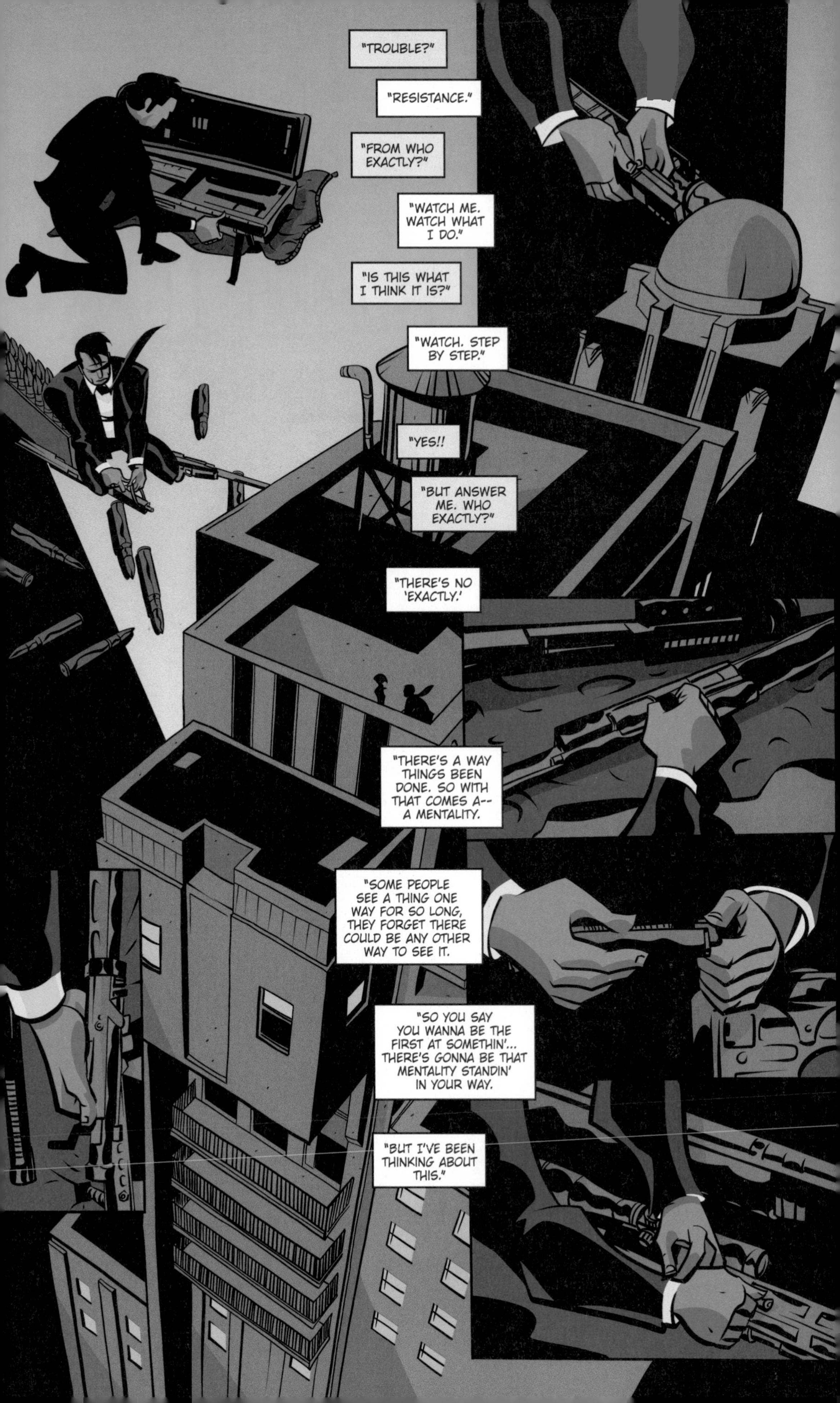
"TROUBLE?"
"RESISTANCE."
"FROM WHO EXACTLY?"
"WATCH ME. WATCH WHAT I DO."
"IS THIS WHAT I THINK IT IS?"
"WATCH. STEP BY STEP."
"YES!!
"BUT ANSWER ME. WHO EXACTLY?"
"THERE'S NO 'EXACTLY.'
"THERE'S A WAY THINGS BEEN DONE. SO WITH THAT COMES A-- A MENTALITY.
"SOME PEOPLE SEE A THING ONE WAY FOR SO LONG, THEY FORGET THERE COULD BE ANY OTHER WAY TO SEE IT.
"SO YOU SAY YOU WANNA BE THE FIRST AT SOMETHIN'... THERE'S GONNA BE THAT MENTALITY STANDIN' IN YOUR WAY.
"BUT I'VE BEEN THINKING ABOUT THIS."

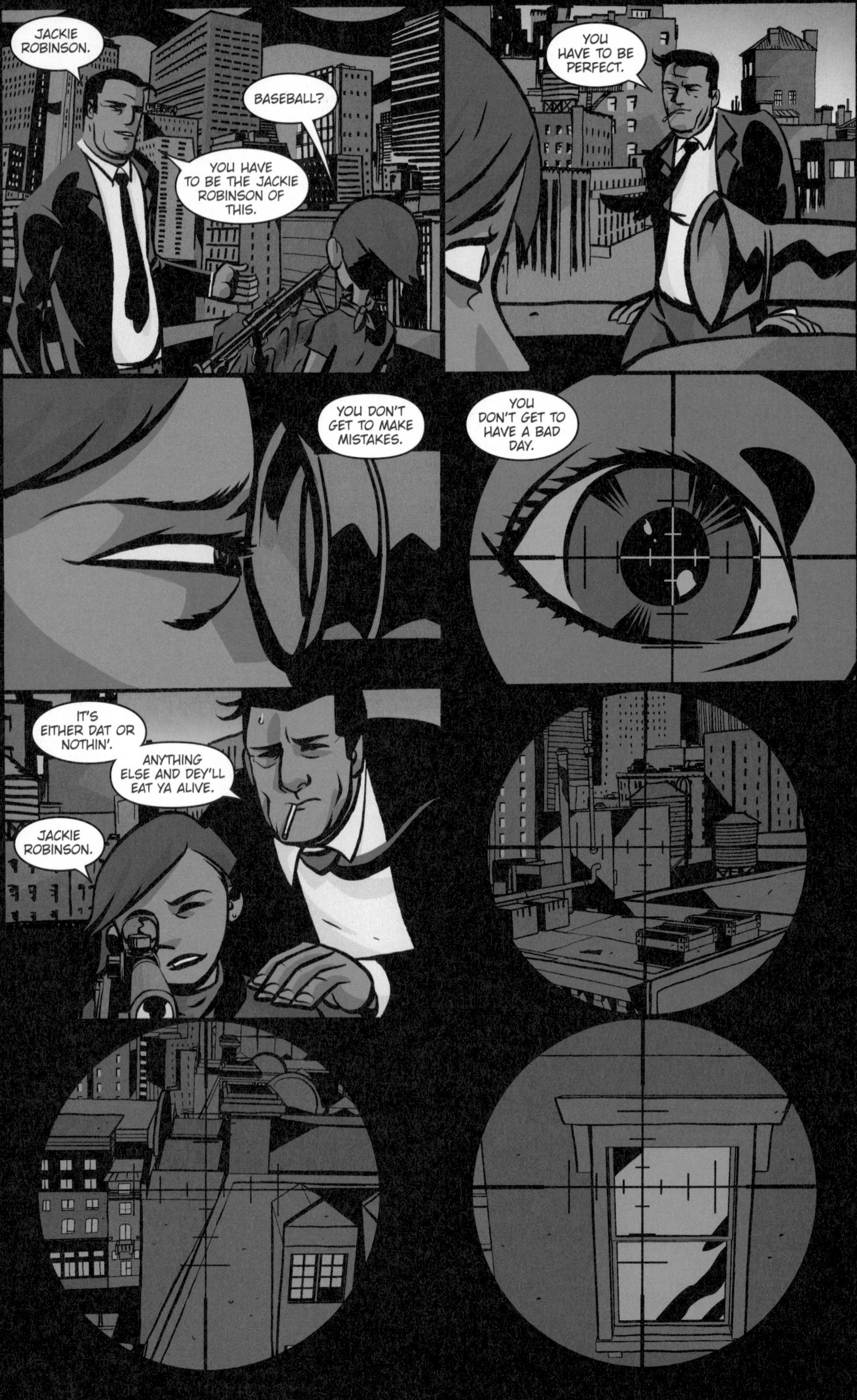
JACKIE ROBINSON.
BASEBALL?
YOU HAVE TO BE THE JACKIE ROBINSON OF THIS.
YOU HAVE TO BE PERFECT.
YOU DON'T GET TO MAKE MISTAKES.
YOU DON'T GET TO HAVE A BAD DAY.
IT'S EITHER DAT OR NOTHIN'.
ANYTHING ELSE AND DEY'LL EAT YA ALIVE.
JACKIE ROBINSON.

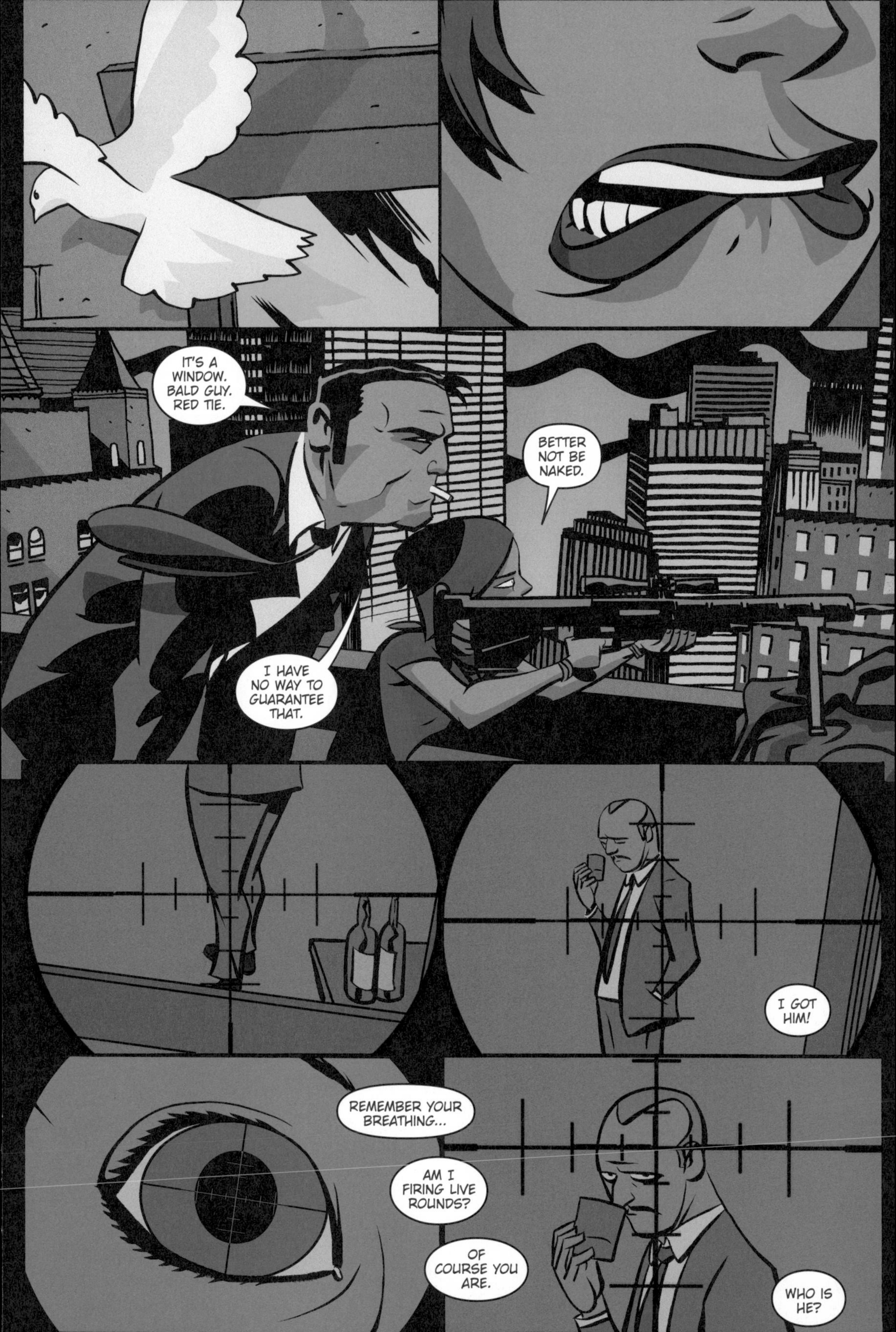
IT'S A WINDOW. BALD GUY. RED TIE.
BETTER NOT BE NAKED.
I HAVE NO WAY TO GUARANTEE THAT.
I GOT HIM!
REMEMBER YOUR BREATHING...
AM I FIRING LIVE ROUNDS?
OF COURSE YOU ARE.
WHO IS HE?

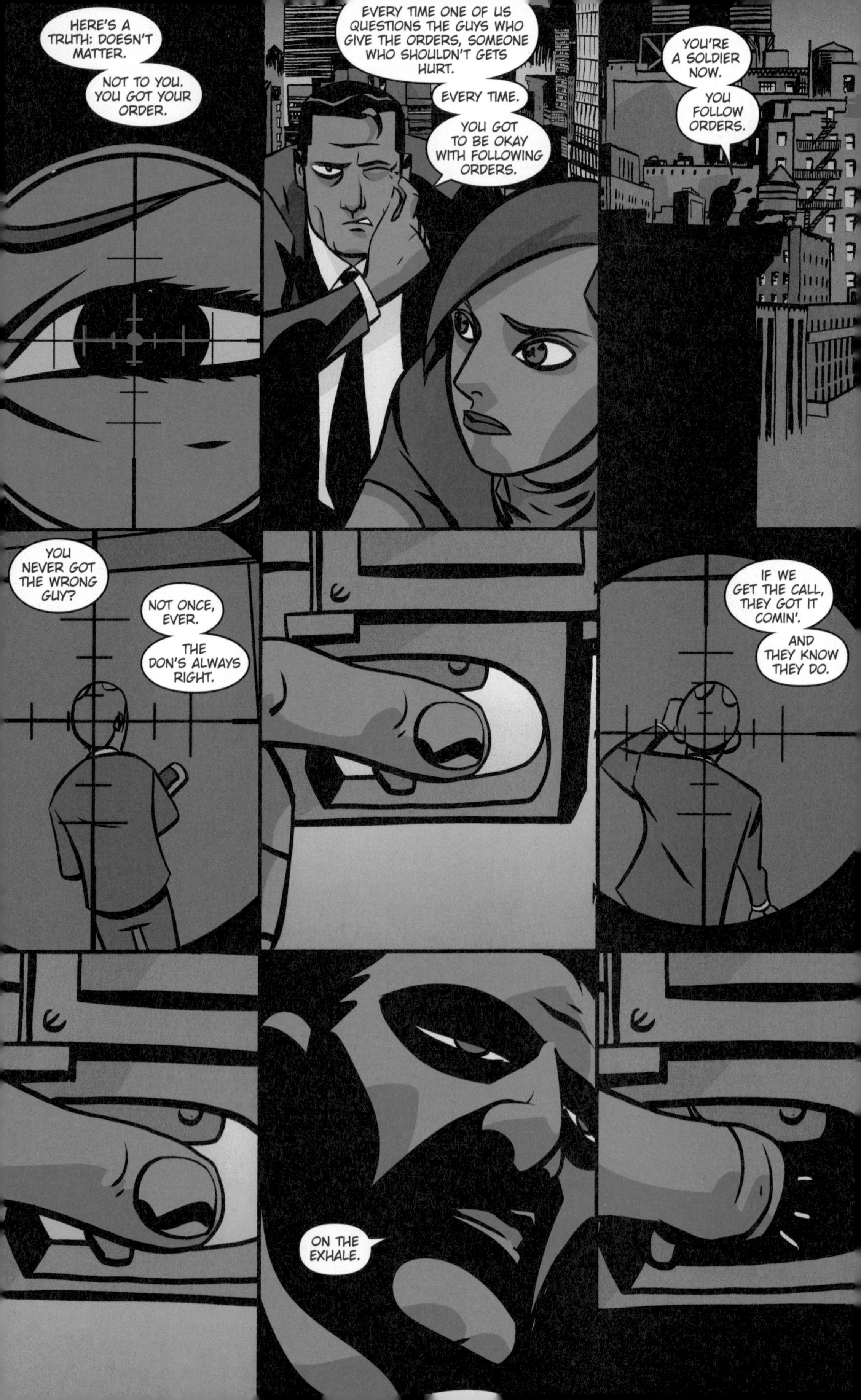
HERE'S A TRUTH: DOESN'T MATTER.
NOT TO YOU. YOU GOT YOUR ORDER.
EVERY TIME ONE OF US QUESTIONS THE GUYS WHO GIVE THE ORDERS, SOMEONE WHO SHOULDN'T GETS HURT.
EVERY TIME.
YOU GOT TO BE OKAY WITH FOLLOWING ORDERS.
YOU'RE A SOLDIER NOW.
YOU FOLLOW ORDERS.
YOU NEVER GOT THE WRONG GUY?
NOT ONCE, EVER.
THE DON'S ALWAYS RIGHT.
IF WE GET THE CALL, THEY GOT IT COMIN'.
AND THEY KNOW THEY DO.
ON THE EXHALE.

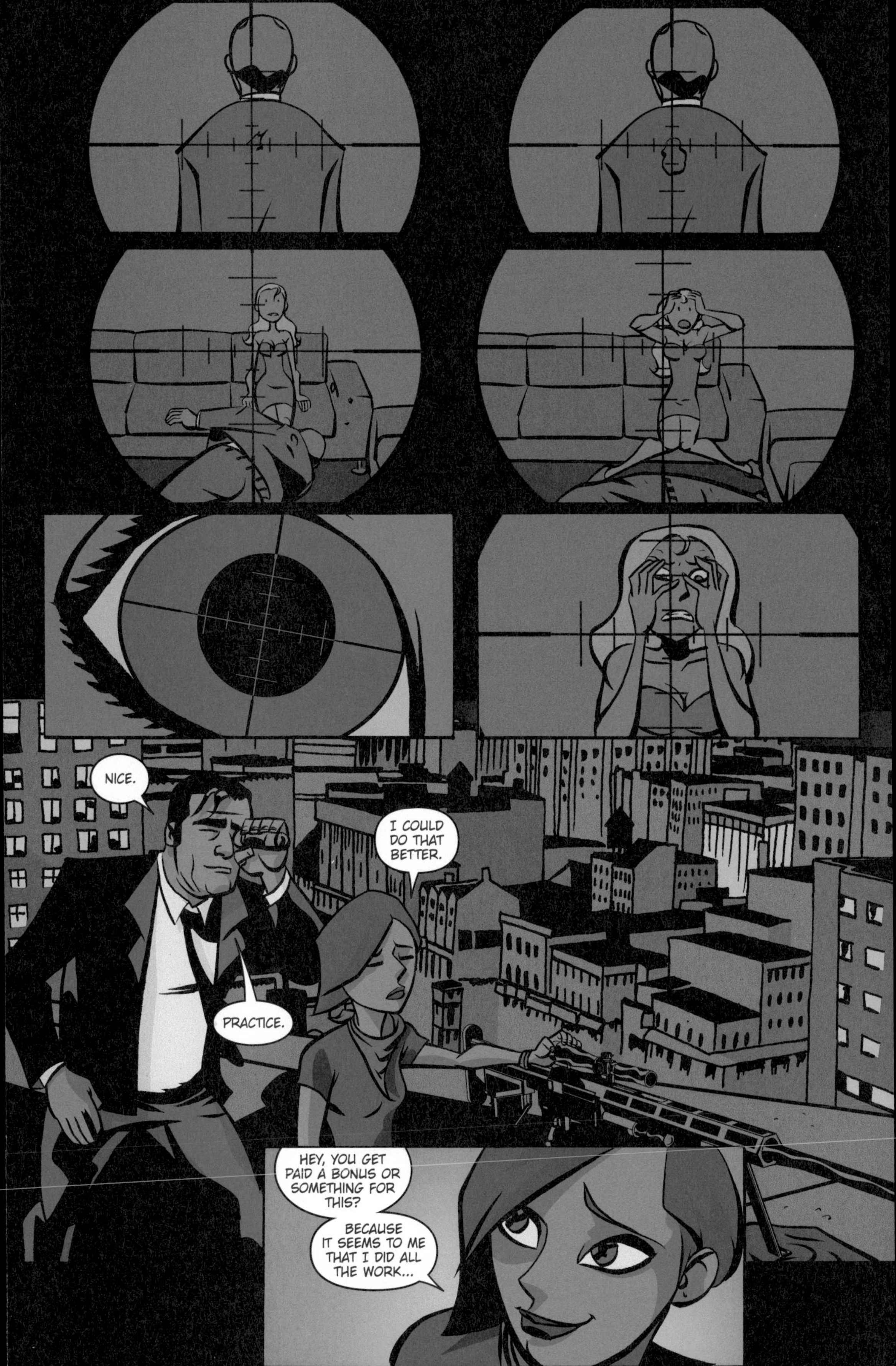
NICE.
I COULD DO THAT BETTER.
PRACTICE.
HEY, YOU GET PAID A BONUS OR SOMETHING FOR THIS?
BECAUSE IT SEEMS TO ME THAT I DID ALL THE WORK...

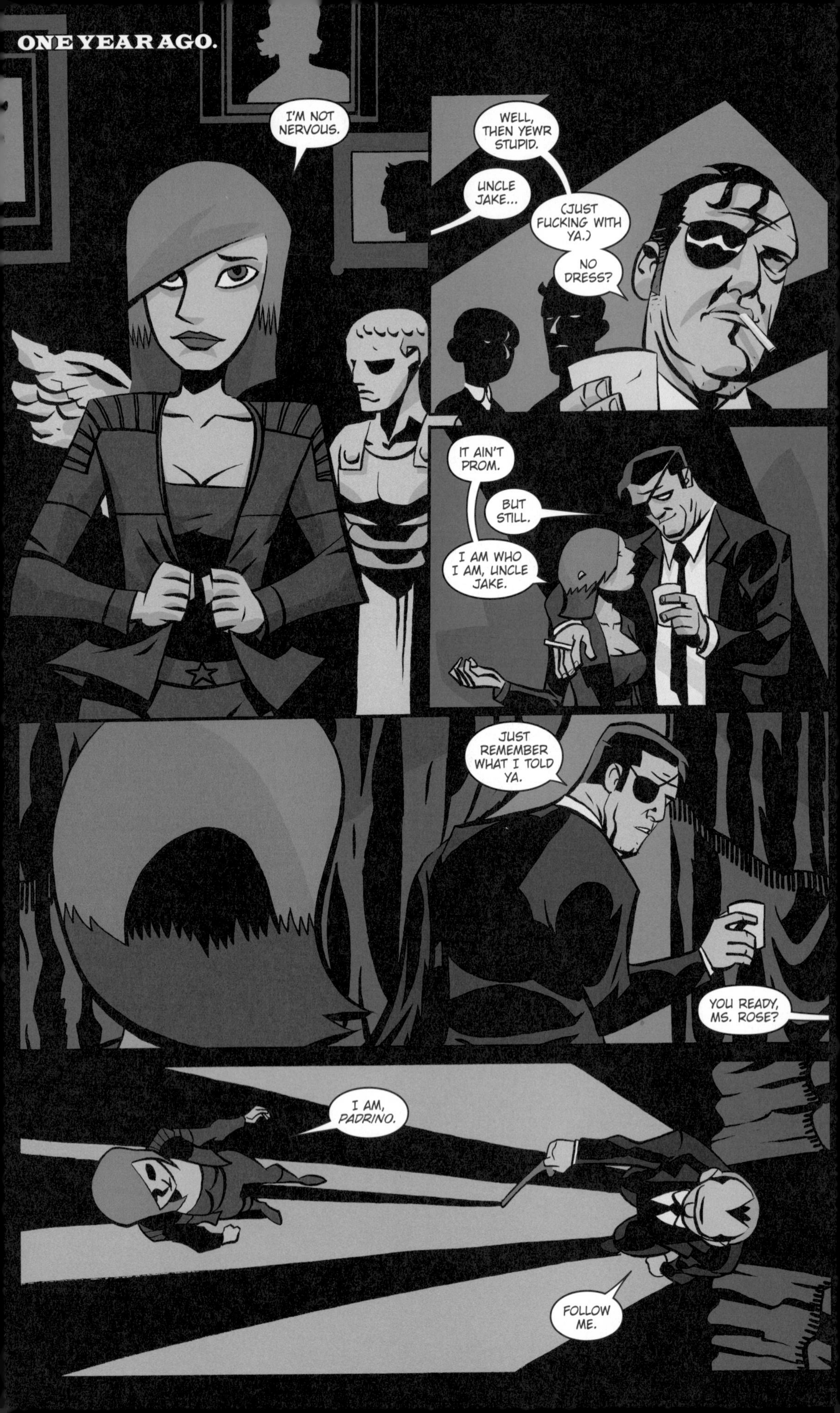
ONE YEAR AGO.
I'M NOT NERVOUS.
WELL, THEN YEWR STUPID.
UNCLE JAKE...
(JUST FUCKING WITH YA.)
NO DRESS?
IT AIN'T PROM.
BUT STILL.
I AM WHO I AM, UNCLE JAKE.
JUST REMEMBER WHAT I TOLD YA.
YOU READY, MS. ROSE?
I AM, *PADRINO.*
FOLLOW ME.

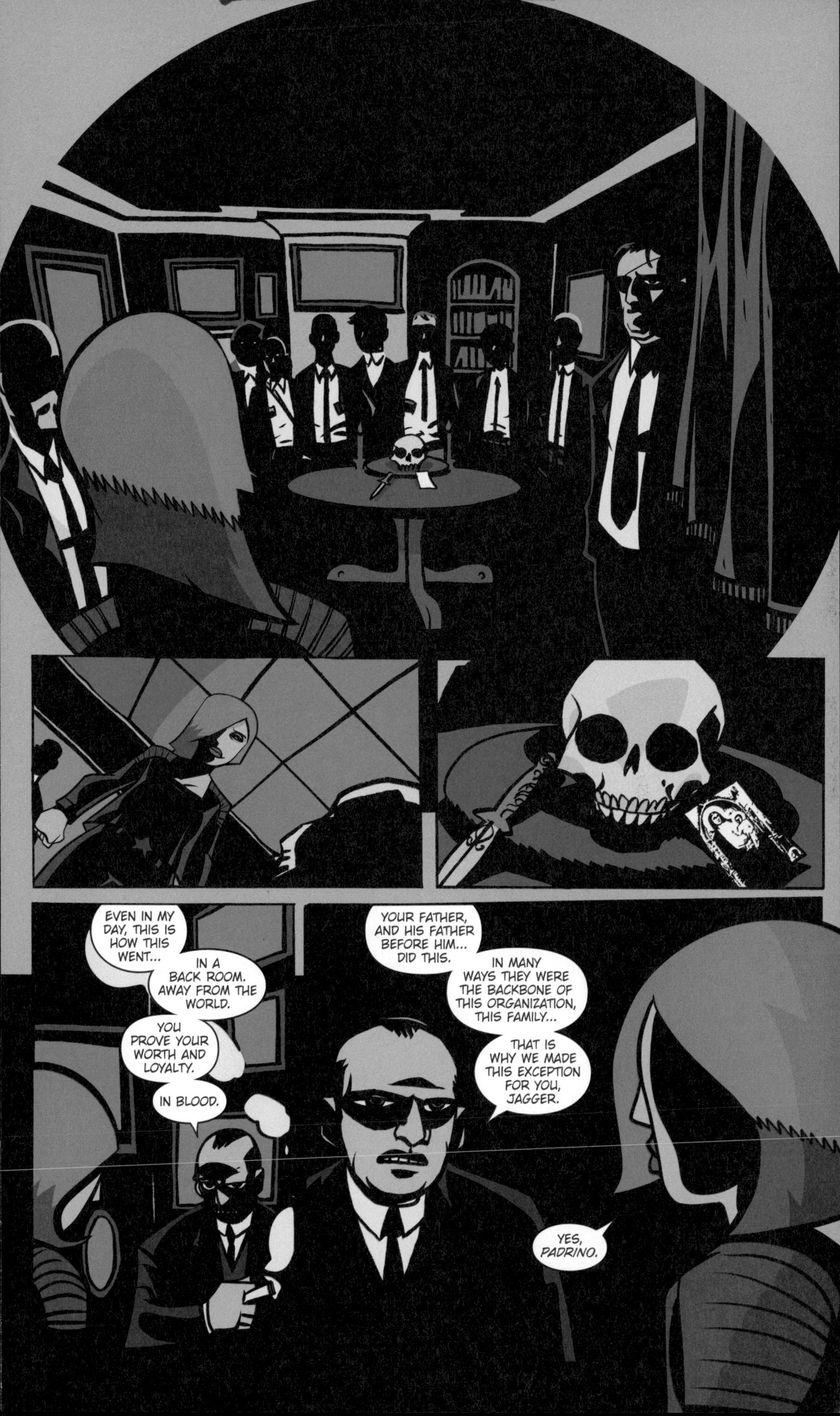
EVEN IN MY DAY, THIS IS HOW THIS WENT...
IN A BACK ROOM. AWAY FROM THE WORLD.
YOU PROVE YOUR WORTH AND LOYALTY.
IN BLOOD.
YOUR FATHER, AND HIS FATHER BEFORE HIM... DID THIS.
IN MANY WAYS THEY WERE THE BACKBONE OF THIS ORGANIZATION, THIS FAMILY...
THAT IS WHY WE MADE THIS EXCEPTION FOR YOU, JAGGER.
YES, PADRINO.

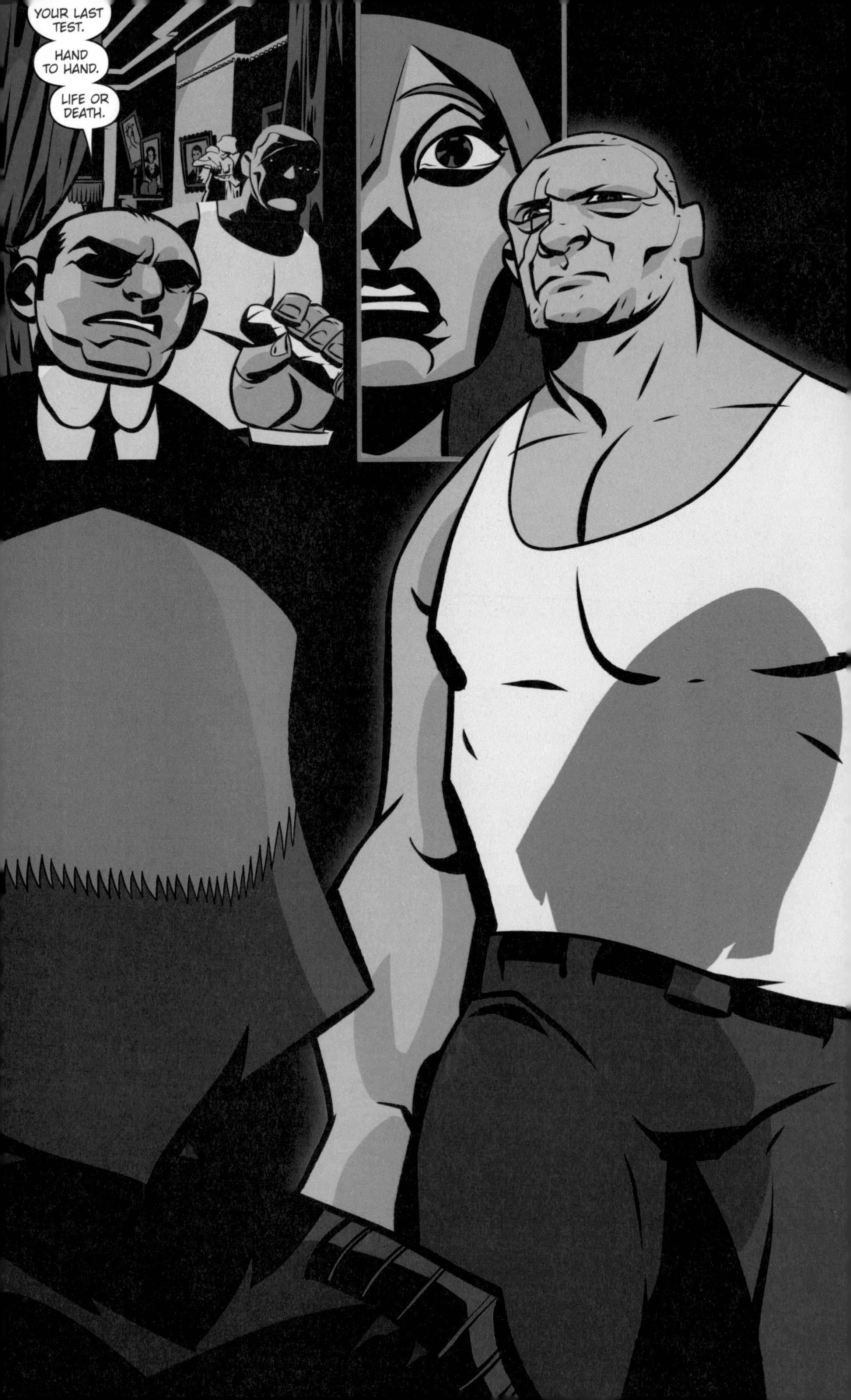
YOUR LAST TEST.
HAND TO HAND.
LIFE OR DEATH.

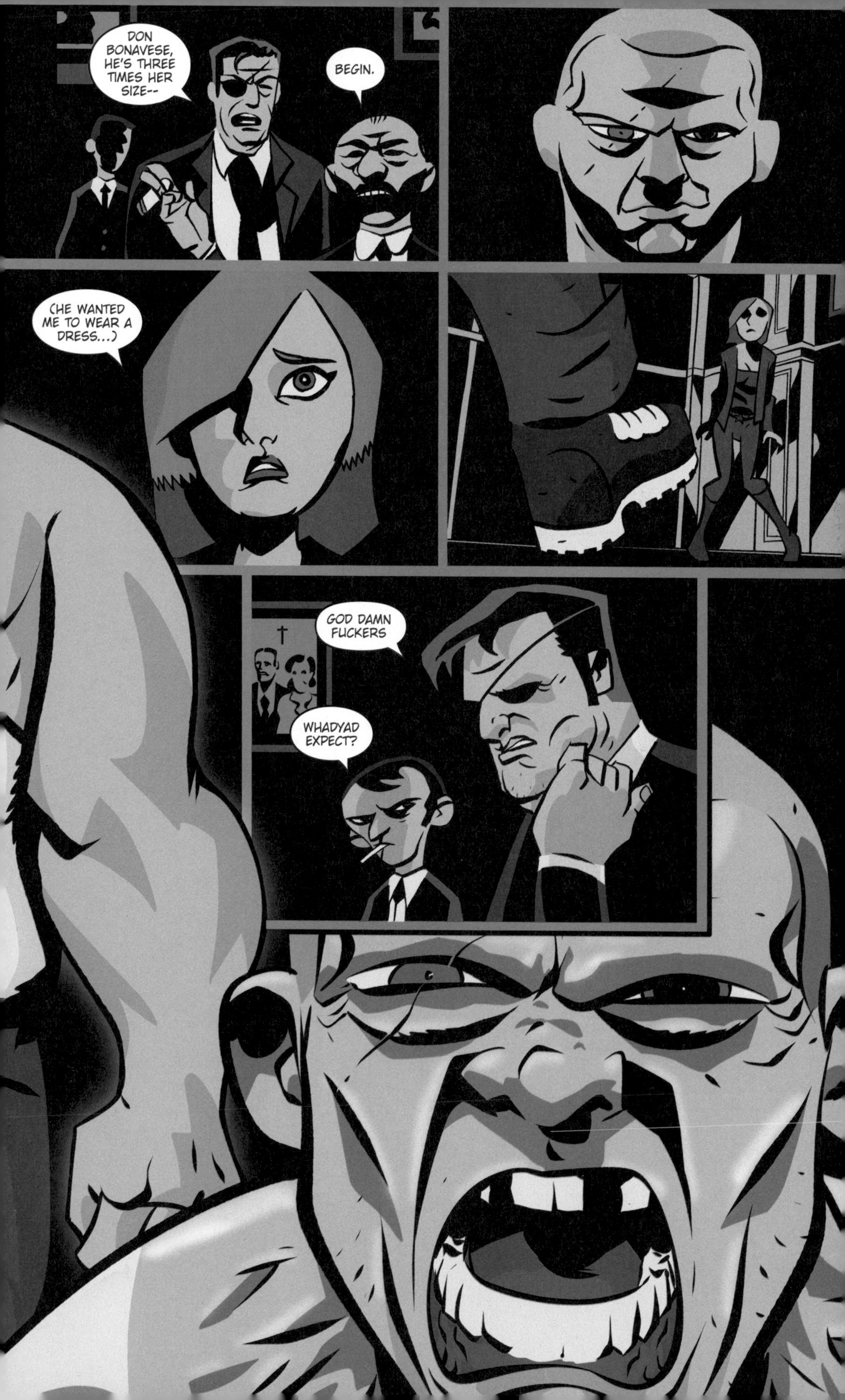
DON BONAVESE, HE'S THREE TIMES HER SIZE--
BEGIN.
(HE WANTED ME TO WEAR A DRESS...)
GOD DAMN FUCKERS
WHADYAD EXPECT?

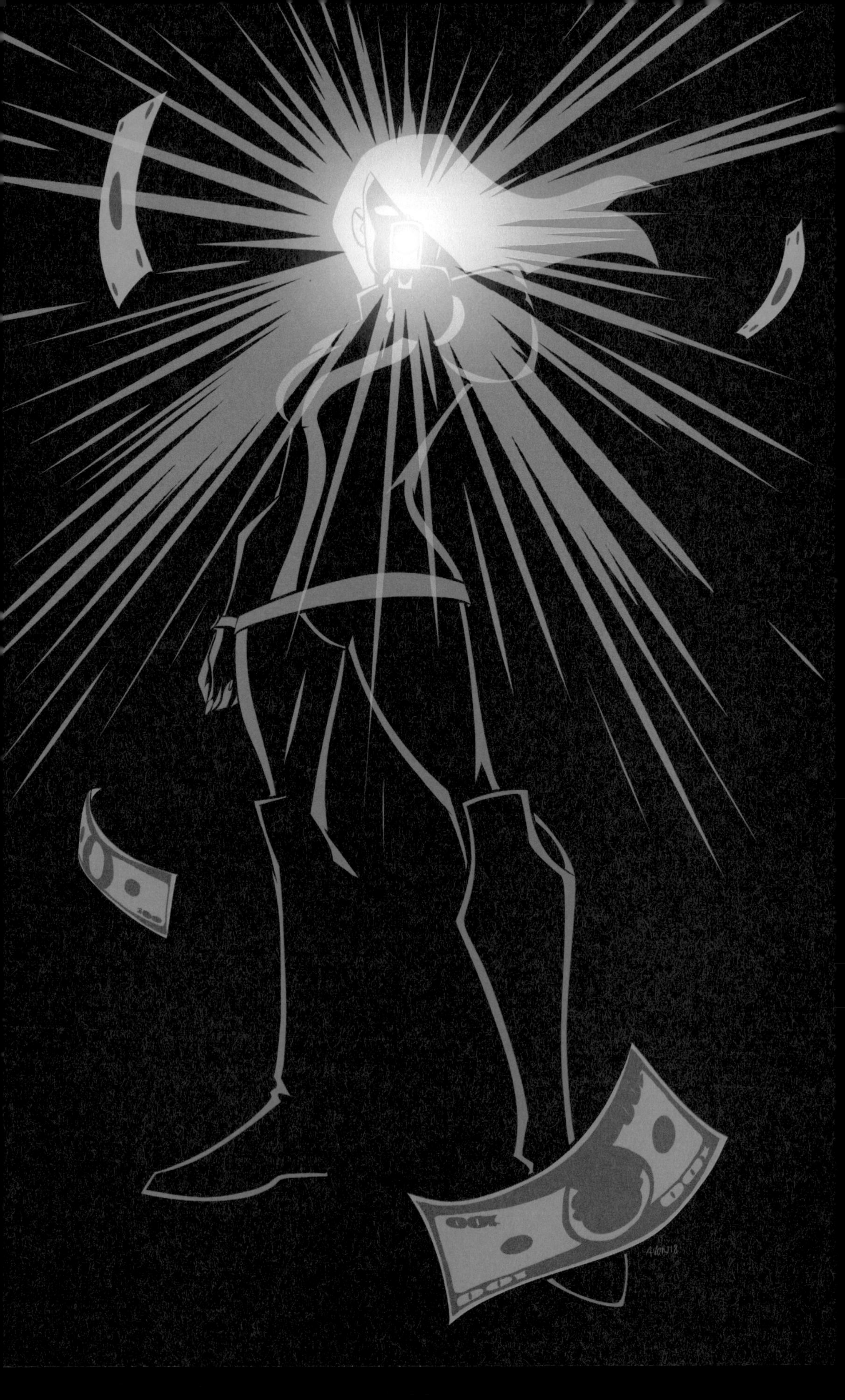

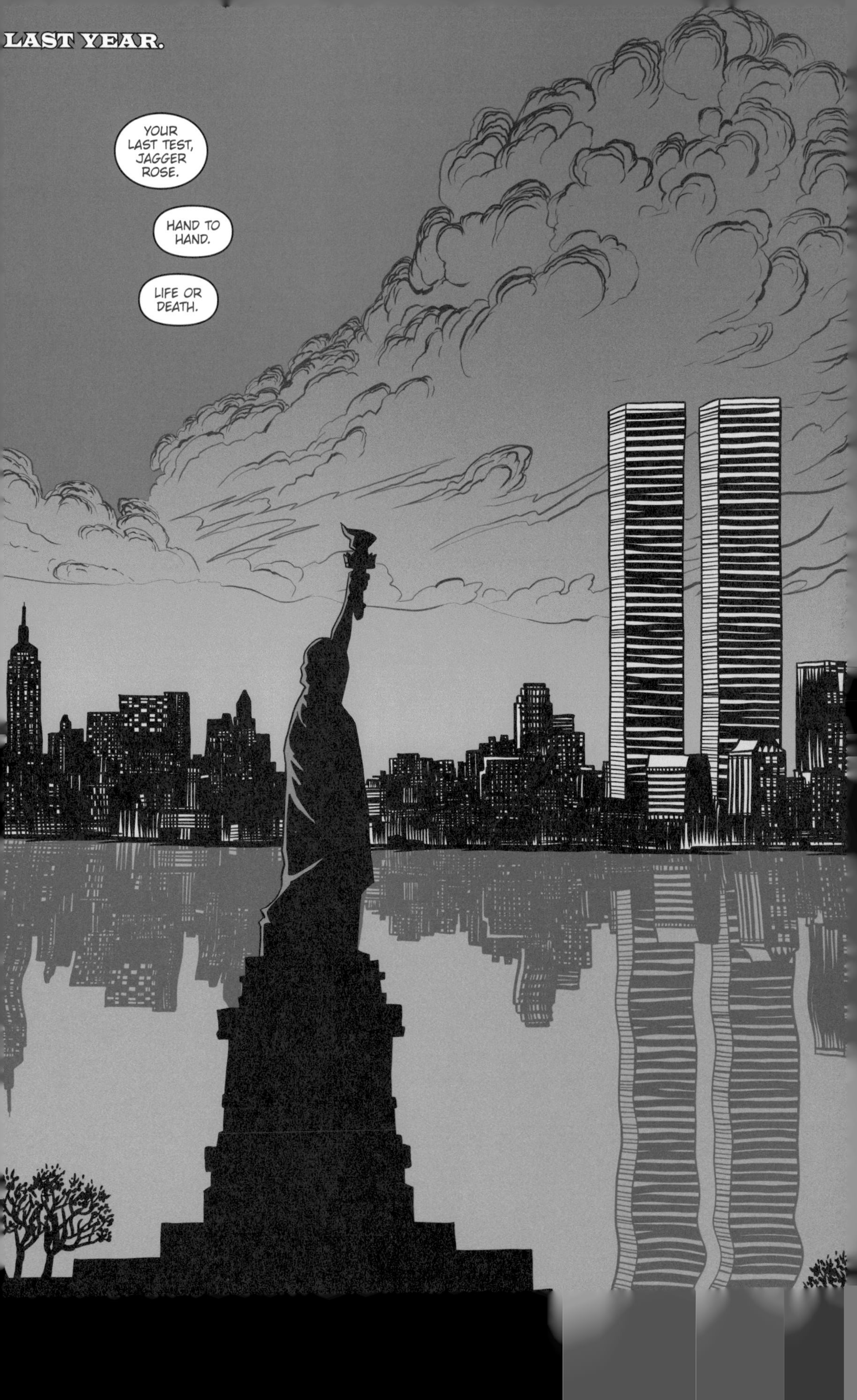
LAST YEAR.
YOUR LAST TEST, JAGGER ROSE.
HAND TO HAND.
LIFE OR DEATH.

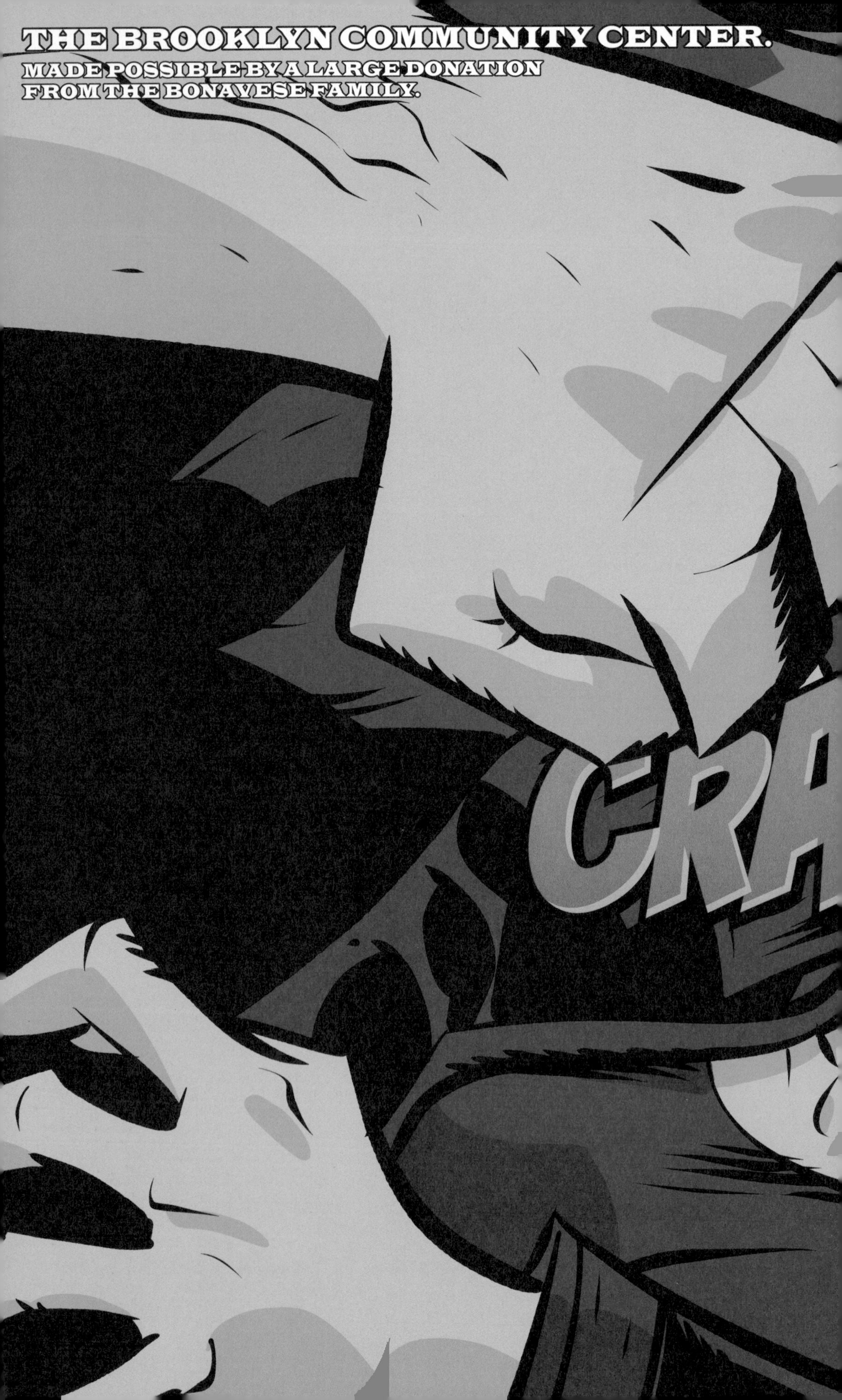
THE BROOKLYN COMMUNITY CENTER.
MADE POSSIBLE BY A LARGE DONATION FROM THE BONAVESE FAMILY.
CRA

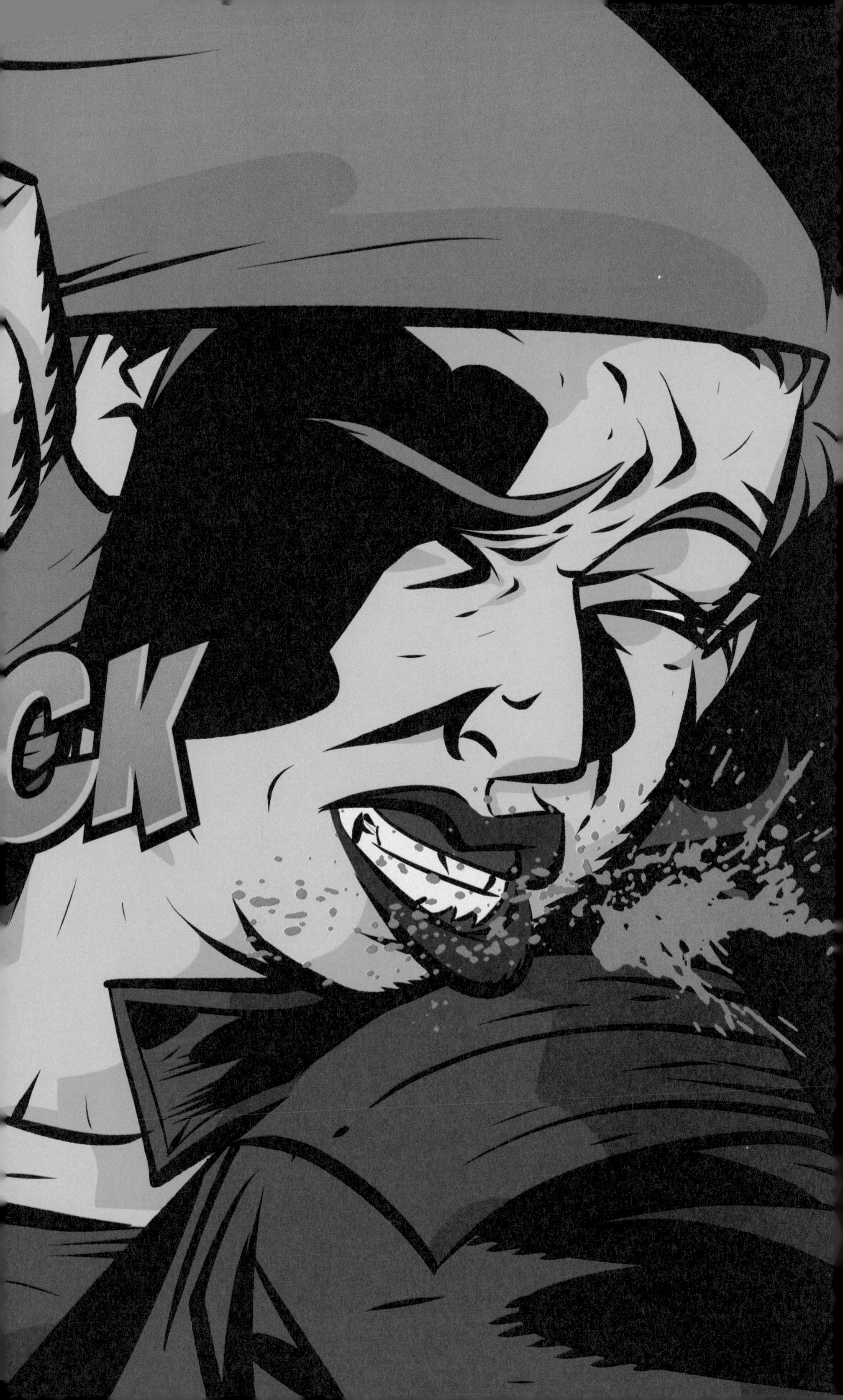
CK

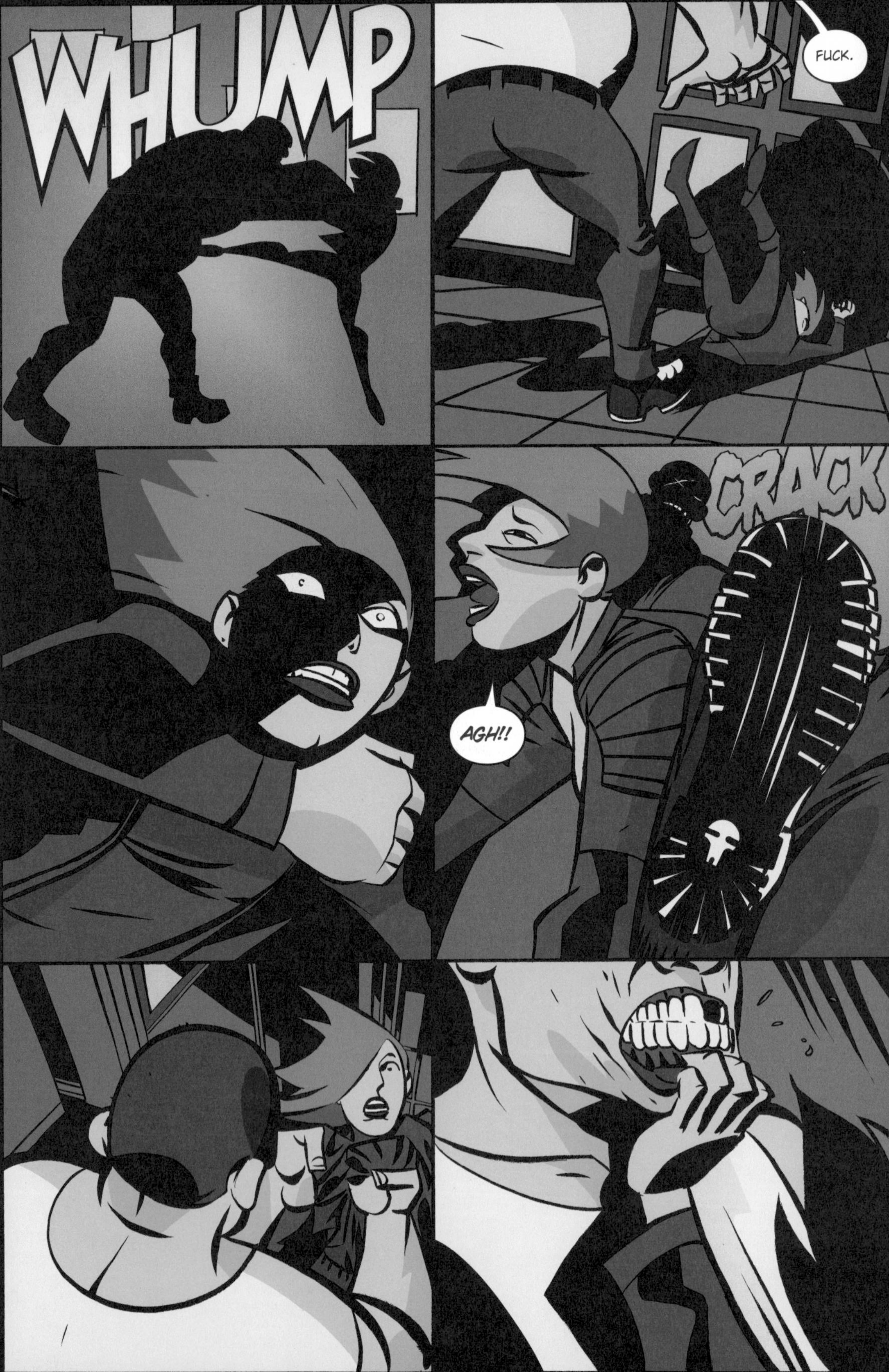
WHUMP
FUCK.
CRACK
AGH!!

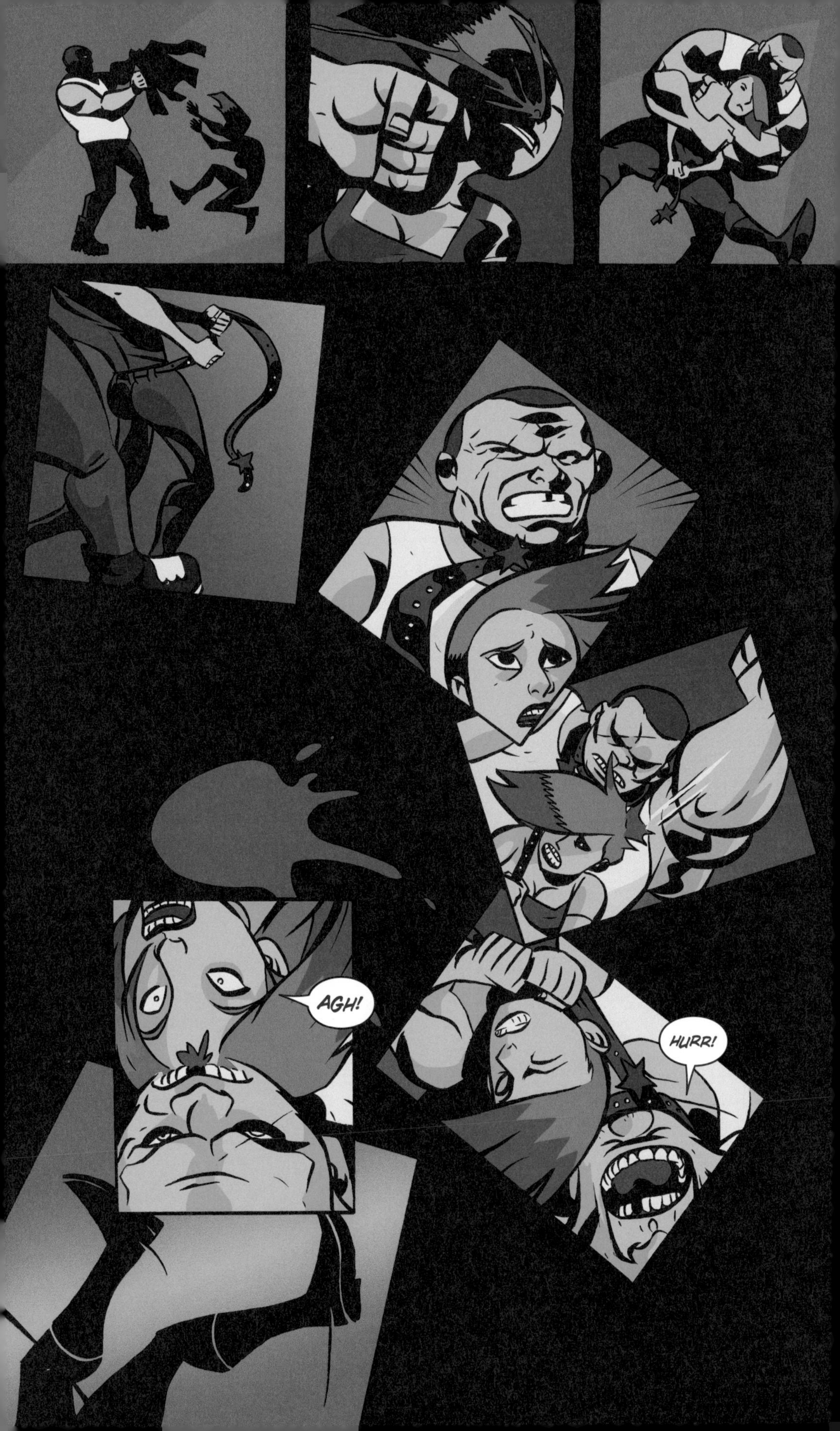
AGH!
HURR!

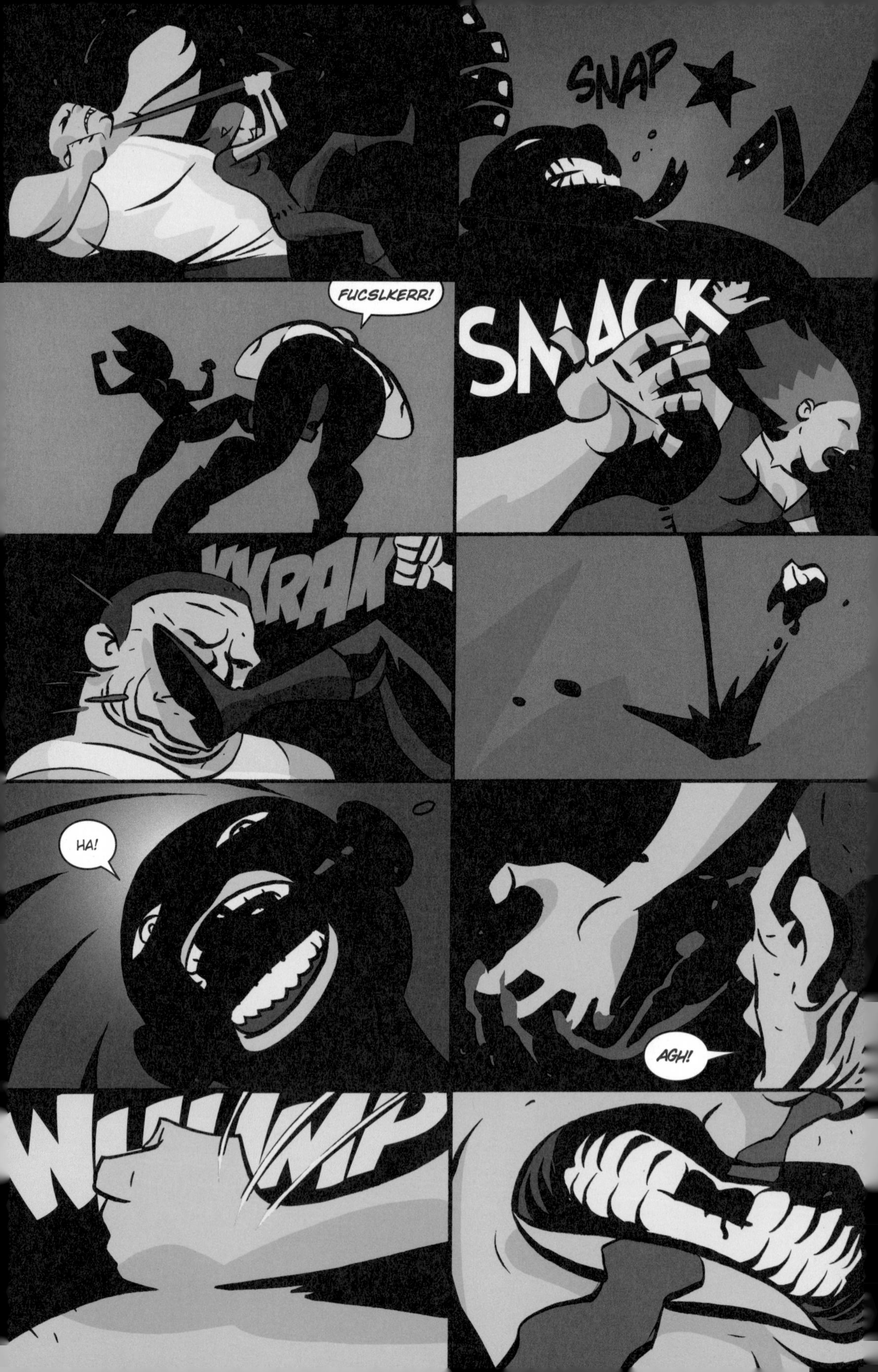
SNAP
FUCSLKERR!
SMACK
KRAK
HA!
AGH!
WHUMP

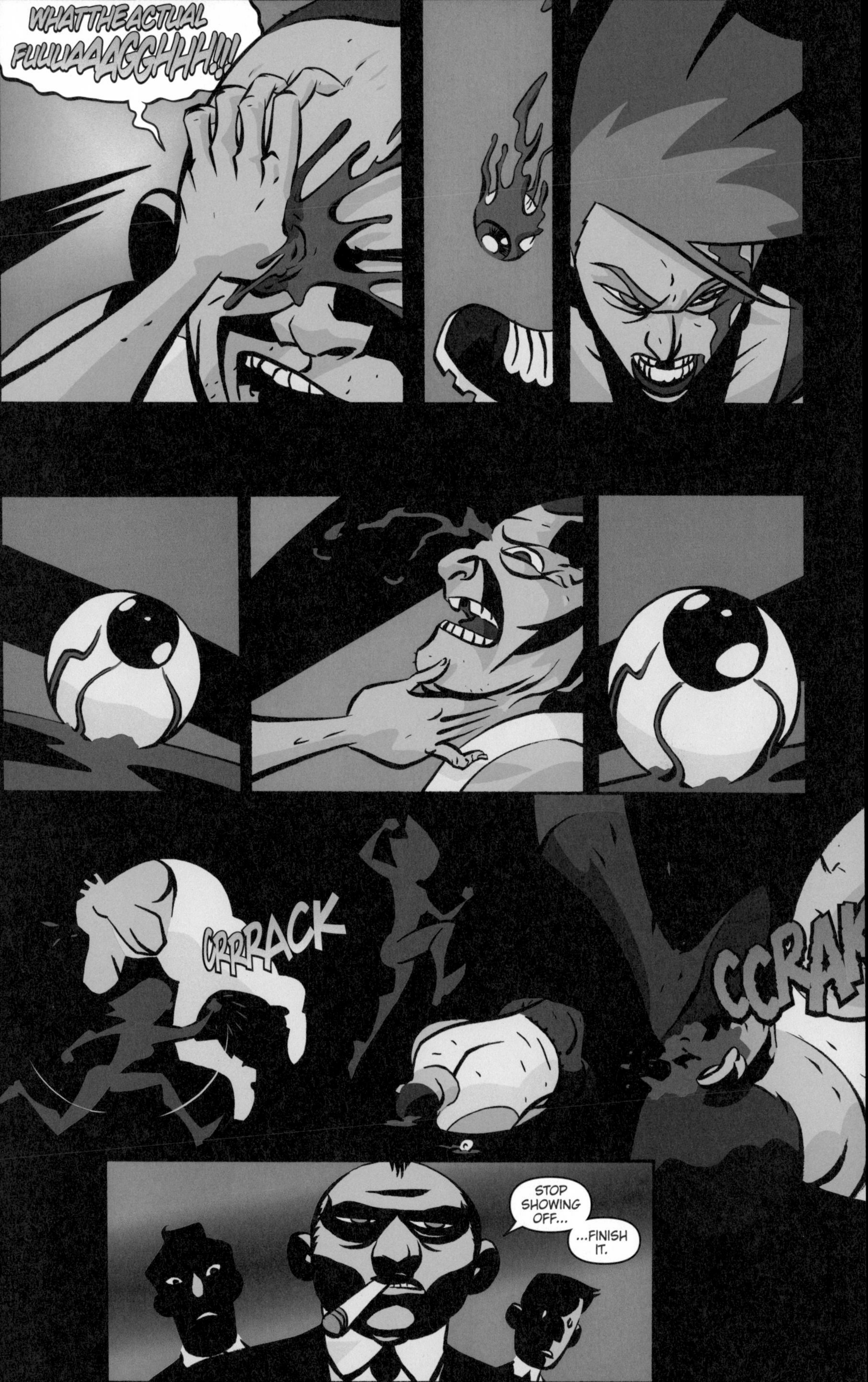
WHATTHEACTUAL FUUUAAAAGGHHH!!!
CRRRACK
CCRAK
STOP SHOWING OFF...
...FINISH IT.

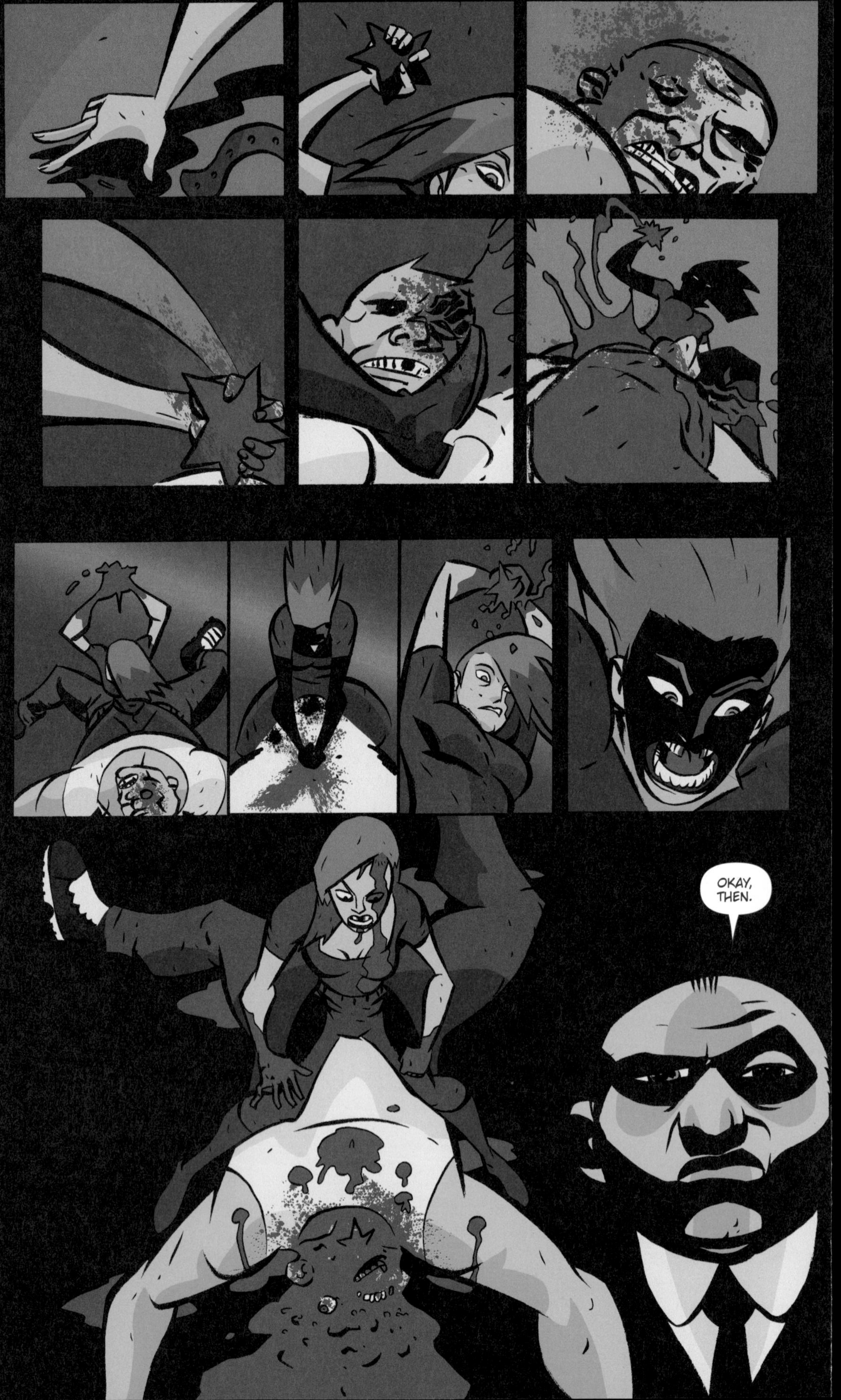
OKAY, THEN.

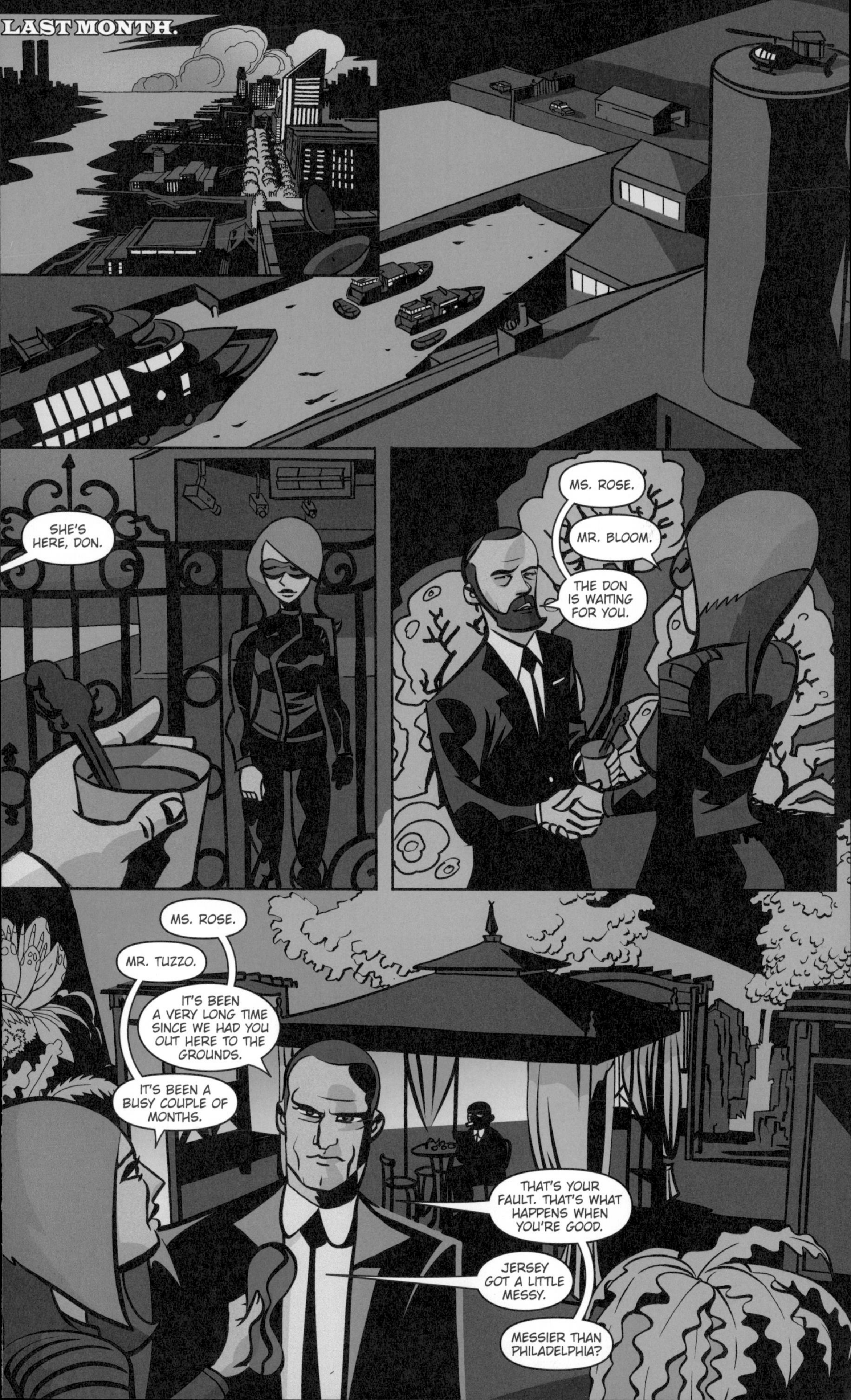
LAST MONTH.
SHE'S HERE, DON.
MS. ROSE.
MR. BLOOM.
THE DON IS WAITING FOR YOU.
MS. ROSE.
MR. TUZZO.
IT'S BEEN A VERY LONG TIME SINCE WE HAD YOU OUT HERE TO THE GROUNDS.
IT'S BEEN A BUSY COUPLE OF MONTHS.
THAT'S YOUR FAULT. THAT'S WHAT HAPPENS WHEN YOU'RE GOOD.
JERSEY GOT A LITTLE MESSY.
MESSIER THAN PHILADELPHIA?

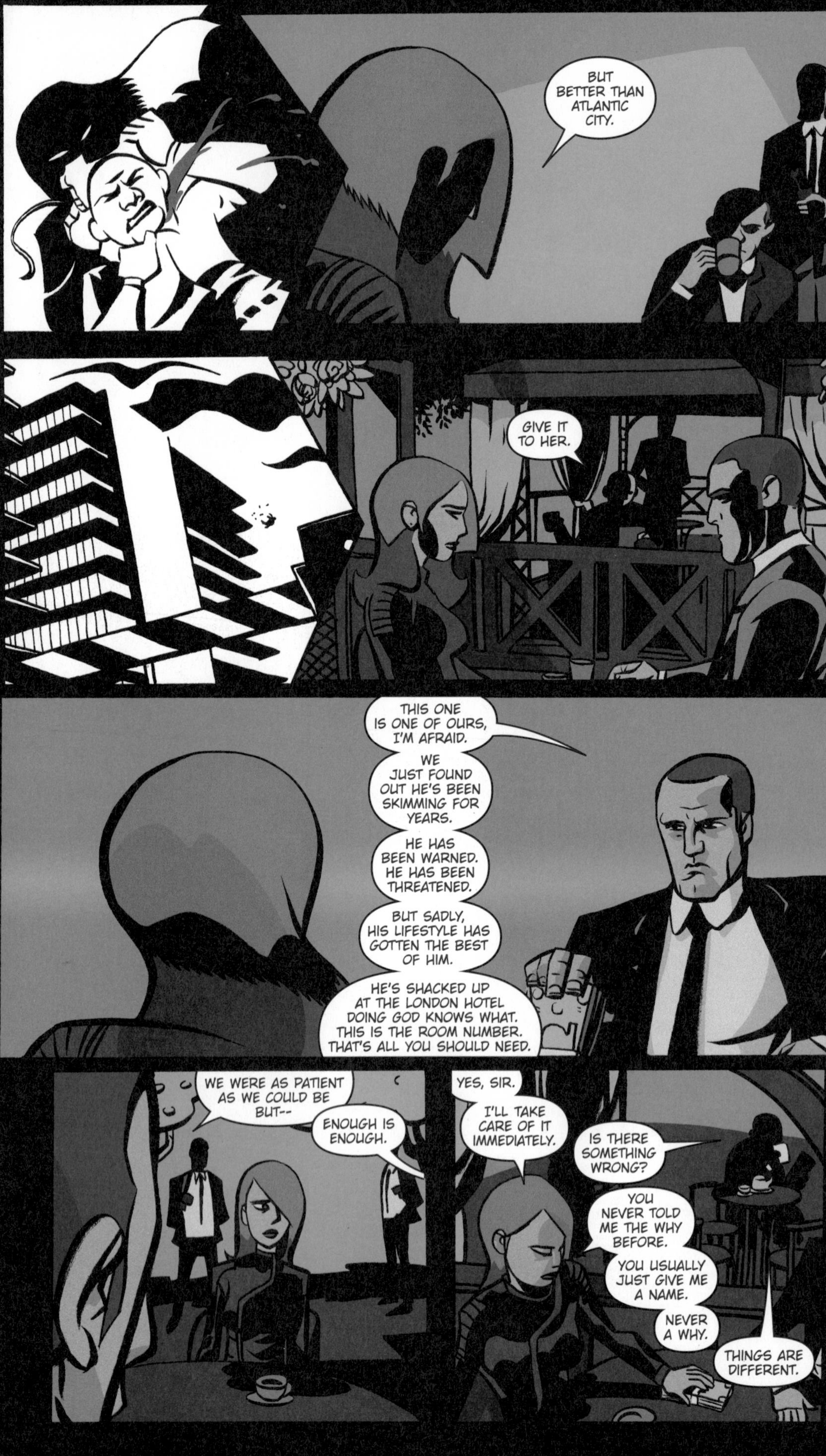
BUT BETTER THAN ATLANTIC CITY.
GIVE IT TO HER.
THIS ONE IS ONE OF OURS, I'M AFRAID.
WE JUST FOUND OUT HE'S BEEN SKIMMING FOR YEARS.
HE HAS BEEN WARNED. HE HAS BEEN THREATENED.
BUT SADLY, HIS LIFESTYLE HAS GOTTEN THE BEST OF HIM.
HE'S SHACKED UP AT THE LONDON HOTEL DOING GOD KNOWS WHAT. THIS IS THE ROOM NUMBER. THAT'S ALL YOU SHOULD NEED.
WE WERE AS PATIENT AS WE COULD BE BUT--
ENOUGH IS ENOUGH.
YES, SIR.
I'LL TAKE CARE OF IT IMMEDIATELY.
IS THERE SOMETHING WRONG?
YOU NEVER TOLD ME THE WHY BEFORE.
YOU USUALLY JUST GIVE ME A NAME.
NEVER A WHY.
THINGS ARE DIFFERENT.

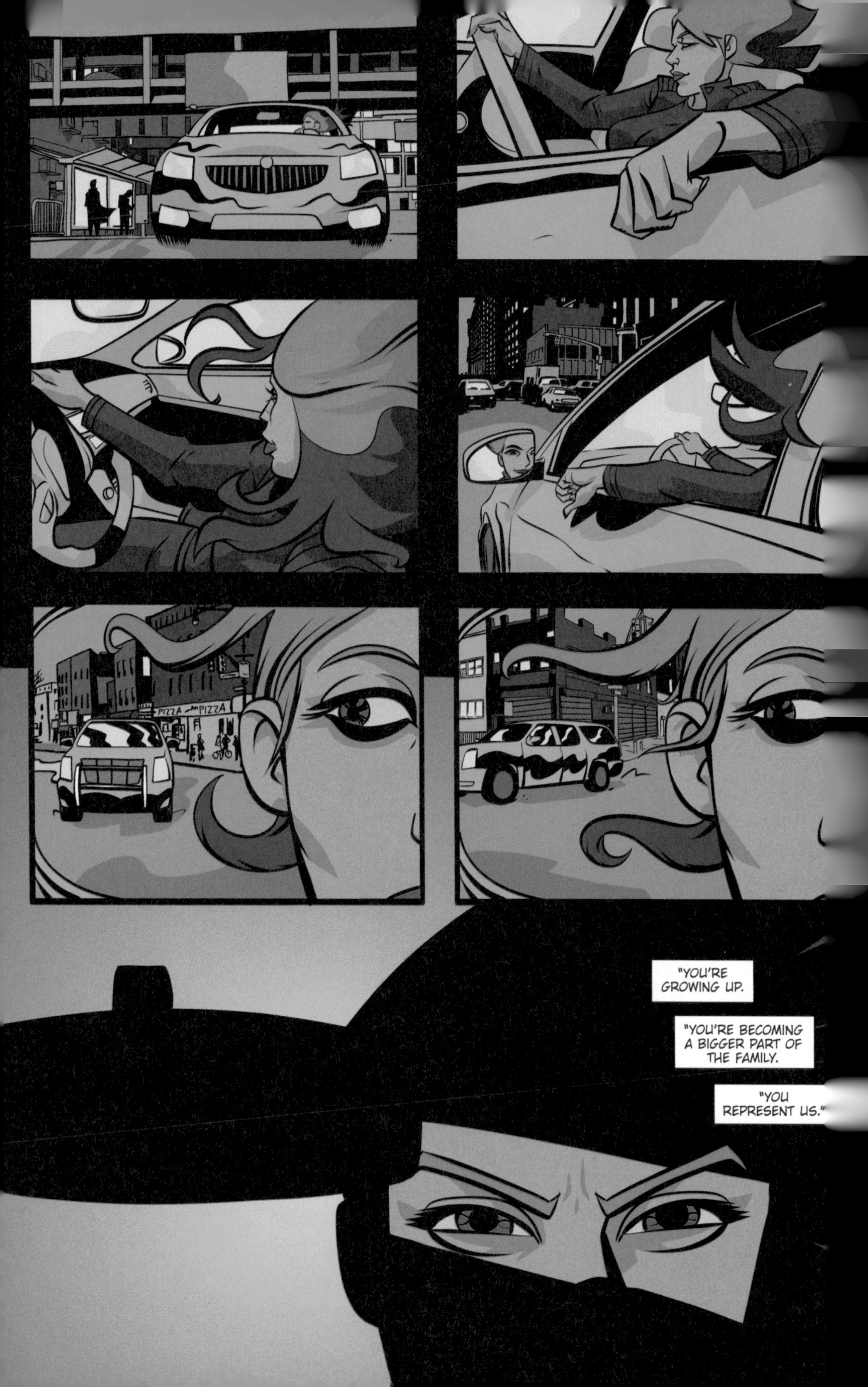
PIZZA PIZZA
"YOU'RE GROWING UP.
"YOU'RE BECOMING A BIGGER PART OF THE FAMILY.
"YOU REPRESENT US."

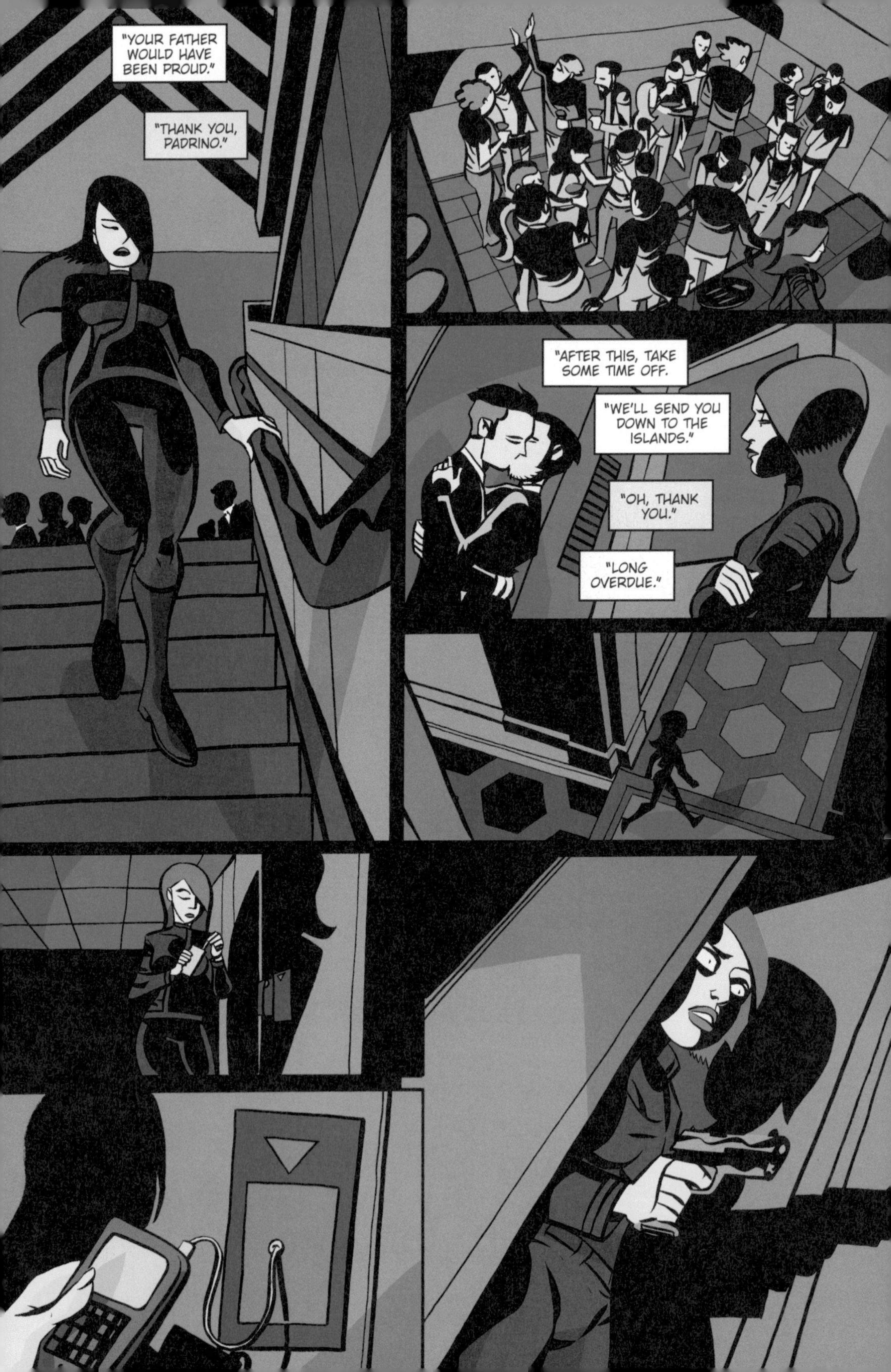
"YOUR FATHER WOULD HAVE BEEN PROUD."
"THANK YOU, PADRINO."
"AFTER THIS, TAKE SOME TIME OFF.
"WE'LL SEND YOU DOWN TO THE ISLANDS."
"OH, THANK YOU."
"LONG OVERDUE."

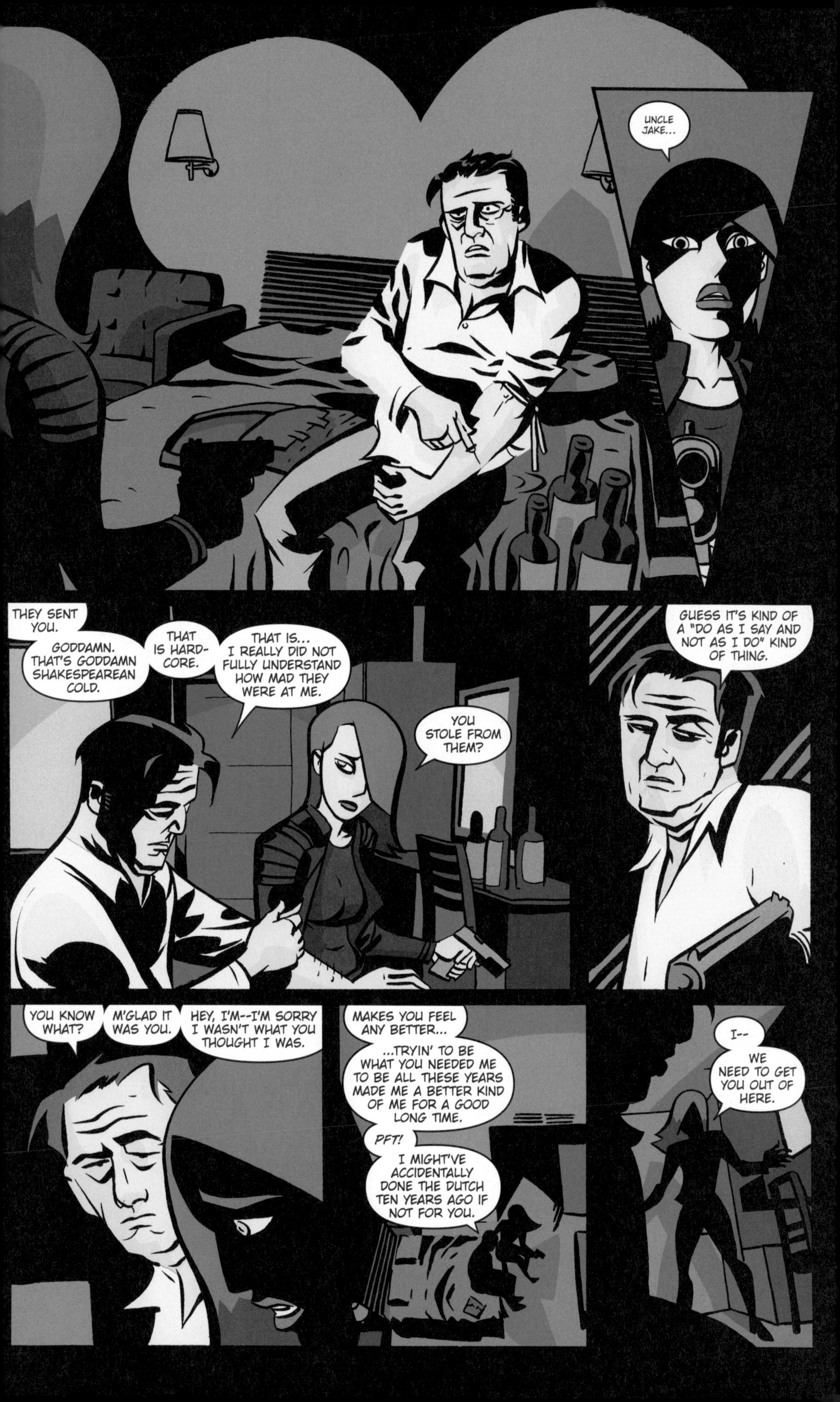

UNCLE JAKE...
THEY SENT YOU.
GODDAMN. THAT'S GODDAMN SHAKESPEAREAN COLD.
THAT IS HARD-CORE.
THAT IS... I REALLY DID NOT FULLY UNDERSTAND HOW MAD THEY WERE AT ME.
YOU STOLE FROM THEM?
GUESS IT'S KIND OF A "DO AS I SAY AND NOT AS I DO" KIND OF THING.
YOU KNOW WHAT?
M'GLAD IT WAS YOU.
HEY, I'M--I'M SORRY I WASN'T WHAT YOU THOUGHT I WAS.
MAKES YOU FEEL ANY BETTER...
...TRYIN' TO BE WHAT YOU NEEDED ME TO BE ALL THESE YEARS MADE ME A BETTER KIND OF ME FOR A GOOD LONG TIME.
PFT!
I MIGHT'VE ACCIDENTALLY DONE THE DUTCH TEN YEARS AGO IF NOT FOR YOU.
I--
WE NEED TO GET YOU OUT OF HERE.

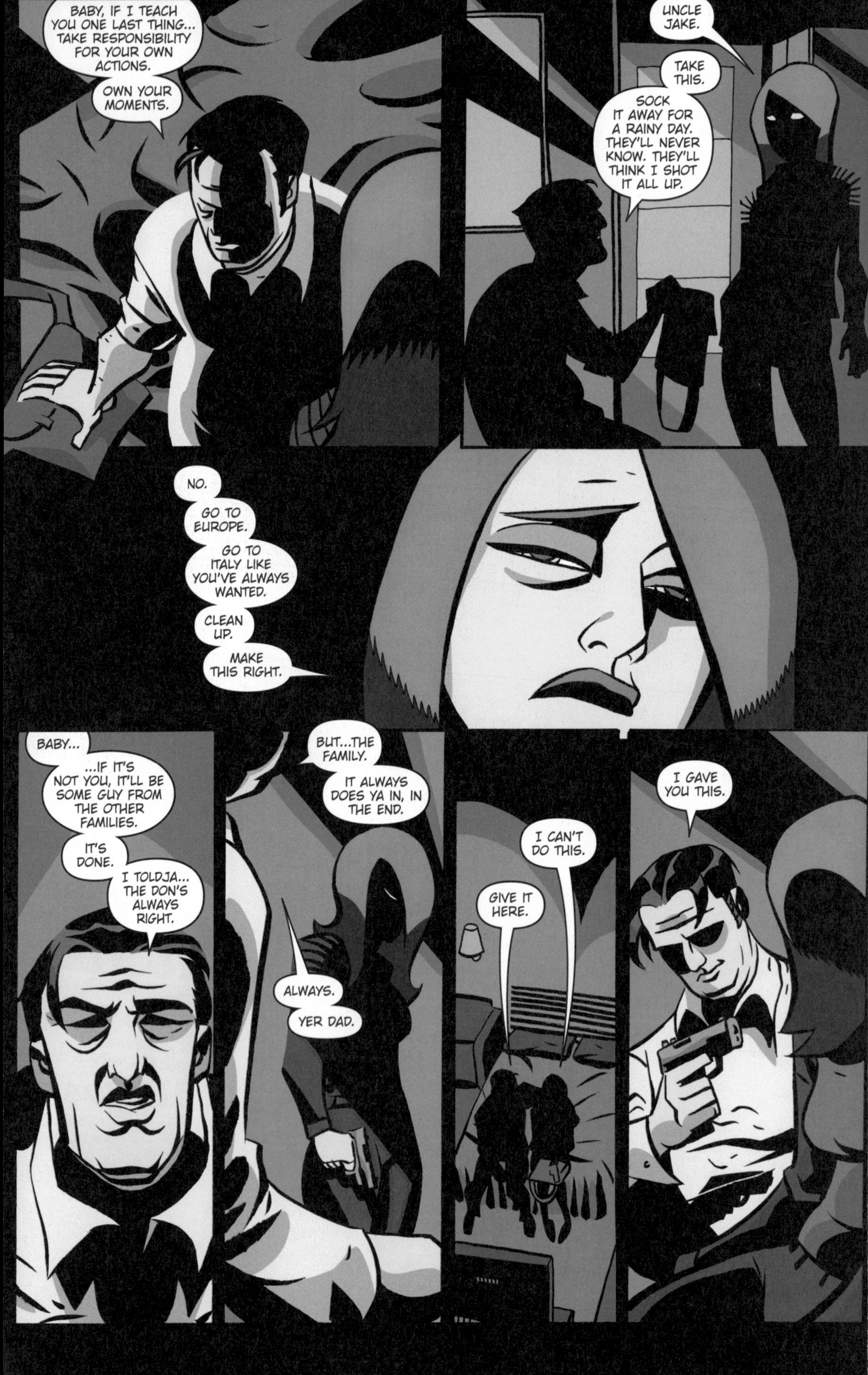
BABY, IF I TEACH YOU ONE LAST THING... TAKE RESPONSIBILITY FOR YOUR OWN ACTIONS.
OWN YOUR MOMENTS.
UNCLE JAKE.
TAKE THIS.
SOCK IT AWAY FOR A RAINY DAY. THEY'LL NEVER KNOW. THEY'LL THINK I SHOT IT ALL UP.
NO.
GO TO EUROPE.
GO TO ITALY LIKE YOU'VE ALWAYS WANTED.
CLEAN UP.
MAKE THIS RIGHT.
BABY...
...IF IT'S NOT YOU, IT'LL BE SOME GUY FROM THE OTHER FAMILIES.
IT'S DONE.
I TOLDJA... THE DON'S ALWAYS RIGHT.
BUT...THE FAMILY.
IT ALWAYS DOES YA IN, IN THE END.
ALWAYS.
YER DAD.
I CAN'T DO THIS.
GIVE IT HERE.
I GAVE YOU THIS.

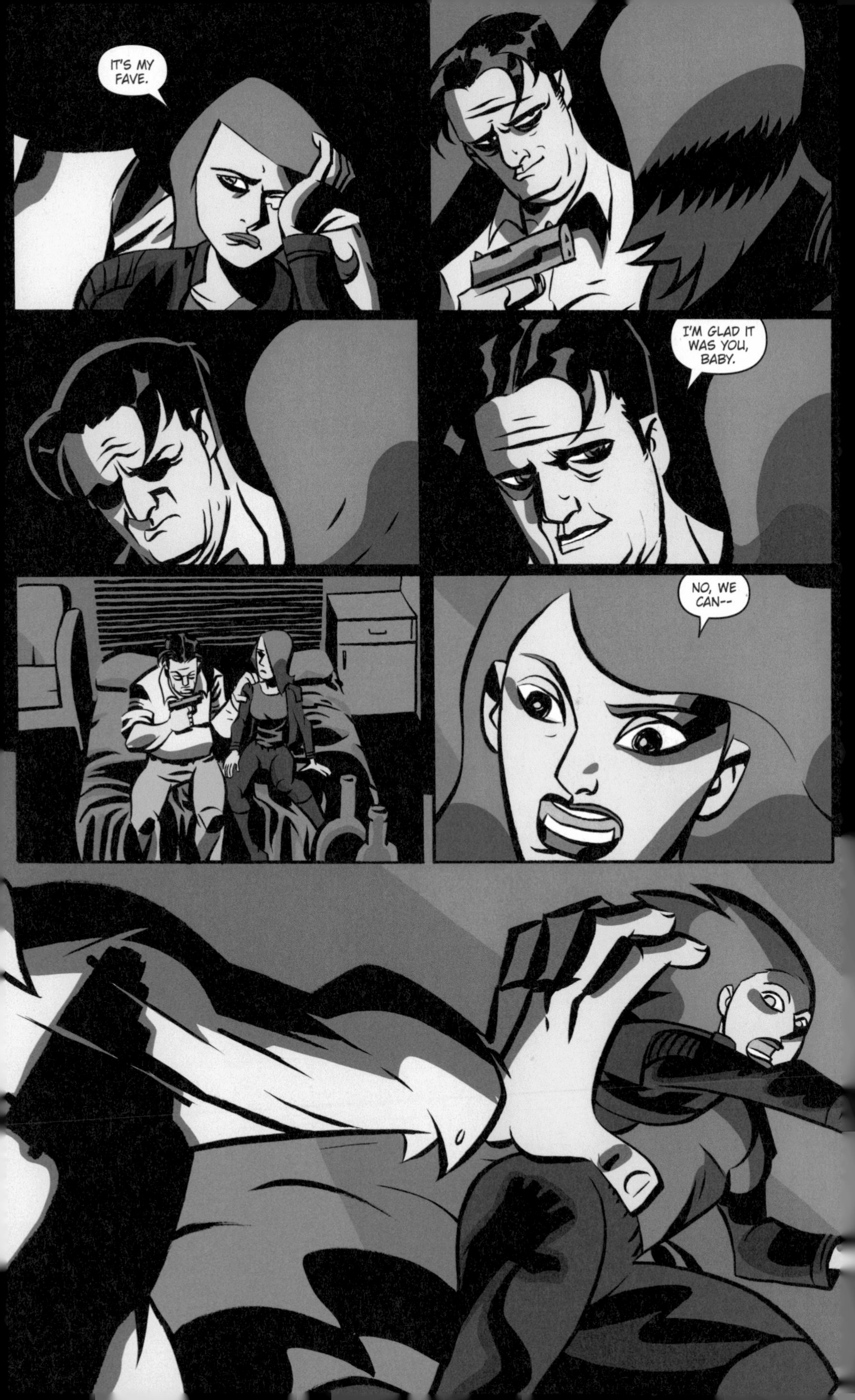
IT'S MY FAVE.
I'M GLAD IT WAS YOU, BABY.
NO, WE CAN--

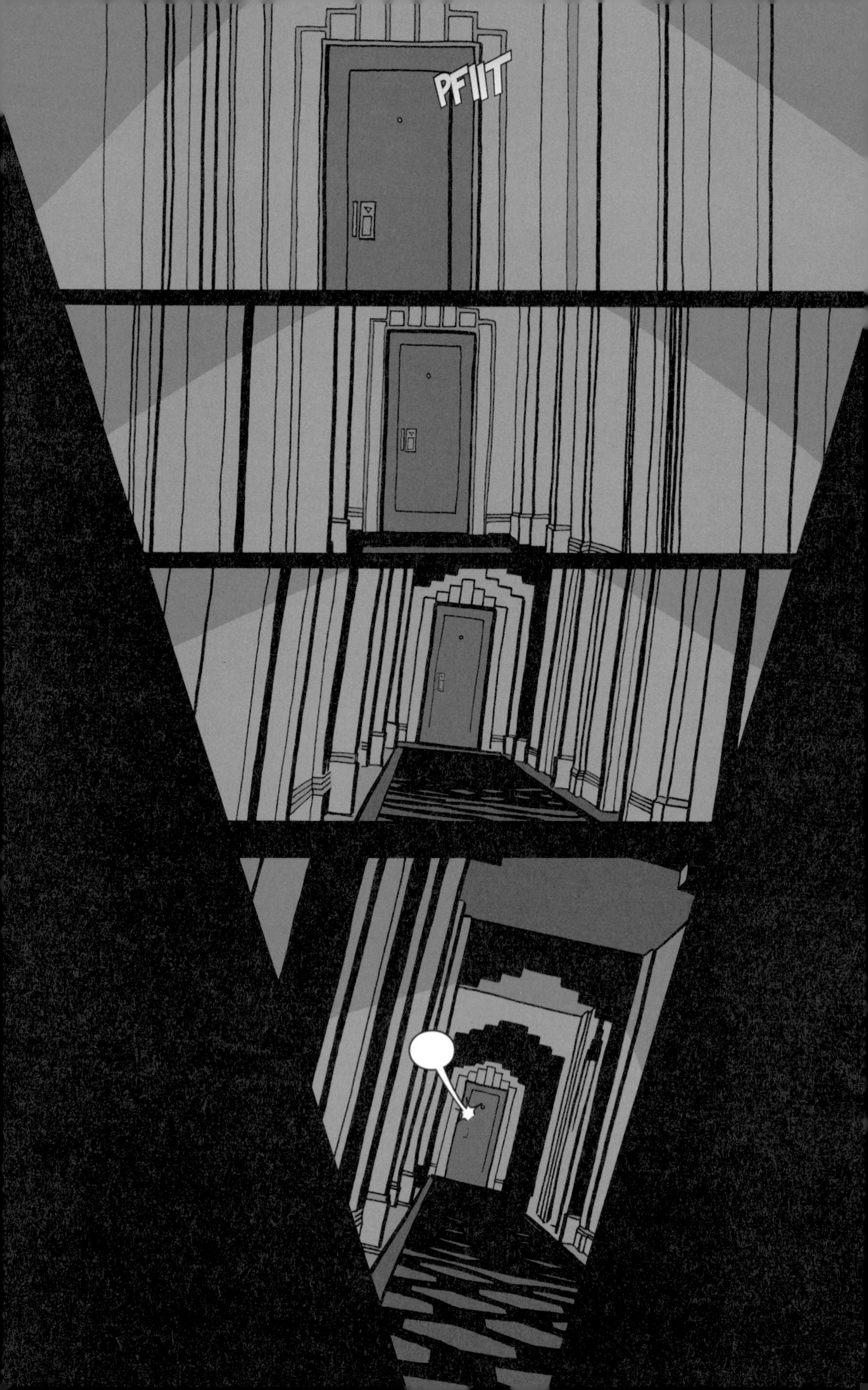
PFIIT

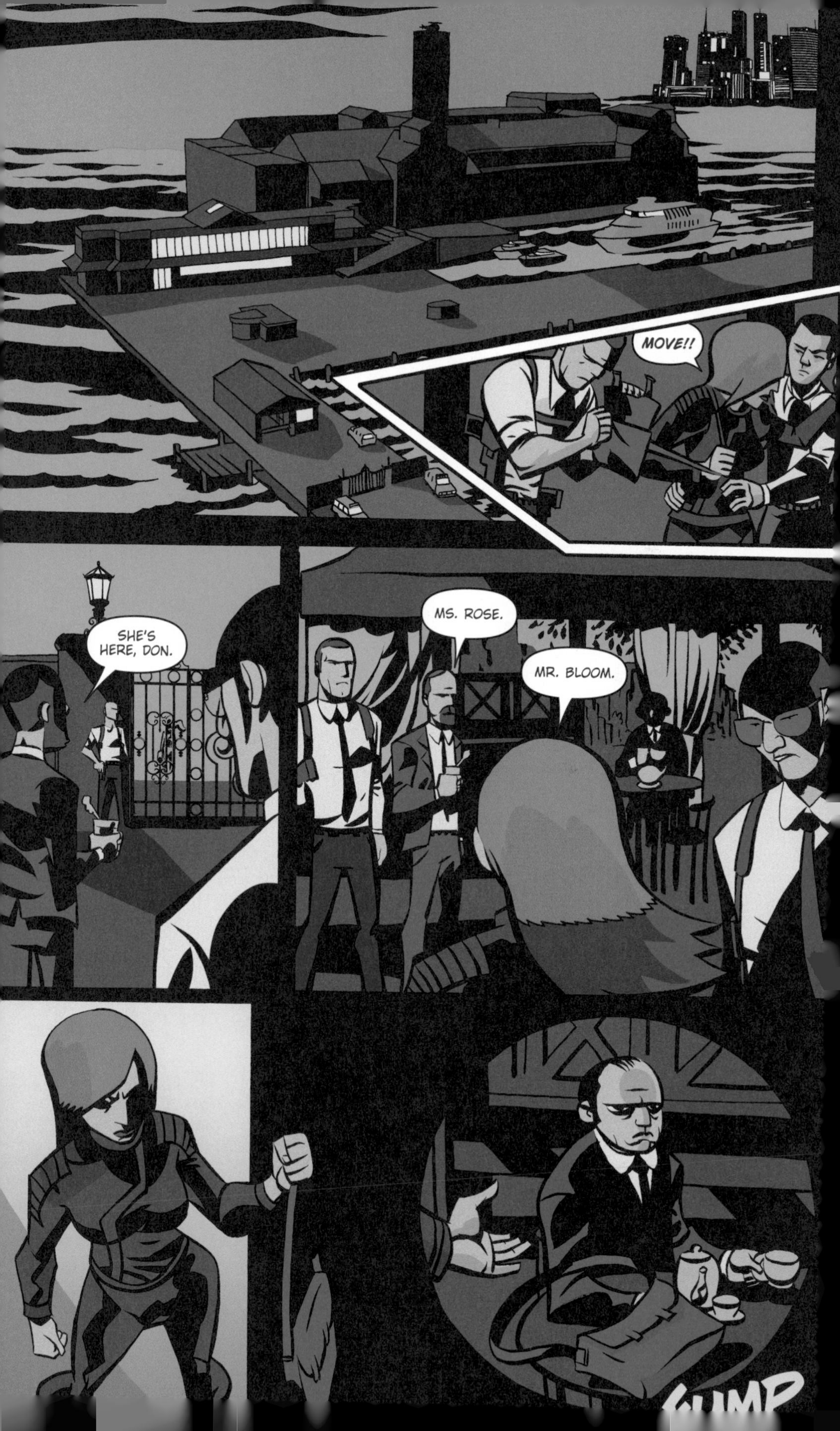
MOVE!!
SHE'S HERE, DON.
MS. ROSE.
MR. BLOOM.

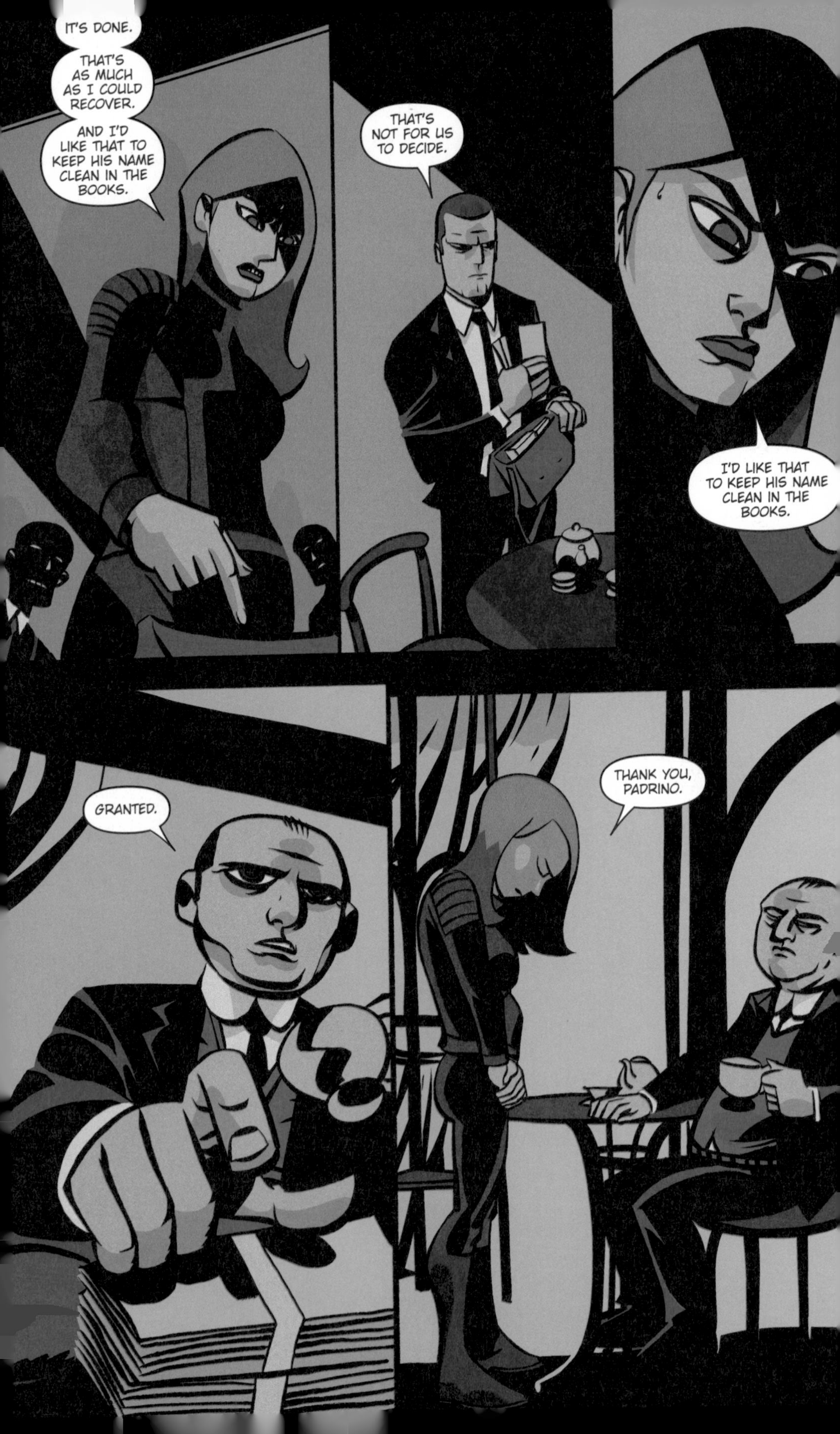
IT'S DONE.
THAT'S AS MUCH AS I COULD RECOVER.
AND I'D LIKE THAT TO KEEP HIS NAME CLEAN IN THE BOOKS.
THAT'S NOT FOR US TO DECIDE.
I'D LIKE THAT TO KEEP HIS NAME CLEAN IN THE BOOKS.
GRANTED.
THANK YOU, PADRINO.

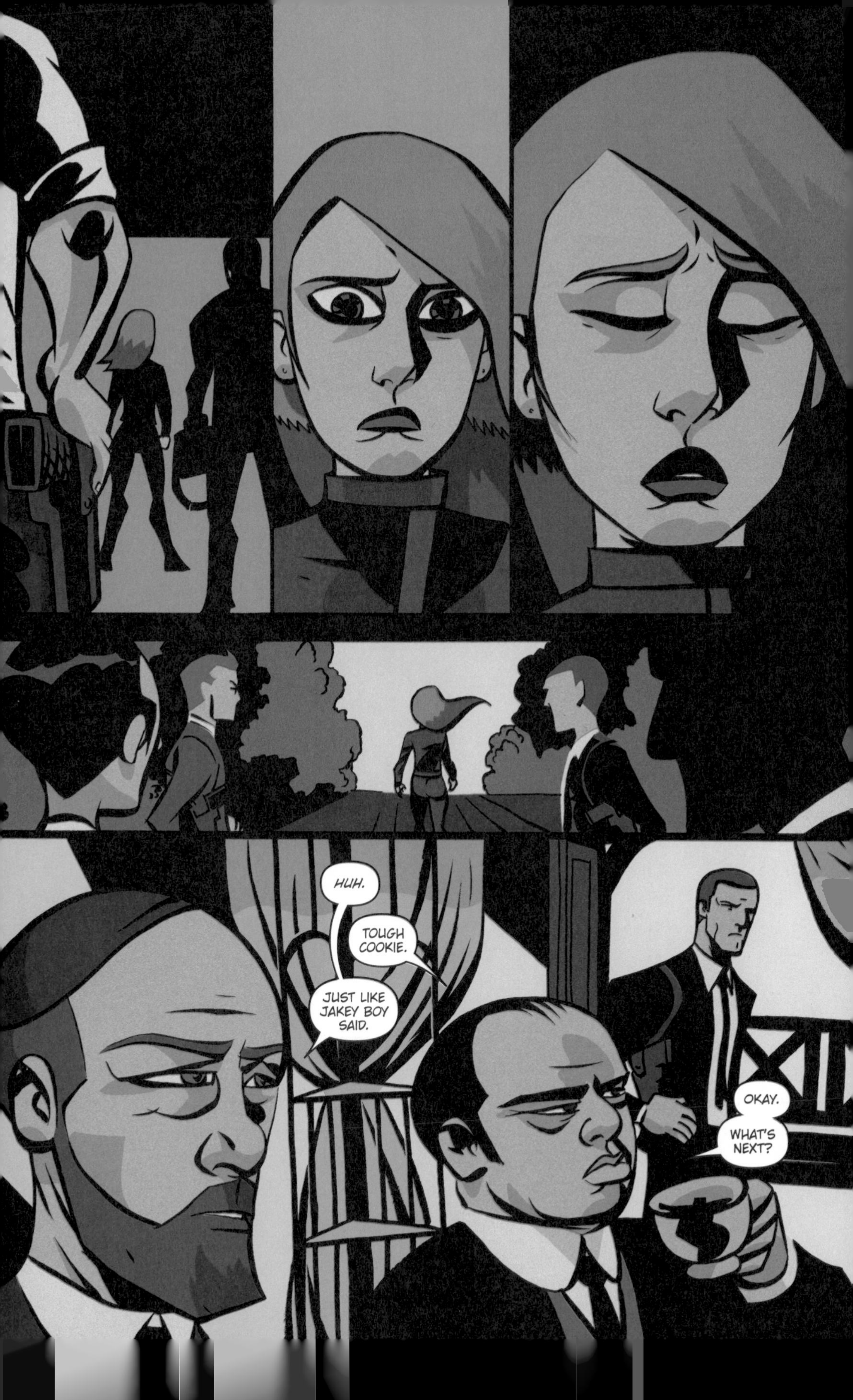
HUH.
TOUGH COOKIE.
JUST LIKE JAKEY BOY SAID.
OKAY.
WHAT'S NEXT?

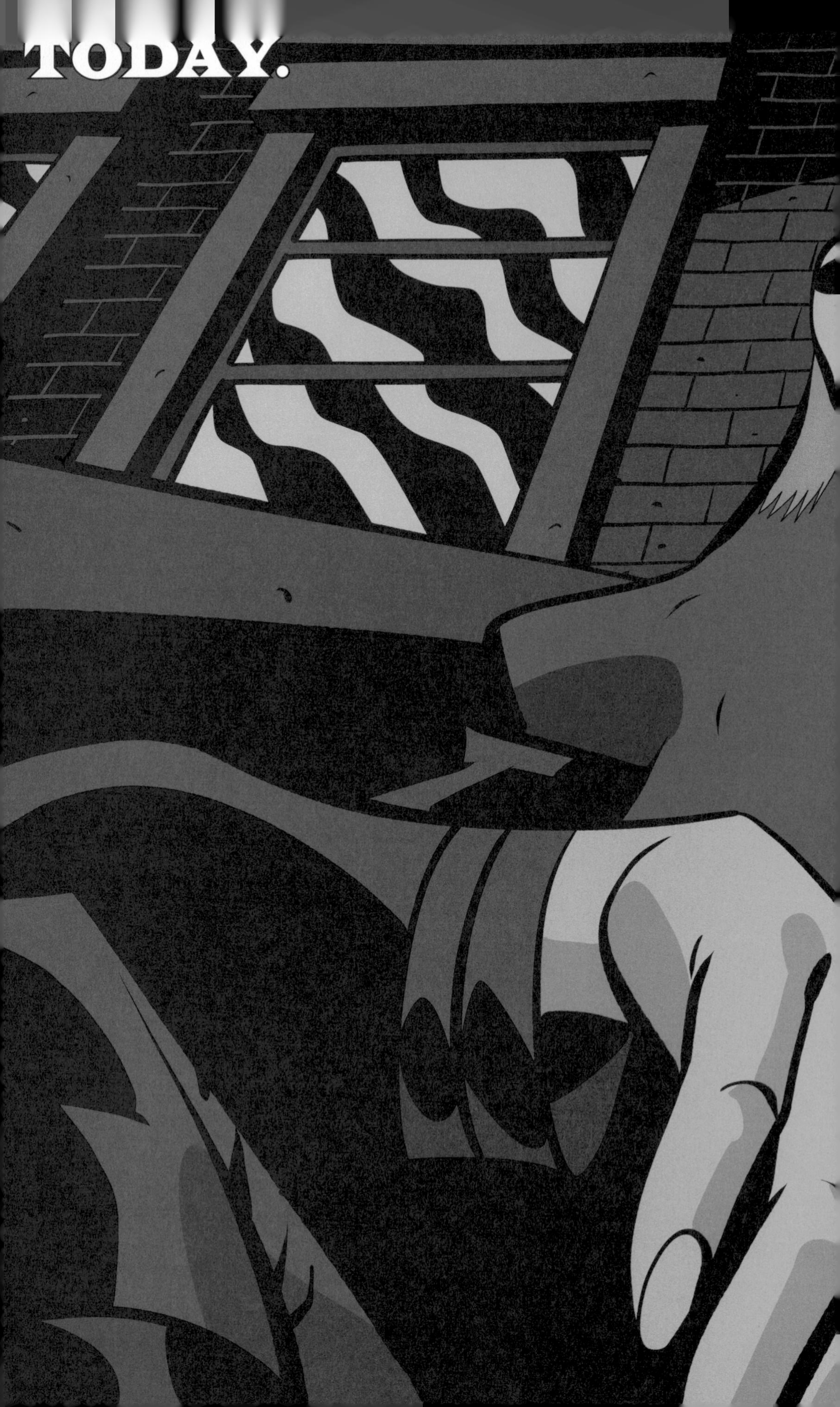
TODAY.

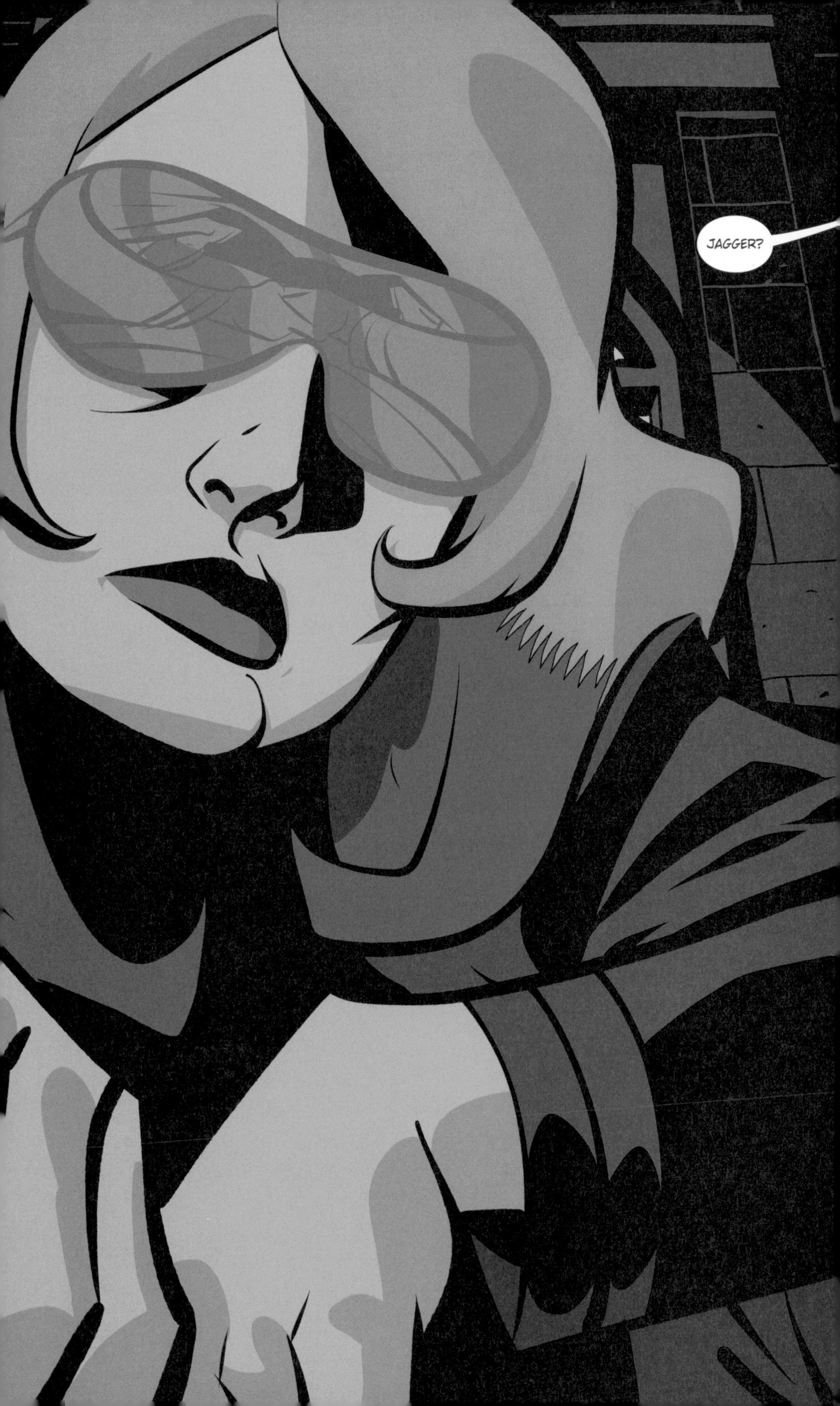
JAGGER?

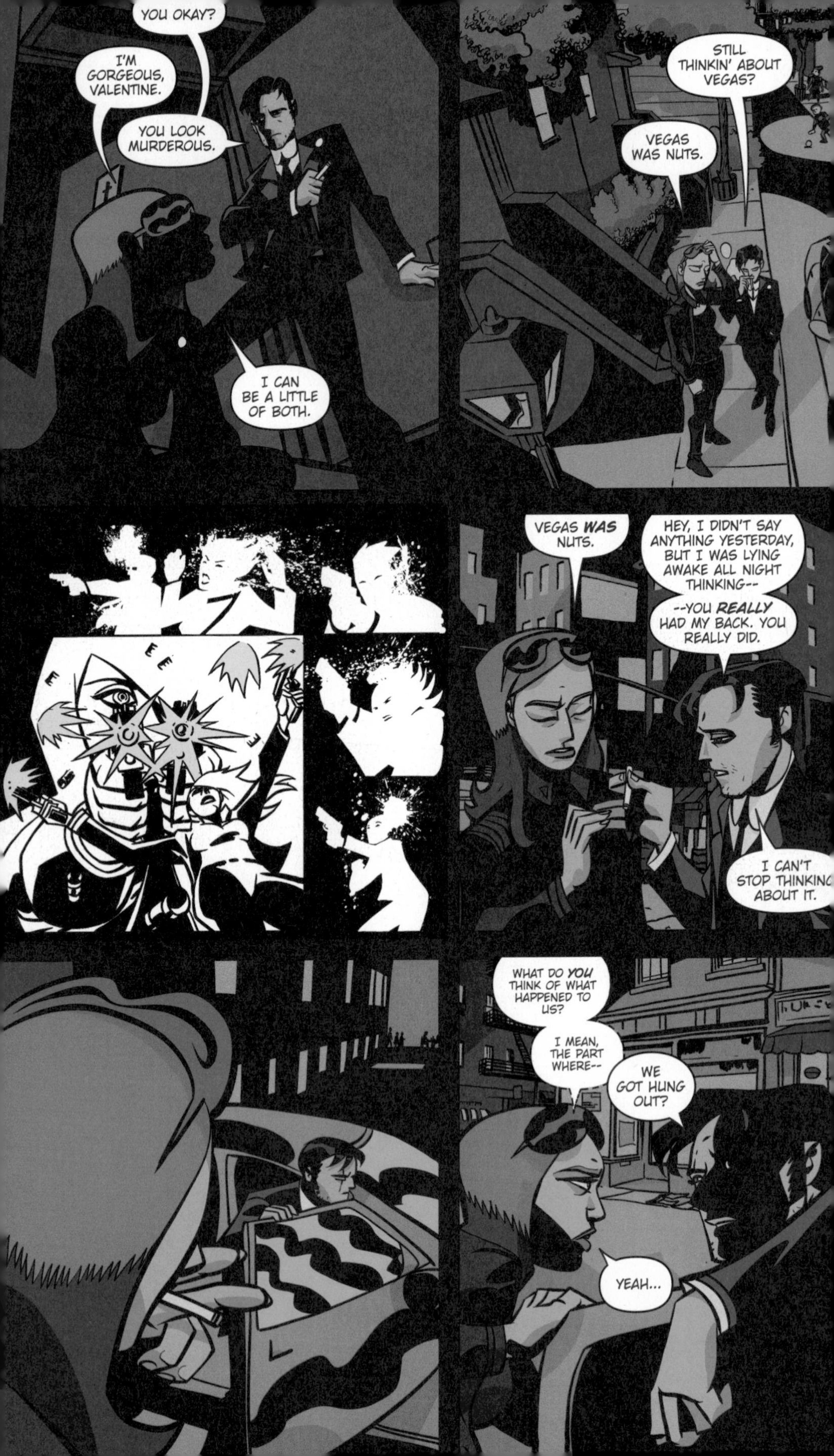
YOU OKAY?
I'M GORGEOUS, VALENTINE.
YOU LOOK MURDEROUS.
I CAN BE A LITTLE OF BOTH.
STILL THINKIN' ABOUT VEGAS?
VEGAS WAS NUTS.
VEGAS WAS NUTS.
HEY, I DIDN'T SAY ANYTHING YESTERDAY, BUT I WAS LYING AWAKE ALL NIGHT THINKING--
--YOU REALLY HAD MY BACK. YOU REALLY DID.
I CAN'T STOP THINKING ABOUT IT.
WHAT DO YOU THINK OF WHAT HAPPENED TO US?
I MEAN, THE PART WHERE--
WE GOT HUNG OUT?
YEAH...

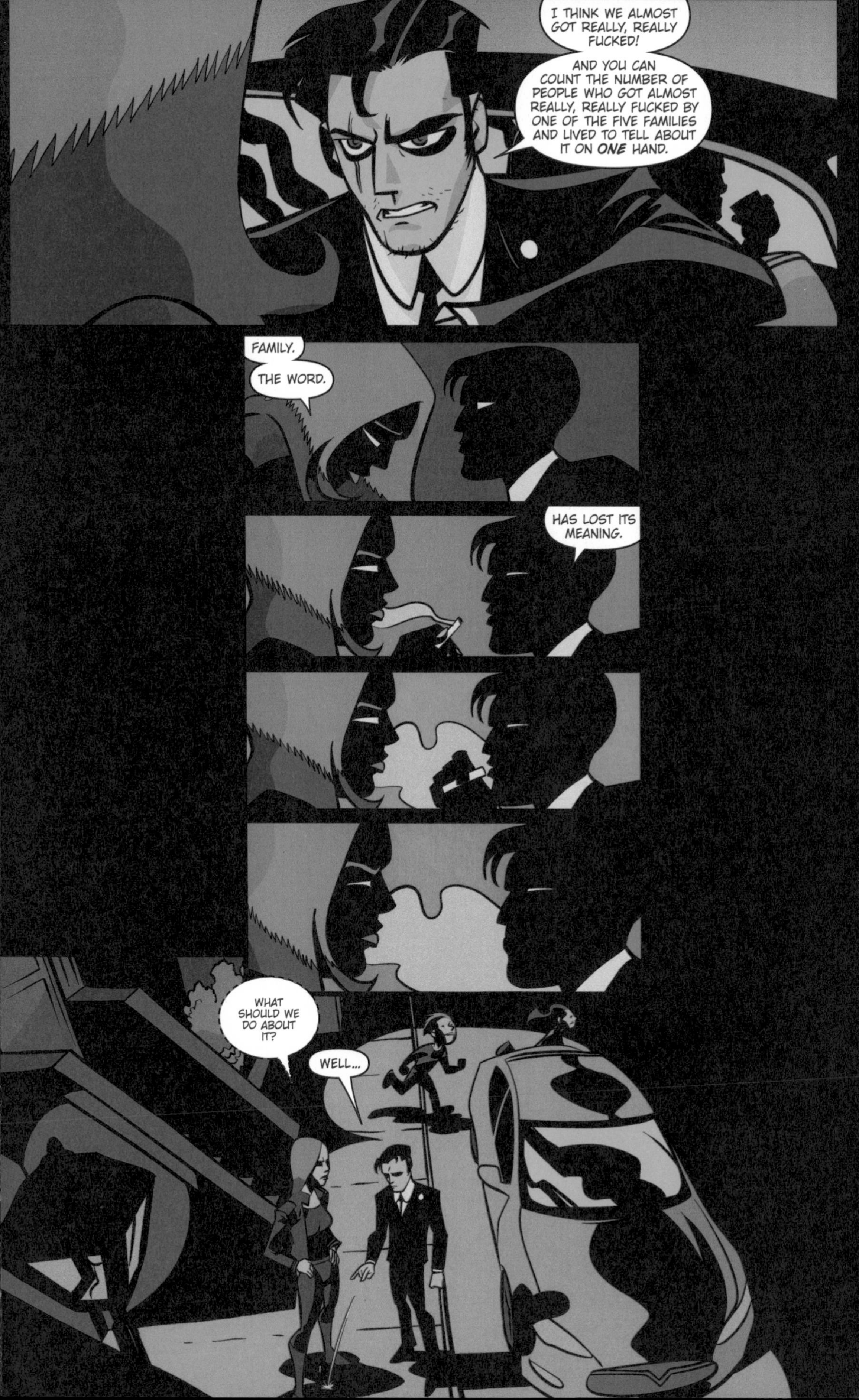
I THINK WE ALMOST GOT REALLY, REALLY FUCKED!
AND YOU CAN COUNT THE NUMBER OF PEOPLE WHO GOT ALMOST REALLY, REALLY FUCKED BY ONE OF THE FIVE FAMILIES AND LIVED TO TELL ABOUT IT ON *ONE* HAND.
FAMILY.
THE WORD.
HAS LOST ITS MEANING.
WHAT SHOULD WE DO ABOUT IT?
WELL...

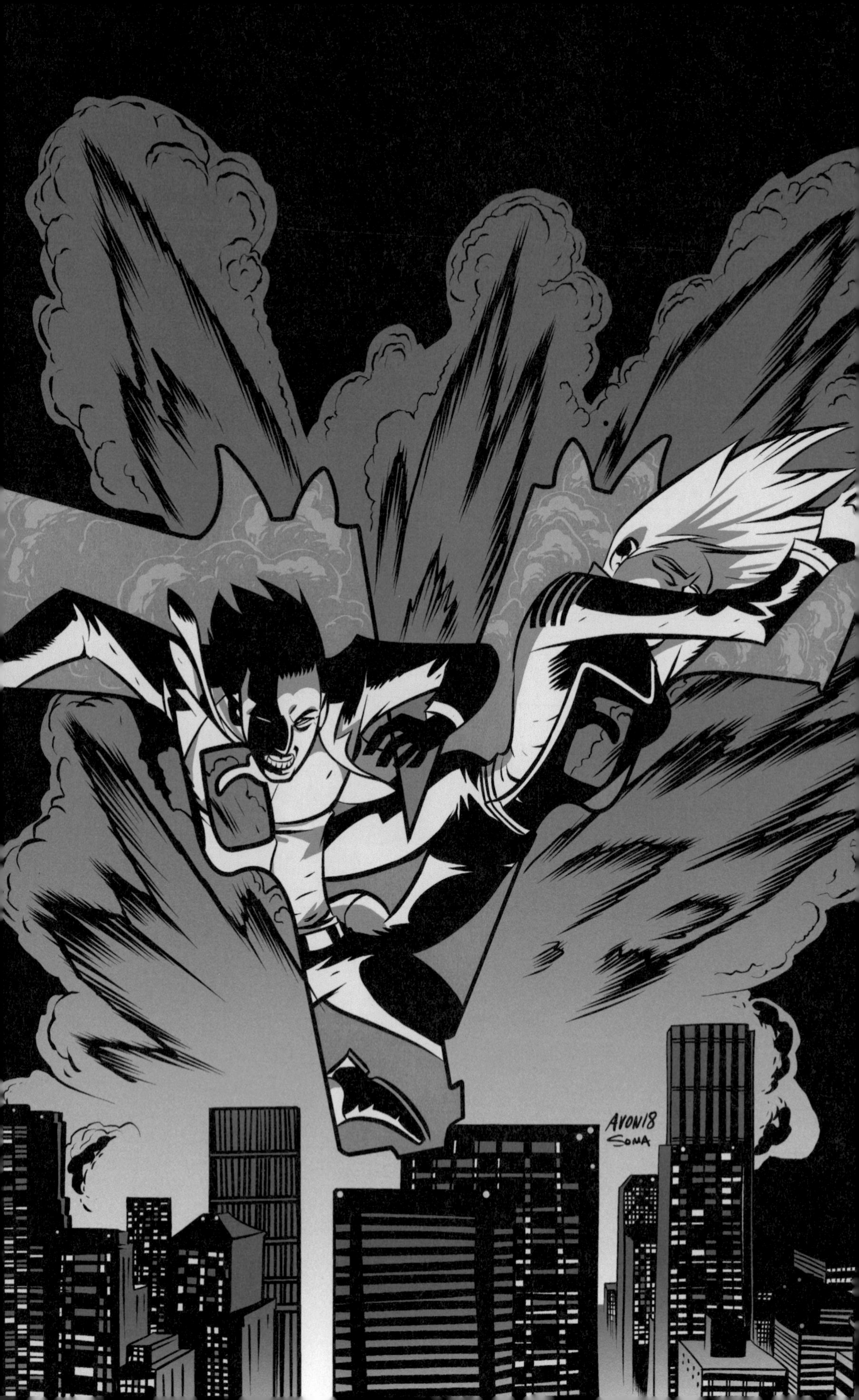
AVON18
SONA

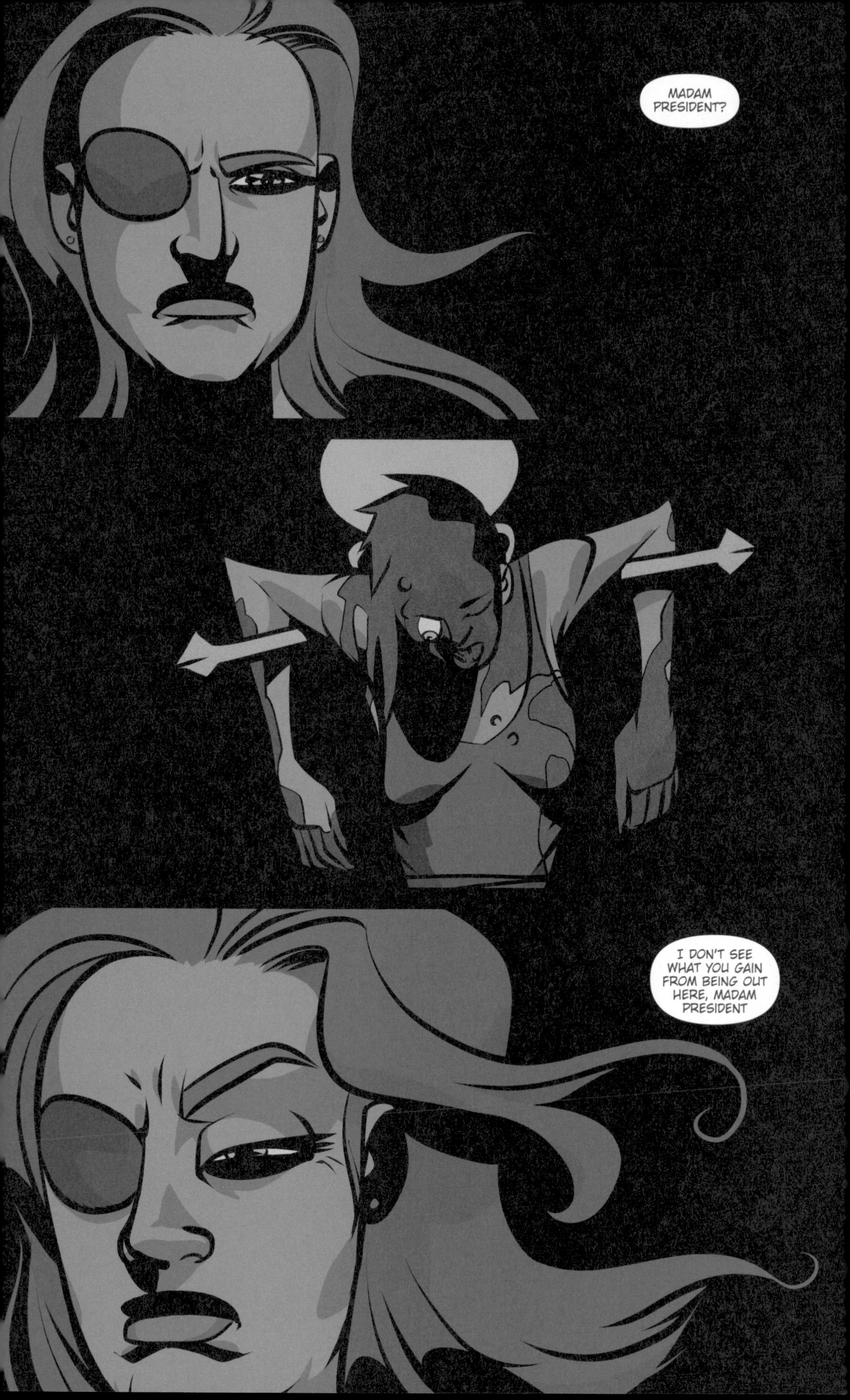
MADAM PRESIDENT?
I DON'T SEE WHAT YOU GAIN FROM BEING OUT HERE, MADAM PRESIDENT

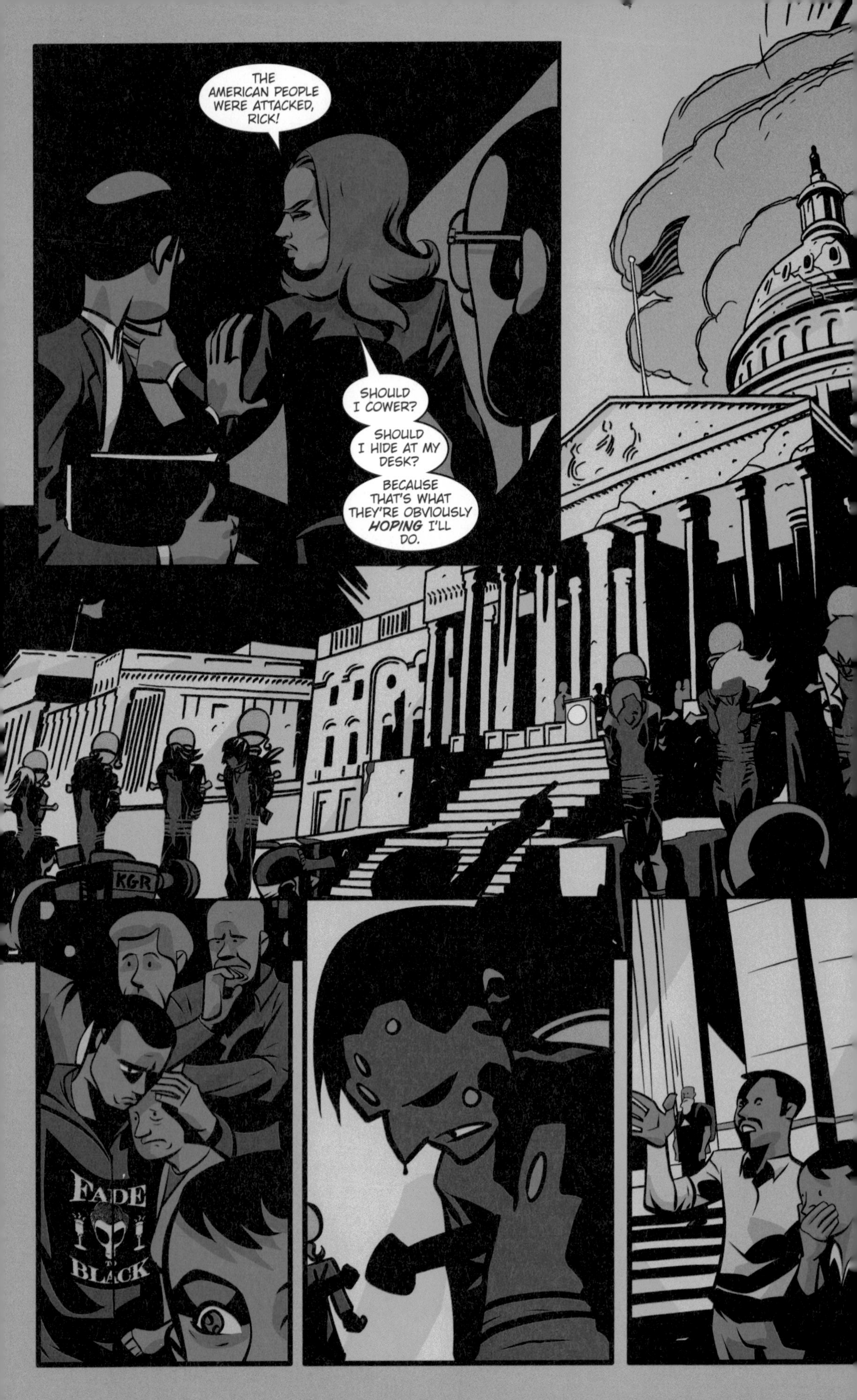
THE AMERICAN PEOPLE WERE ATTACKED, RICK!
SHOULD I COWER?
SHOULD I HIDE AT MY DESK?
BECAUSE THAT'S WHAT THEY'RE OBVIOUSLY *HOPING* I'LL DO.
KGR
FADE TO BLACK

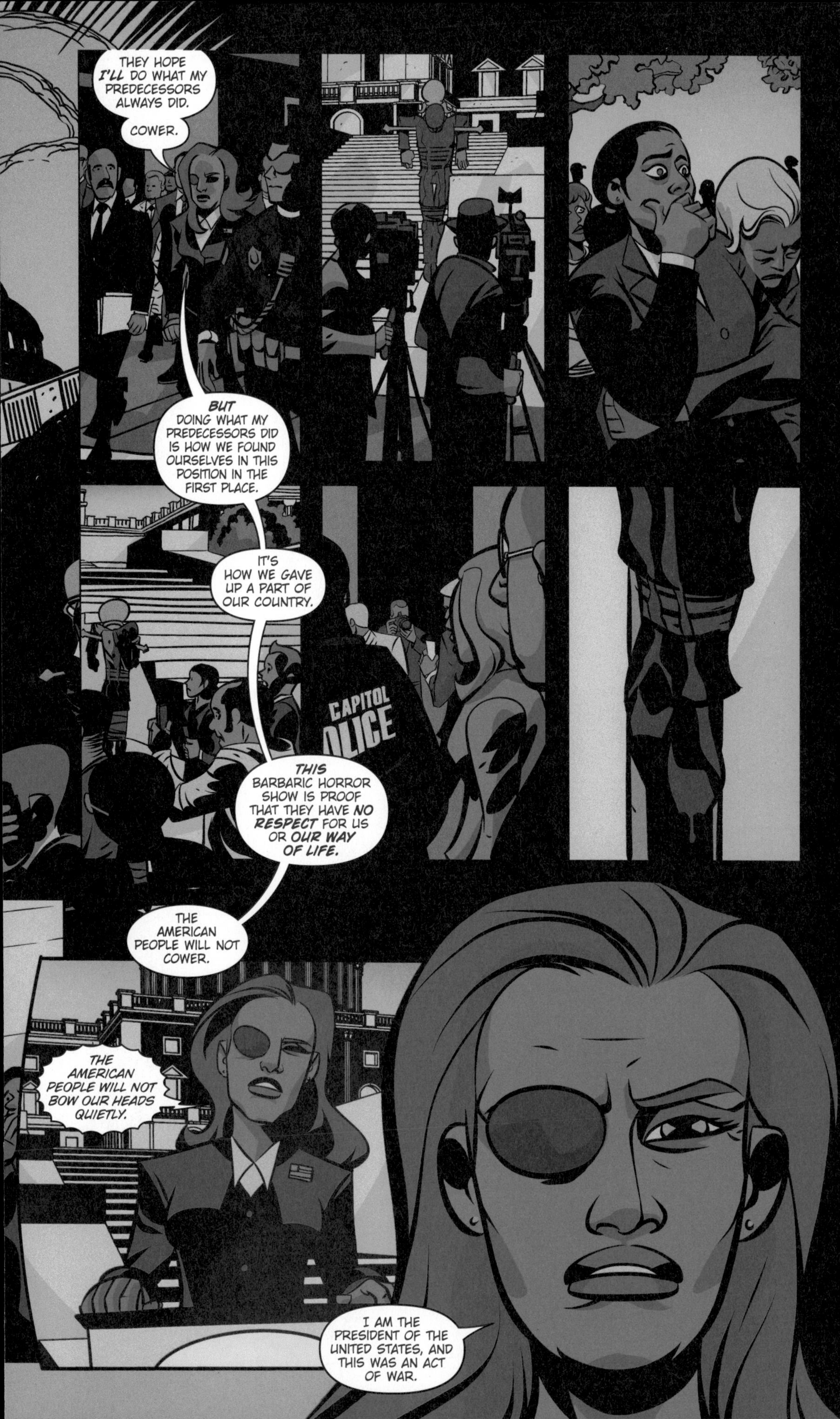

THEY HOPE *I'LL* DO WHAT MY PREDECESSORS ALWAYS DID.
COWER.
BUT DOING WHAT MY PREDECESSORS DID IS HOW WE FOUND OURSELVES IN THIS POSITION IN THE FIRST PLACE.
IT'S HOW WE GAVE UP A PART OF OUR COUNTRY.
CAPITOL
OLICE
THIS BARBARIC HORROR SHOW IS PROOF THAT THEY HAVE *NO RESPECT* FOR US OR *OUR WAY OF LIFE.*
THE AMERICAN PEOPLE WILL NOT COWER.
THE AMERICAN PEOPLE WILL NOT BOW OUR HEADS QUIETLY.
I AM THE PRESIDENT OF THE UNITED STATES, AND THIS WAS AN ACT OF WAR.

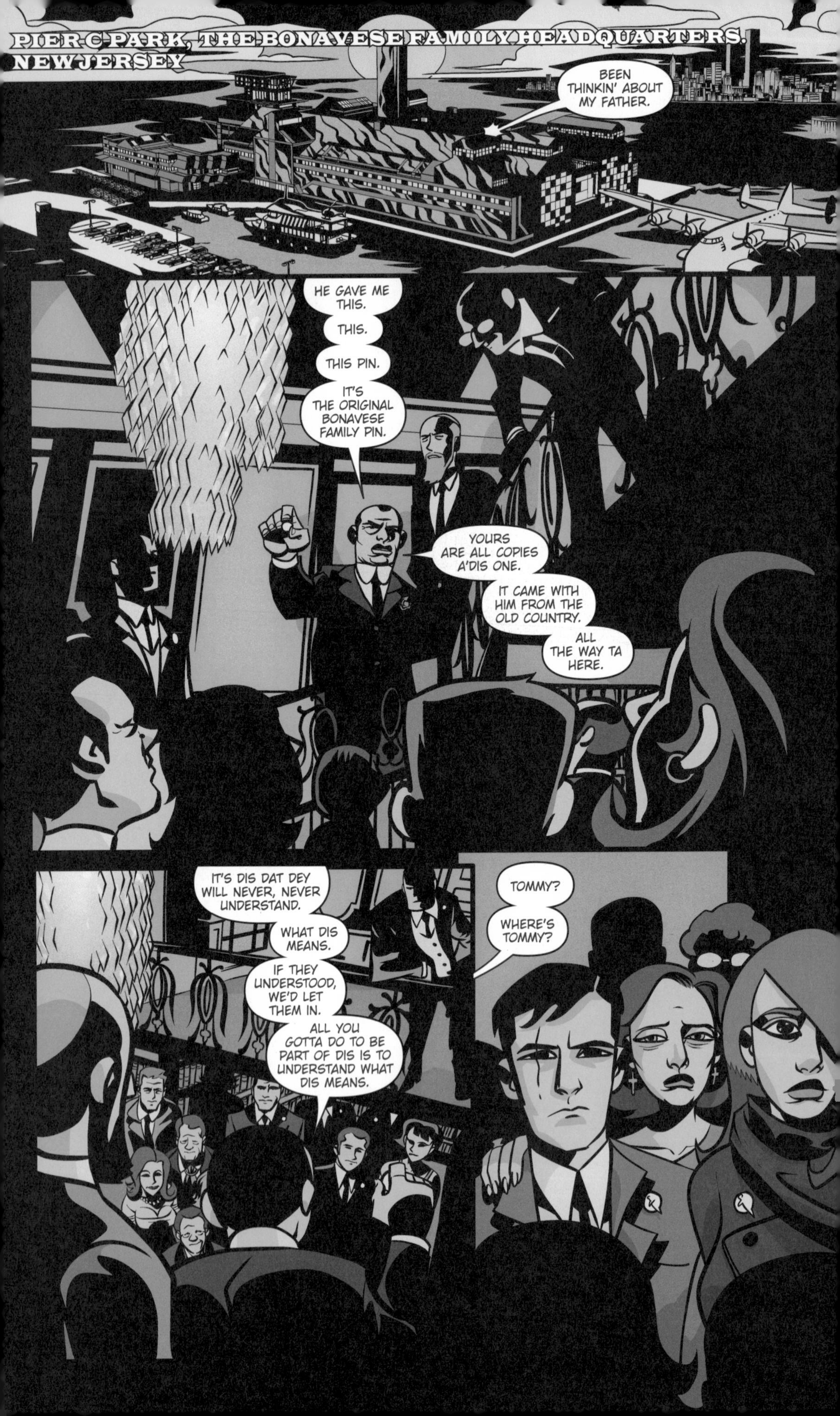
PIER C PARK, THE BONAVESE FAMILY HEADQUARTERS. NEW JERSEY
BEEN THINKIN' ABOUT MY FATHER.
HE GAVE ME THIS.
THIS.
THIS PIN.
IT'S THE ORIGINAL BONAVESE FAMILY PIN.
YOURS ARE ALL COPIES A'DIS ONE.
IT CAME WITH HIM FROM THE OLD COUNTRY.
ALL THE WAY TA HERE.
IT'S DIS DAT DEY WILL NEVER, NEVER UNDERSTAND.
WHAT DIS MEANS.
IF THEY UNDERSTOOD, WE'D LET THEM IN.
ALL YOU GOTTA DO TO BE PART OF DIS IS TO UNDERSTAND WHAT DIS MEANS.
TOMMY?
WHERE'S TOMMY?

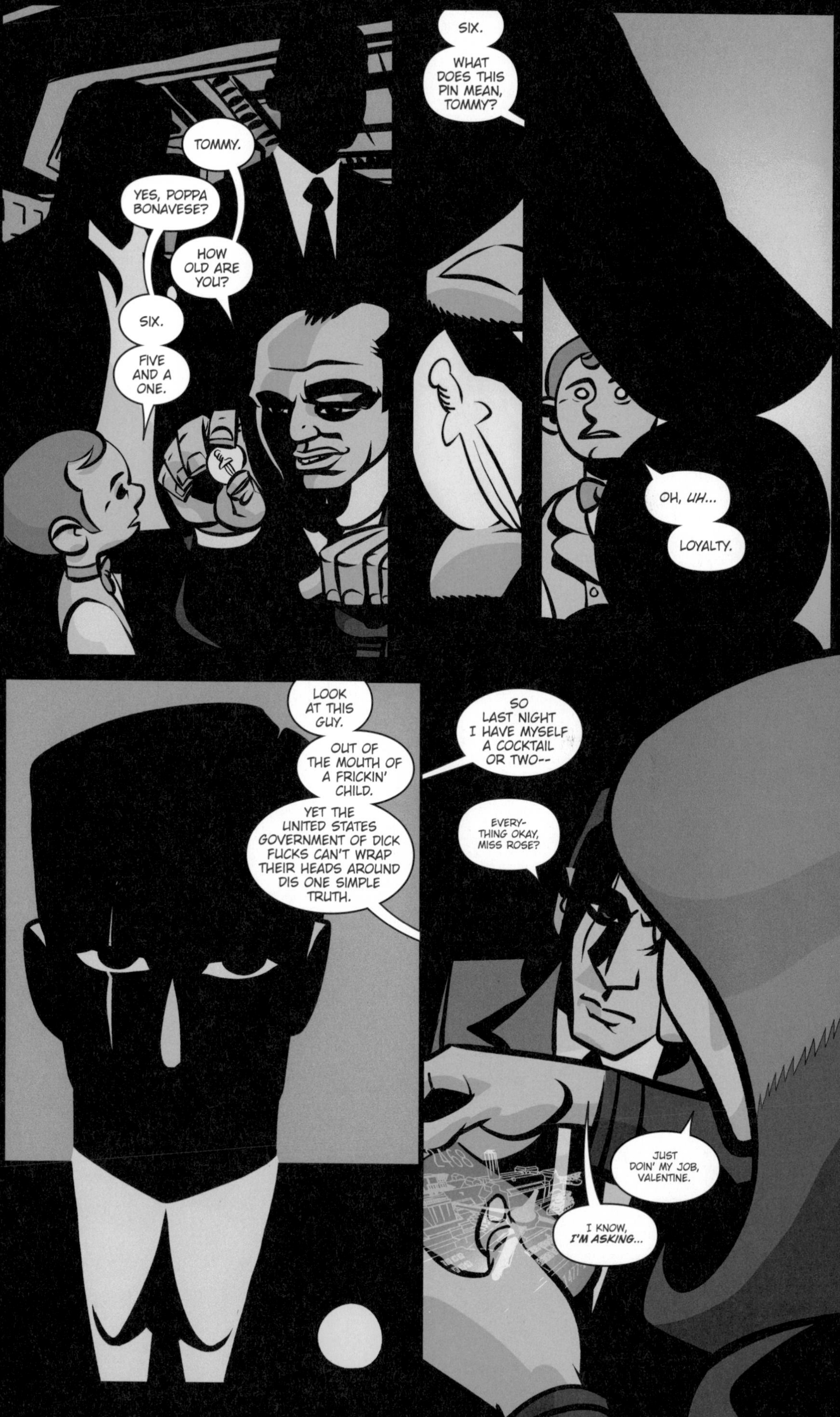
TOMMY.
YES, POPPA BONAVESE?
HOW OLD ARE YOU?
SIX.
FIVE AND A ONE.
SIX.
WHAT DOES THIS PIN MEAN, TOMMY?
OH, UH...
LOYALTY.
LOOK AT THIS GUY.
OUT OF THE MOUTH OF A FRICKIN' CHILD.
YET THE UNITED STATES GOVERNMENT OF DICK FUCKS CAN'T WRAP THEIR HEADS AROUND DIS ONE SIMPLE TRUTH.
SO LAST NIGHT I HAVE MYSELF A COCKTAIL OR TWO--
EVERY-THING OKAY, MISS ROSE?
JUST DOIN' MY JOB, VALENTINE.
I KNOW, I'M ASKING...

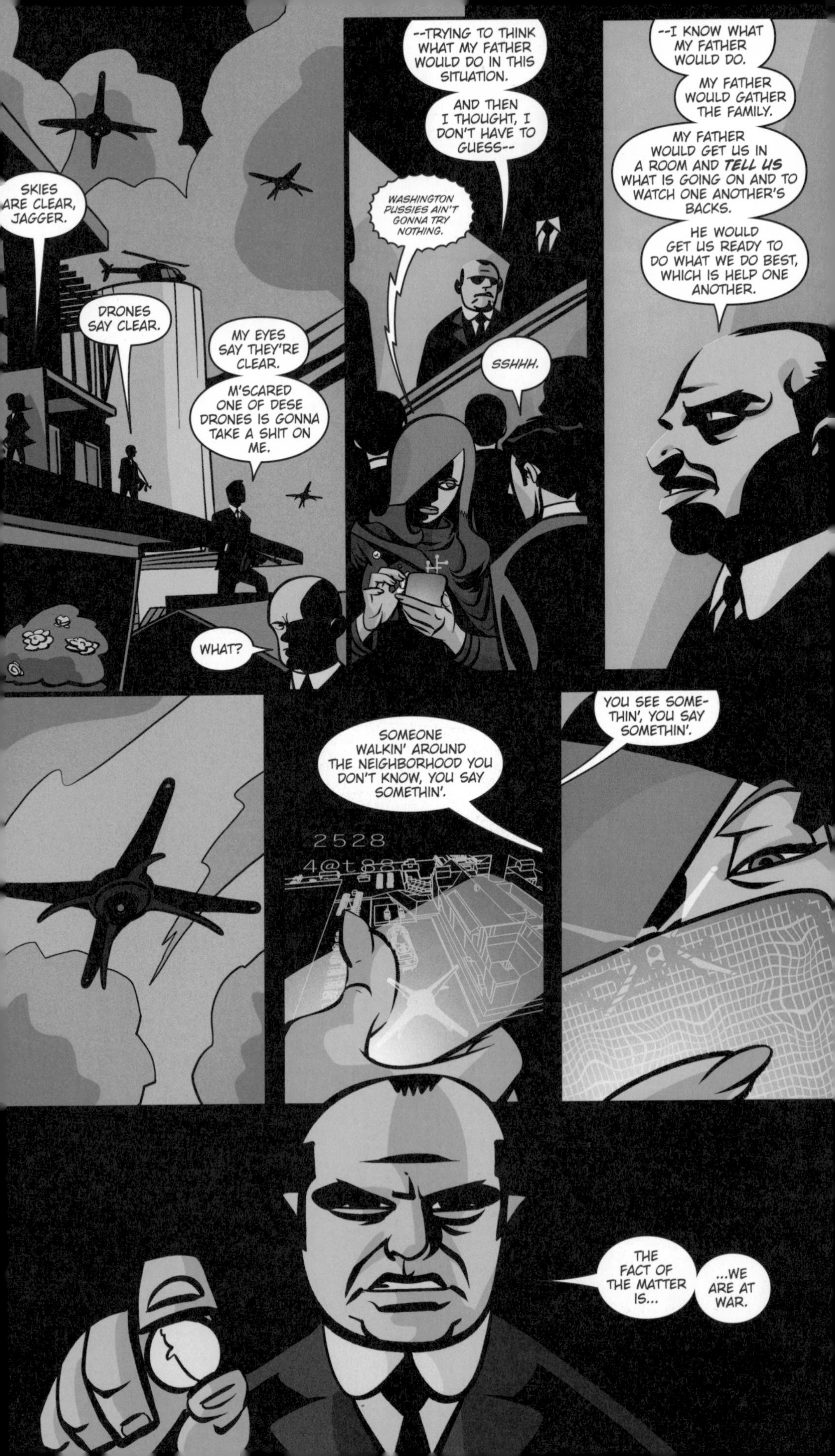

SKIES ARE CLEAR, JAGGER.
DRONES SAY CLEAR.
MY EYES SAY THEY'RE CLEAR.
M'SCARED ONE OF DESE DRONES IS GONNA TAKE A SHIT ON ME.
WHAT?
--TRYING TO THINK WHAT MY FATHER WOULD DO IN THIS SITUATION.
AND THEN I THOUGHT, I DON'T HAVE TO GUESS--
WASHINGTON PUSSIES AIN'T GONNA TRY NOTHING.
SSHHH.
--I KNOW WHAT MY FATHER WOULD DO.
MY FATHER WOULD GATHER THE FAMILY.
MY FATHER WOULD GET US IN A ROOM AND TELL US WHAT IS GOING ON AND TO WATCH ONE ANOTHER'S BACKS.
HE WOULD GET US READY TO DO WHAT WE DO BEST, WHICH IS HELP ONE ANOTHER.
SOMEONE WALKIN' AROUND THE NEIGHBORHOOD YOU DON'T KNOW, YOU SAY SOMETHIN'.
2528
4@t88
YOU SEE SOMETHIN', YOU SAY SOMETHIN'.
THE FACT OF THE MATTER IS...
...WE ARE AT WAR.

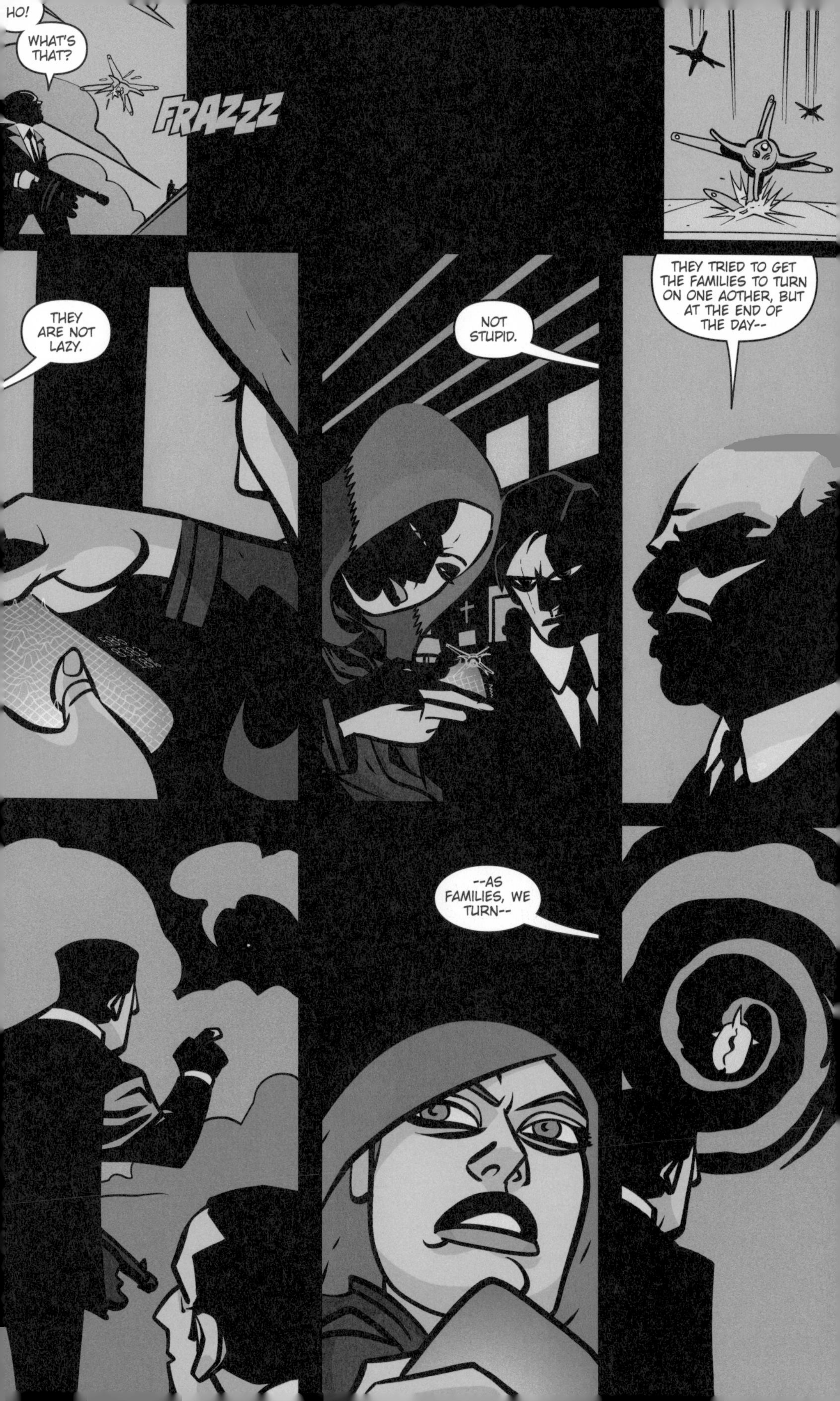
HO!
WHAT'S THAT?
FRAZZZ
THEY ARE NOT LAZY.
NOT STUPID.
THEY TRIED TO GET THE FAMILIES TO TURN ON ONE AOTHER, BUT AT THE END OF THE DAY--
--AS FAMILIES, WE TURN--

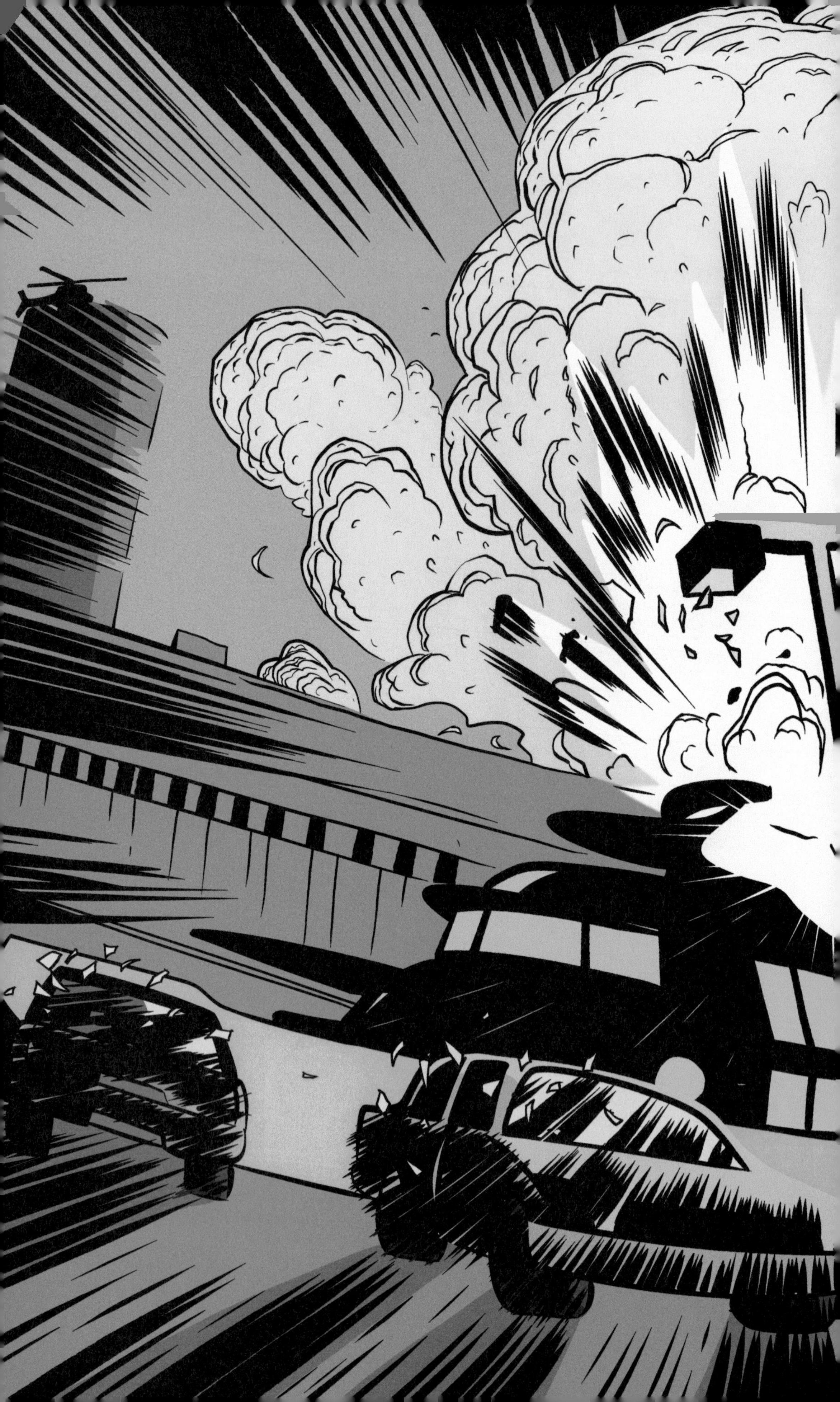

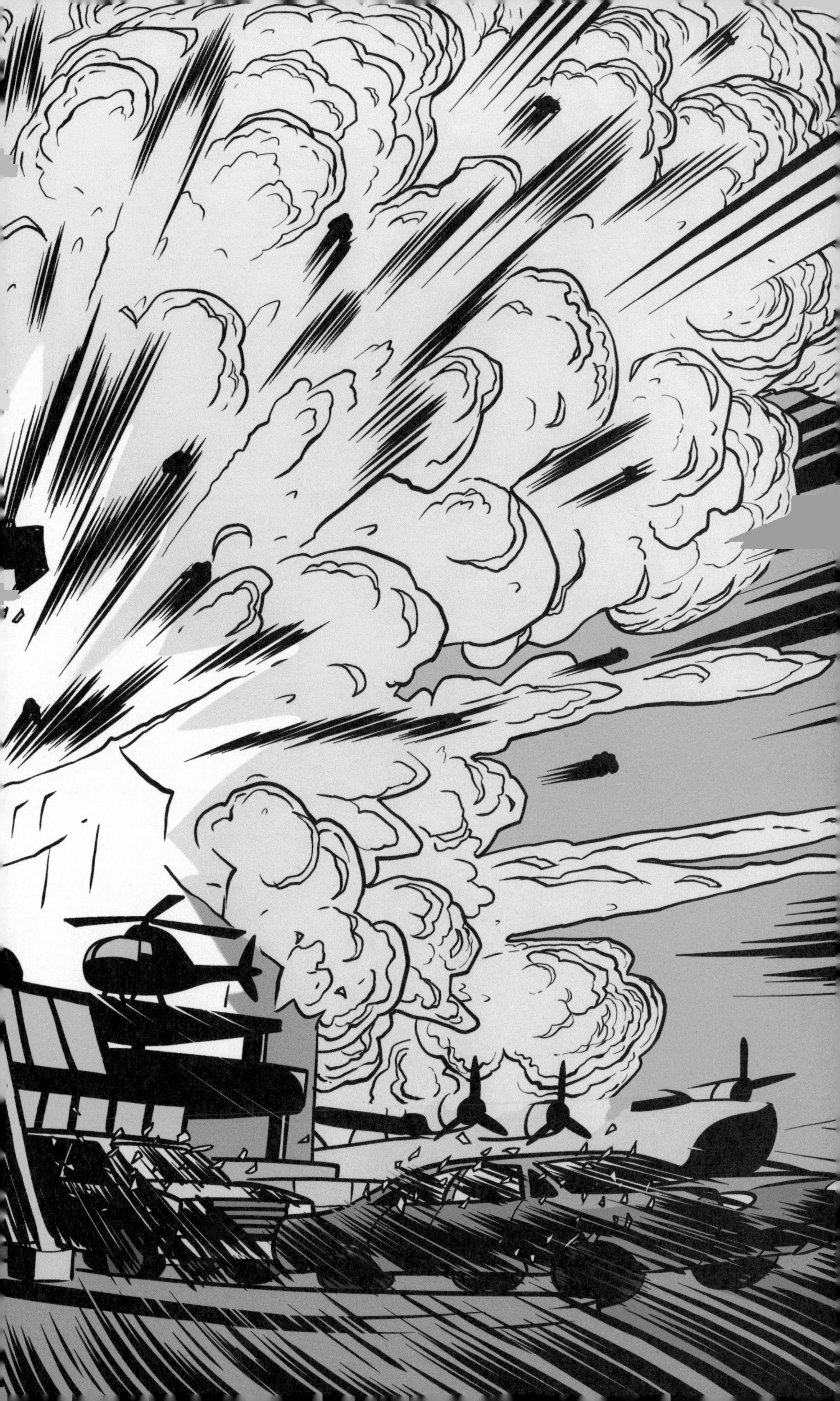

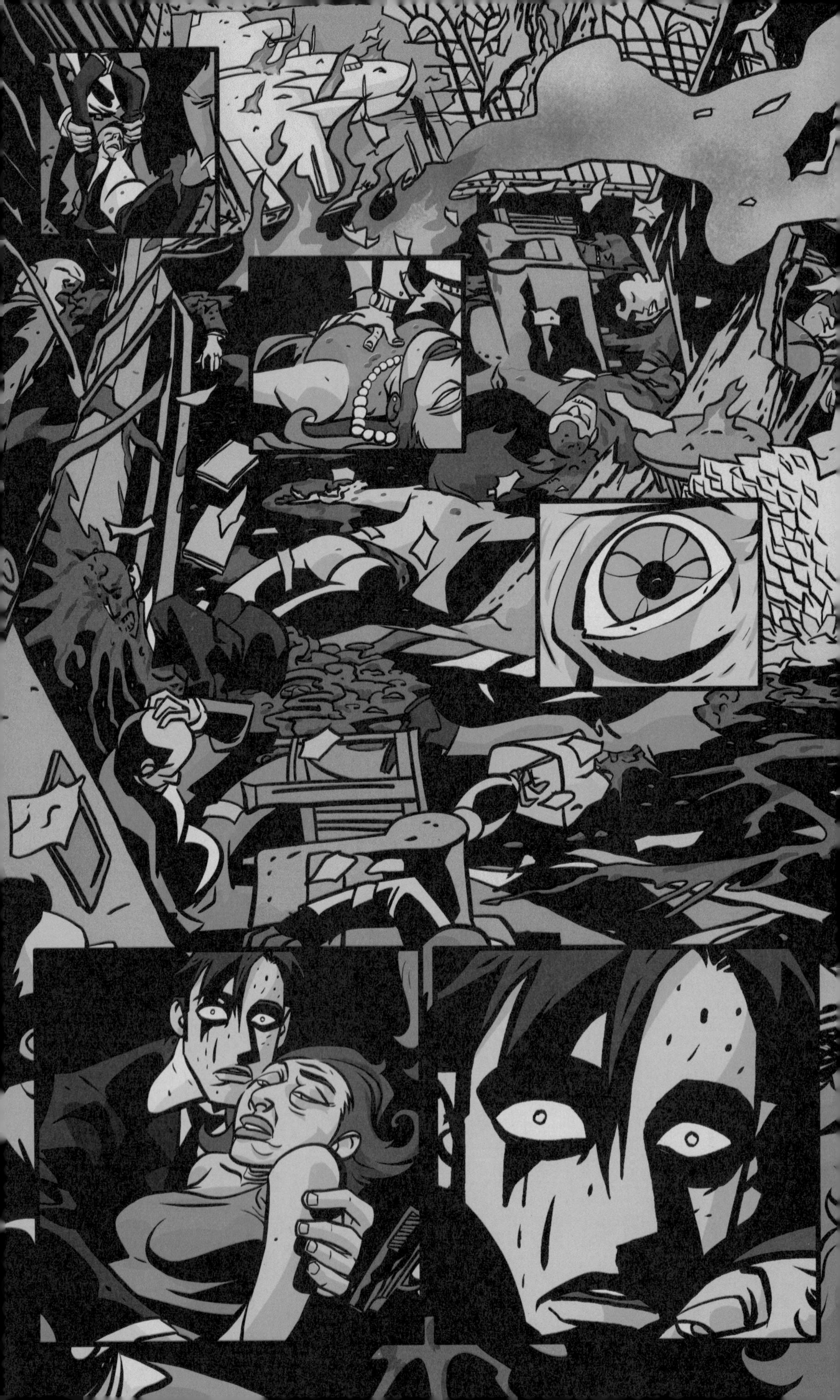

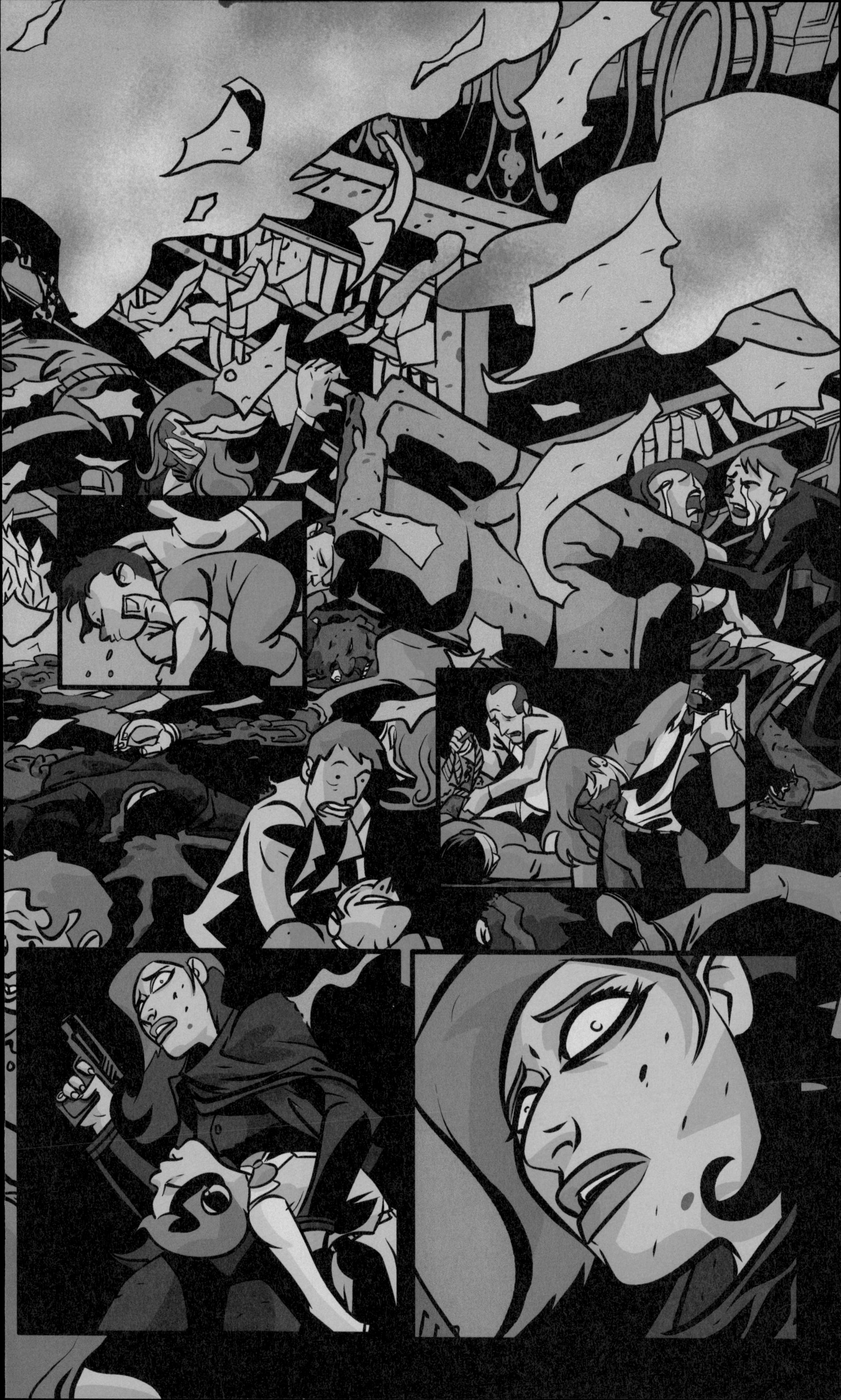

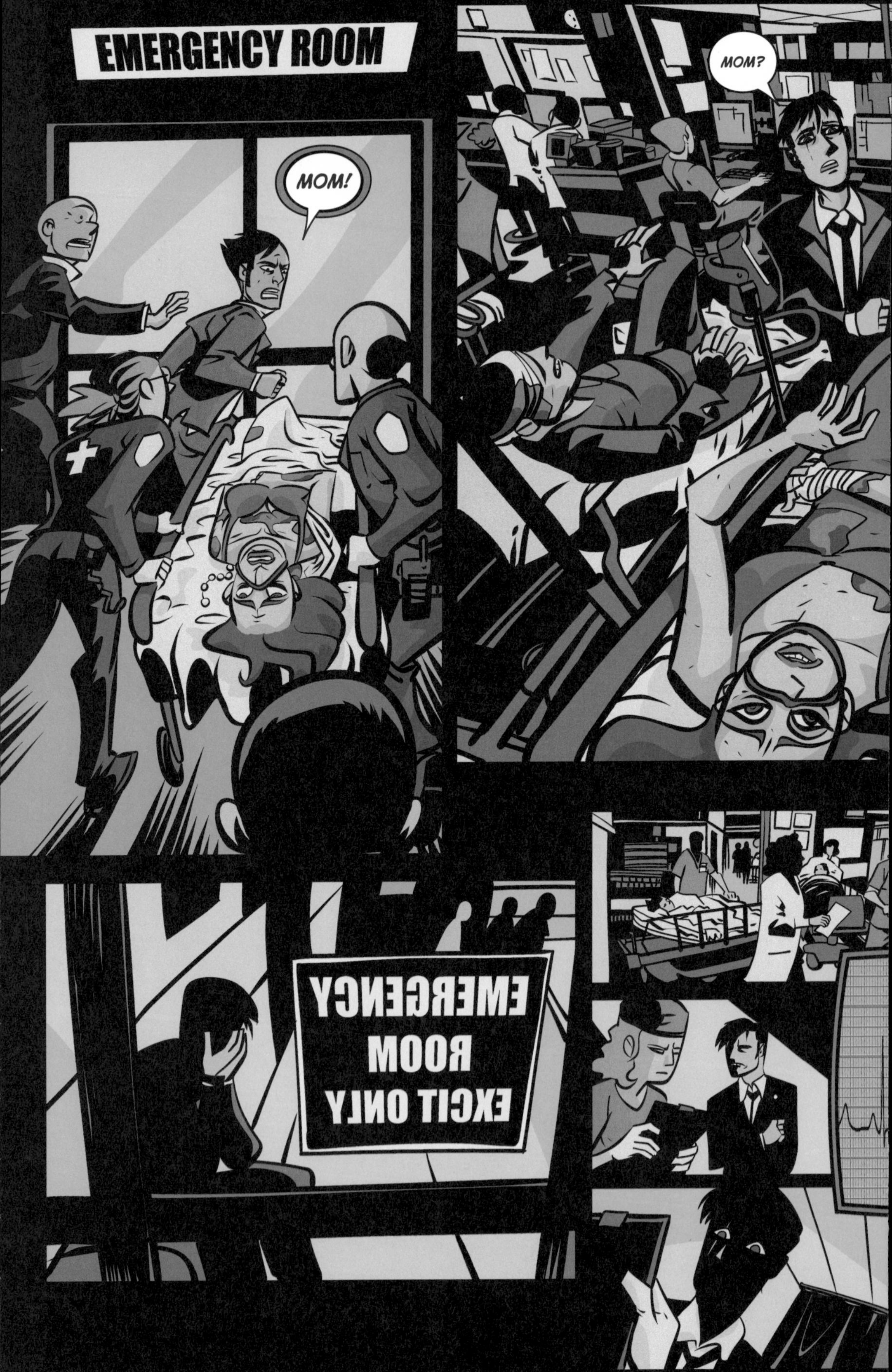
EMERGENCY ROOM
MOM!
MOM?
EMERGENCY
ROOM
EXCIT ONLY

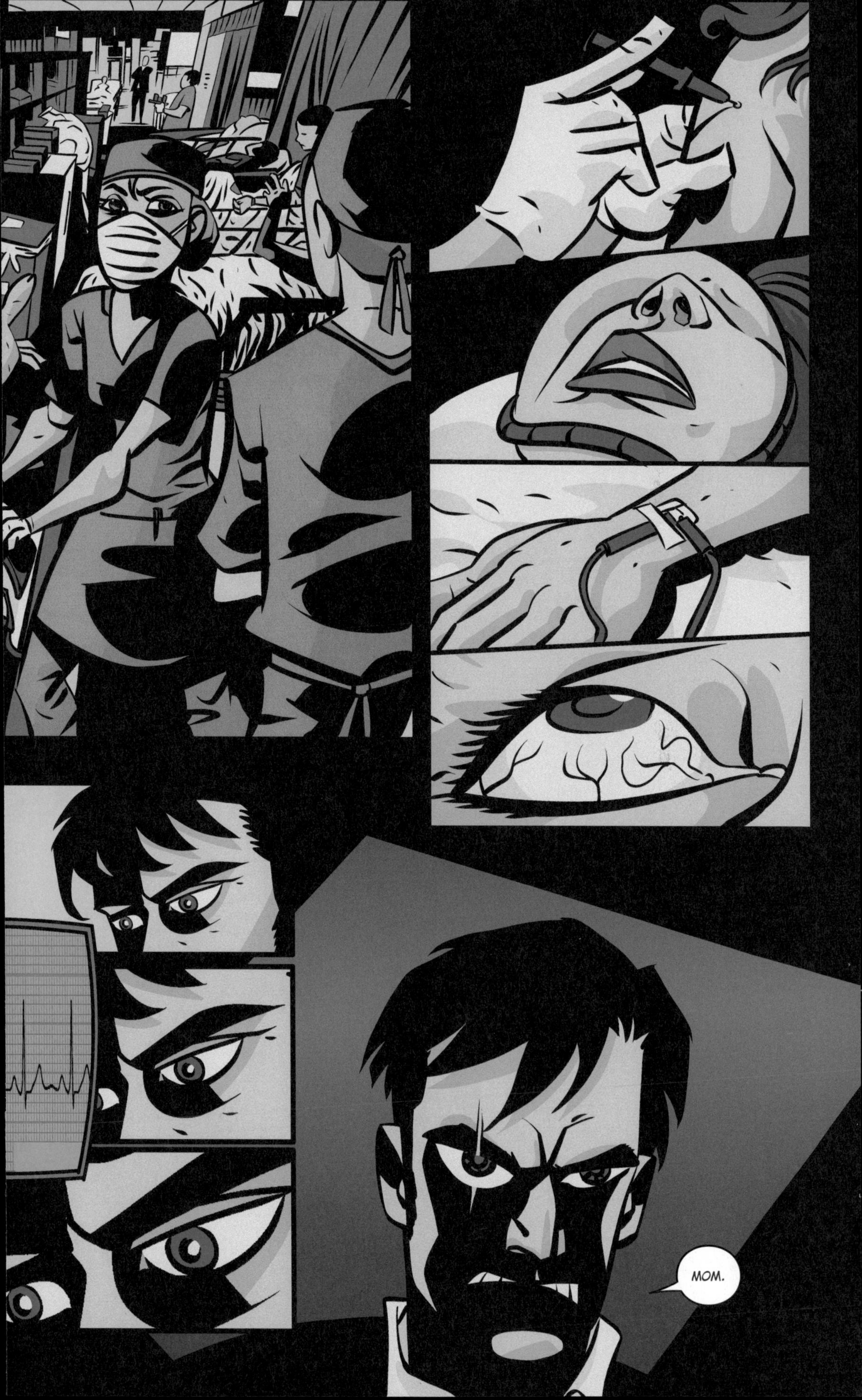
MOM.

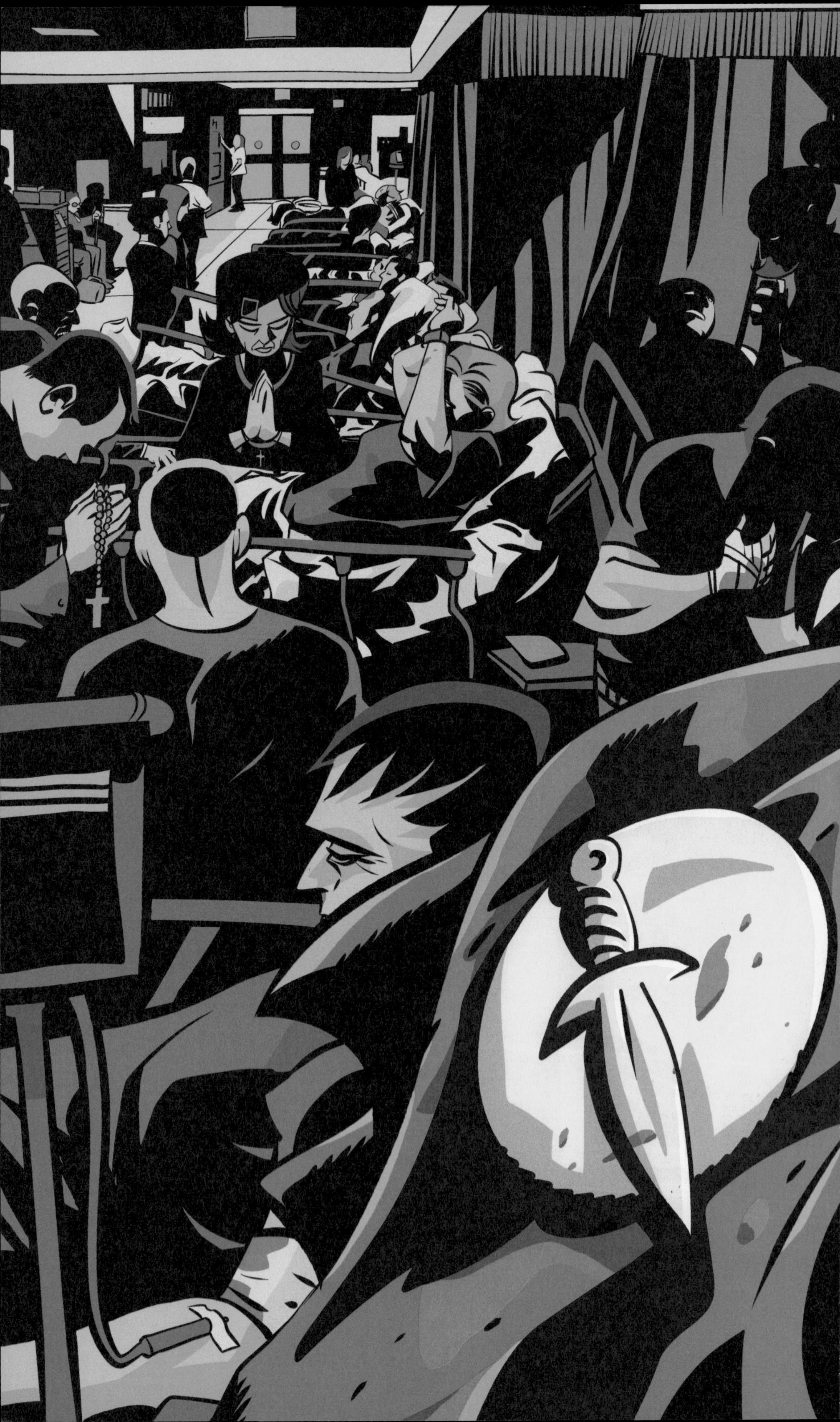

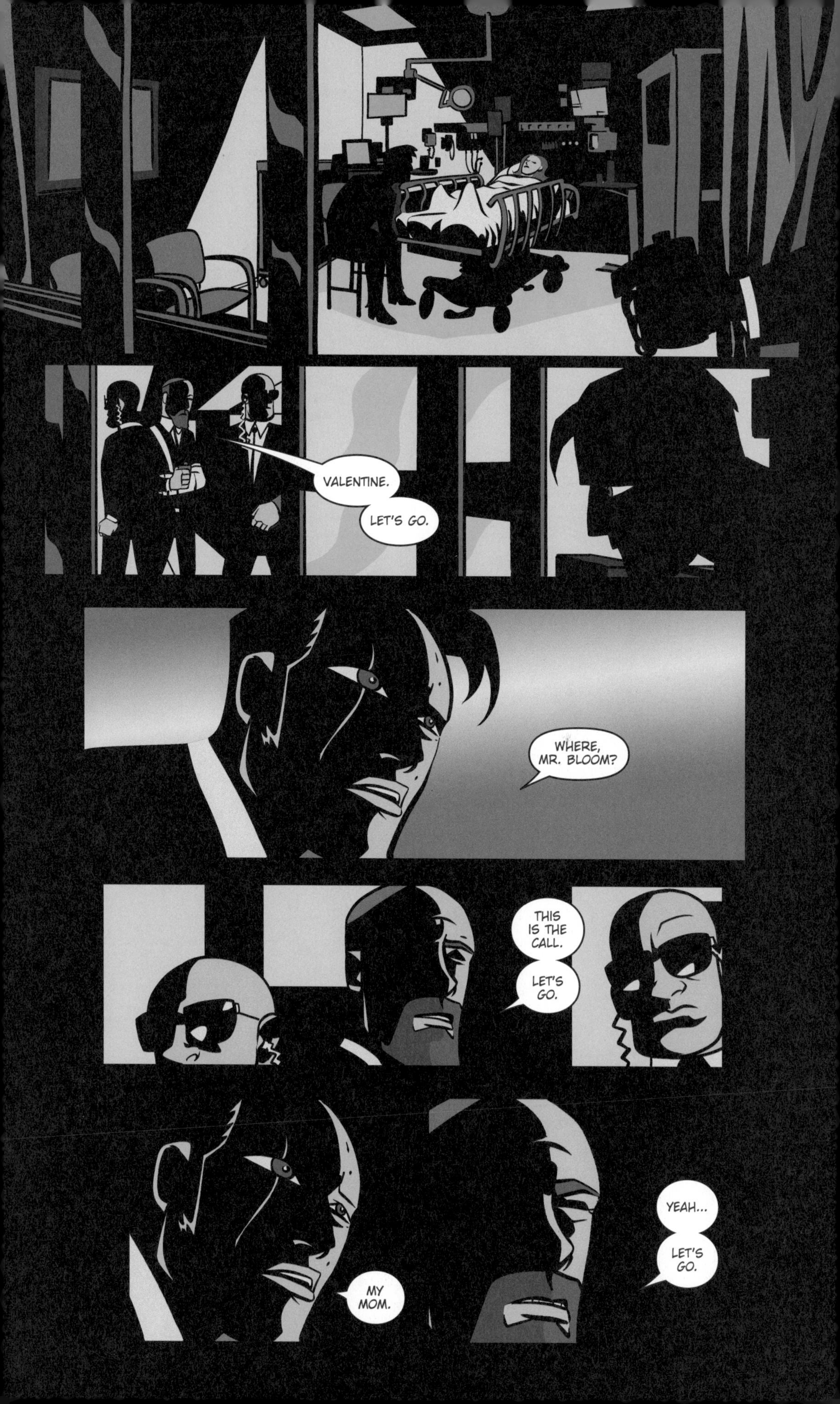
VALENTINE.
LET'S GO.
WHERE, MR. BLOOM?
THIS IS THE CALL.
LET'S GO.
MY MOM.
YEAH...
LET'S GO.

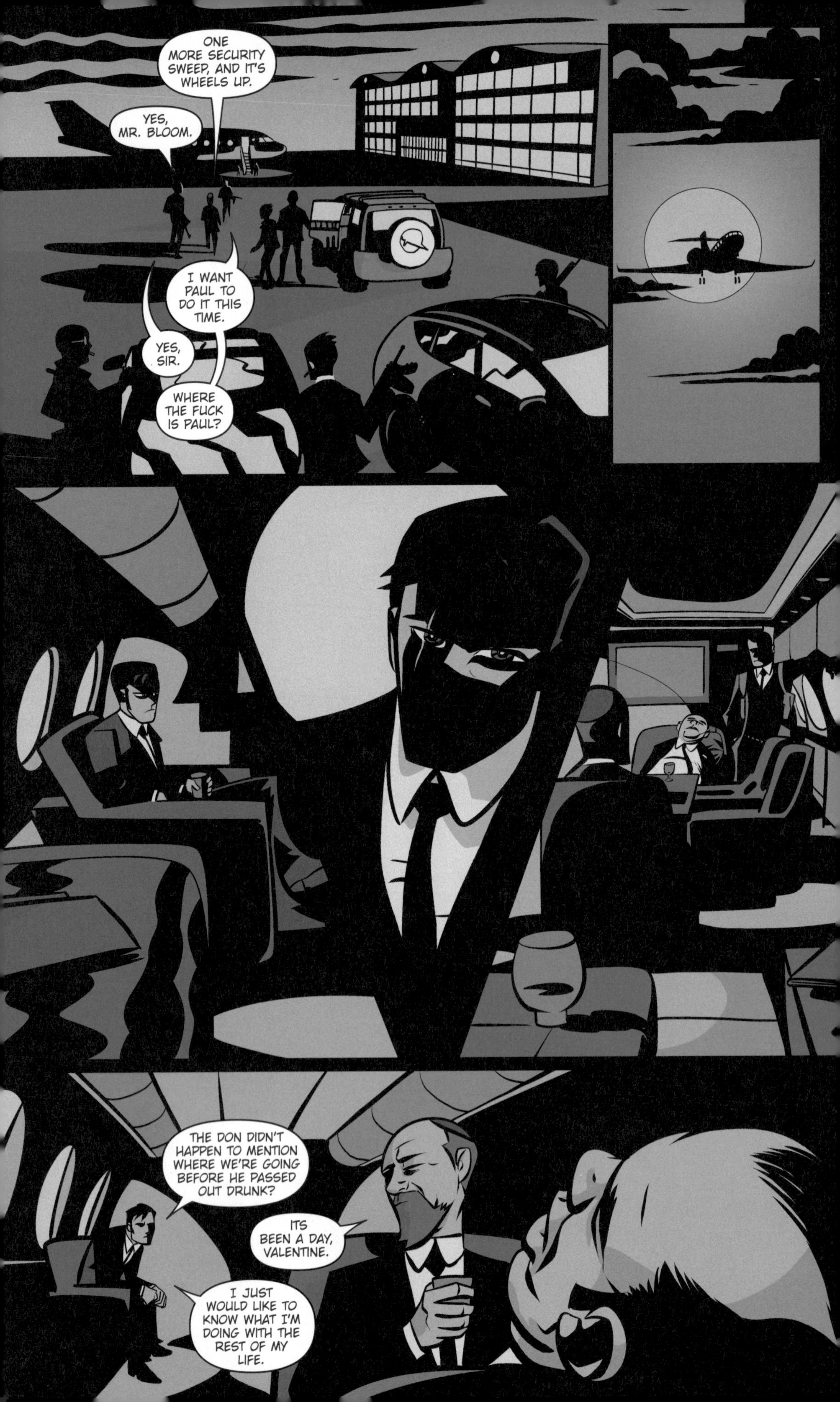
ONE MORE SECURITY SWEEP, AND IT'S WHEELS UP.
YES, MR. BLOOM.
I WANT PAUL TO DO IT THIS TIME.
YES, SIR.
WHERE THE FUCK IS PAUL?
THE DON DIDN'T HAPPEN TO MENTION WHERE WE'RE GOING BEFORE HE PASSED OUT DRUNK?
ITS BEEN A DAY, VALENTINE.
I JUST WOULD LIKE TO KNOW WHAT I'M DOING WITH THE REST OF MY LIFE.

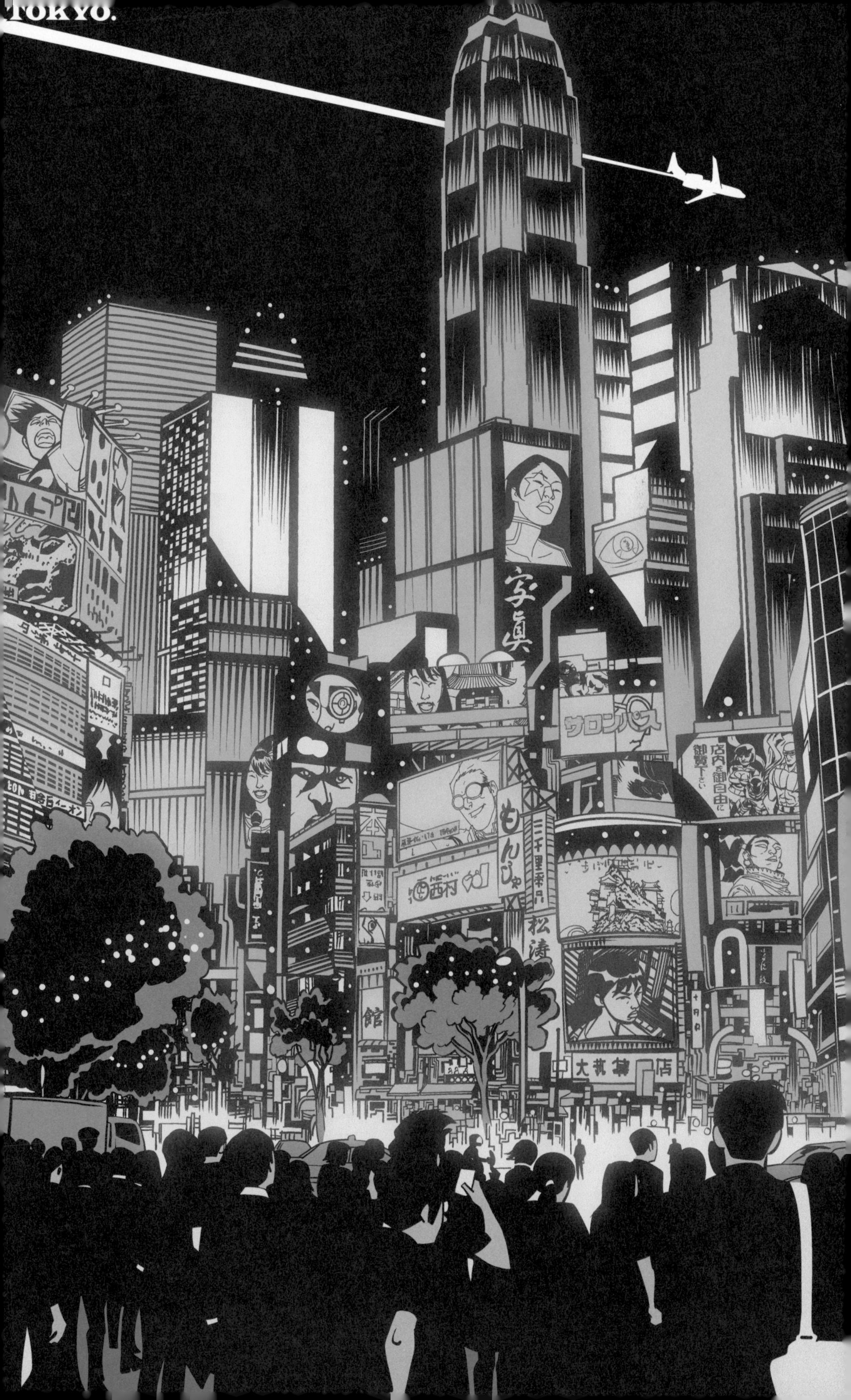
TOKYO.
サロンパス
もんじゃ

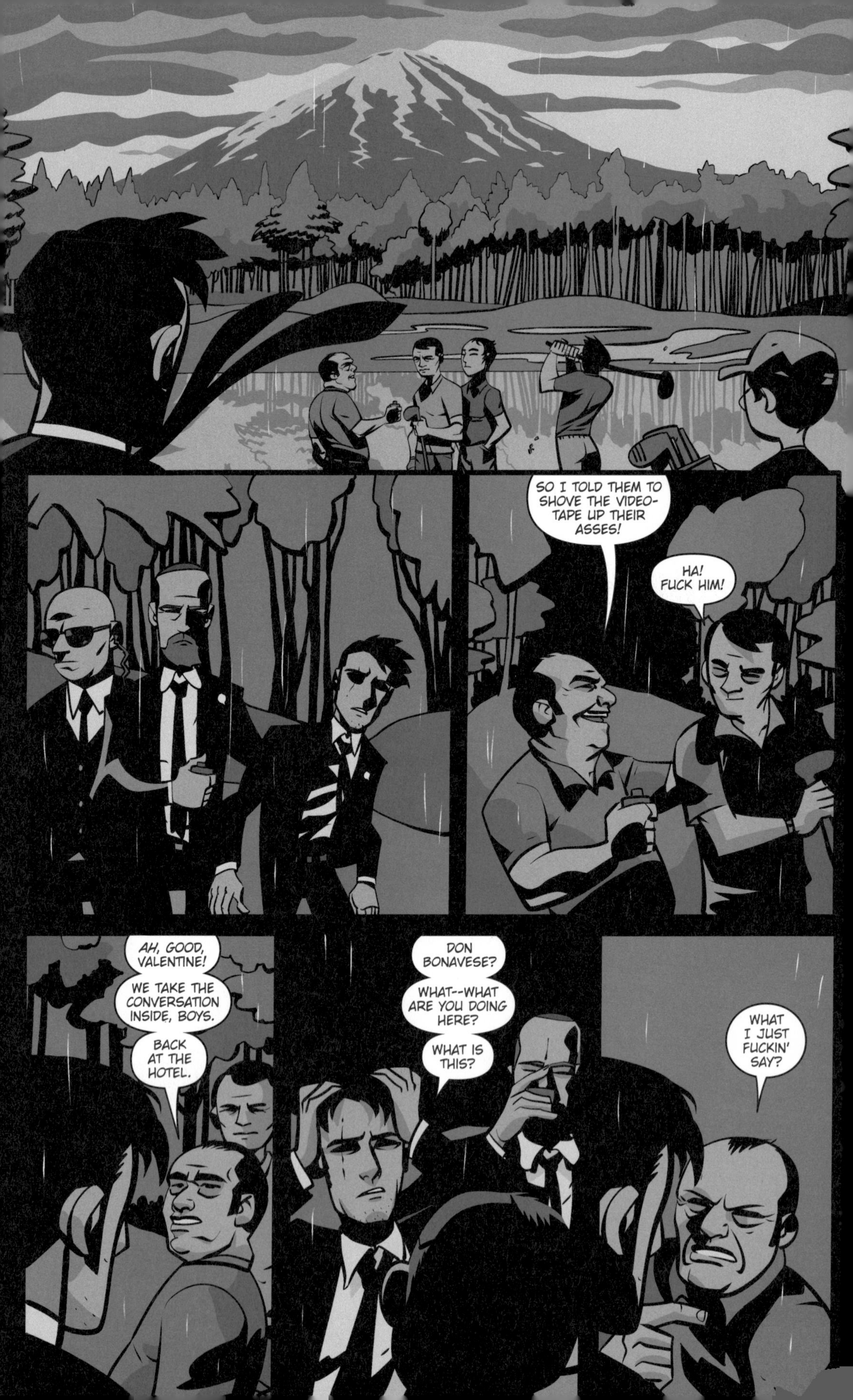
SO I TOLD THEM TO SHOVE THE VIDEO-TAPE UP THEIR ASSES!
HA! FUCK HIM!
AH, GOOD, VALENTINE!
WE TAKE THE CONVERSATION INSIDE, BOYS.
BACK AT THE HOTEL.
DON BONAVESE?
WHAT--WHAT ARE YOU DOING HERE?
WHAT IS THIS?
WHAT I JUST FUCKIN' SAY?

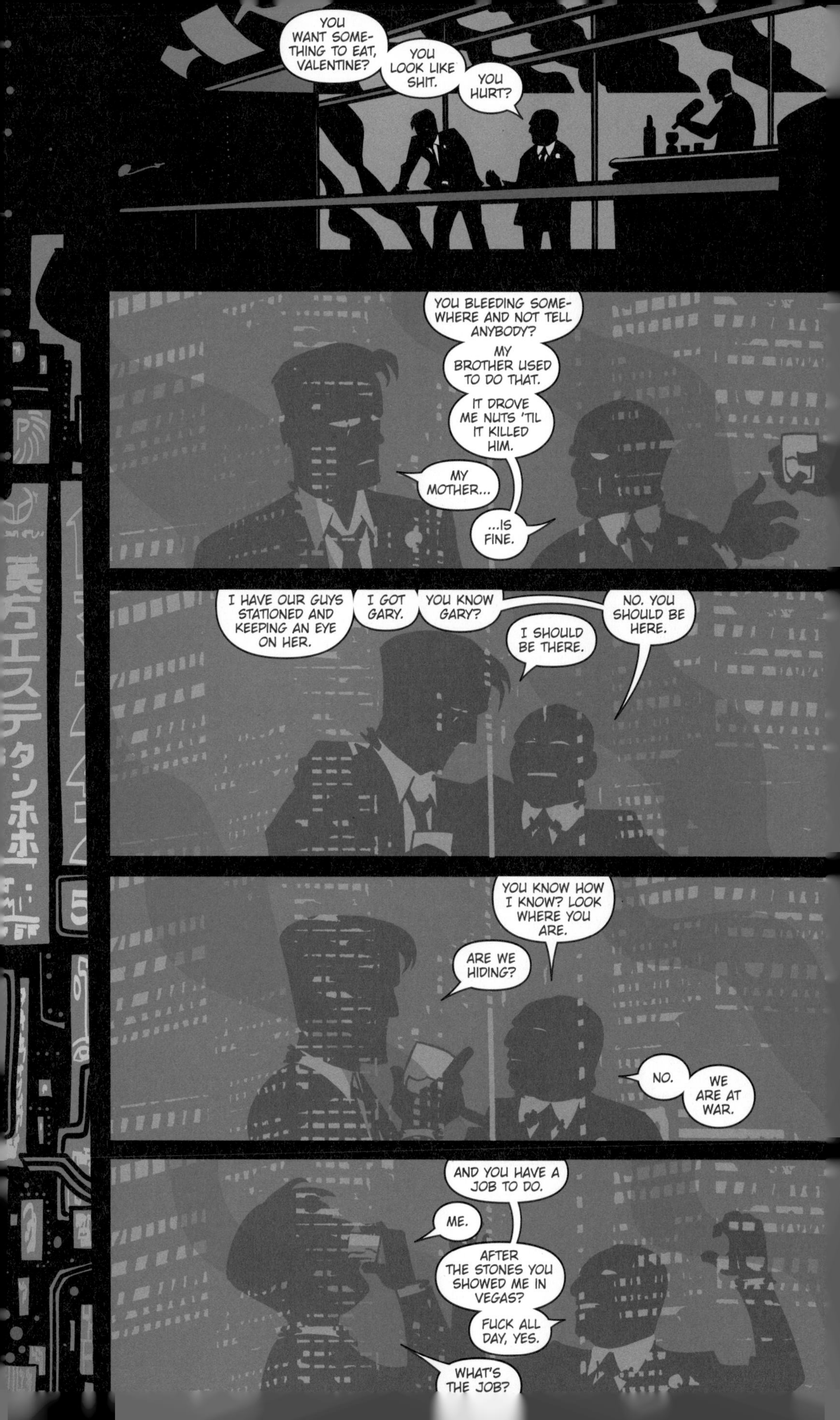
YOU WANT SOME-THING TO EAT, VALENTINE?
YOU LOOK LIKE SHIT.
YOU HURT?
YOU BLEEDING SOME-WHERE AND NOT TELL ANYBODY?
MY BROTHER USED TO DO THAT.
IT DROVE ME NUTS 'TIL IT KILLED HIM.
MY MOTHER...
...IS FINE.
I HAVE OUR GUYS STATIONED AND KEEPING AN EYE ON HER.
I GOT GARY.
YOU KNOW GARY?
I SHOULD BE THERE.
NO. YOU SHOULD BE HERE.
YOU KNOW HOW I KNOW? LOOK WHERE YOU ARE.
ARE WE HIDING?
NO.
WE ARE AT WAR.
AND YOU HAVE A JOB TO DO.
ME.
AFTER THE STONES YOU SHOWED ME IN VEGAS?
FUCK ALL DAY, YES.
WHAT'S THE JOB?

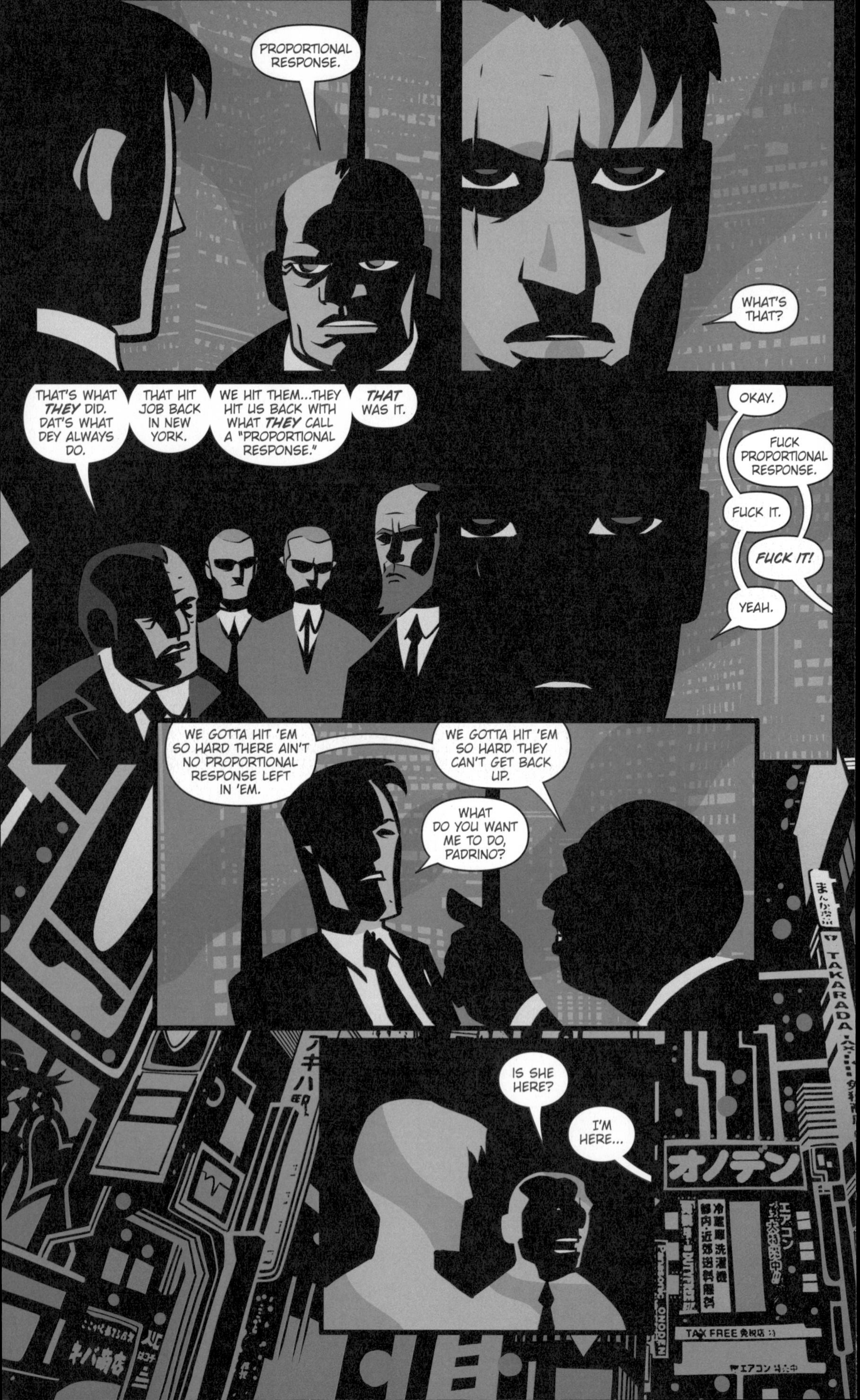
PROPORTIONAL RESPONSE.
WHAT'S THAT?
THAT'S WHAT THEY DID. DAT'S WHAT DEY ALWAYS DO.
THAT HIT JOB BACK IN NEW YORK.
WE HIT THEM...THEY HIT US BACK WITH WHAT THEY CALL A "PROPORTIONAL RESPONSE."
THAT WAS IT.
OKAY.
FUCK PROPORTIONAL RESPONSE.
FUCK IT.
FUCK IT!
YEAH.
WE GOTTA HIT 'EM SO HARD THERE AIN'T NO PROPORTIONAL RESPONSE LEFT IN 'EM.
WE GOTTA HIT 'EM SO HARD THEY CAN'T GET BACK UP.
WHAT DO YOU WANT ME TO DO, PADRINO?
TAKARADA
IS SHE HERE?
I'M HERE...
オノデン
エアコン
TAX FREE 免税店
キバ商店

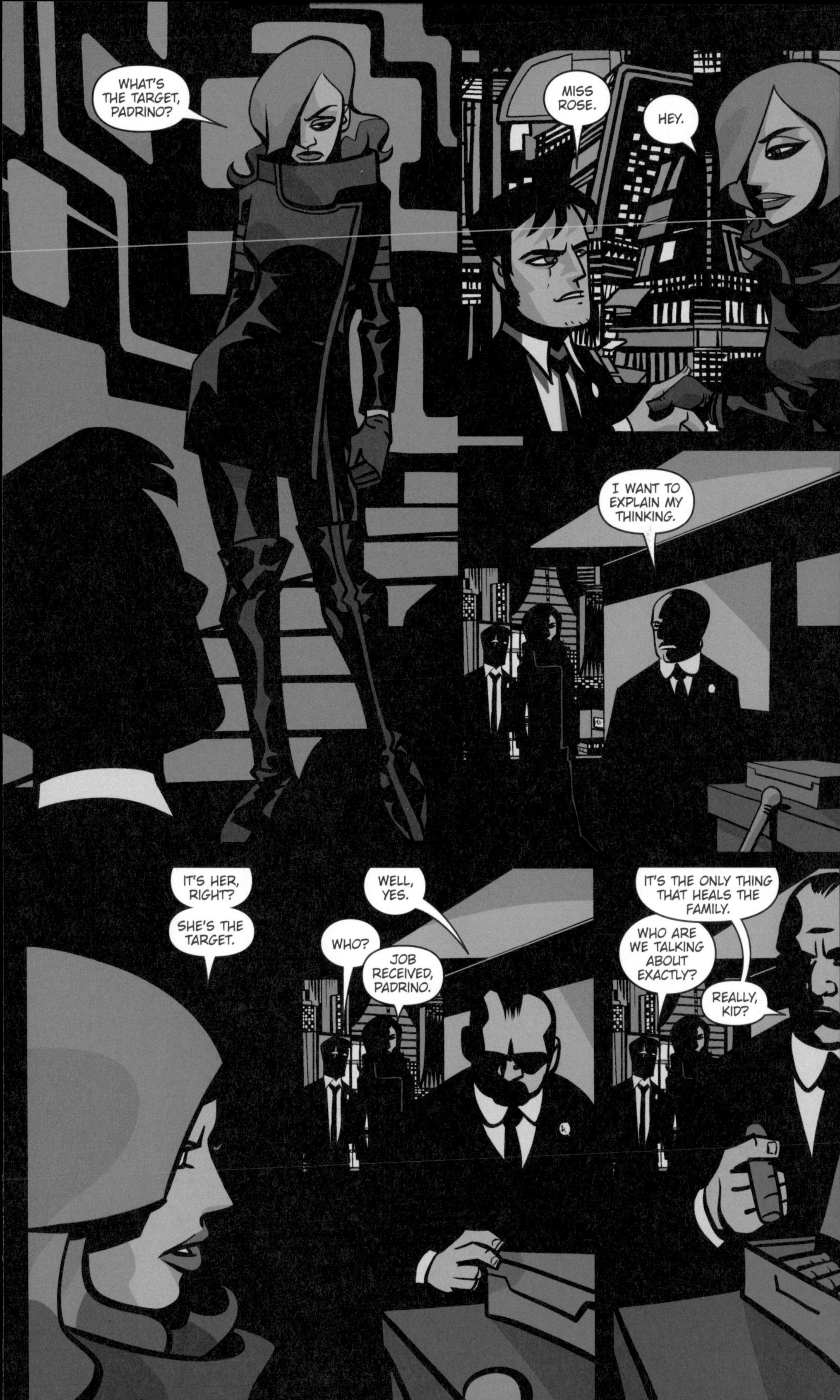
WHAT'S THE TARGET, PADRINO?
MISS ROSE.
HEY.
I WANT TO EXPLAIN MY THINKING.
IT'S HER, RIGHT?
SHE'S THE TARGET.
WELL, YES.
WHO?
JOB RECEIVED, PADRINO.
IT'S THE ONLY THING THAT HEALS THE FAMILY.
WHO ARE WE TALKING ABOUT EXACTLY?
REALLY, KID?

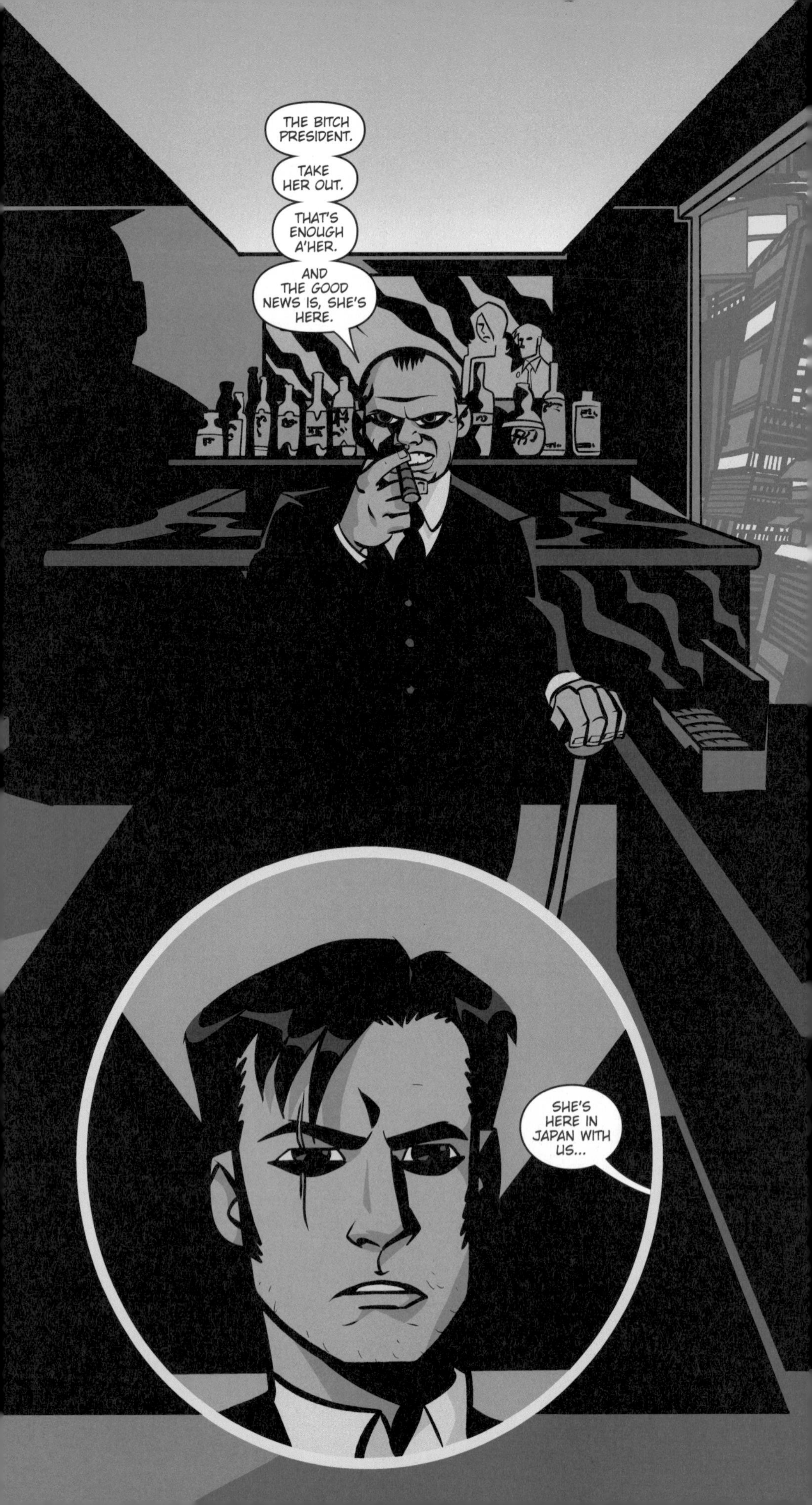
THE BITCH PRESIDENT.
TAKE HER OUT.
THAT'S ENOUGH A'HER.
AND THE GOOD NEWS IS, SHE'S HERE.
SHE'S HERE IN JAPAN WITH US...

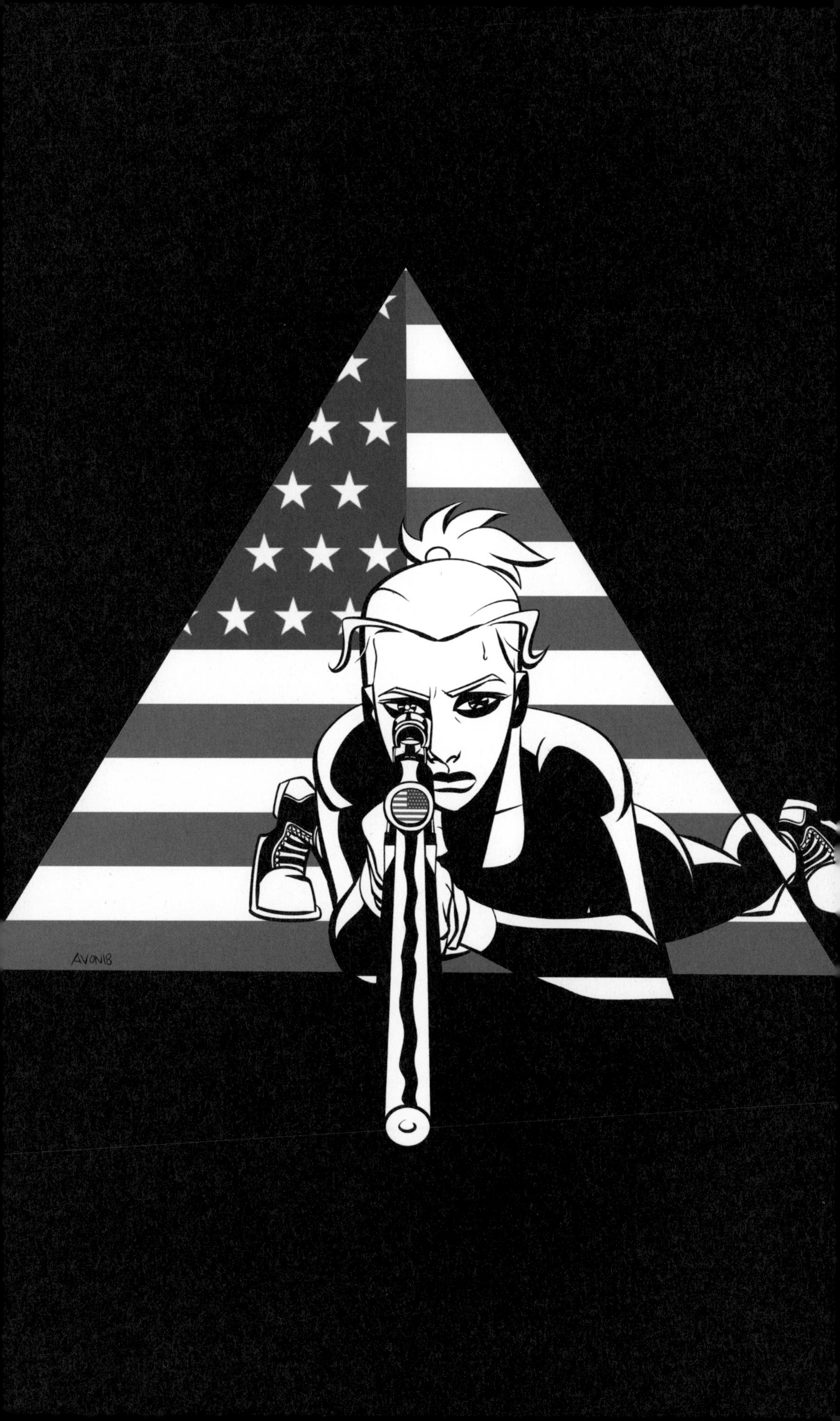
AVON18

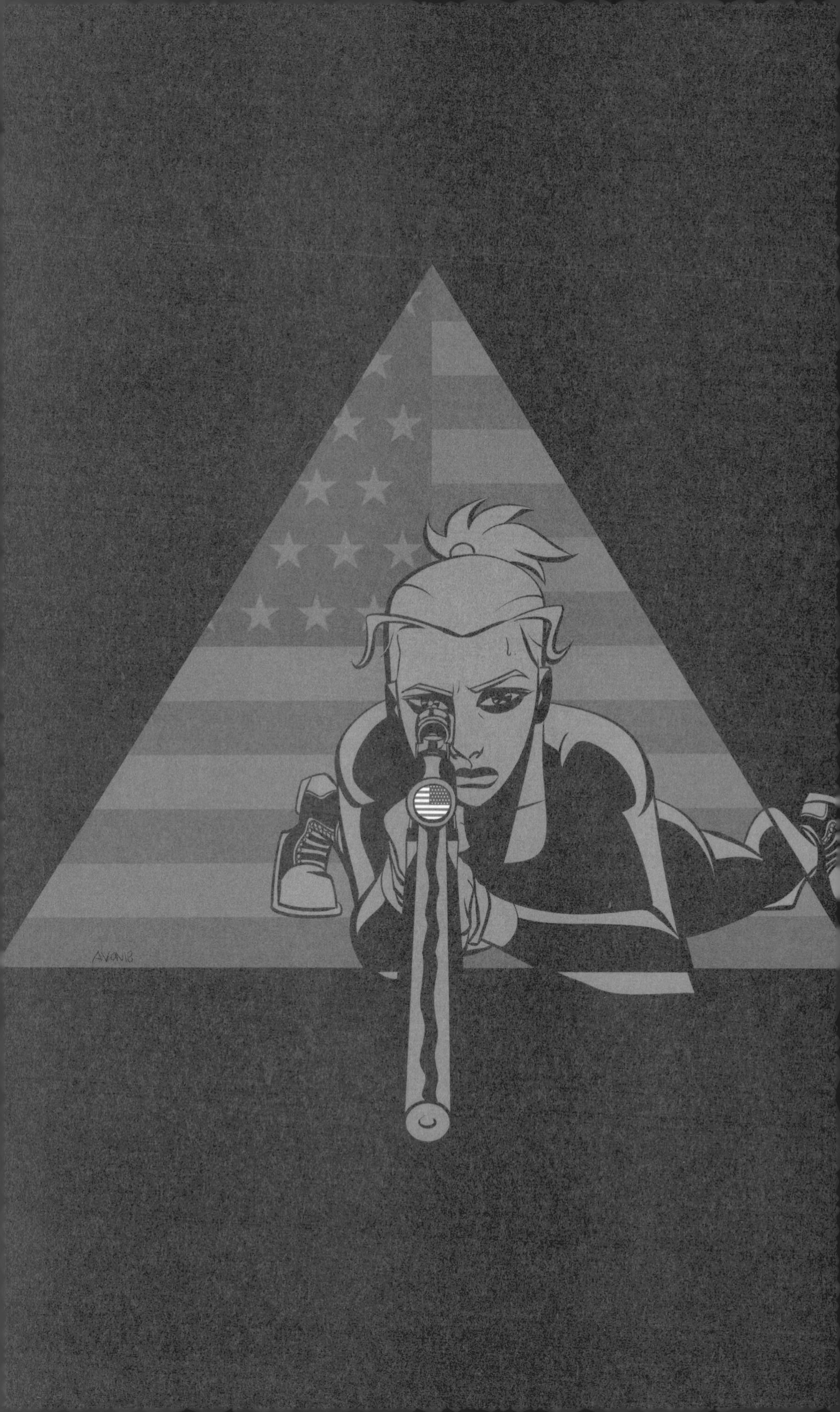

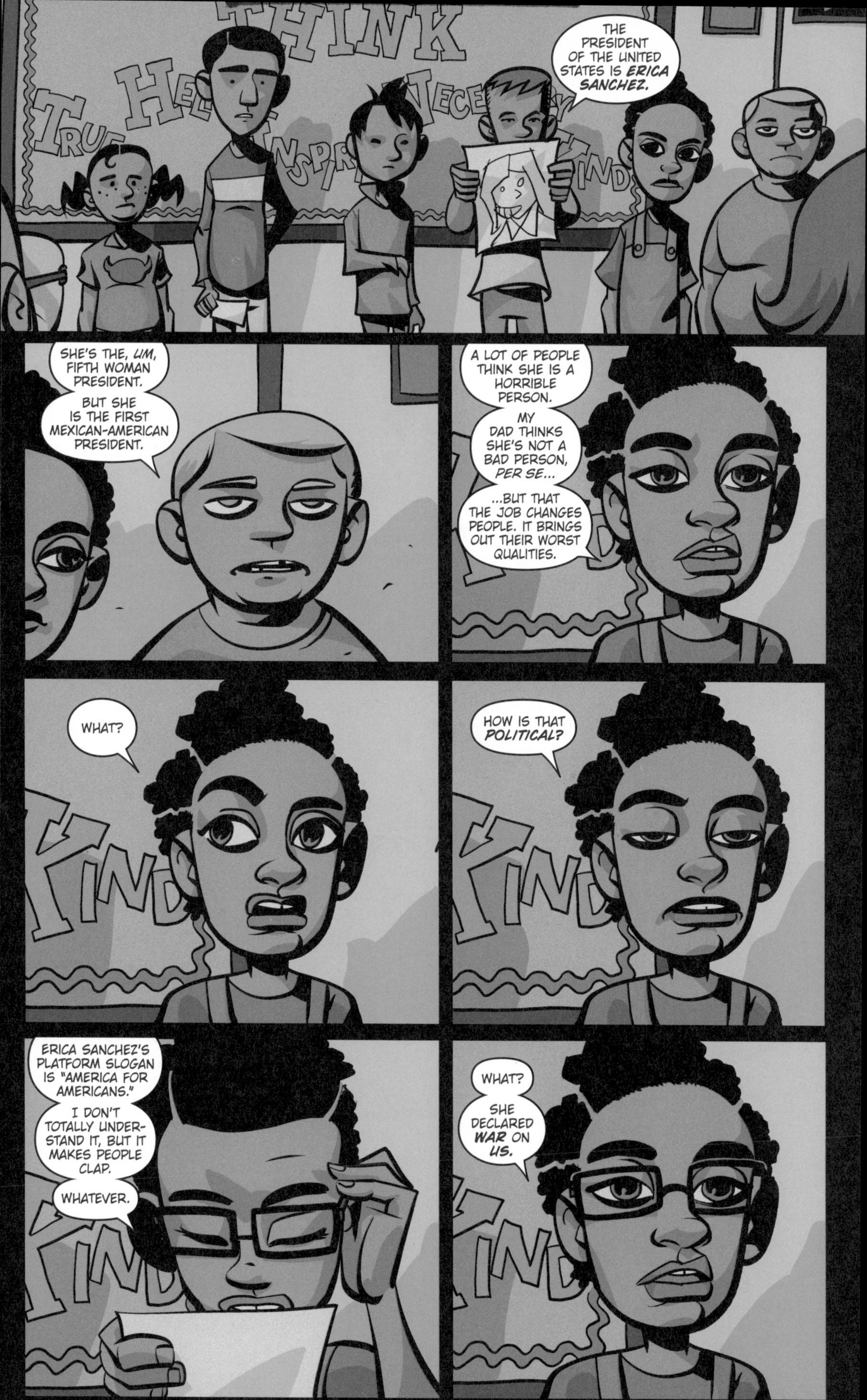
THINK
TRUE
HELPFUL
INSPIRING
NECESSARY
KIND
THE PRESIDENT OF THE UNITED STATES IS *ERICA SANCHEZ.*
SHE'S THE, *UM,* FIFTH WOMAN PRESIDENT.
BUT SHE IS THE FIRST MEXICAN-AMERICAN PRESIDENT.
A LOT OF PEOPLE THINK SHE IS A HORRIBLE PERSON.
MY DAD THINKS SHE'S NOT A BAD PERSON, *PER SE...*
...BUT THAT THE JOB CHANGES PEOPLE. IT BRINGS OUT THEIR WORST QUALITIES.
WHAT?
HOW IS THAT ***POLITICAL?***
ERICA SANCHEZ'S PLATFORM SLOGAN IS "AMERICA FOR AMERICANS."
I DON'T TOTALLY UNDER-STAND IT, BUT IT MAKES PEOPLE CLAP.
WHATEVER.
WHAT?
SHE DECLARED ***WAR*** ON ***US.***

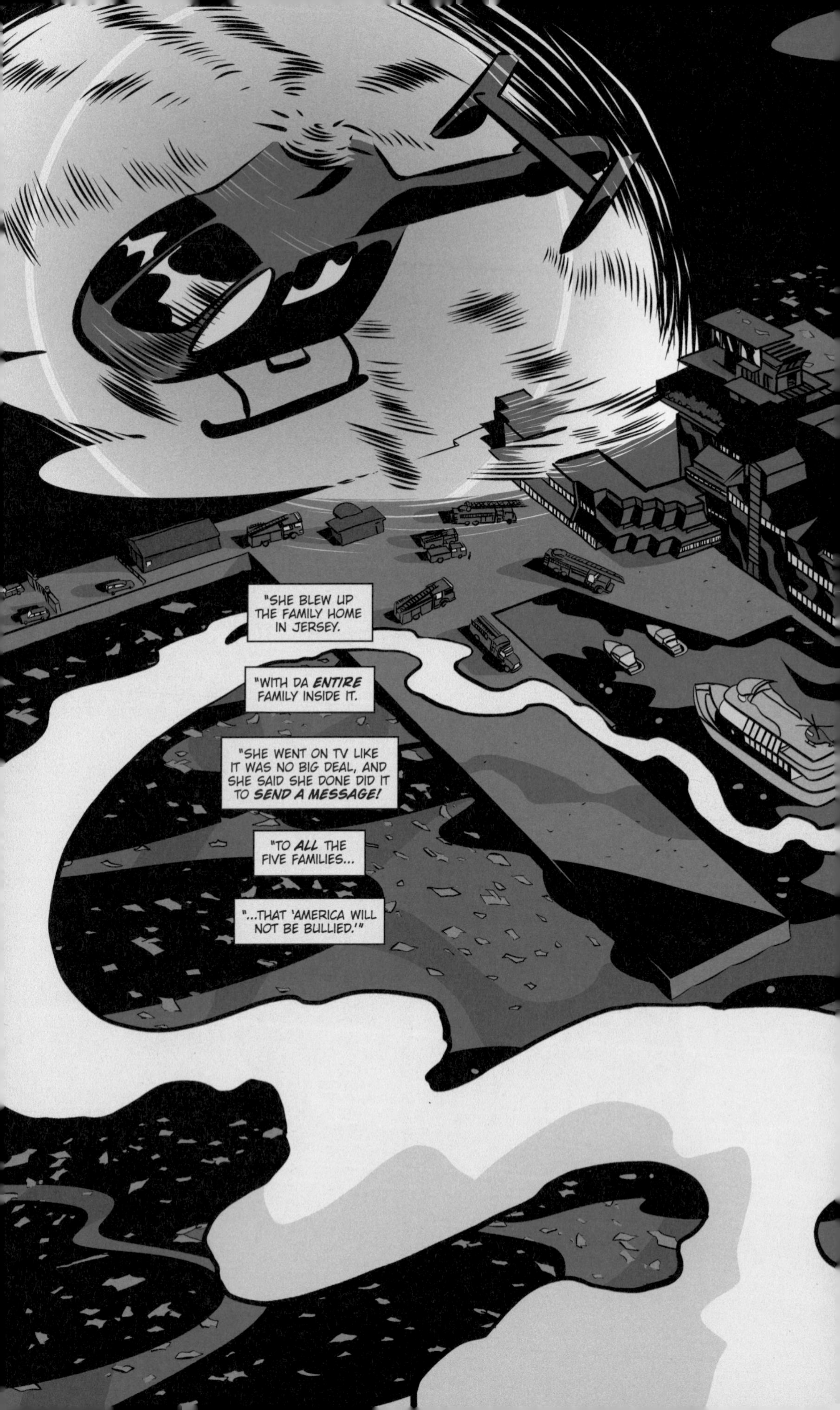
"SHE BLEW UP THE FAMILY HOME IN JERSEY.
"WITH DA ENTIRE FAMILY INSIDE IT.
"SHE WENT ON TV LIKE IT WAS NO BIG DEAL, AND SHE SAID SHE DONE DID IT TO SEND A MESSAGE!
"TO ALL THE FIVE FAMILIES...
"...THAT 'AMERICA WILL NOT BE BULLIED.'"

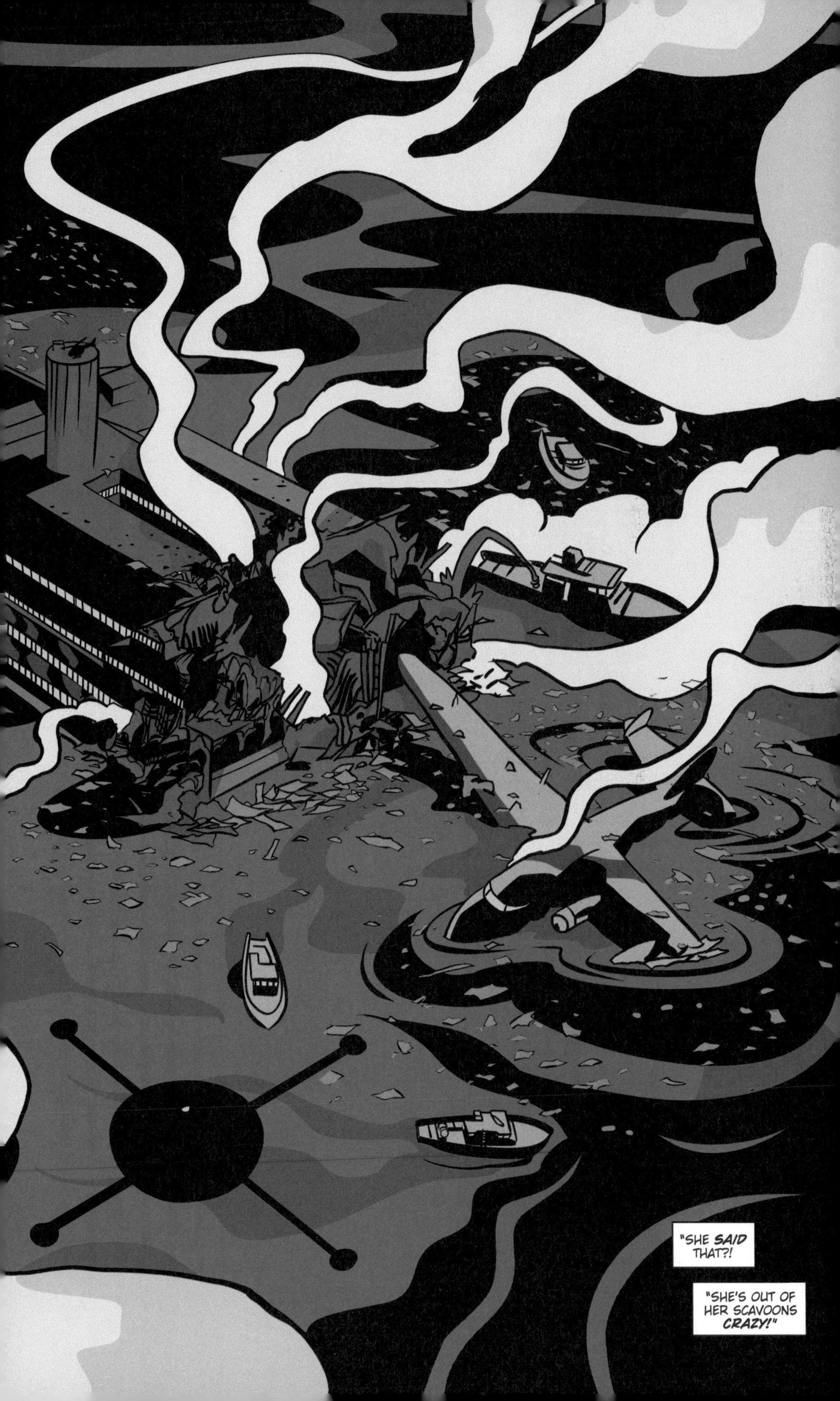
"SHE *SAID* THAT?!
"SHE'S OUT OF HER SCAVOONS *CRAZY!*"

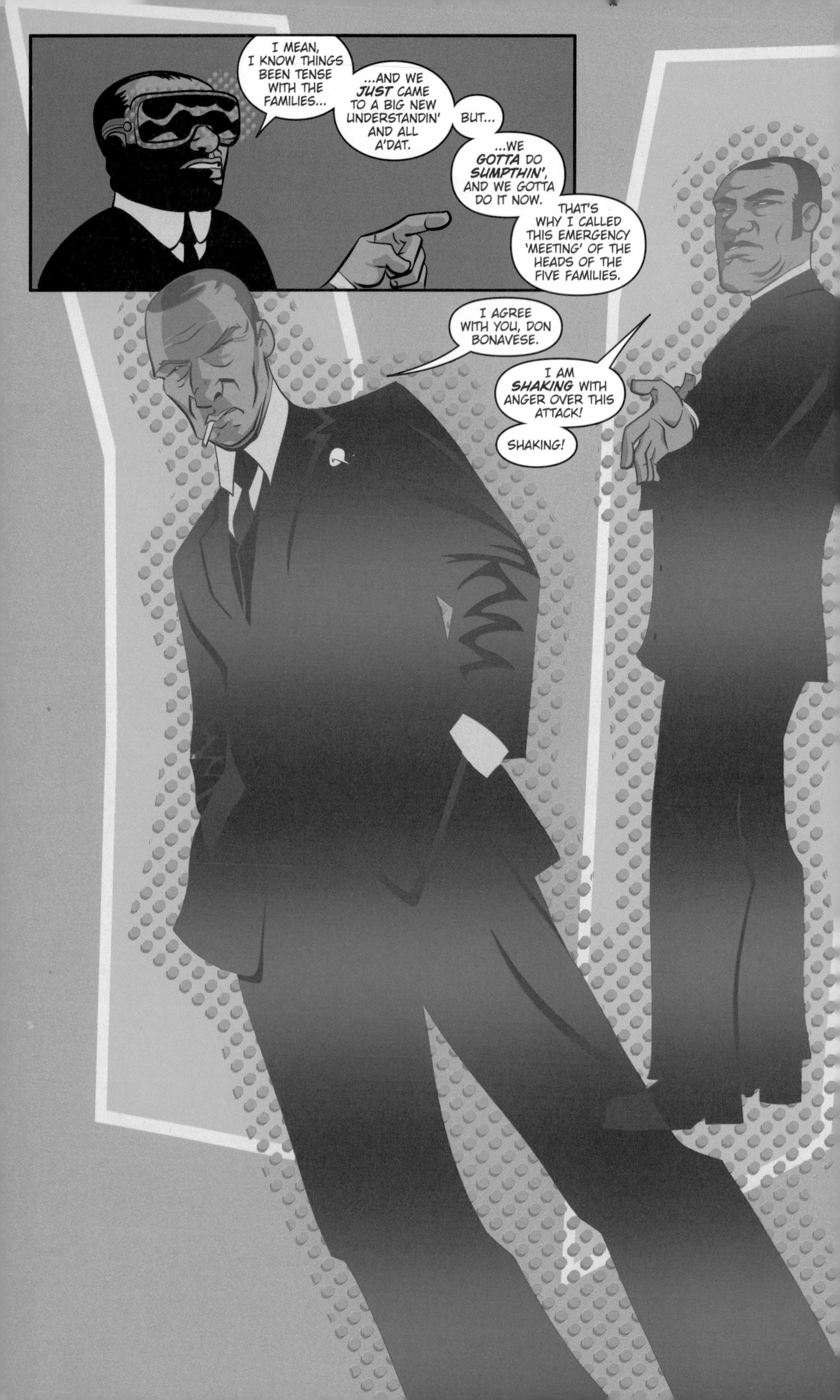
I MEAN, I KNOW THINGS BEEN TENSE WITH THE FAMILIES...
...AND WE JUST CAME TO A BIG NEW UNDERSTANDIN' AND ALL A'DAT.
BUT...
...WE GOTTA DO SUMPTHIN', AND WE GOTTA DO IT NOW.
THAT'S WHY I CALLED THIS EMERGENCY 'MEETING' OF THE HEADS OF THE FIVE FAMILIES.
I AGREE WITH YOU, DON BONAVESE.
I AM SHAKING WITH ANGER OVER THIS ATTACK!
SHAKING!

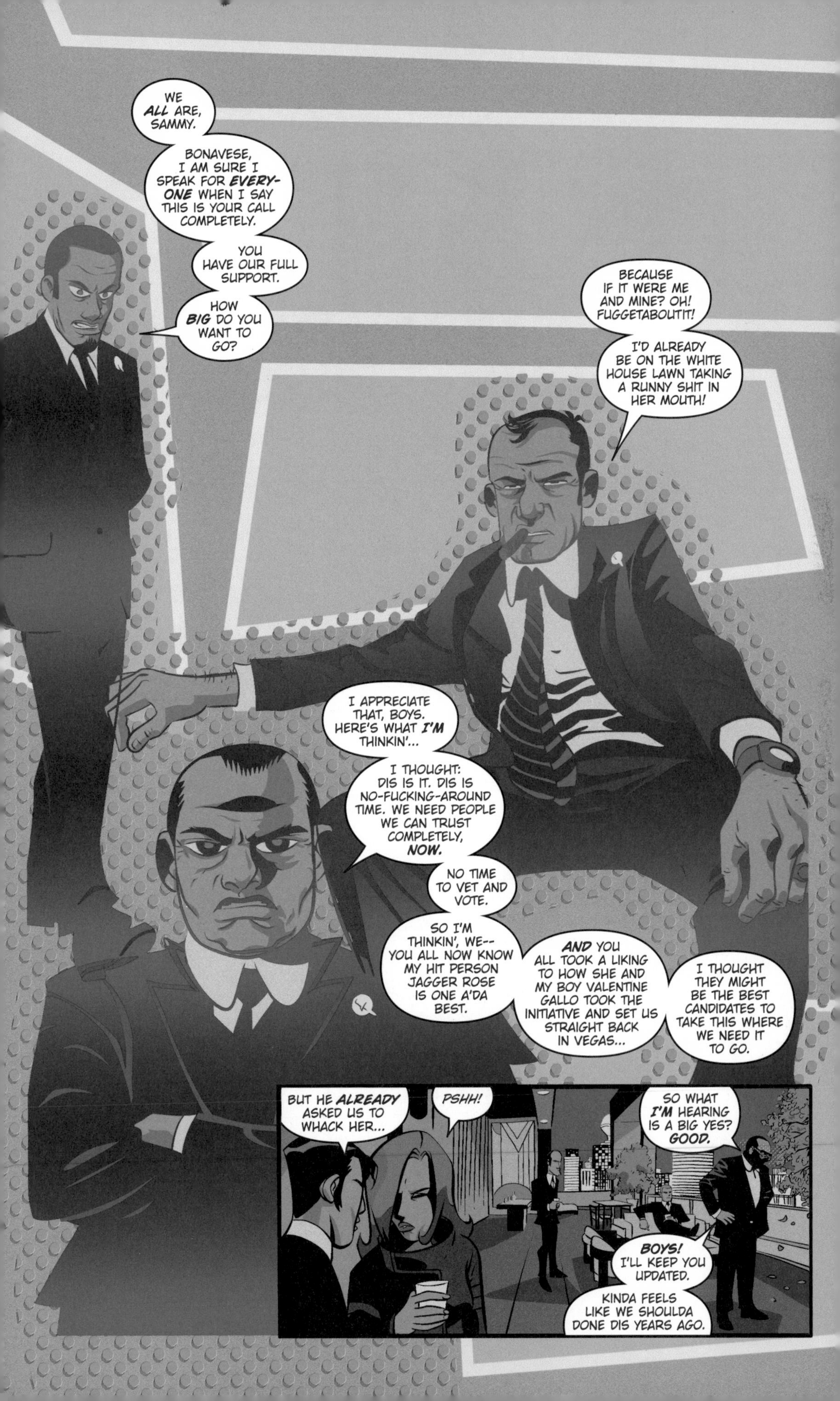
WE ALL ARE, SAMMY.
BONAVESE, I AM SURE I SPEAK FOR EVERY-ONE WHEN I SAY THIS IS YOUR CALL COMPLETELY.
YOU HAVE OUR FULL SUPPORT.
HOW BIG DO YOU WANT TO GO?
BECAUSE IF IT WERE ME AND MINE? OH! FUGGETABOUTIT!
I'D ALREADY BE ON THE WHITE HOUSE LAWN TAKING A RUNNY SHIT IN HER MOUTH!
I APPRECIATE THAT, BOYS. HERE'S WHAT I'M THINKIN'...
I THOUGHT: DIS IS IT. DIS IS NO-FUCKING-AROUND TIME. WE NEED PEOPLE WE CAN TRUST COMPLETELY, NOW.
NO TIME TO VET AND VOTE.
SO I'M THINKIN', WE-- YOU ALL NOW KNOW MY HIT PERSON JAGGER ROSE IS ONE A'DA BEST.
AND YOU ALL TOOK A LIKING TO HOW SHE AND MY BOY VALENTINE GALLO TOOK THE INITIATIVE AND SET US STRAIGHT BACK IN VEGAS...
I THOUGHT THEY MIGHT BE THE BEST CANDIDATES TO TAKE THIS WHERE WE NEED IT TO GO.
BUT HE ALREADY ASKED US TO WHACK HER...
PSHH!
SO WHAT I'M HEARING IS A BIG YES? GOOD.
BOYS! I'LL KEEP YOU UPDATED.
KINDA FEELS LIKE WE SHOULDA DONE DIS YEARS AGO.

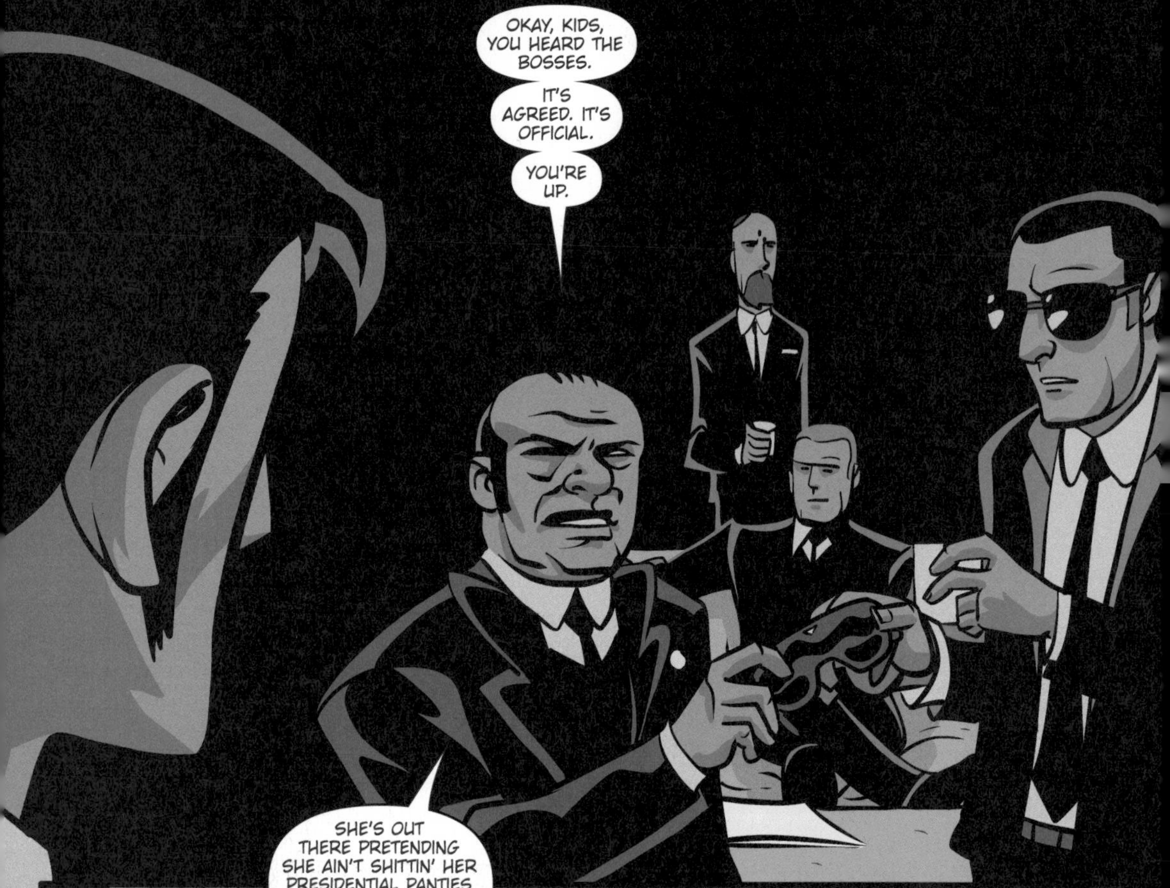
OKAY, KIDS, YOU HEARD THE BOSSES.
IT'S AGREED. IT'S OFFICIAL.
YOU'RE UP.
SHE'S OUT THERE PRETENDING SHE AIN'T SHITTIN' HER PRESIDENTIAL PANTIES WAITIN' TO SEE WHAT ***WE'LL*** DO TO HER AND HERS.

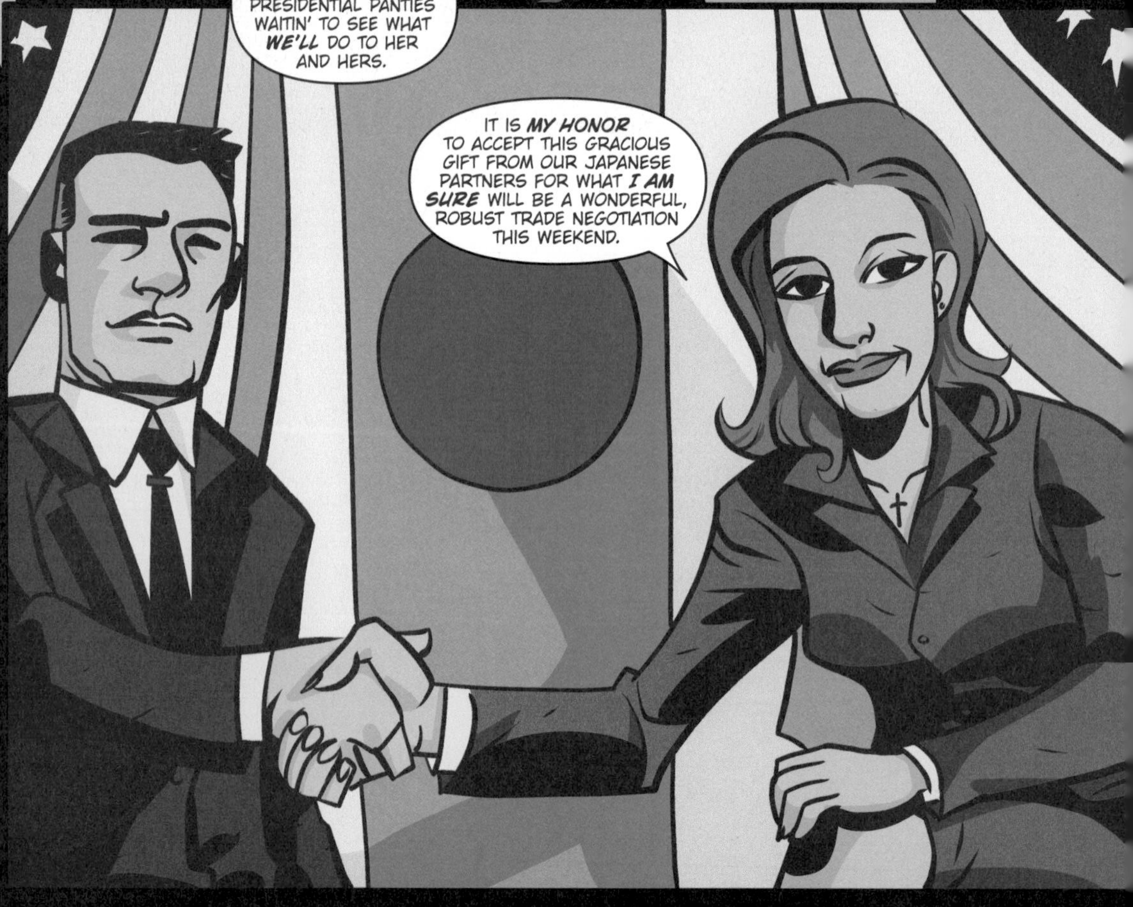
IT IS ***MY HONOR*** TO ACCEPT THIS GRACIOUS GIFT FROM OUR JAPANESE PARTNERS FOR WHAT ***I AM SURE*** WILL BE A WONDERFUL, ROBUST TRADE NEGOTIATION THIS WEEKEND.

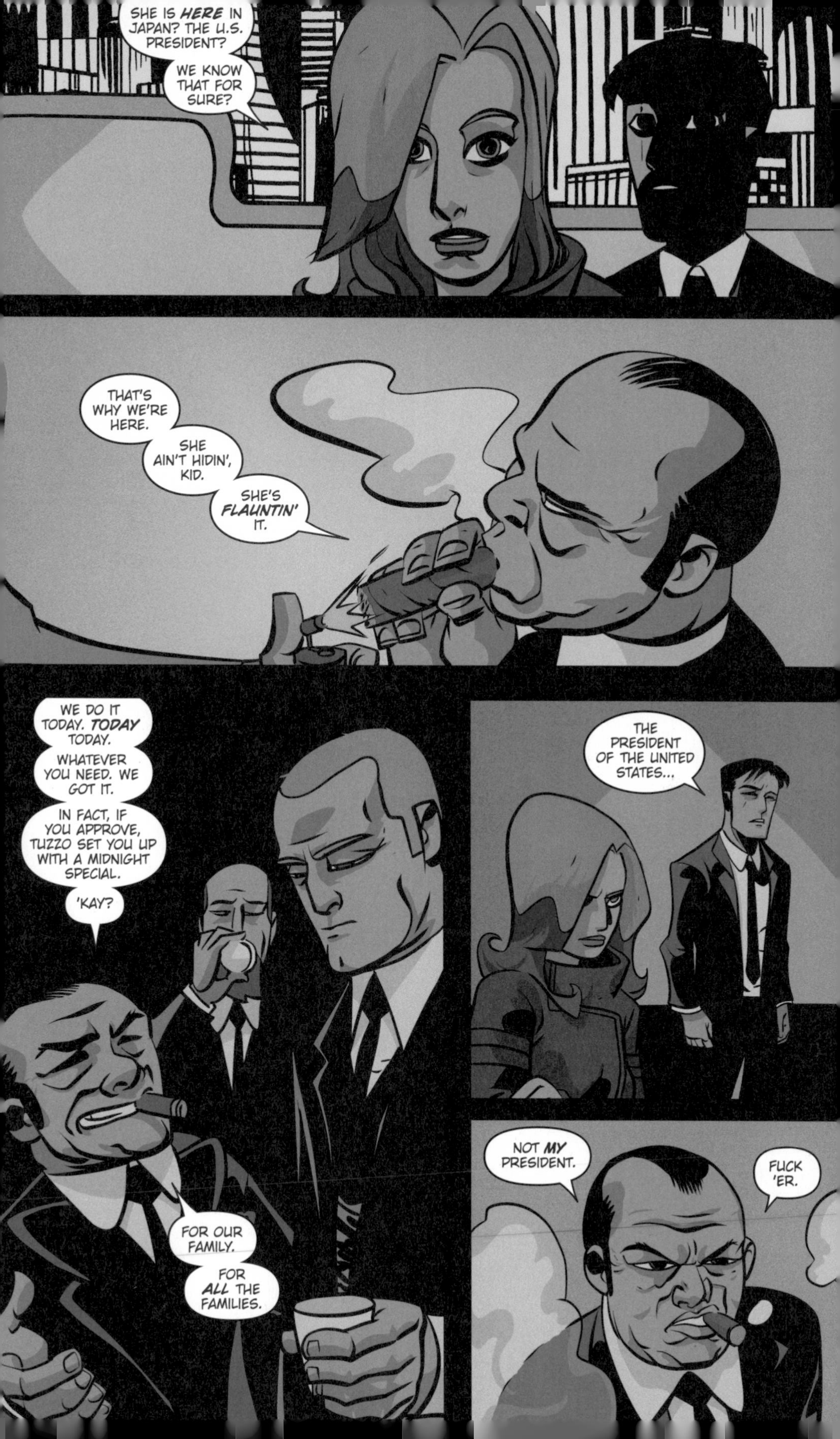
SHE IS HERE IN JAPAN? THE U.S. PRESIDENT?
WE KNOW THAT FOR SURE?
THAT'S WHY WE'RE HERE.
SHE AIN'T HIDIN', KID.
SHE'S FLAUNTIN' IT.
WE DO IT TODAY. TODAY TODAY.
WHATEVER YOU NEED. WE GOT IT.
IN FACT, IF YOU APPROVE, TUZZO SET YOU UP WITH A MIDNIGHT SPECIAL.
'KAY?
FOR OUR FAMILY.
FOR ALL THE FAMILIES.
THE PRESIDENT OF THE UNITED STATES...
NOT MY PRESIDENT.
FUCK 'ER.

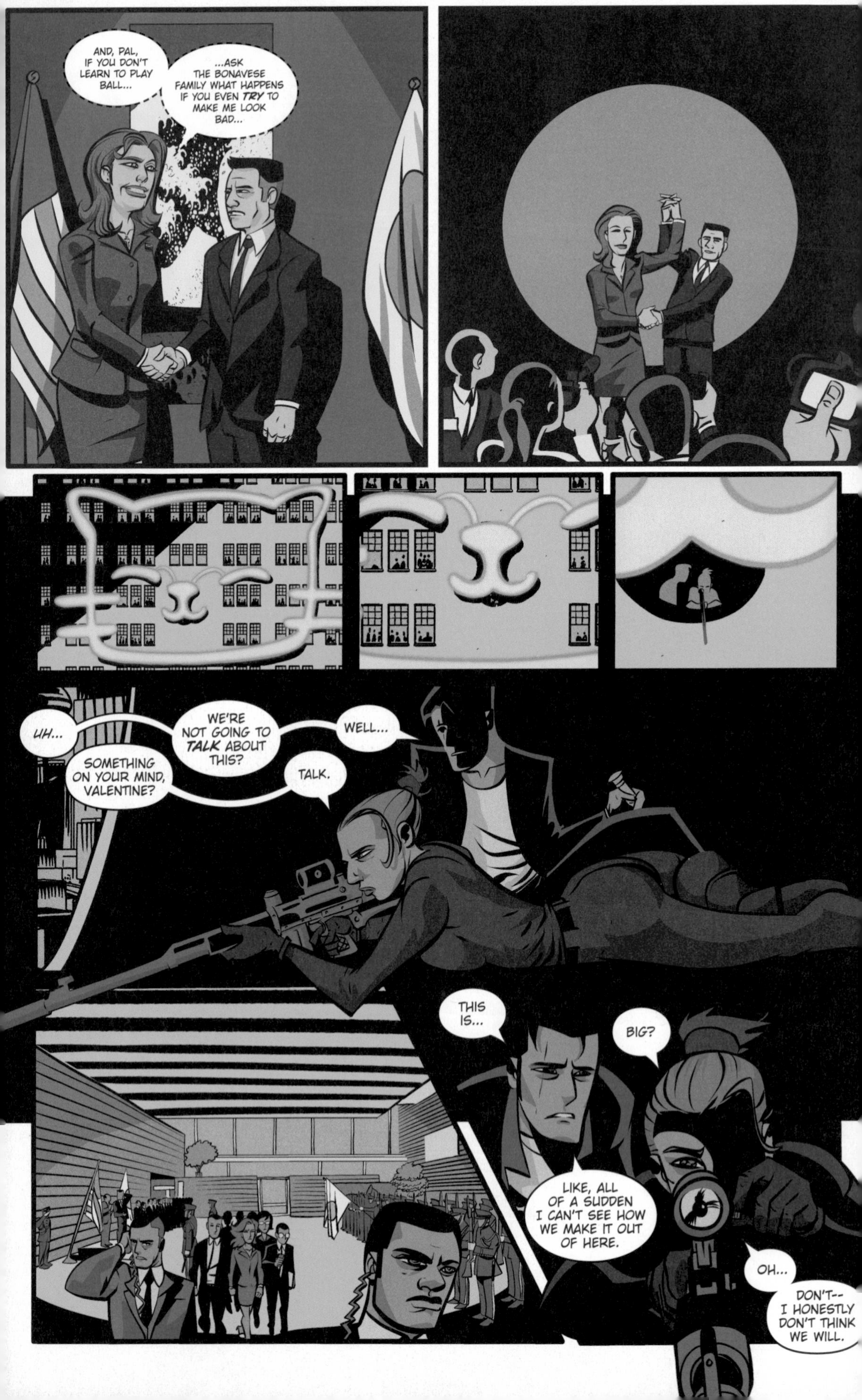
AND, PAL, IF YOU DON'T LEARN TO PLAY BALL...
...ASK THE BONAVESE FAMILY WHAT HAPPENS IF YOU EVEN TRY TO MAKE ME LOOK BAD...
UH...
SOMETHING ON YOUR MIND, VALENTINE?
WE'RE NOT GOING TO TALK ABOUT THIS?
TALK.
WELL...
THIS IS...
BIG?
LIKE, ALL OF A SUDDEN I CAN'T SEE HOW WE MAKE IT OUT OF HERE.
OH...
DON'T-- I HONESTLY DON'T THINK WE WILL.

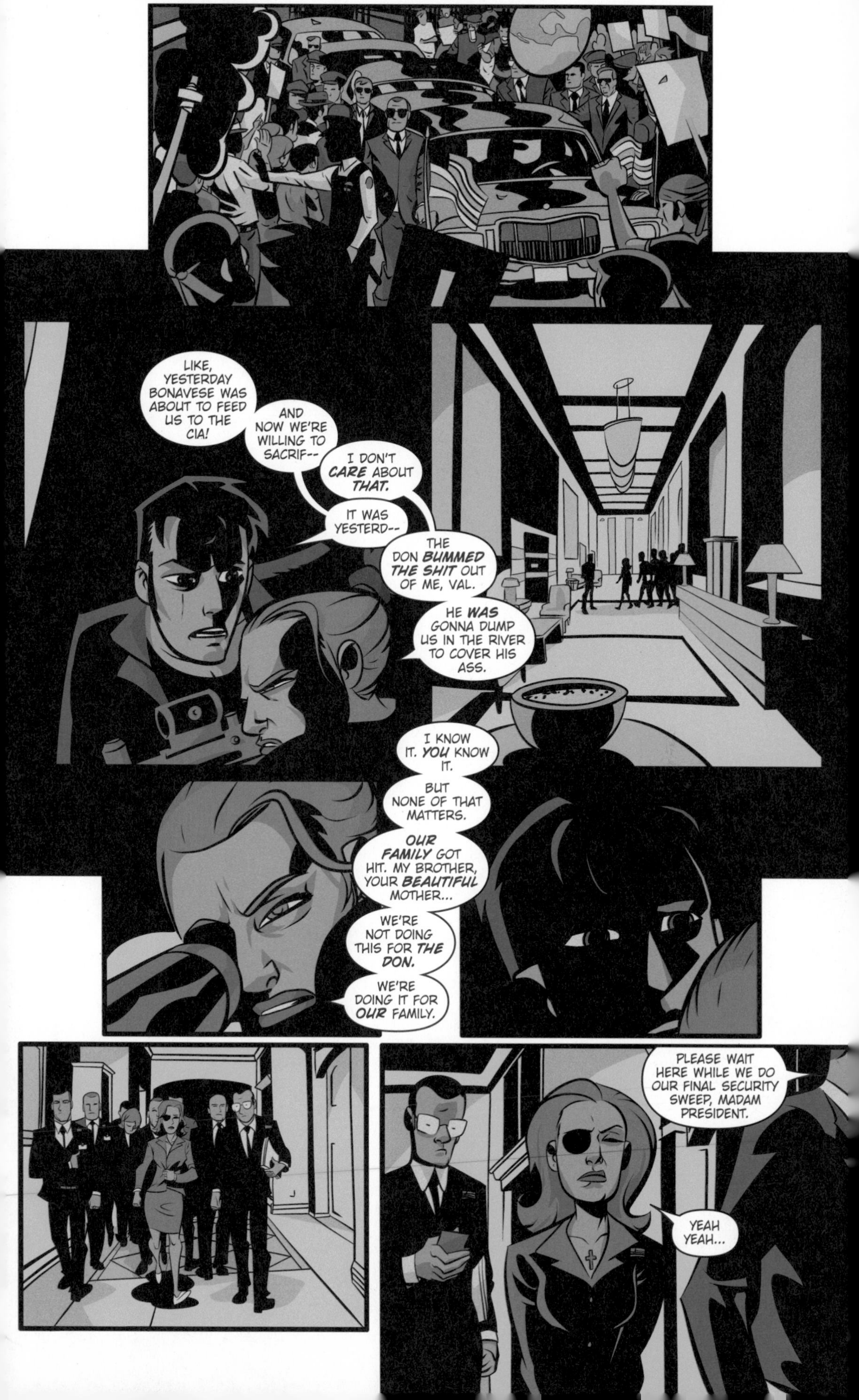

LIKE, YESTERDAY BONAVESE WAS ABOUT TO FEED US TO THE CIA!
AND NOW WE'RE WILLING TO SACRIF--
I DON'T *CARE* ABOUT *THAT.*
IT WAS YESTERD--
THE DON *BUMMED THE SHIT* OUT OF ME, VAL.
HE *WAS* GONNA DUMP US IN THE RIVER TO COVER HIS ASS.
I KNOW IT. *YOU* KNOW IT.
BUT NONE OF THAT MATTERS.
OUR FAMILY GOT HIT. MY BROTHER, YOUR *BEAUTIFUL* MOTHER...
WE'RE NOT DOING THIS FOR *THE DON.*
WE'RE DOING IT FOR *OUR* FAMILY.
PLEASE WAIT HERE WHILE WE DO OUR FINAL SECURITY SWEEP, MADAM PRESIDENT.
YEAH YEAH...

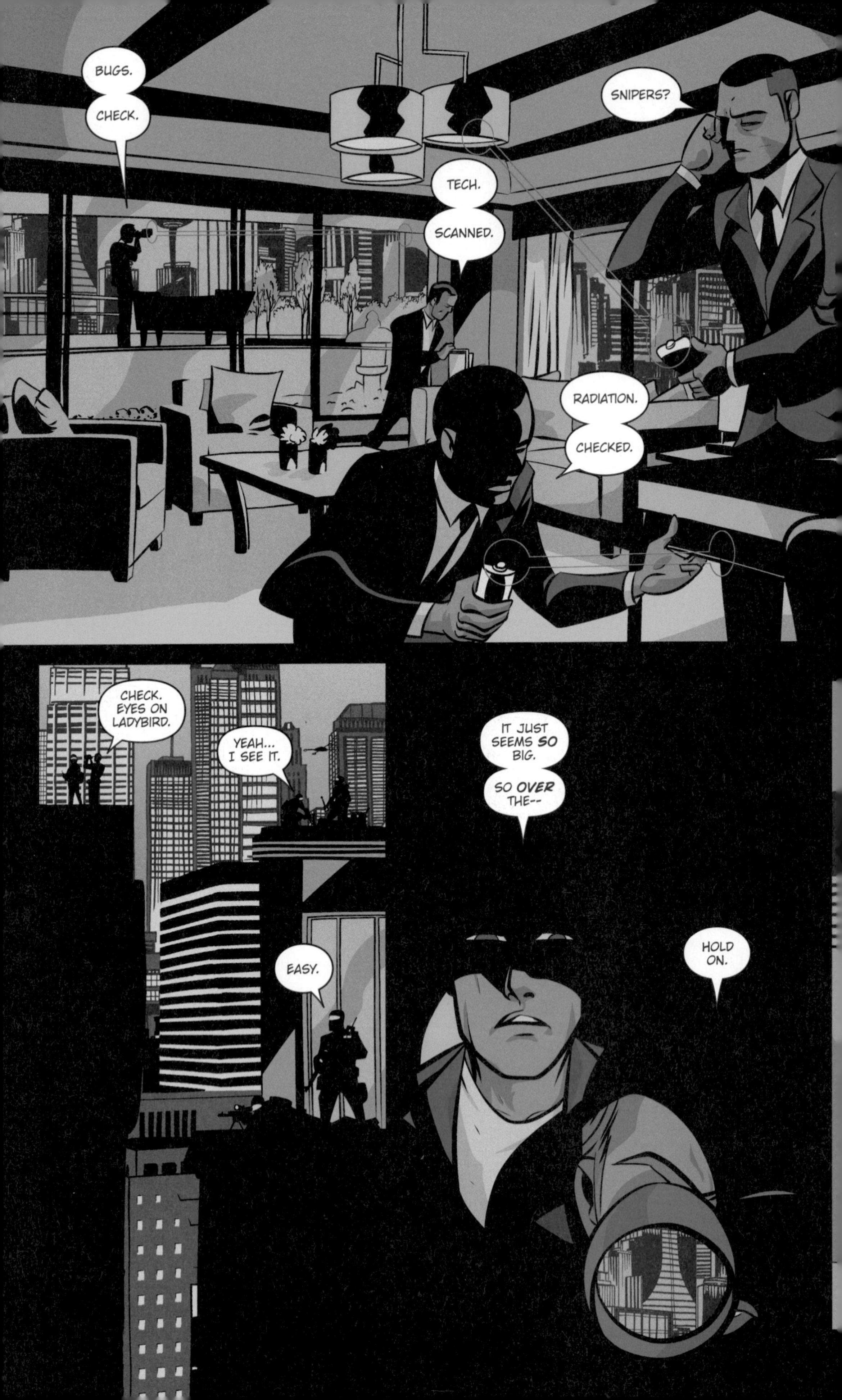
BUGS.
CHECK.
SNIPERS?
TECH.
SCANNED.
RADIATION.
CHECKED.
CHECK. EYES ON LADYBIRD.
YEAH... I SEE IT.
IT JUST SEEMS SO BIG.
SO OVER THE--
EASY.
HOLD ON.

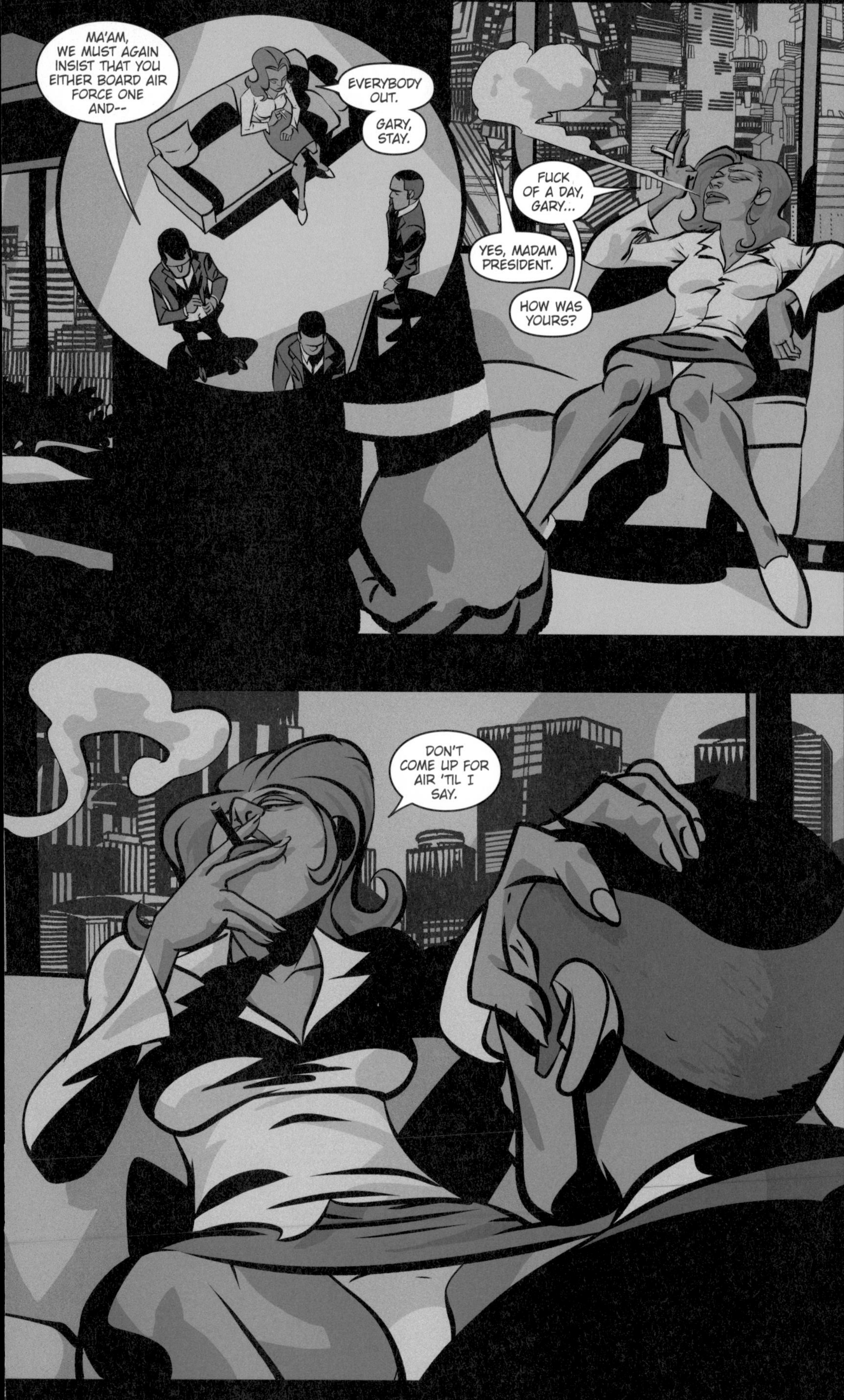
MA'AM, WE MUST AGAIN INSIST THAT YOU EITHER BOARD AIR FORCE ONE AND--
EVERYBODY OUT.
GARY, STAY.
FUCK OF A DAY, GARY...
YES, MADAM PRESIDENT.
HOW WAS YOURS?
DON'T COME UP FOR AIR 'TIL I SAY.

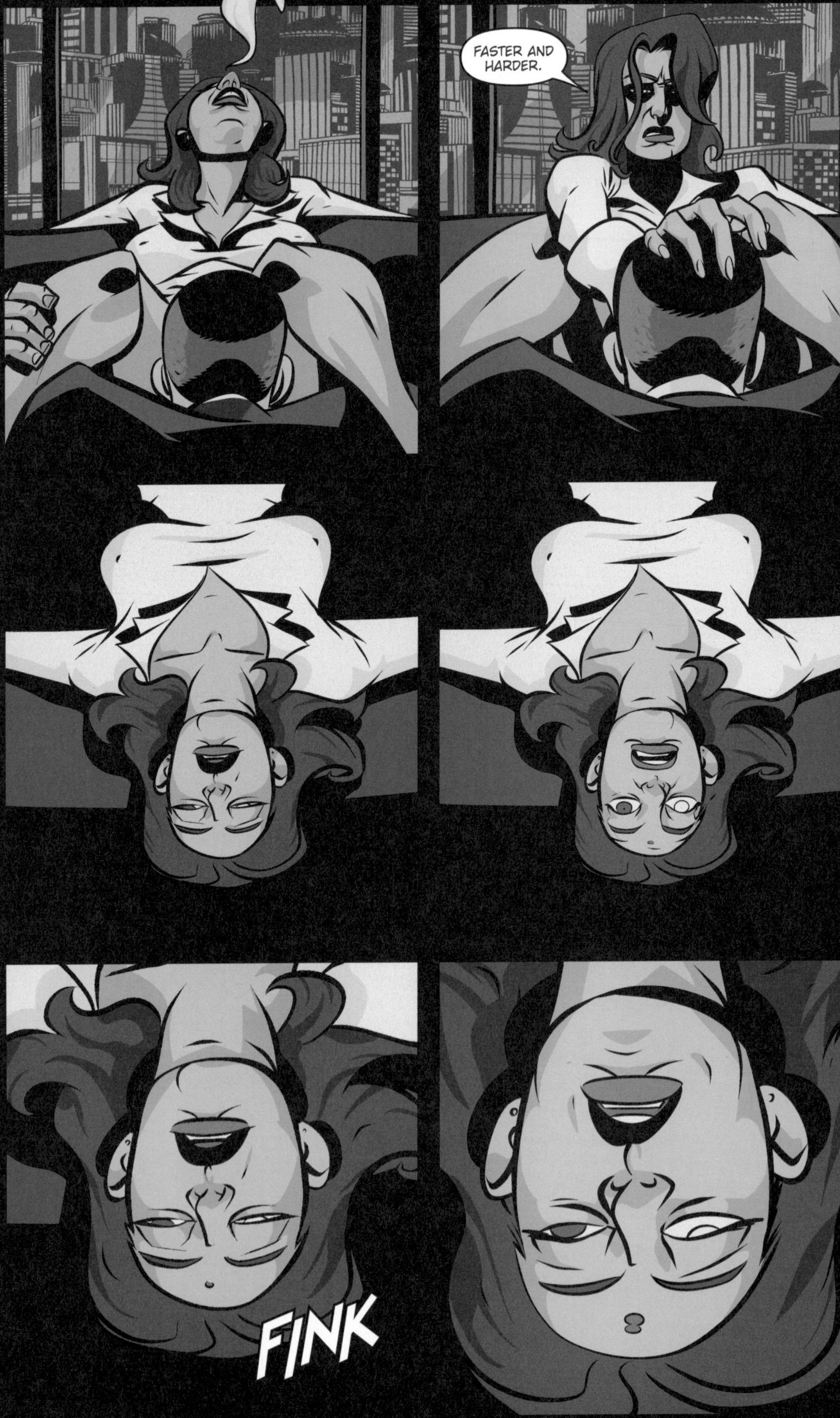

FASTER AND HARDER.
FINK

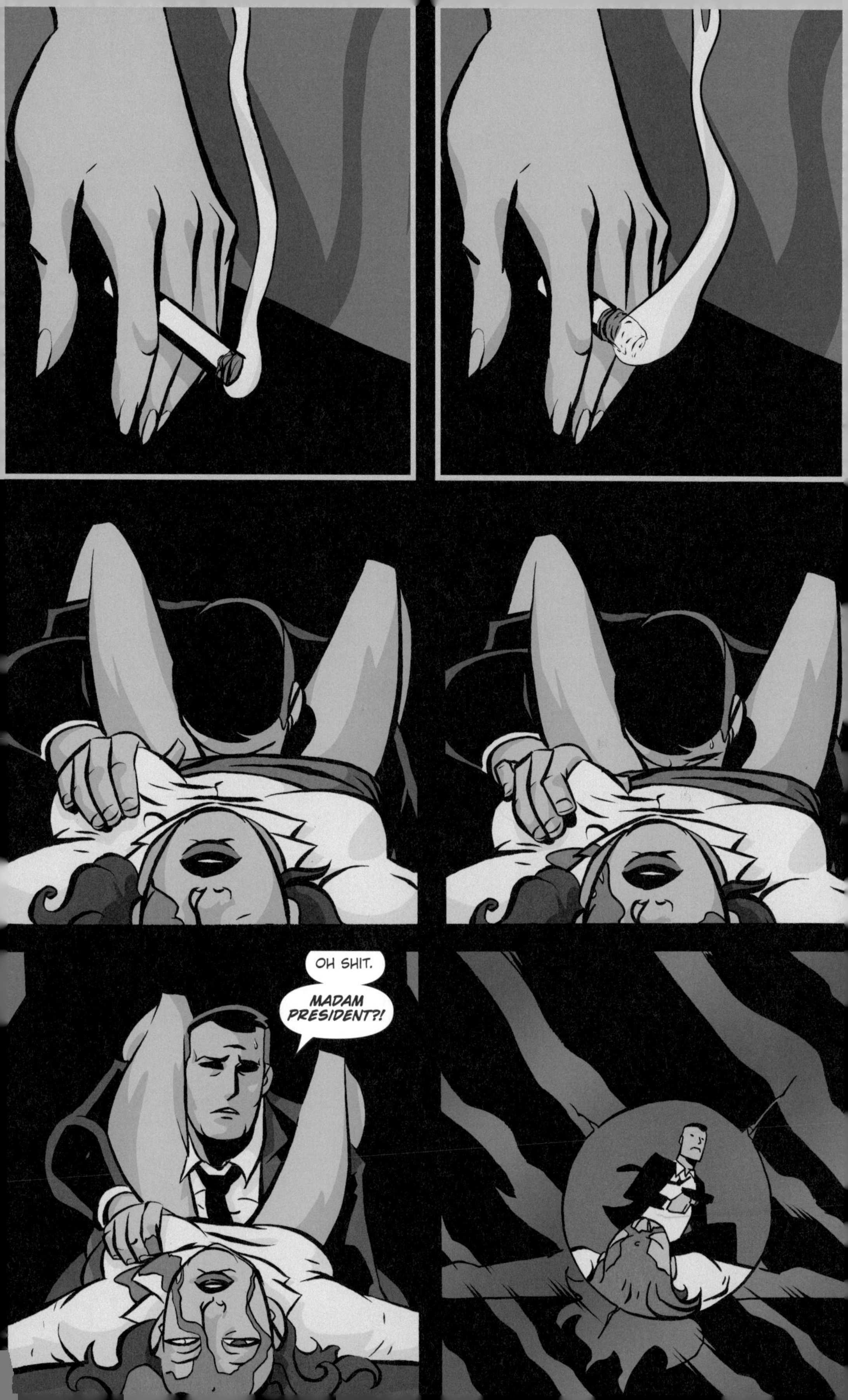
OH SHIT.
MADAM PRESIDENT?!

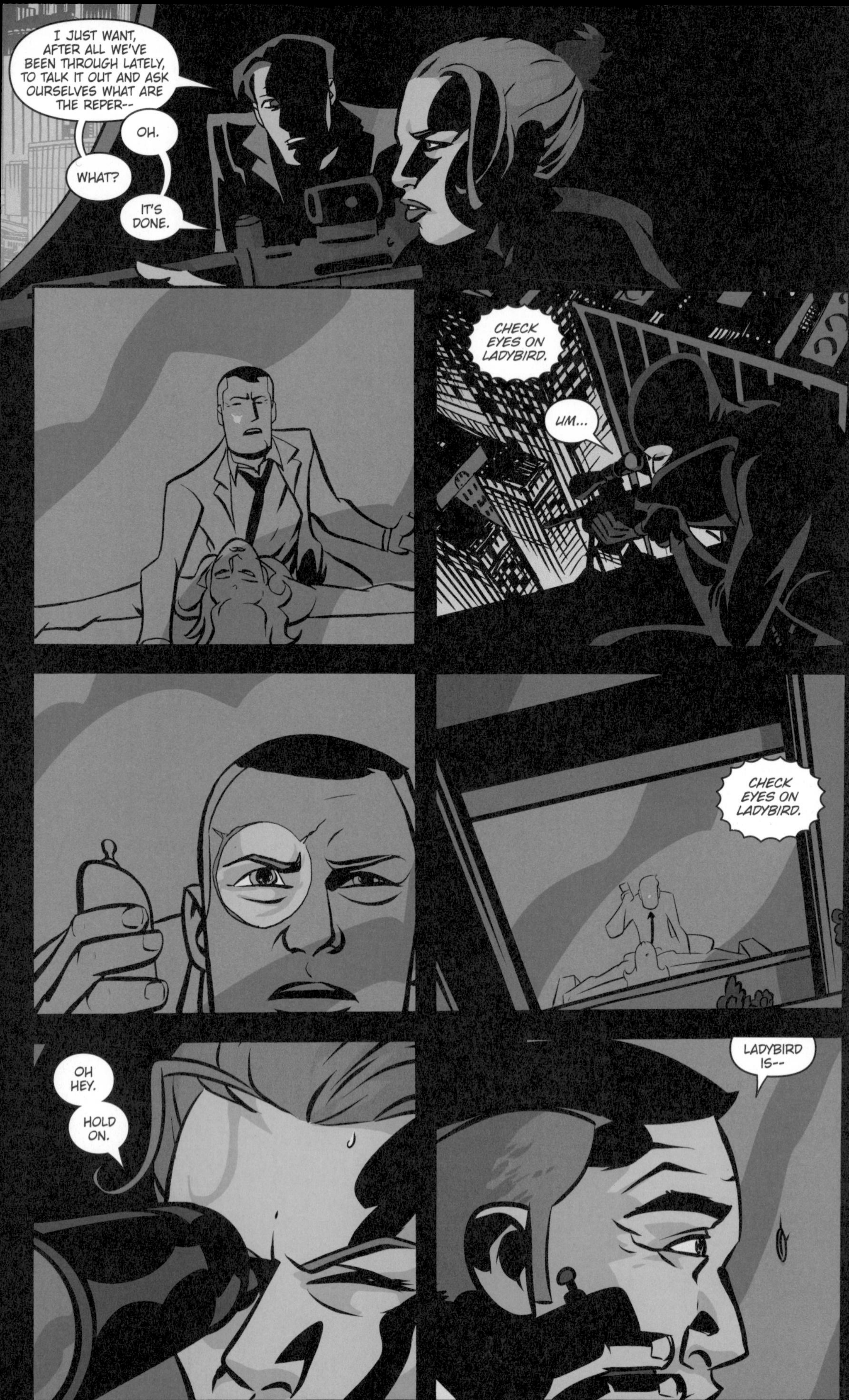
I JUST WANT, AFTER ALL WE'VE BEEN THROUGH LATELY, TO TALK IT OUT AND ASK OURSELVES WHAT ARE THE REPER--
OH.
WHAT?
IT'S DONE.
CHECK EYES ON LADYBIRD.
UM...
CHECK EYES ON LADYBIRD.
OH HEY.
HOLD ON.
LADYBIRD IS--

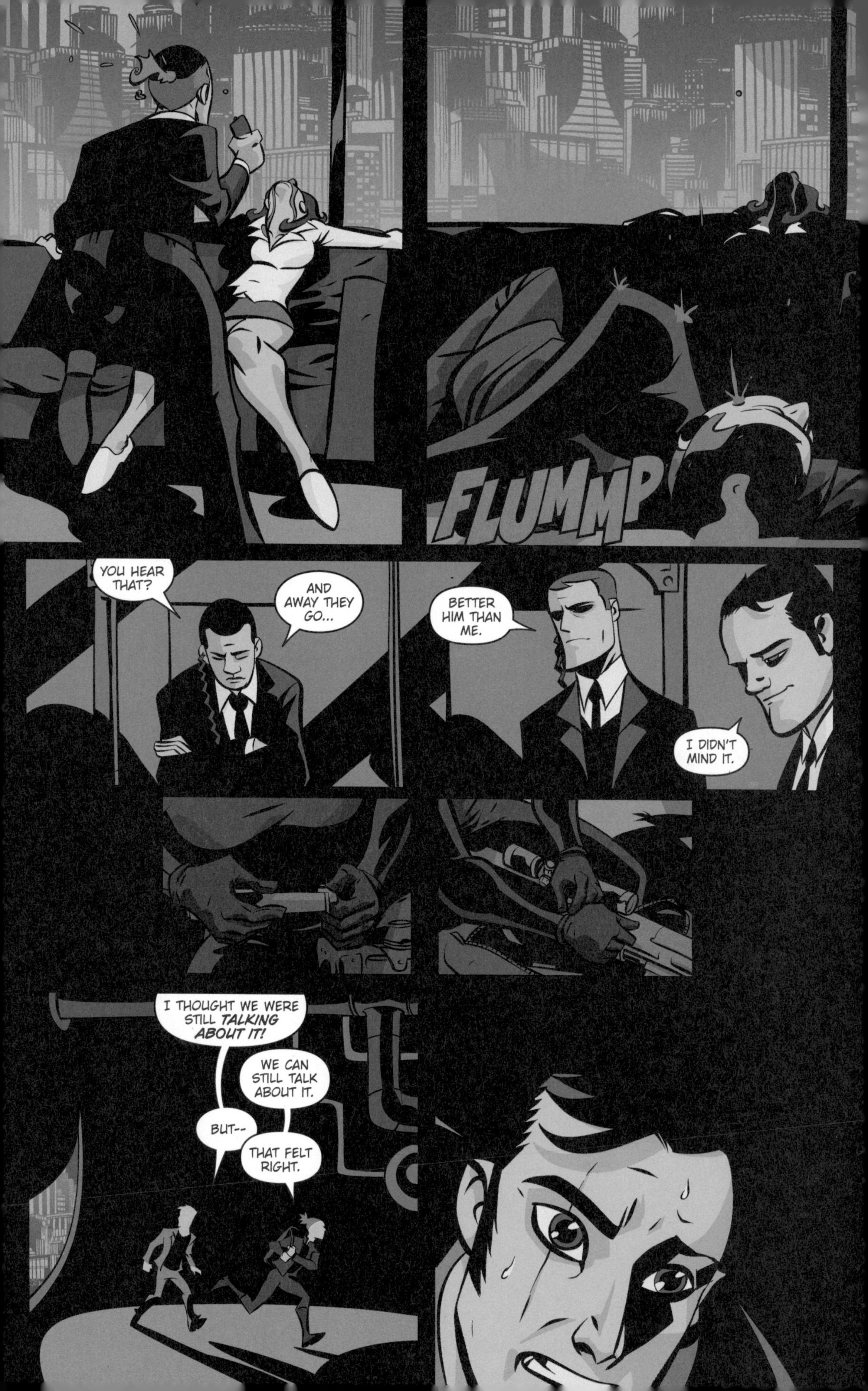
FLUMMP
YOU HEAR THAT?
AND AWAY THEY GO...
BETTER HIM THAN ME.
I DIDN'T MIND IT.
I THOUGHT WE WERE STILL *TALKING ABOUT IT!*
WE CAN STILL TALK ABOUT IT.
BUT--
THAT FELT RIGHT.

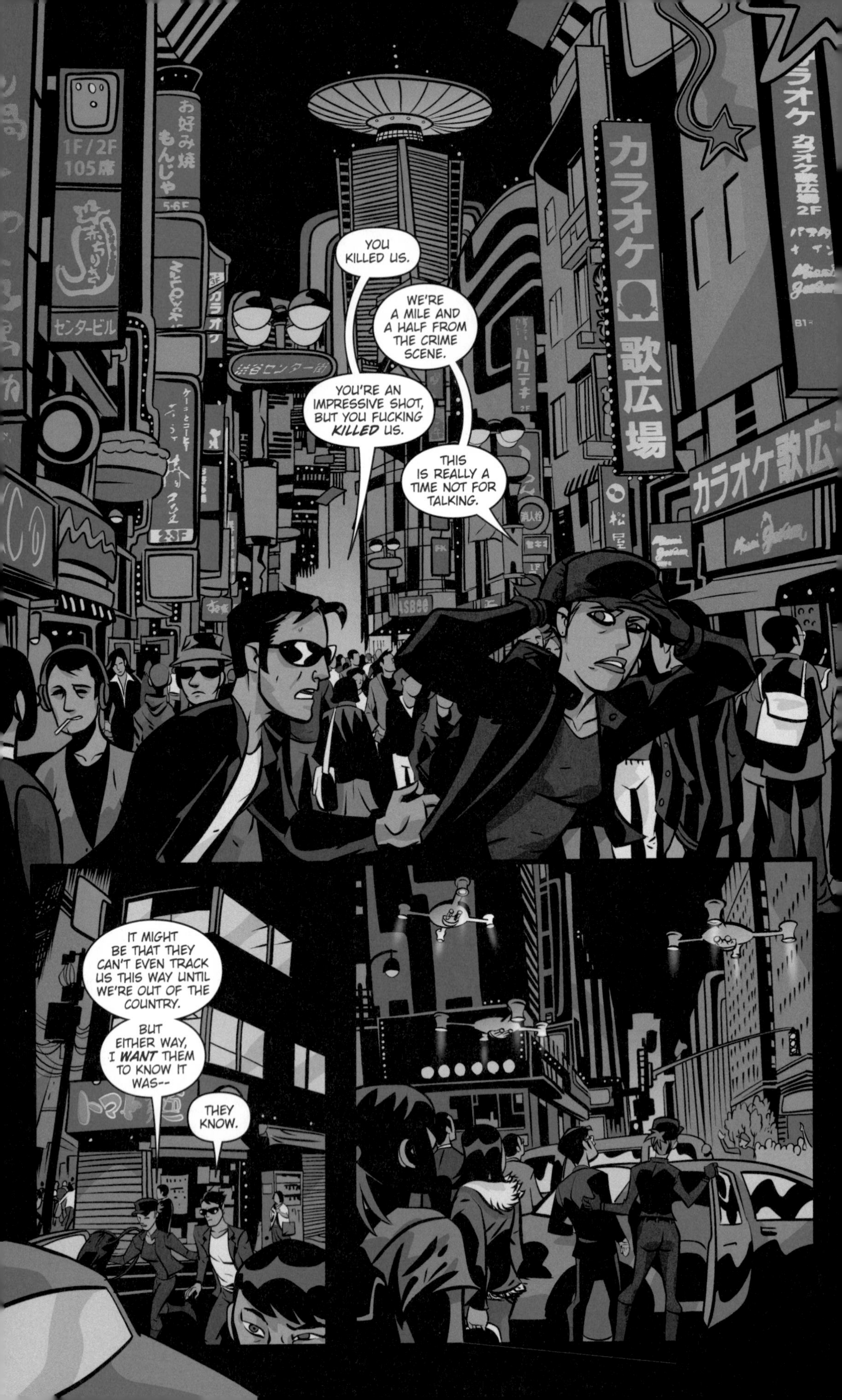

1F/2F
105席
お好み焼
もんじゃ
センタービル
渋谷センター街
カラオケ
歌広場
カラオケ歌広
YOU KILLED US.
WE'RE A MILE AND A HALF FROM THE CRIME SCENE.
YOU'RE AN IMPRESSIVE SHOT, BUT YOU FUCKING ***KILLED*** US.
THIS IS REALLY A TIME NOT FOR TALKING.
IT MIGHT BE THAT THEY CAN'T EVEN TRACK US THIS WAY UNTIL WE'RE OUT OF THE COUNTRY.
BUT EITHER WAY, I ***WANT*** THEM TO KNOW IT WAS--
THEY KNOW.

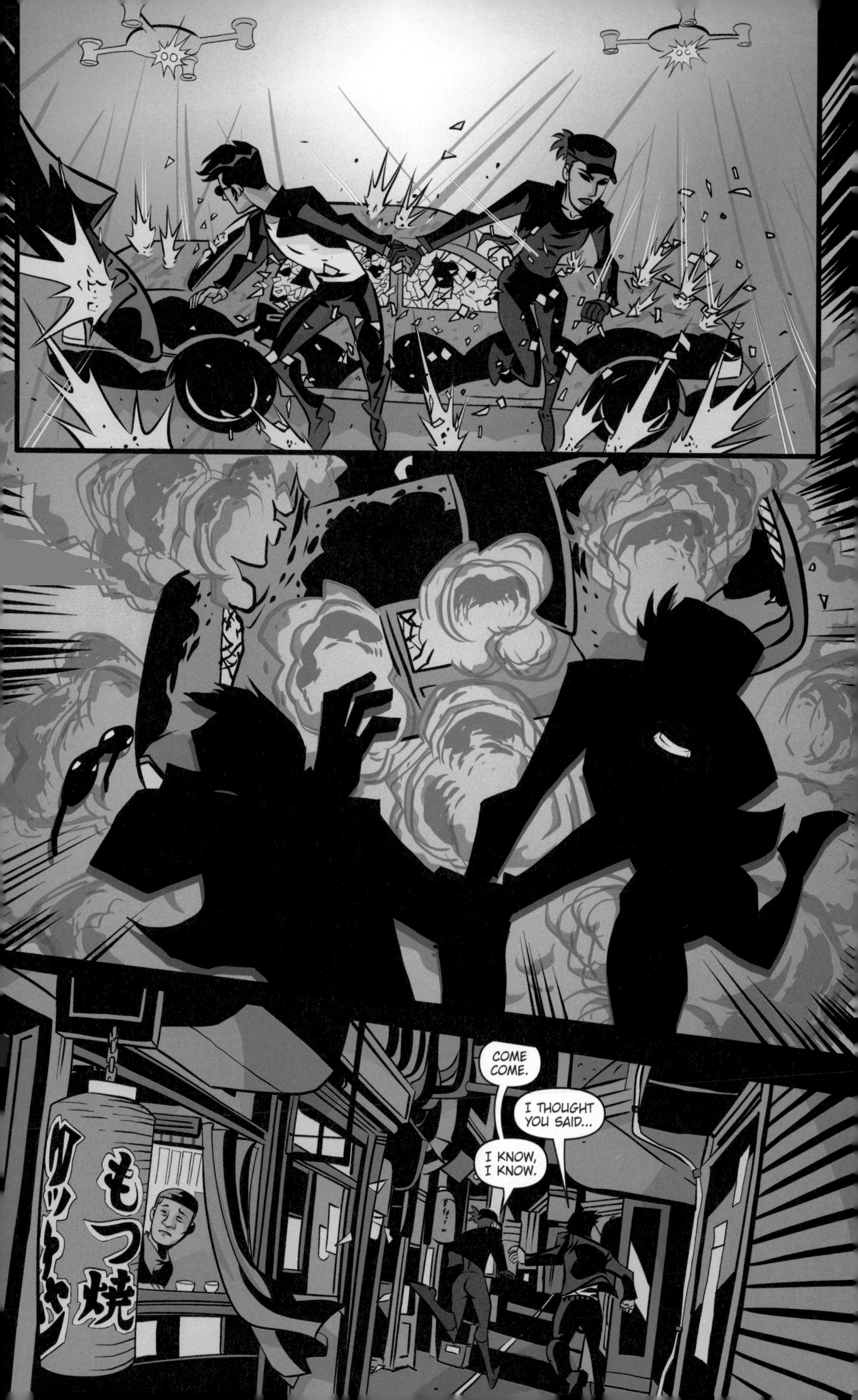
COME COME.
I THOUGHT YOU SAID...
I KNOW, I KNOW.
もつ焼

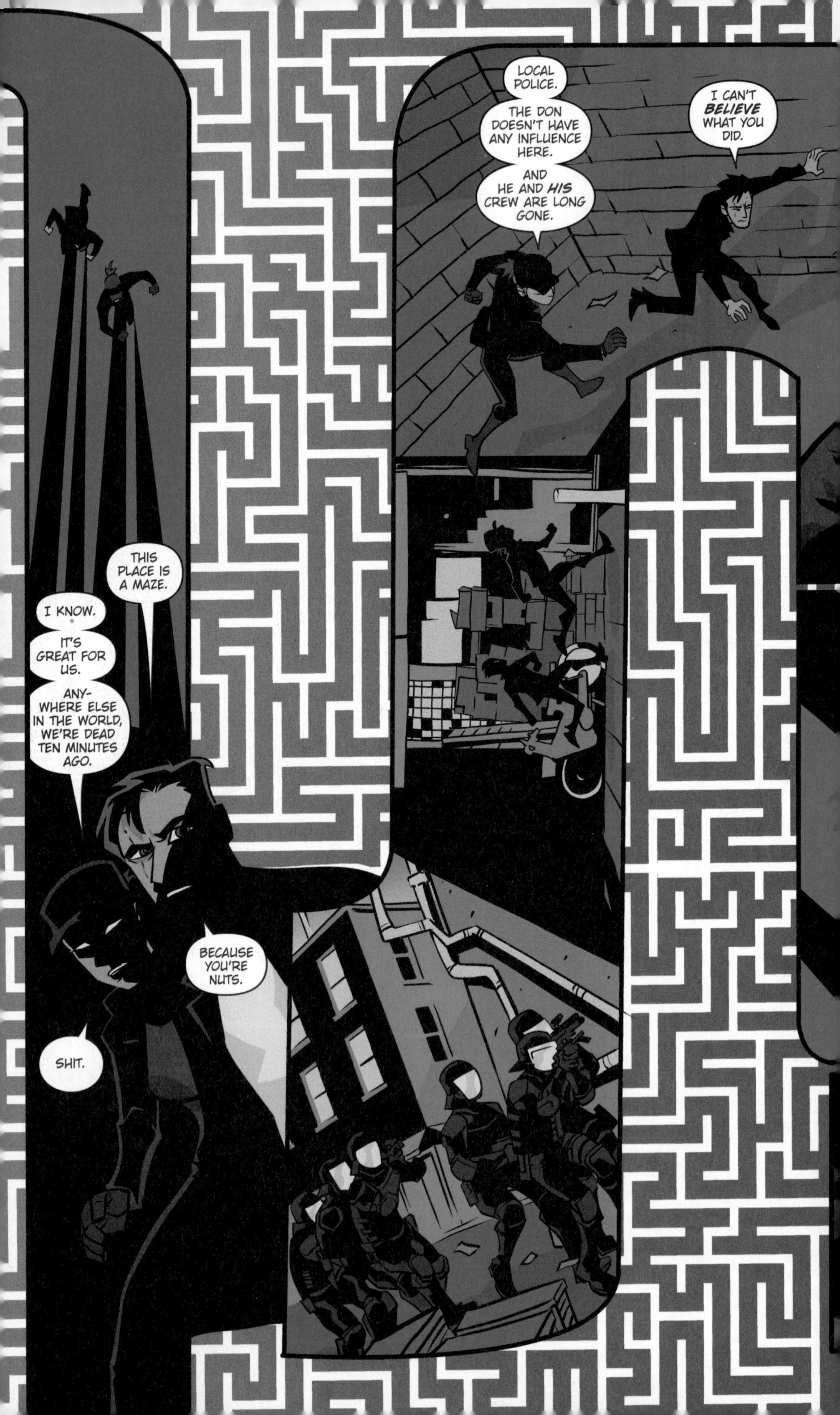
THIS PLACE IS A MAZE.
I KNOW.
IT'S GREAT FOR US.
ANY-WHERE ELSE IN THE WORLD, WE'RE DEAD TEN MINUTES AGO.
BECAUSE YOU'RE NUTS.
SHIT.
LOCAL POLICE.
THE DON DOESN'T HAVE ANY INFLUENCE HERE.
AND HE AND HIS CREW ARE LONG GONE.
I CAN'T BELIEVE WHAT YOU DID.

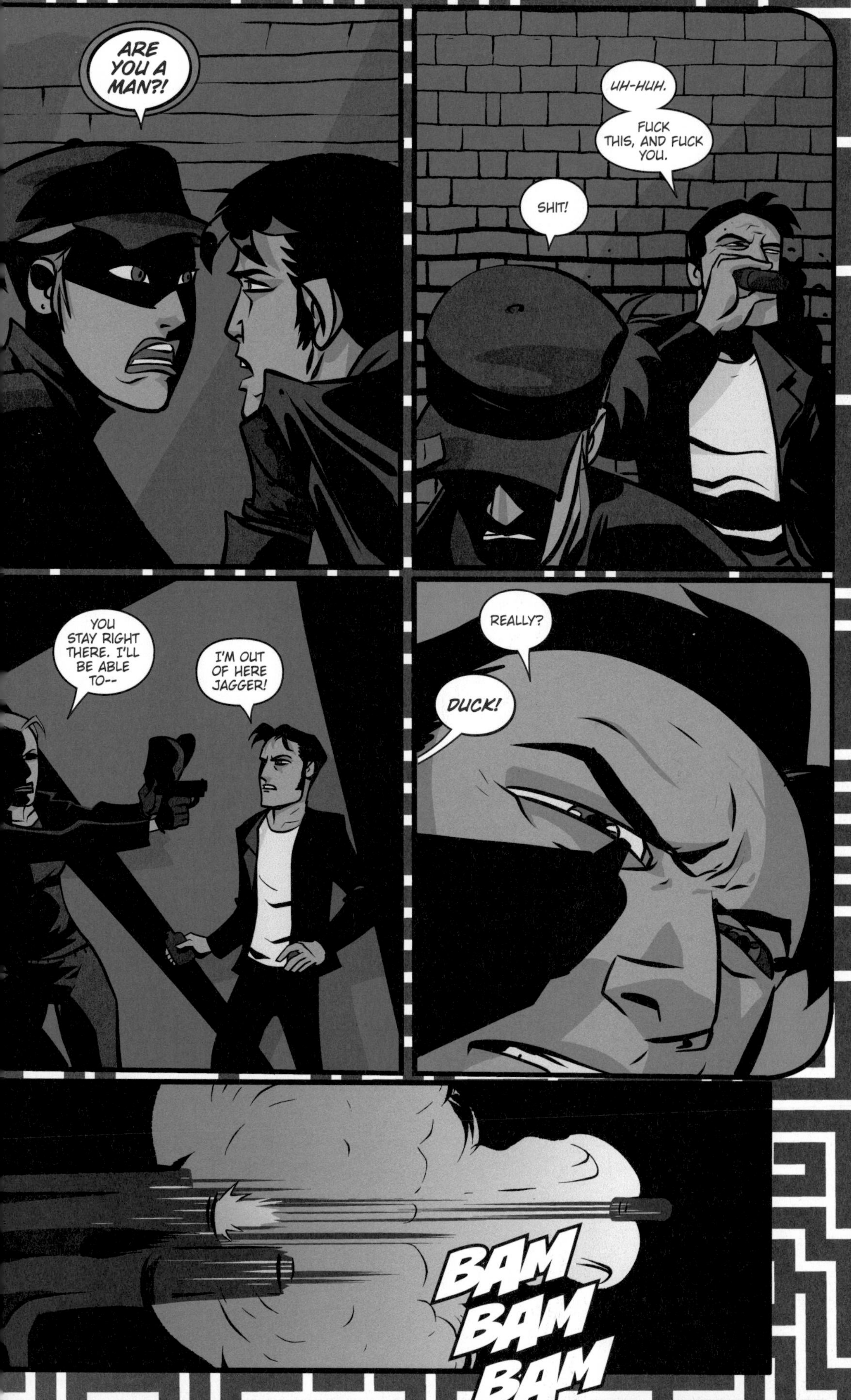
ARE YOU A MAN?!
UH-HUH.
FUCK THIS, AND FUCK YOU.
SHIT!
YOU STAY RIGHT THERE. I'LL BE ABLE TO--
I'M OUT OF HERE JAGGER!
REALLY?
DUCK!
BAM BAM BAM

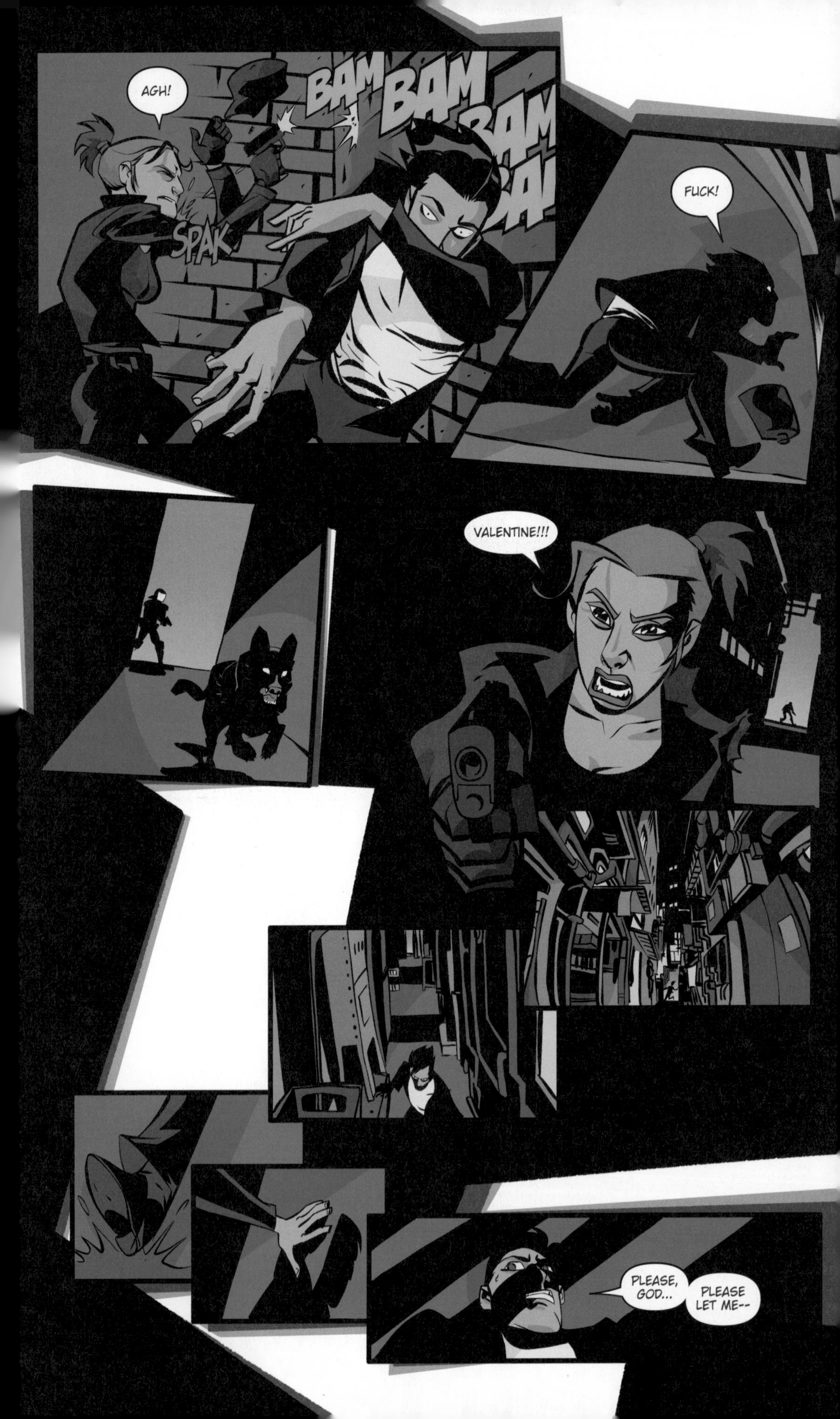
AGH!
BAM
BAM
BAM
SPAK
FUCK!
VALENTINE!!!
PLEASE, GOD...
PLEASE LET ME--

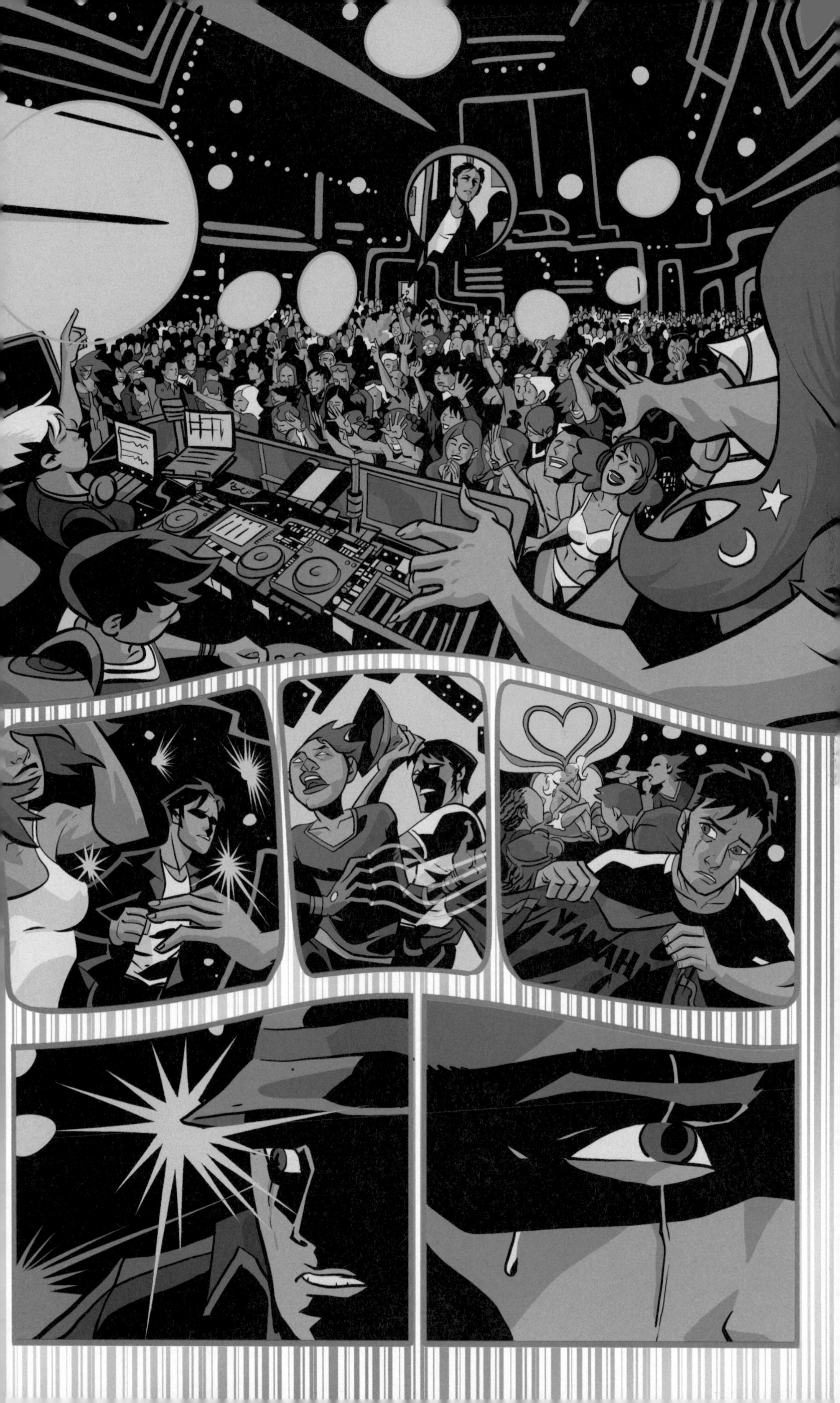

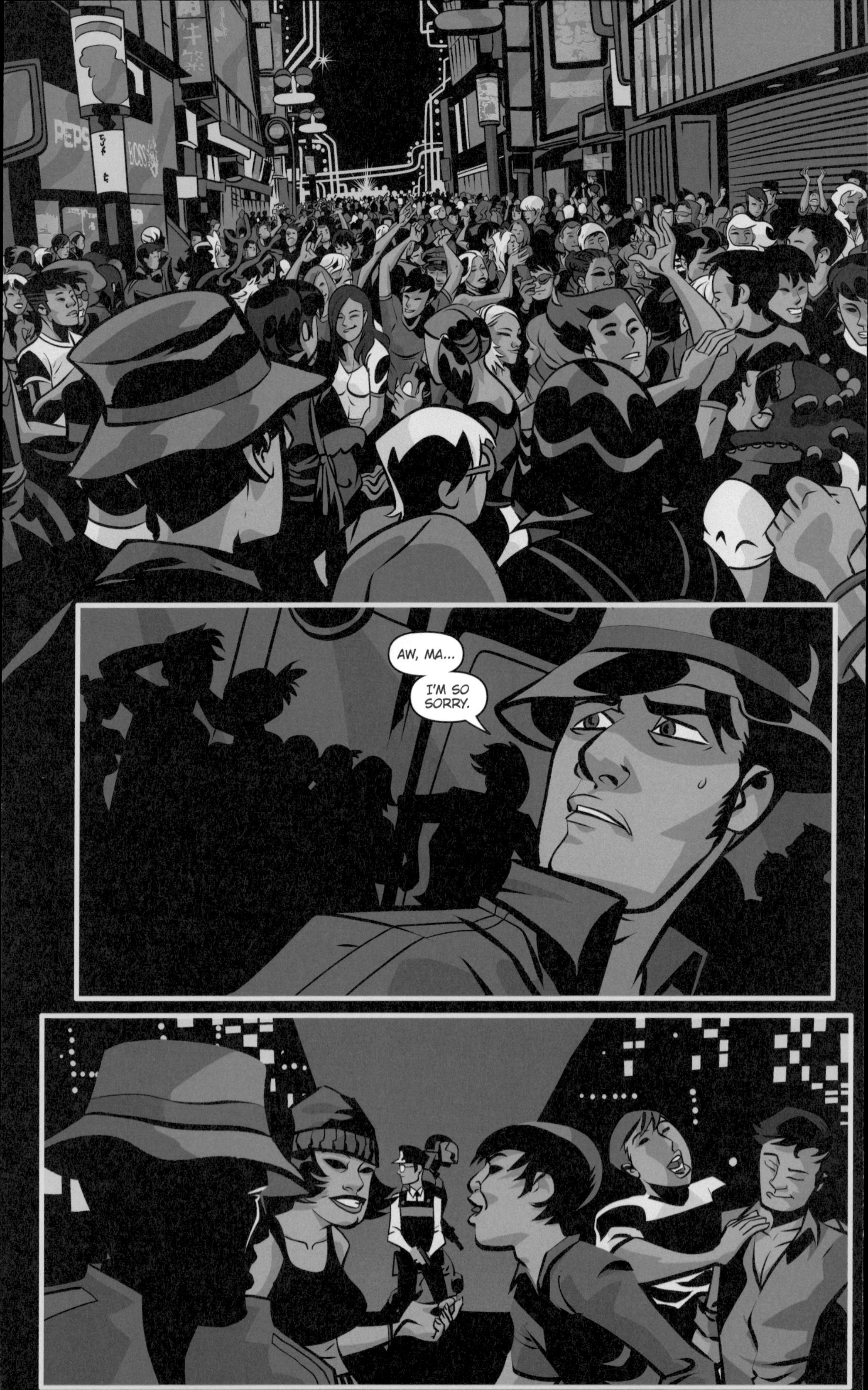
AW, MA...
I'M SO SORRY.

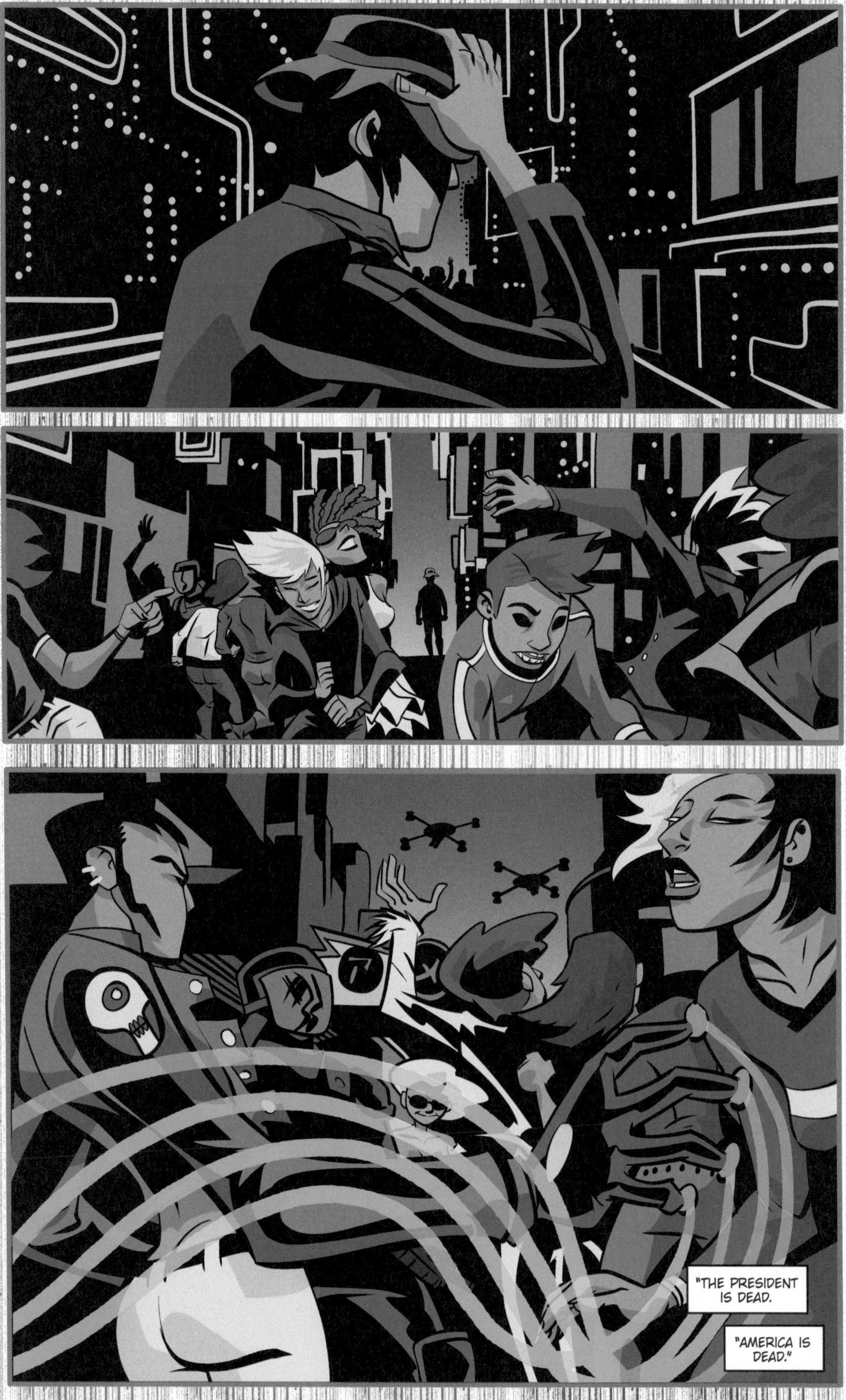
"THE PRESIDENT IS DEAD.
"AMERICA IS DEAD."

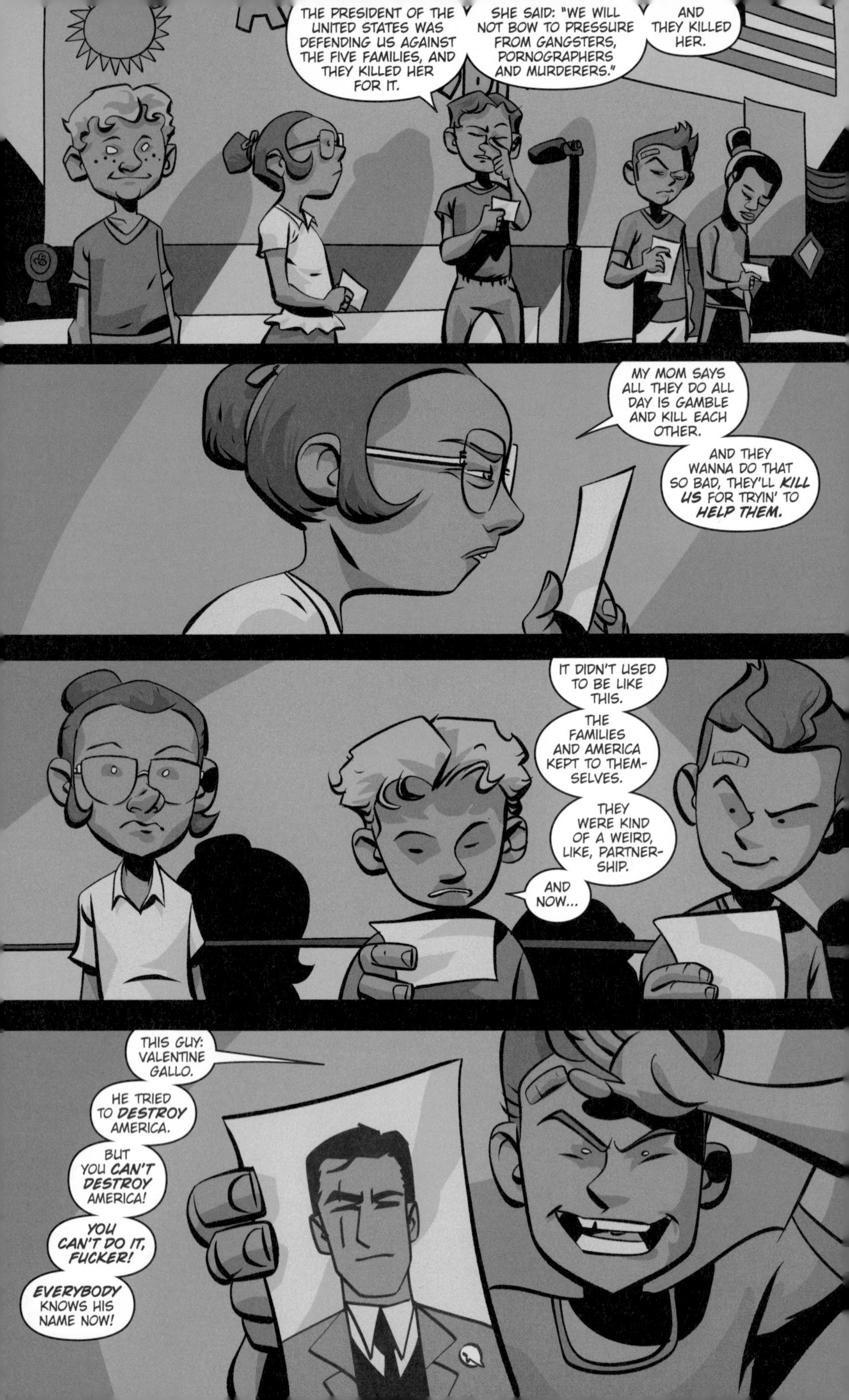
THE PRESIDENT OF THE UNITED STATES WAS DEFENDING US AGAINST THE FIVE FAMILIES, AND THEY KILLED HER FOR IT.
SHE SAID: "WE WILL NOT BOW TO PRESSURE FROM GANGSTERS, PORNOGRAPHERS AND MURDERERS."
AND THEY KILLED HER.
MY MOM SAYS ALL THEY DO ALL DAY IS GAMBLE AND KILL EACH OTHER.
AND THEY WANNA DO THAT SO BAD, THEY'LL ***KILL US*** FOR TRYIN' TO ***HELP THEM.***
IT DIDN'T USED TO BE LIKE THIS.
THE FAMILIES AND AMERICA KEPT TO THEMSELVES.
THEY WERE KIND OF A WEIRD, LIKE, PARTNERSHIP.
AND NOW...
THIS GUY: VALENTINE GALLO.
HE TRIED TO ***DESTROY*** AMERICA.
BUT YOU ***CAN'T DESTROY*** AMERICA!
YOU CAN'T DO IT, FUCKER!
EVERYBODY KNOWS HIS NAME NOW!

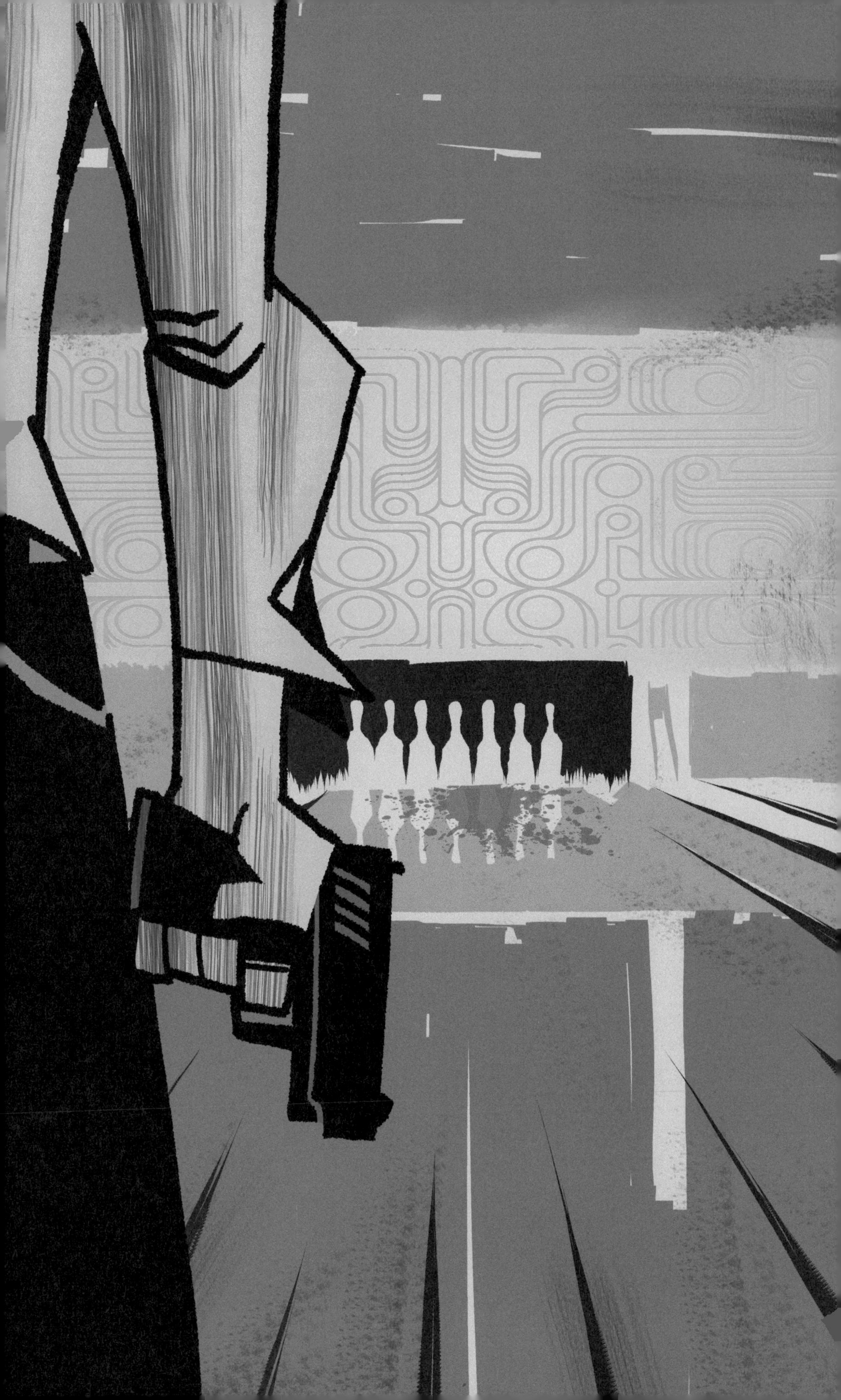

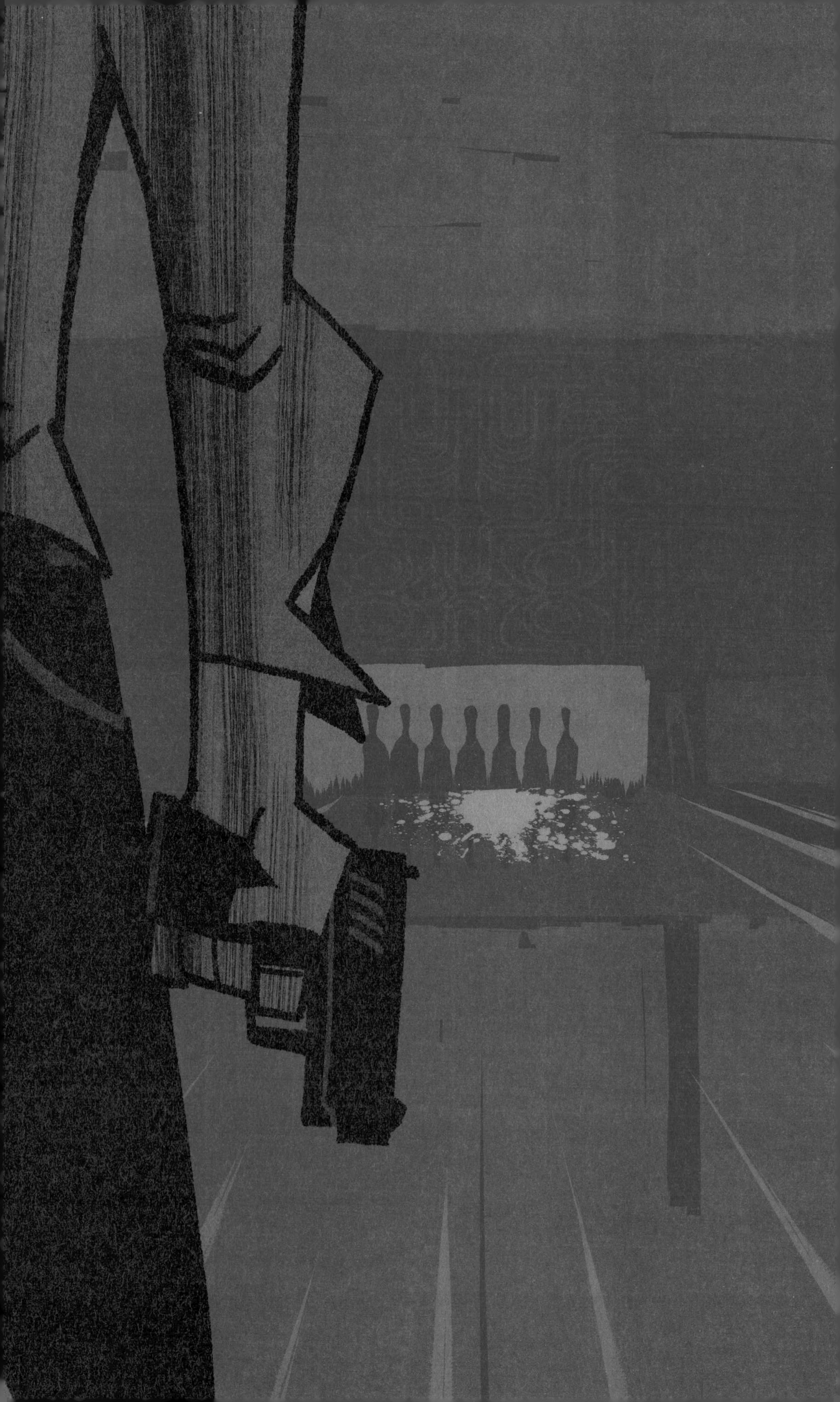

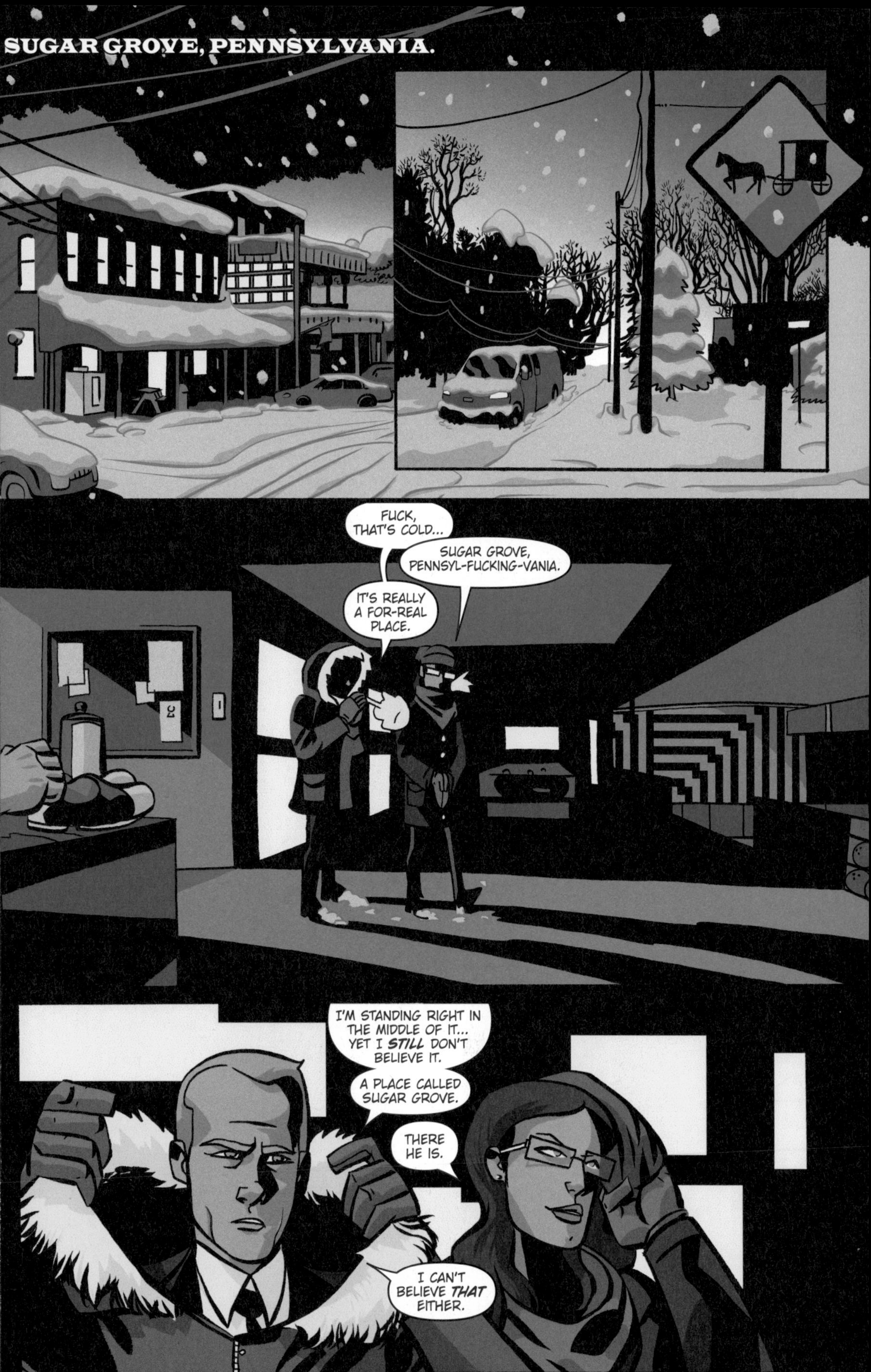
SUGAR GROVE, PENNSYLVANIA.
FUCK, THAT'S COLD...
IT'S REALLY A FOR-REAL PLACE.
SUGAR GROVE, PENNSYL-FUCKING-VANIA.
I'M STANDING RIGHT IN THE MIDDLE OF IT... YET I STILL DON'T BELIEVE IT.
A PLACE CALLED SUGAR GROVE.
THERE HE IS.
I CAN'T BELIEVE THAT EITHER.

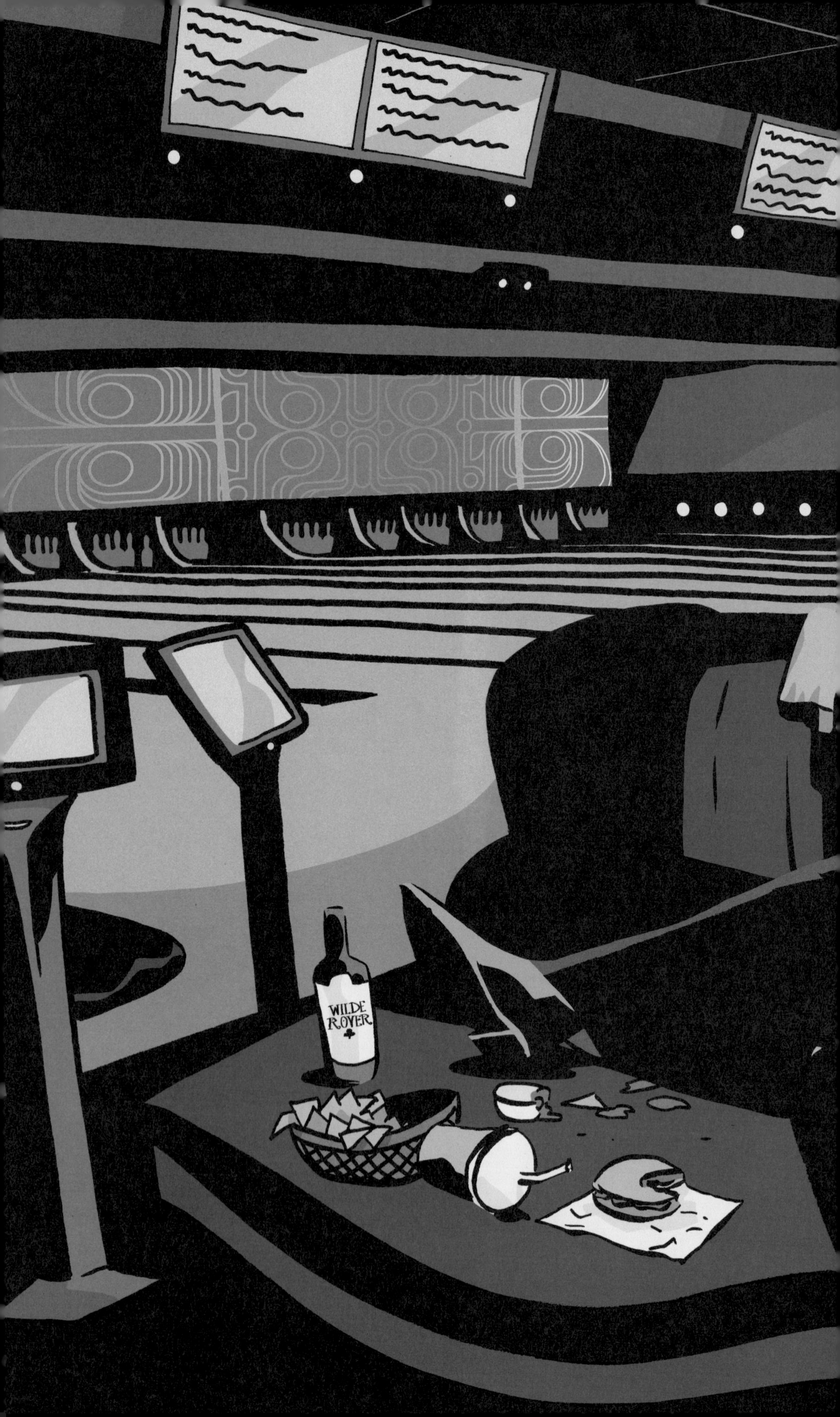
WILDE
ROVER

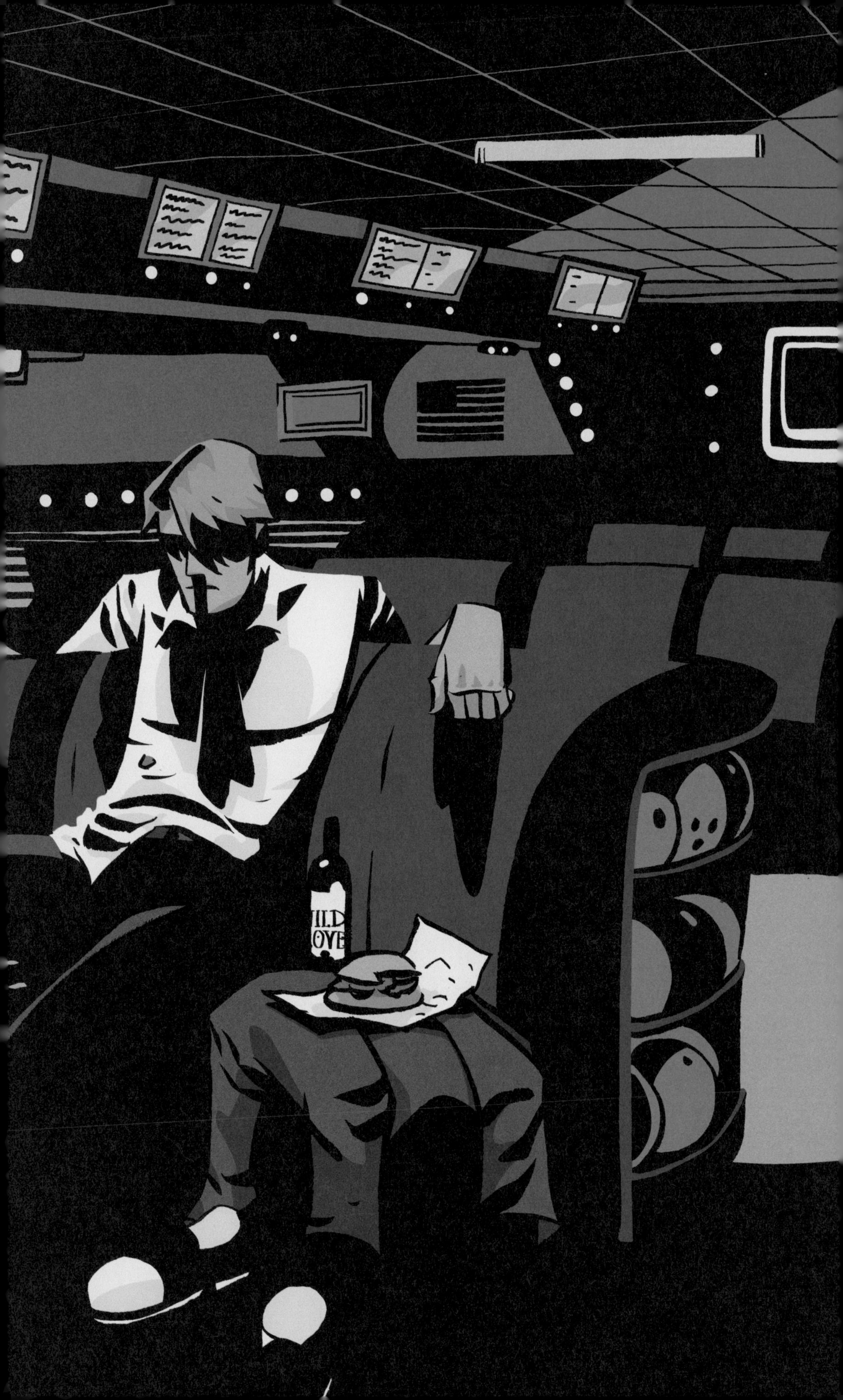

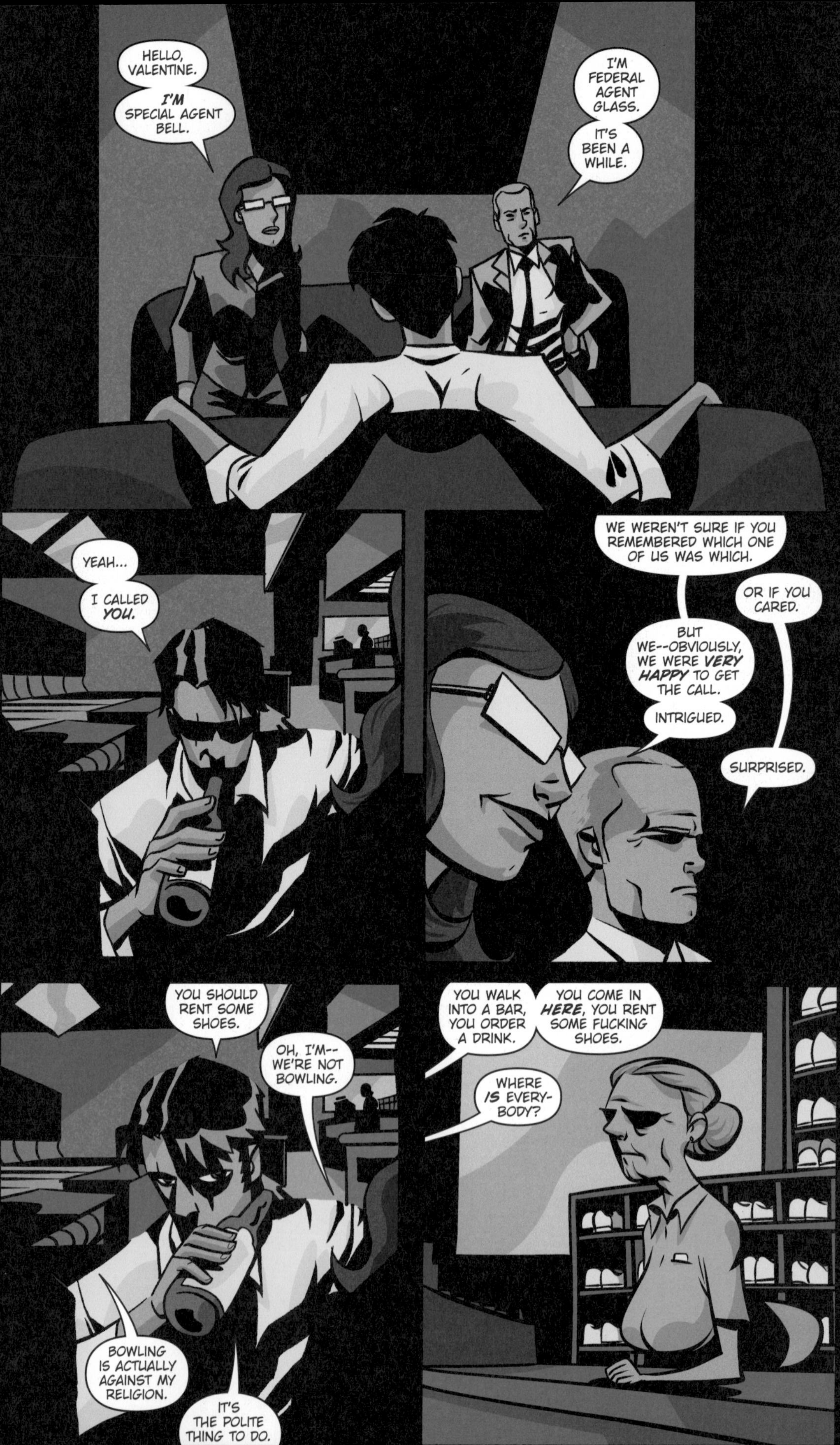
HELLO, VALENTINE.
I'M SPECIAL AGENT BELL.
I'M FEDERAL AGENT GLASS.
IT'S BEEN A WHILE.
YEAH...
I CALLED YOU.
WE WEREN'T SURE IF YOU REMEMBERED WHICH ONE OF US WAS WHICH.
OR IF YOU CARED.
BUT WE--OBVIOUSLY, WE WERE VERY HAPPY TO GET THE CALL.
INTRIGUED.
SURPRISED.
YOU SHOULD RENT SOME SHOES.
OH, I'M-- WE'RE NOT BOWLING.
BOWLING IS ACTUALLY AGAINST MY RELIGION.
IT'S THE POLITE THING TO DO.
YOU WALK INTO A BAR, YOU ORDER A DRINK.
YOU COME IN HERE, YOU RENT SOME FUCKING SHOES.
WHERE IS EVERY-BODY?

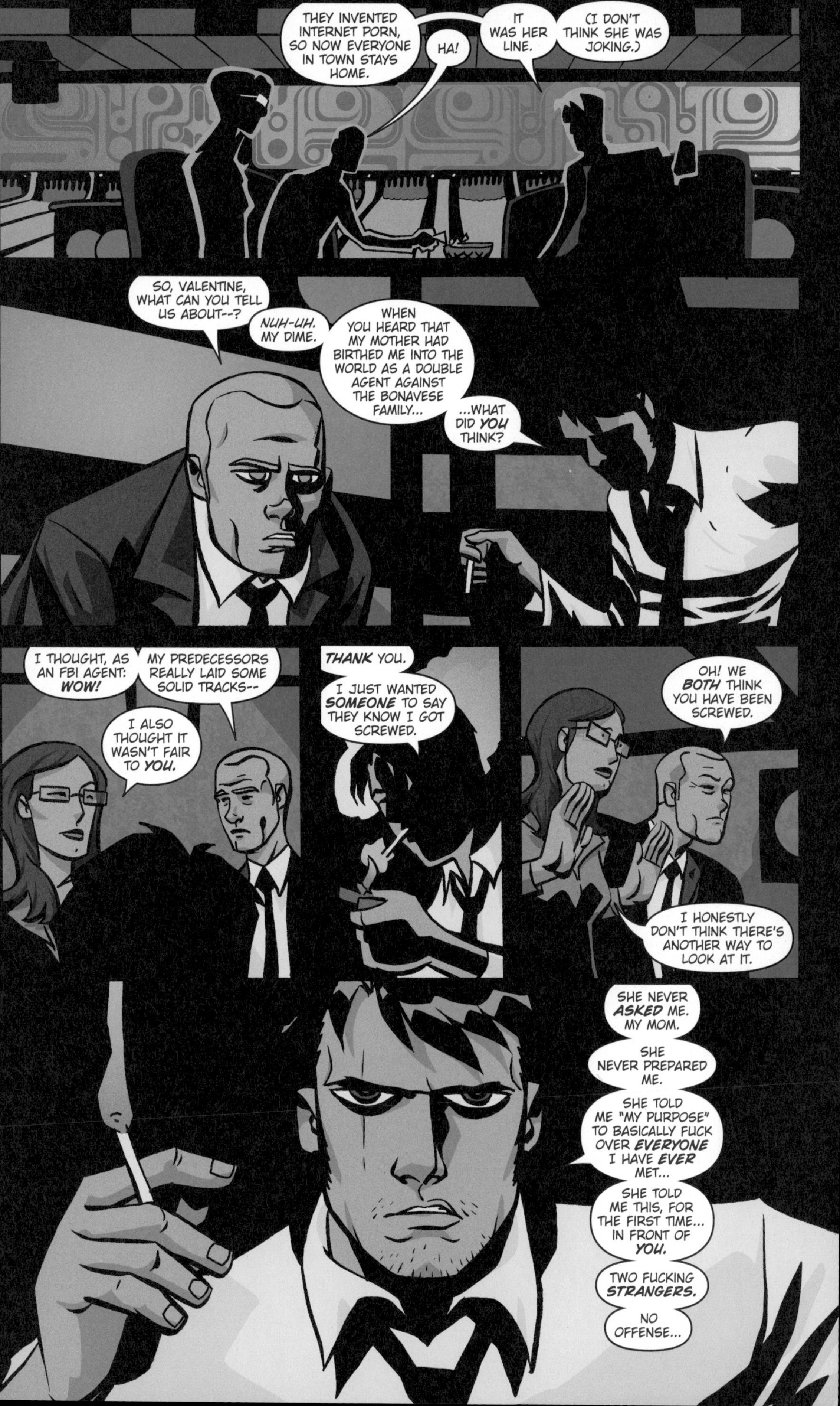
THEY INVENTED INTERNET PORN, SO NOW EVERYONE IN TOWN STAYS HOME.
HA!
IT WAS HER LINE.
(I DON'T THINK SHE WAS JOKING.)
SO, VALENTINE, WHAT CAN YOU TELL US ABOUT--?
NUH-UH. MY DIME.
WHEN YOU HEARD THAT MY MOTHER HAD BIRTHED ME INTO THE WORLD AS A DOUBLE AGENT AGAINST THE BONAVESE FAMILY...
...WHAT DID YOU THINK?
I THOUGHT, AS AN FBI AGENT: WOW!
MY PREDECESSORS REALLY LAID SOME SOLID TRACKS--
I ALSO THOUGHT IT WASN'T FAIR TO YOU.
THANK YOU.
I JUST WANTED SOMEONE TO SAY THEY KNOW I GOT SCREWED.
OH! WE BOTH THINK YOU HAVE BEEN SCREWED.
I HONESTLY DON'T THINK THERE'S ANOTHER WAY TO LOOK AT IT.
SHE NEVER ASKED ME. MY MOM.
SHE NEVER PREPARED ME.
SHE TOLD ME "MY PURPOSE" TO BASICALLY FUCK OVER EVERYONE I HAVE EVER MET...
SHE TOLD ME THIS, FOR THE FIRST TIME... IN FRONT OF YOU.
TWO FUCKING STRANGERS.
NO OFFENSE...

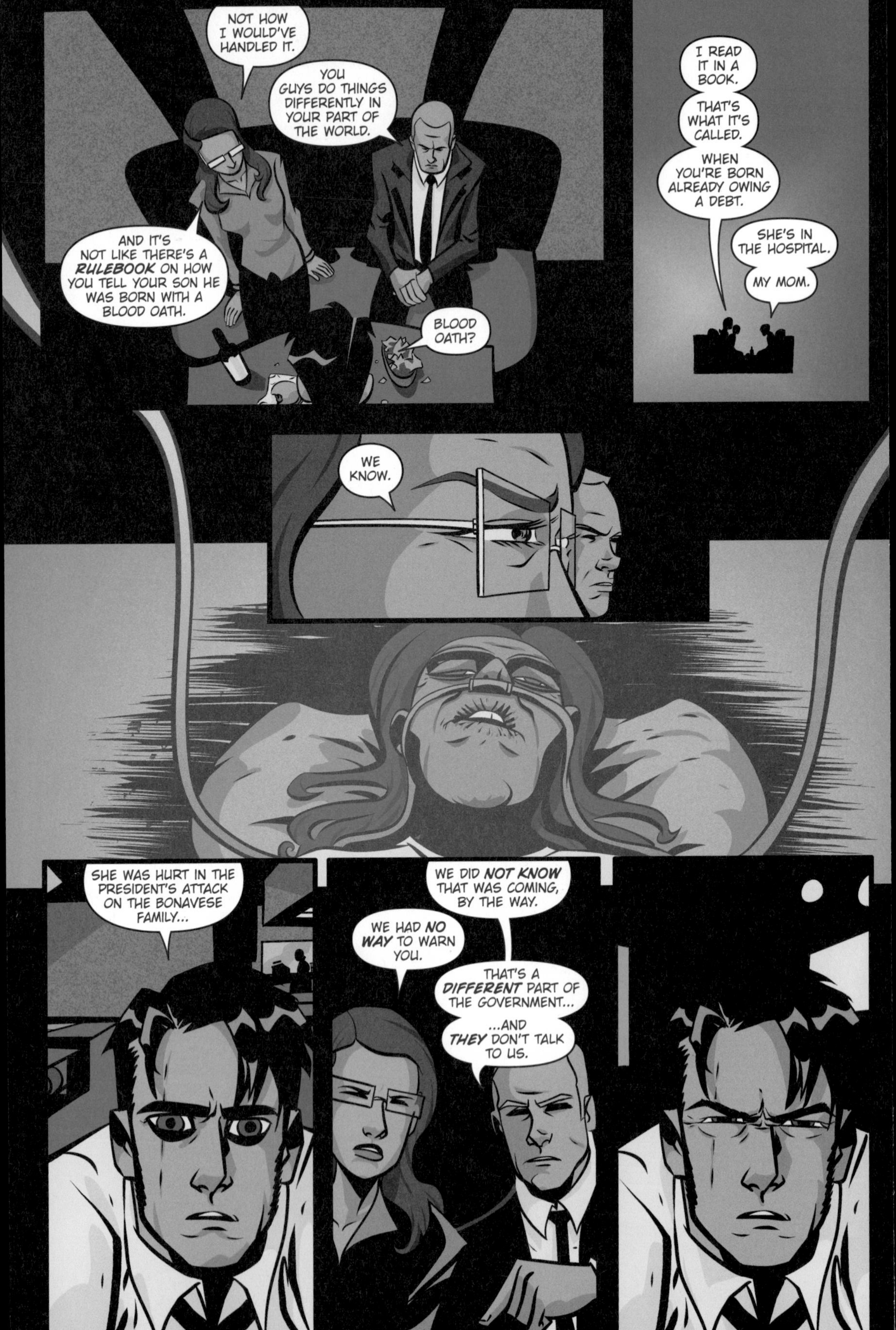
NOT HOW I WOULD'VE HANDLED IT.
YOU GUYS DO THINGS DIFFERENTLY IN YOUR PART OF THE WORLD.
AND IT'S NOT LIKE THERE'S A RULEBOOK ON HOW YOU TELL YOUR SON HE WAS BORN WITH A BLOOD OATH.
BLOOD OATH?
I READ IT IN A BOOK.
THAT'S WHAT IT'S CALLED.
WHEN YOU'RE BORN ALREADY OWING A DEBT.
SHE'S IN THE HOSPITAL.
MY MOM.
WE KNOW.
SHE WAS HURT IN THE PRESIDENT'S ATTACK ON THE BONAVESE FAMILY...
WE HAD NO WAY TO WARN YOU.
WE DID NOT KNOW THAT WAS COMING, BY THE WAY.
THAT'S A DIFFERENT PART OF THE GOVERNMENT...
...AND THEY DON'T TALK TO US.

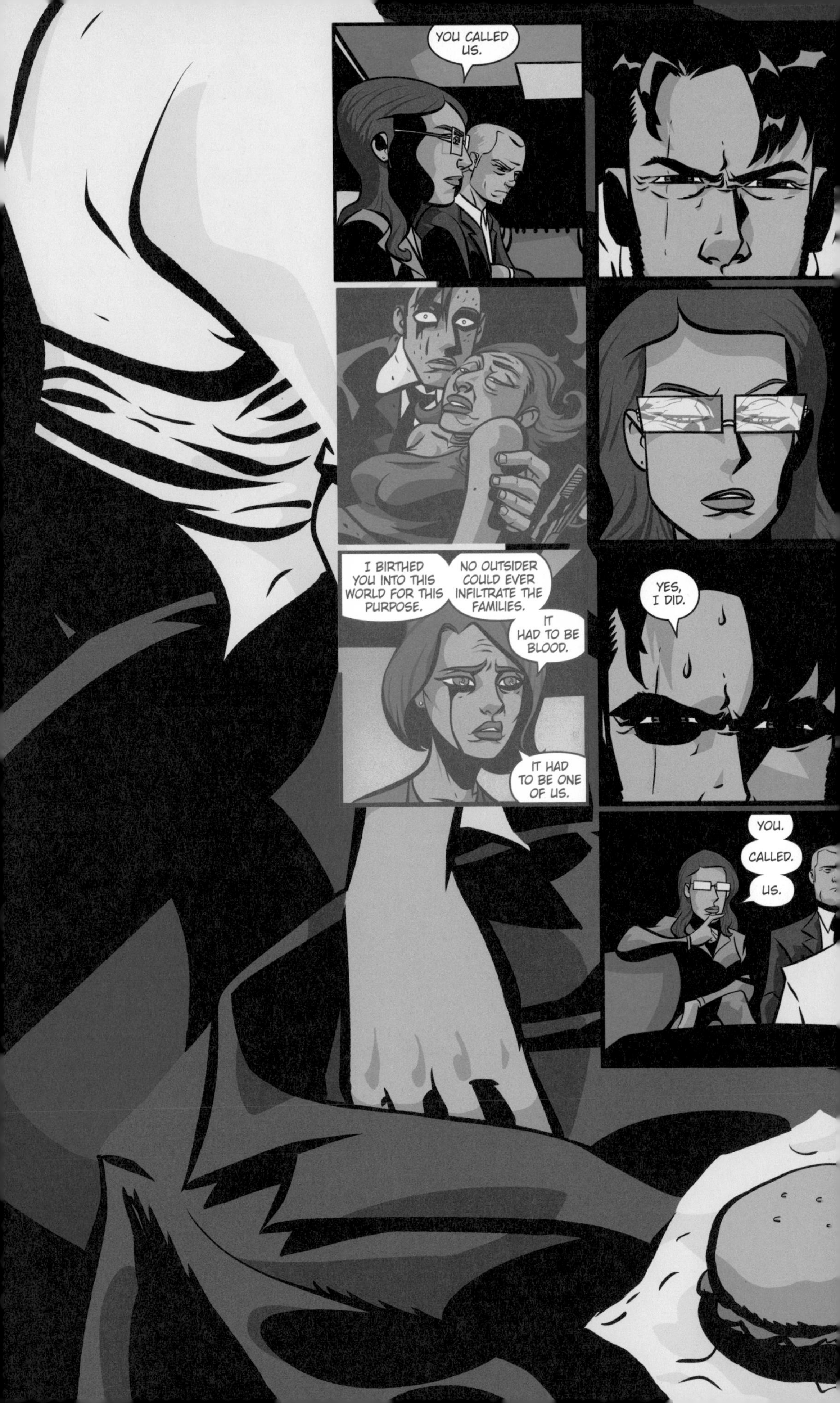
YOU CALLED US.
I BIRTHED YOU INTO THIS WORLD FOR THIS PURPOSE.
NO OUTSIDER COULD EVER INFILTRATE THE FAMILIES.
IT HAD TO BE BLOOD.
IT HAD TO BE ONE OF US.
YES, I DID.
YOU.
CALLED.
US.

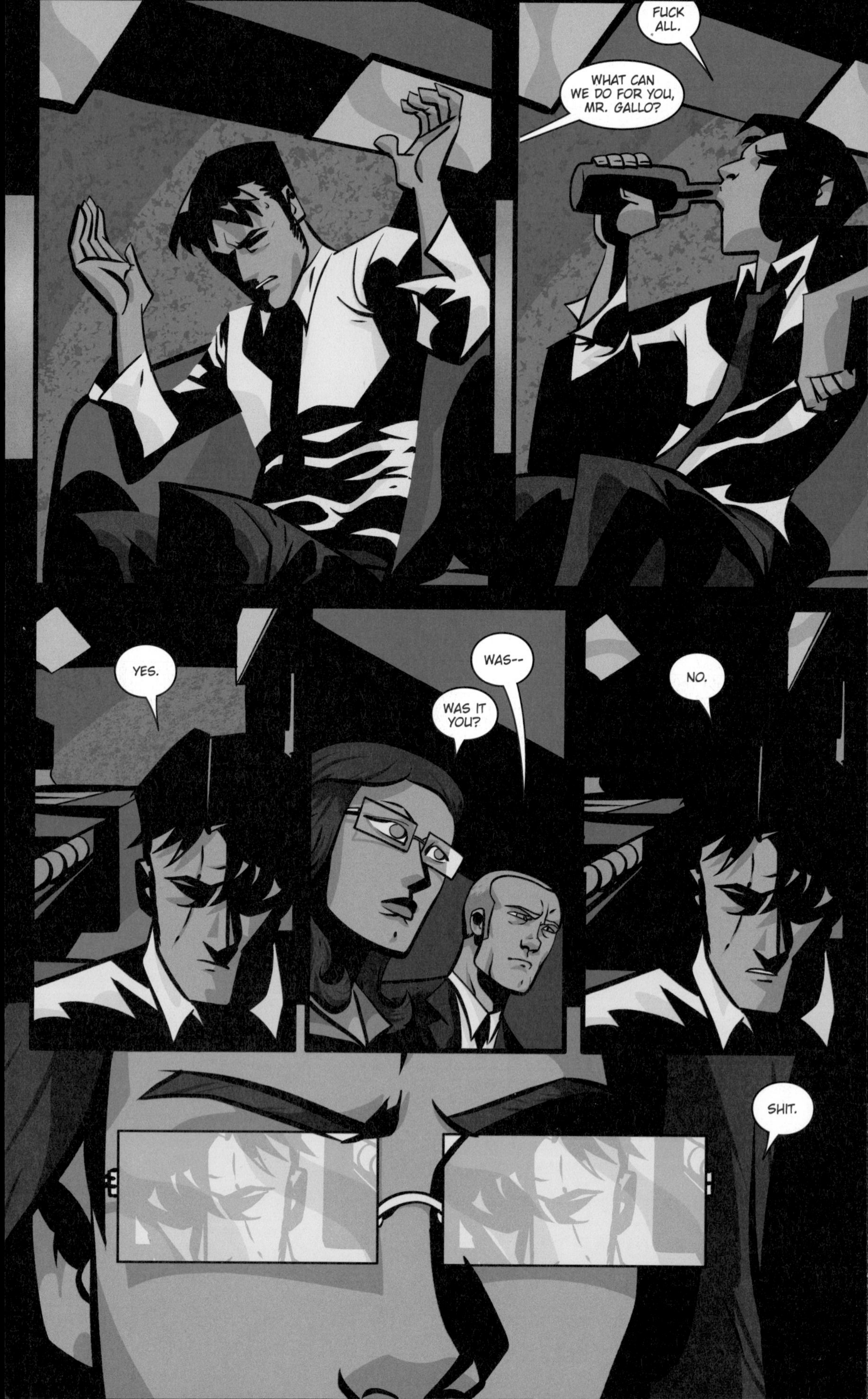
FUCK ALL.
WHAT CAN WE DO FOR YOU, MR. GALLO?
YES.
WAS--
WAS IT YOU?
NO.
SHIT.

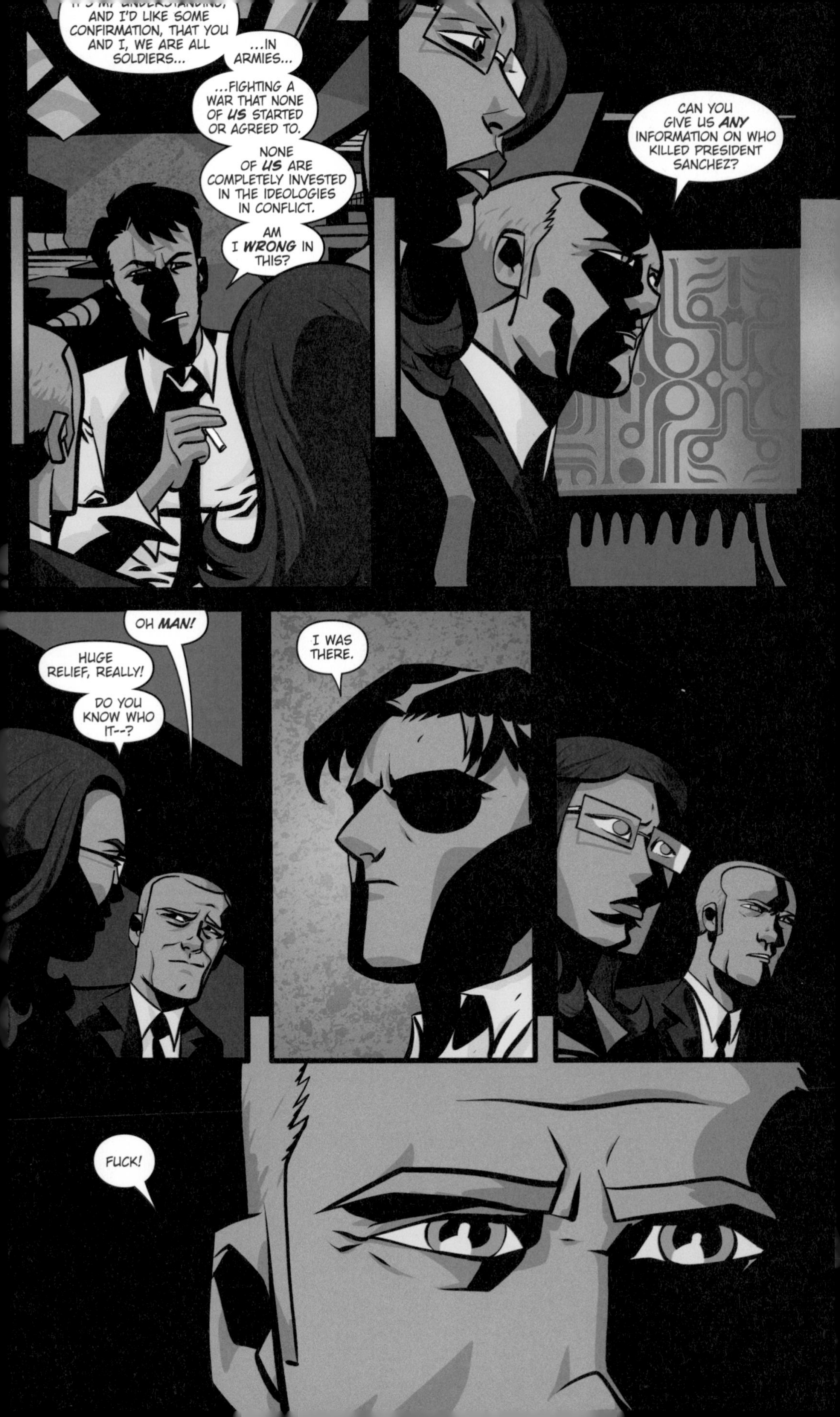
AND I'D LIKE SOME CONFIRMATION, THAT YOU AND I, WE ARE ALL SOLDIERS...
...IN ARMIES...
...FIGHTING A WAR THAT NONE OF US STARTED OR AGREED TO.
NONE OF US ARE COMPLETELY INVESTED IN THE IDEOLOGIES IN CONFLICT.
AM I WRONG IN THIS?
CAN YOU GIVE US ANY INFORMATION ON WHO KILLED PRESIDENT SANCHEZ?
OH MAN!
HUGE RELIEF, REALLY!
DO YOU KNOW WHO IT--?
I WAS THERE.
FUCK!

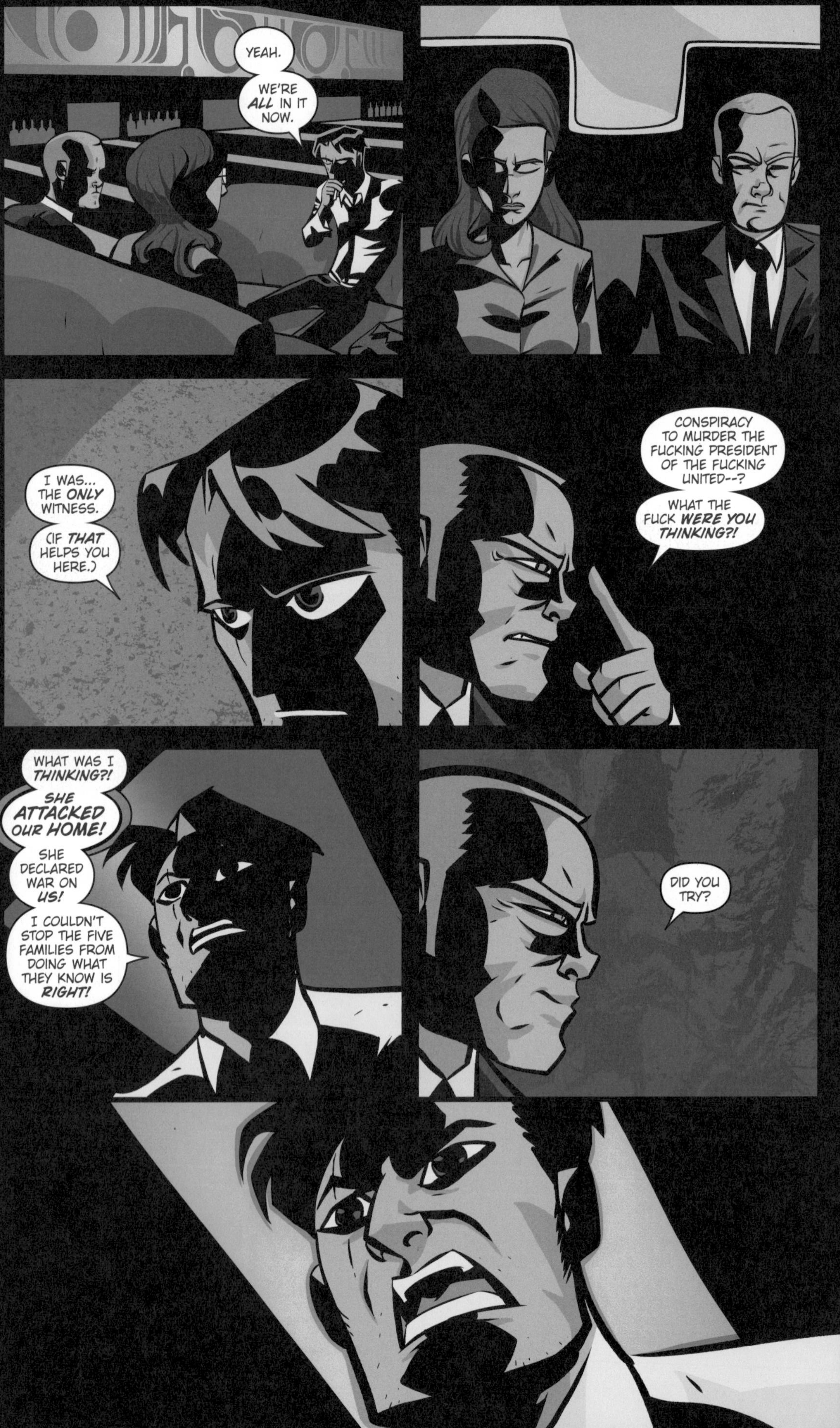
YEAH.
WE'RE ALL IN IT NOW.
I WAS... THE ONLY WITNESS.
(IF THAT HELPS YOU HERE.)
CONSPIRACY TO MURDER THE FUCKING PRESIDENT OF THE FUCKING UNITED--?
WHAT THE FUCK WERE YOU THINKING?!
WHAT WAS I THINKING?!
SHE ATTACKED OUR HOME!
SHE DECLARED WAR ON US!
I COULDN'T STOP THE FIVE FAMILIES FROM DOING WHAT THEY KNOW IS RIGHT!
DID YOU TRY?

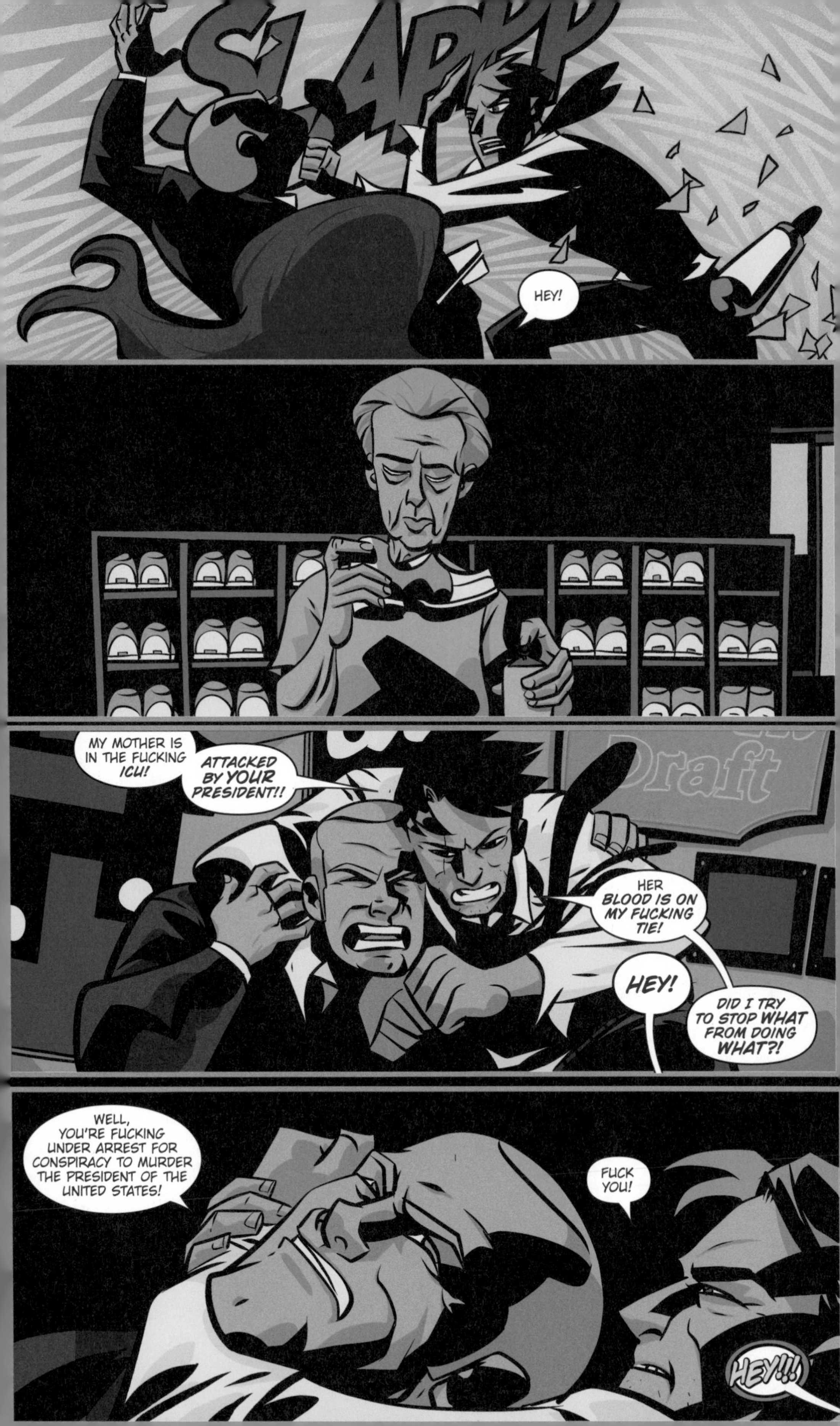
SLAPP
HEY!
MY MOTHER IS IN THE FUCKING ICU!
ATTACKED BY YOUR PRESIDENT!!
Draft
HER BLOOD IS ON MY FUCKING TIE!
HEY!
DID I TRY TO STOP WHAT FROM DOING WHAT?!
WELL, YOU'RE FUCKING UNDER ARREST FOR CONSPIRACY TO MURDER THE PRESIDENT OF THE UNITED STATES!
FUCK YOU!
HEY!!!

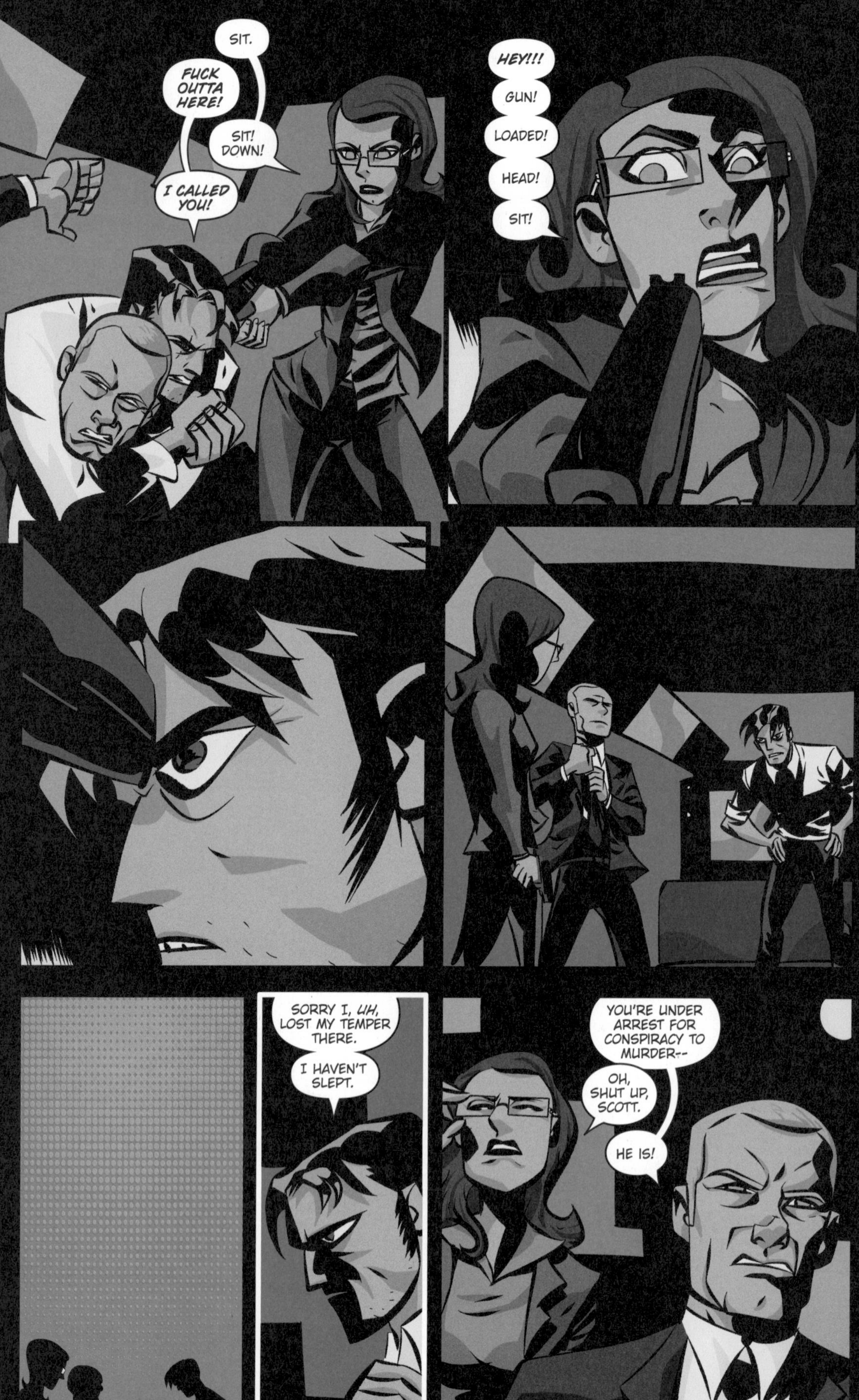
SIT.
FUCK OUTTA HERE!
SIT! DOWN!
I CALLED YOU!
HEY!!!
GUN!
LOADED!
HEAD!
SIT!
SORRY I, UH, LOST MY TEMPER THERE.
I HAVEN'T SLEPT.
YOU'RE UNDER ARREST FOR CONSPIRACY TO MURDER--
OH, SHUT UP, SCOTT.
HE IS!

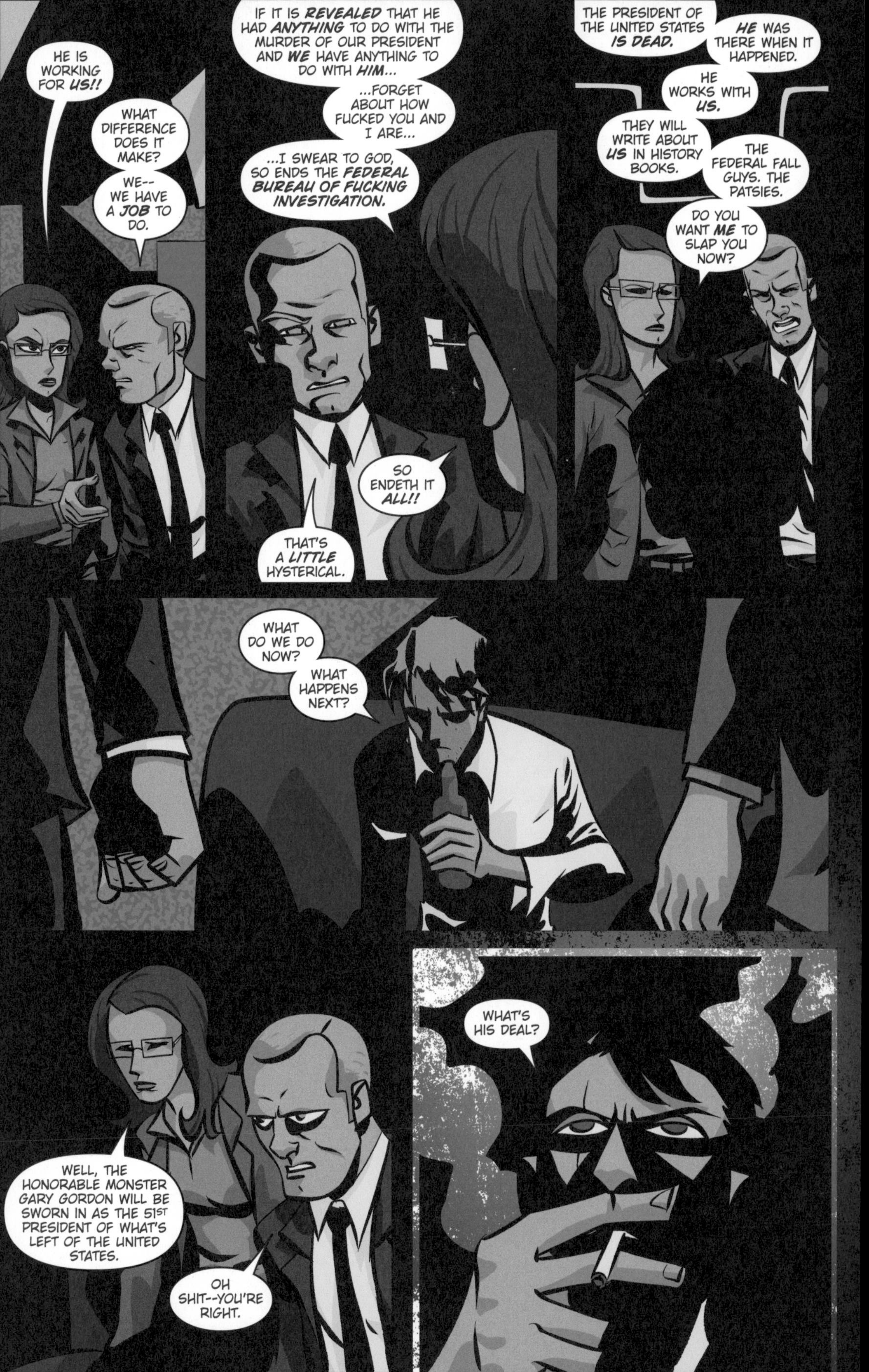
HE IS WORKING FOR US!!
WHAT DIFFERENCE DOES IT MAKE?
WE-- WE HAVE A JOB TO DO.
IF IT IS REVEALED THAT HE HAD ANYTHING TO DO WITH THE MURDER OF OUR PRESIDENT AND WE HAVE ANYTHING TO DO WITH HIM...
...FORGET ABOUT HOW FUCKED YOU AND I ARE...
...I SWEAR TO GOD, SO ENDS THE FEDERAL BUREAU OF FUCKING INVESTIGATION.
SO ENDETH IT ALL!!
THAT'S A LITTLE HYSTERICAL.
THE PRESIDENT OF THE UNITED STATES IS DEAD.
HE WAS THERE WHEN IT HAPPENED.
HE WORKS WITH US.
THEY WILL WRITE ABOUT US IN HISTORY BOOKS.
THE FEDERAL FALL GUYS. THE PATSIES.
DO YOU WANT ME TO SLAP YOU NOW?
WHAT DO WE DO NOW?
WHAT HAPPENS NEXT?
WELL, THE HONORABLE MONSTER GARY GORDON WILL BE SWORN IN AS THE 51ST PRESIDENT OF WHAT'S LEFT OF THE UNITED STATES.
OH SHIT--YOU'RE RIGHT.
WHAT'S HIS DEAL?

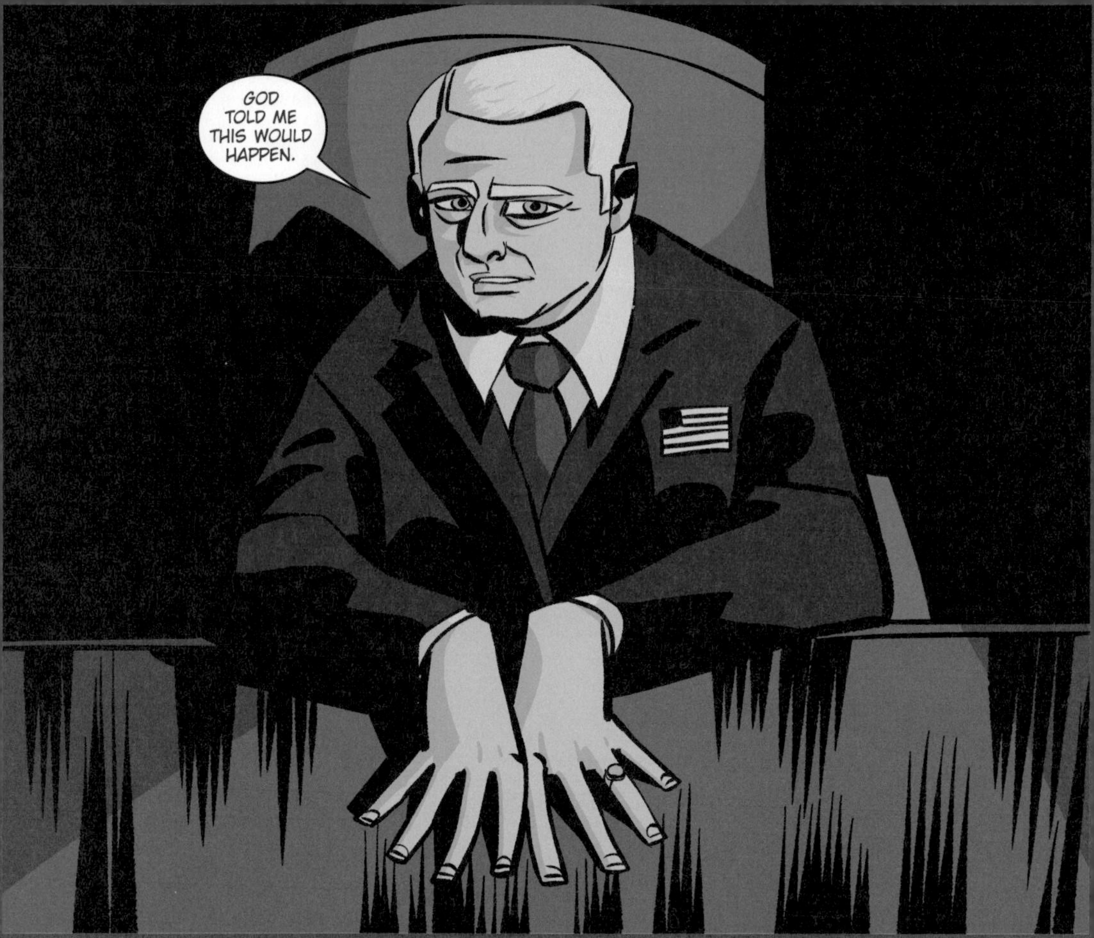
GOD TOLD ME THIS WOULD HAPPEN.

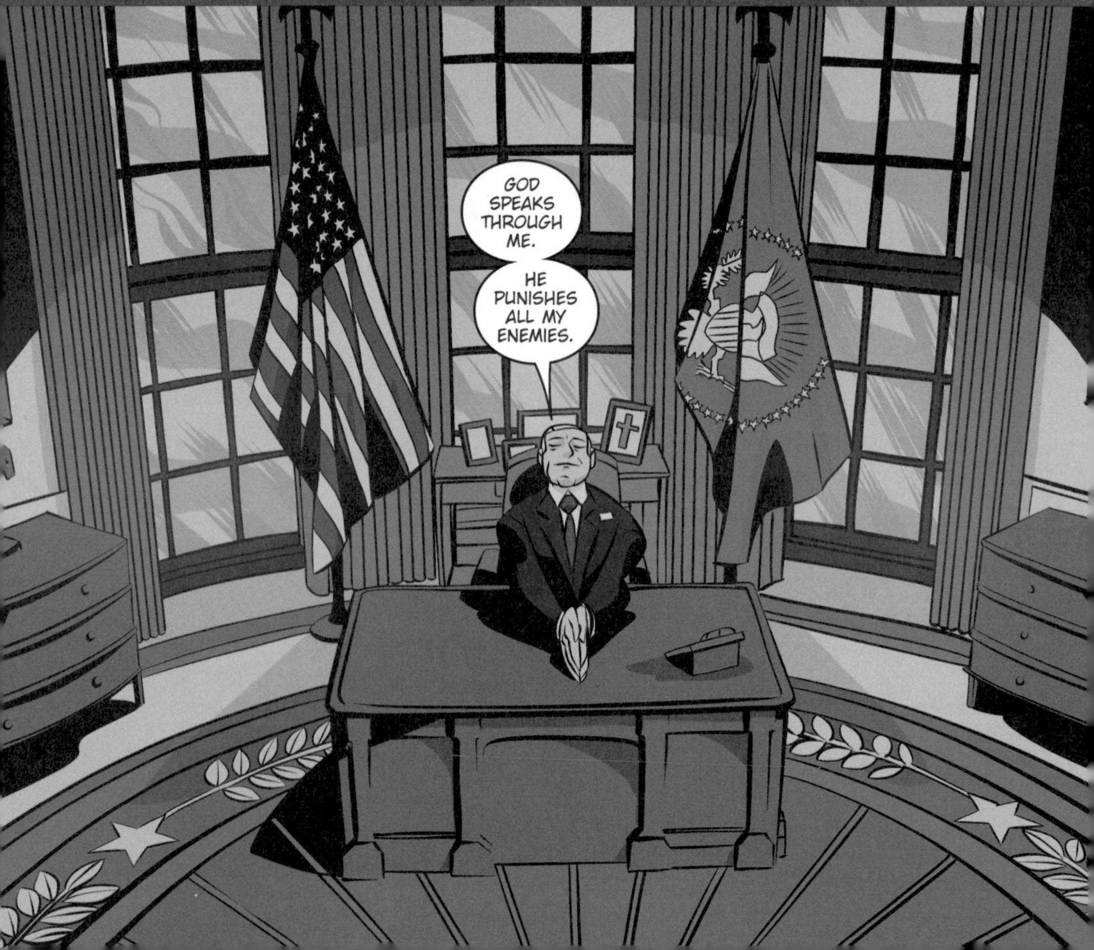
GOD SPEAKS THROUGH ME.
HE PUNISHES ALL MY ENEMIES.

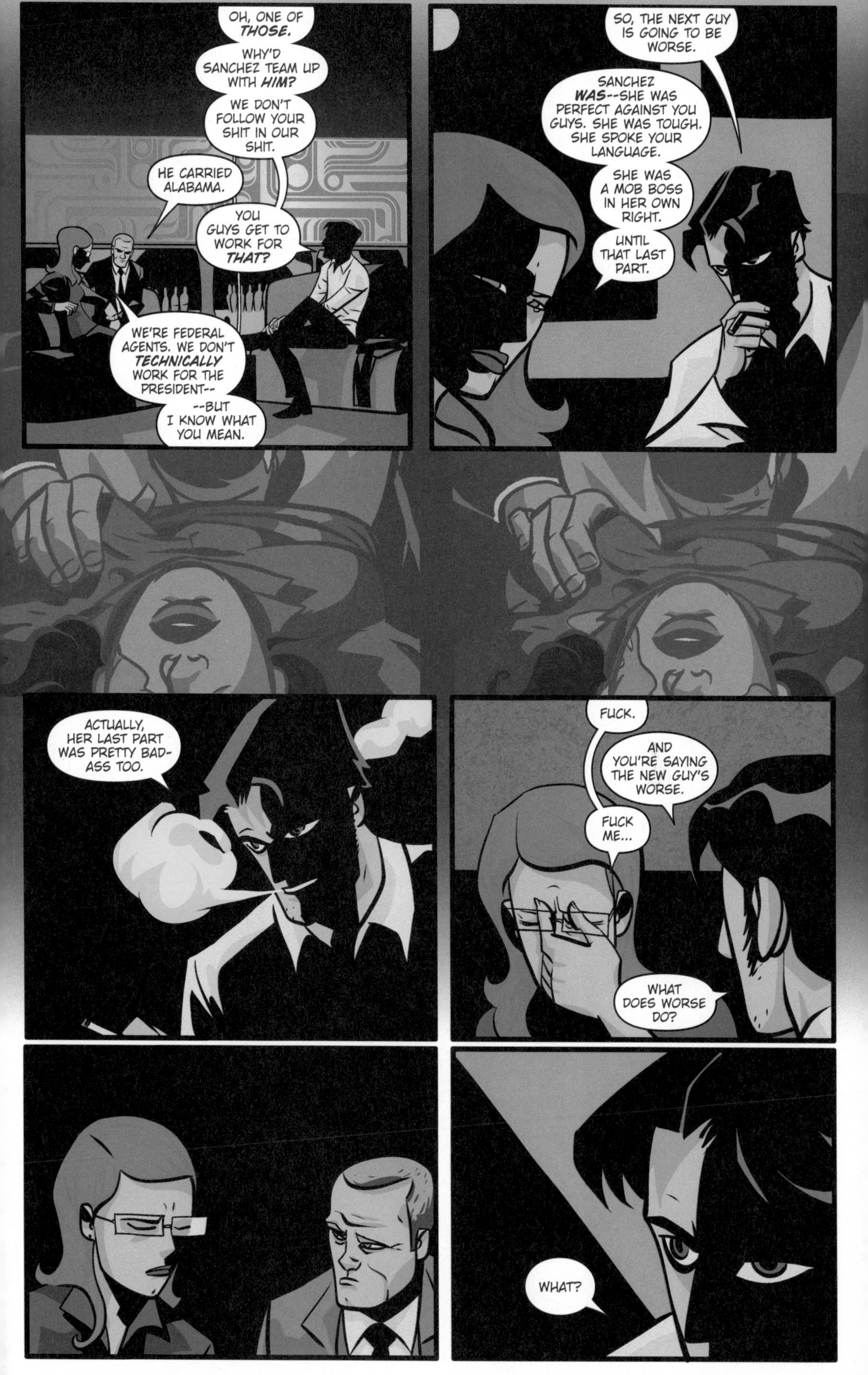
OH, ONE OF *THOSE.*
WHY'D SANCHEZ TEAM UP WITH *HIM?*
WE DON'T FOLLOW YOUR SHIT IN OUR SHIT.
HE CARRIED ALABAMA.
YOU GUYS GET TO WORK FOR *THAT?*
WE'RE FEDERAL AGENTS. WE DON'T *TECHNICALLY* WORK FOR THE PRESIDENT--
--BUT I KNOW WHAT YOU MEAN.
SO, THE NEXT GUY IS GOING TO BE WORSE.
SANCHEZ *WAS*--SHE WAS PERFECT AGAINST YOU GUYS. SHE WAS TOUGH. SHE SPOKE YOUR LANGUAGE.
SHE WAS A MOB BOSS IN HER OWN RIGHT.
UNTIL THAT LAST PART.
ACTUALLY, HER LAST PART WAS PRETTY BAD-ASS TOO.
FUCK.
AND YOU'RE SAYING THE NEW GUY'S WORSE.
FUCK ME...
WHAT DOES WORSE DO?
WHAT?

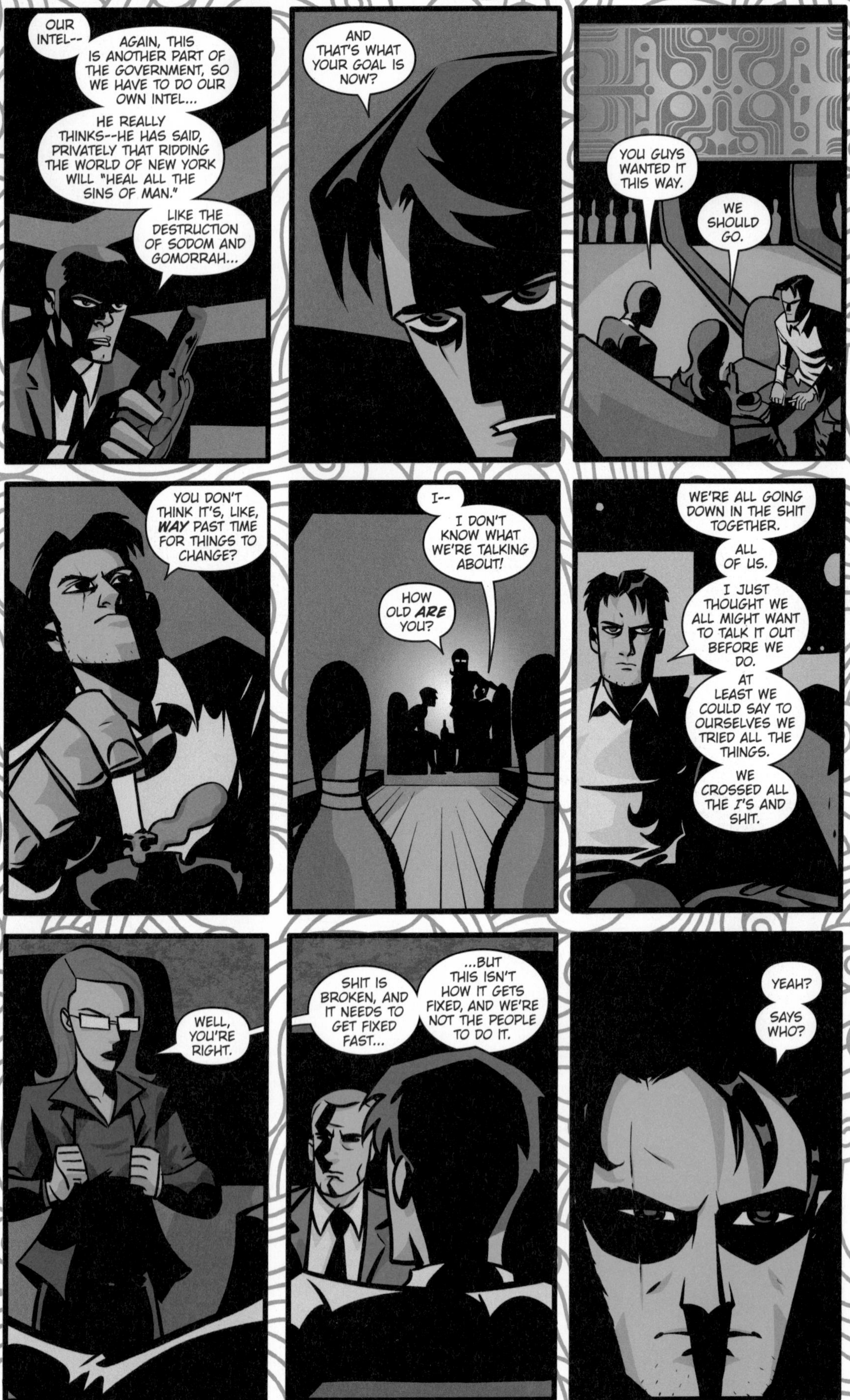

OUR INTEL--
AGAIN, THIS IS ANOTHER PART OF THE GOVERNMENT, SO WE HAVE TO DO OUR OWN INTEL...
HE REALLY THINKS--HE HAS SAID, PRIVATELY THAT RIDDING THE WORLD OF NEW YORK WILL "HEAL ALL THE SINS OF MAN."
LIKE THE DESTRUCTION OF SODOM AND GOMORRAH...
AND THAT'S WHAT YOUR GOAL IS NOW?
YOU GUYS WANTED IT THIS WAY.
WE SHOULD GO.
YOU DON'T THINK IT'S, LIKE, *WAY* PAST TIME FOR THINGS TO CHANGE?
I--
I DON'T KNOW WHAT WE'RE TALKING ABOUT!
HOW OLD *ARE* YOU?
WE'RE ALL GOING DOWN IN THE SHIT TOGETHER.
ALL OF US.
I JUST THOUGHT WE ALL MIGHT WANT TO TALK IT OUT BEFORE WE DO.
AT LEAST WE COULD SAY TO OURSELVES WE TRIED ALL THE THINGS.
WE CROSSED ALL THE *I*'S AND SHIT.
WELL, YOU'RE RIGHT.
SHIT IS BROKEN, AND IT NEEDS TO GET FIXED FAST...
...BUT THIS ISN'T HOW IT GETS FIXED, AND WE'RE NOT THE PEOPLE TO DO IT.
YEAH?
SAYS WHO?

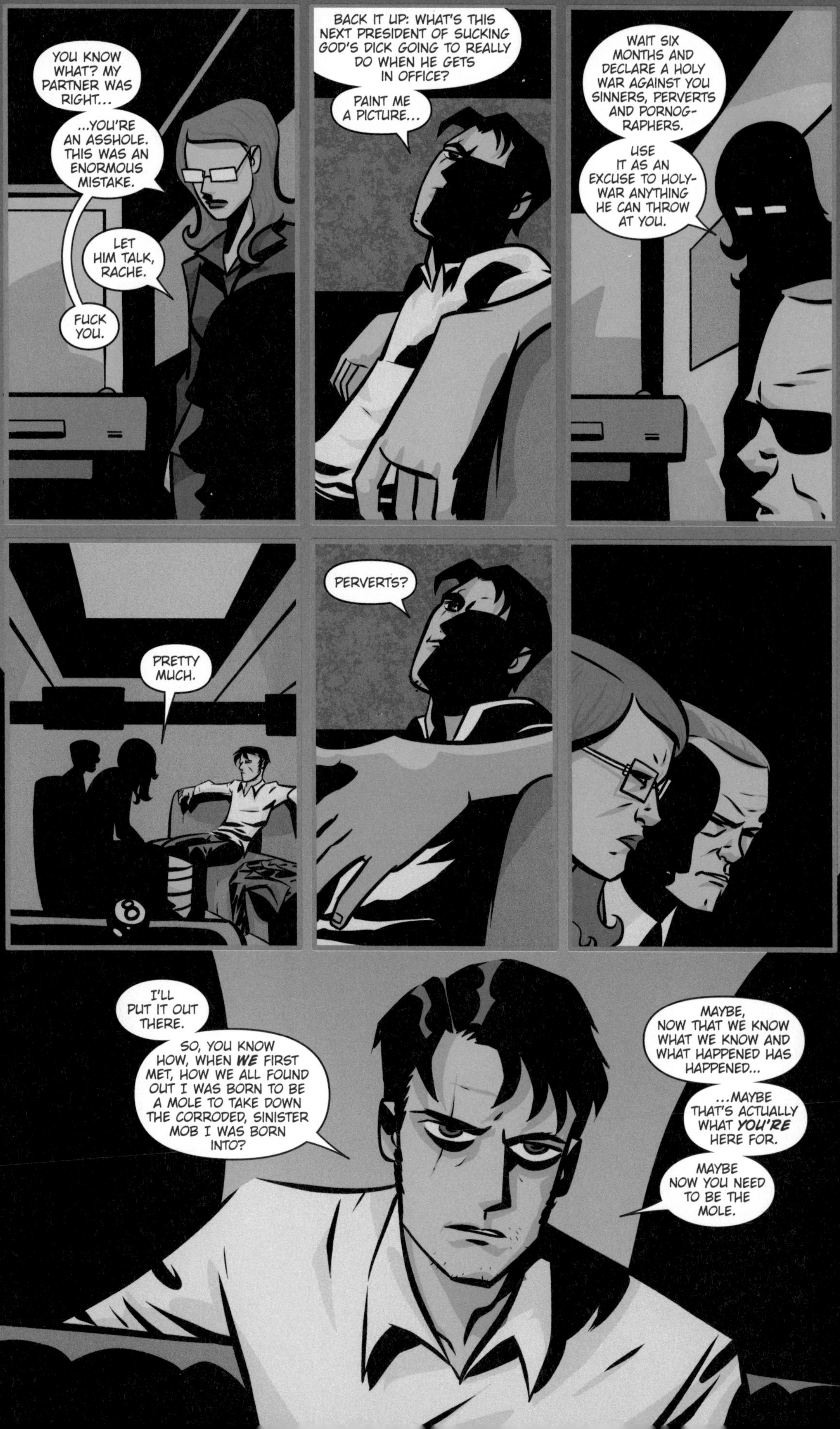
YOU KNOW WHAT? MY PARTNER WAS RIGHT...
...YOU'RE AN ASSHOLE. THIS WAS AN ENORMOUS MISTAKE.
LET HIM TALK, RACHE.
FUCK YOU.
BACK IT UP: WHAT'S THIS NEXT PRESIDENT OF SUCKING GOD'S DICK GOING TO REALLY DO WHEN HE GETS IN OFFICE?
PAINT ME A PICTURE...
WAIT SIX MONTHS AND DECLARE A HOLY WAR AGAINST YOU SINNERS, PERVERTS AND PORNOGRAPHERS.
USE IT AS AN EXCUSE TO HOLY-WAR ANYTHING HE CAN THROW AT YOU.
PERVERTS?
PRETTY MUCH.
I'LL PUT IT OUT THERE.
SO, YOU KNOW HOW, WHEN WE FIRST MET, HOW WE ALL FOUND OUT I WAS BORN TO BE A MOLE TO TAKE DOWN THE CORRODED, SINISTER MOB I WAS BORN INTO?
MAYBE, NOW THAT WE KNOW WHAT WE KNOW AND WHAT HAPPENED HAS HAPPENED...
...MAYBE THAT'S ACTUALLY WHAT YOU'RE HERE FOR.
MAYBE NOW YOU NEED TO BE THE MOLE.

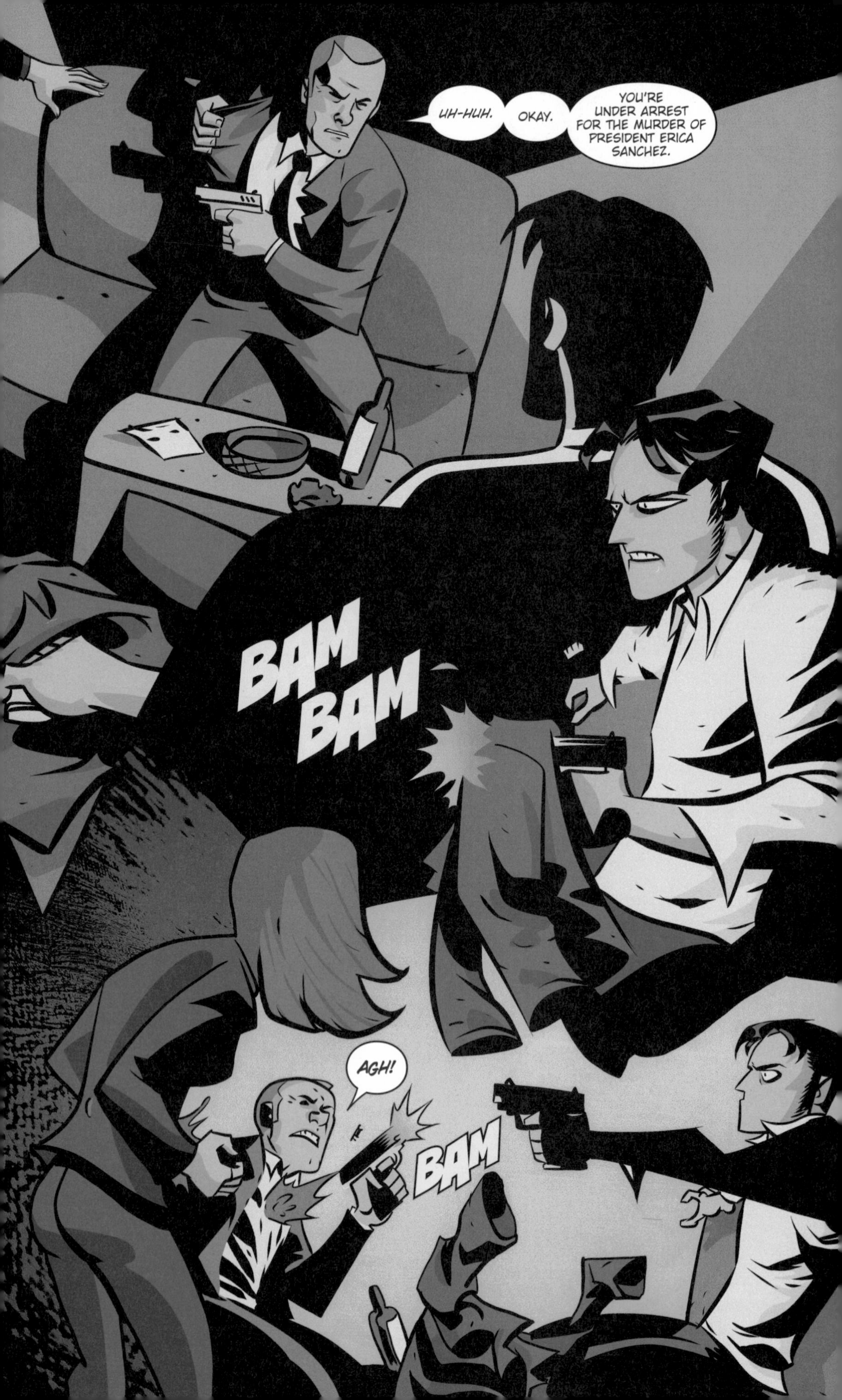
UH-HUH.
OKAY.
YOU'RE UNDER ARREST FOR THE MURDER OF PRESIDENT ERICA SANCHEZ.
BAM BAM
AGH!
BAM

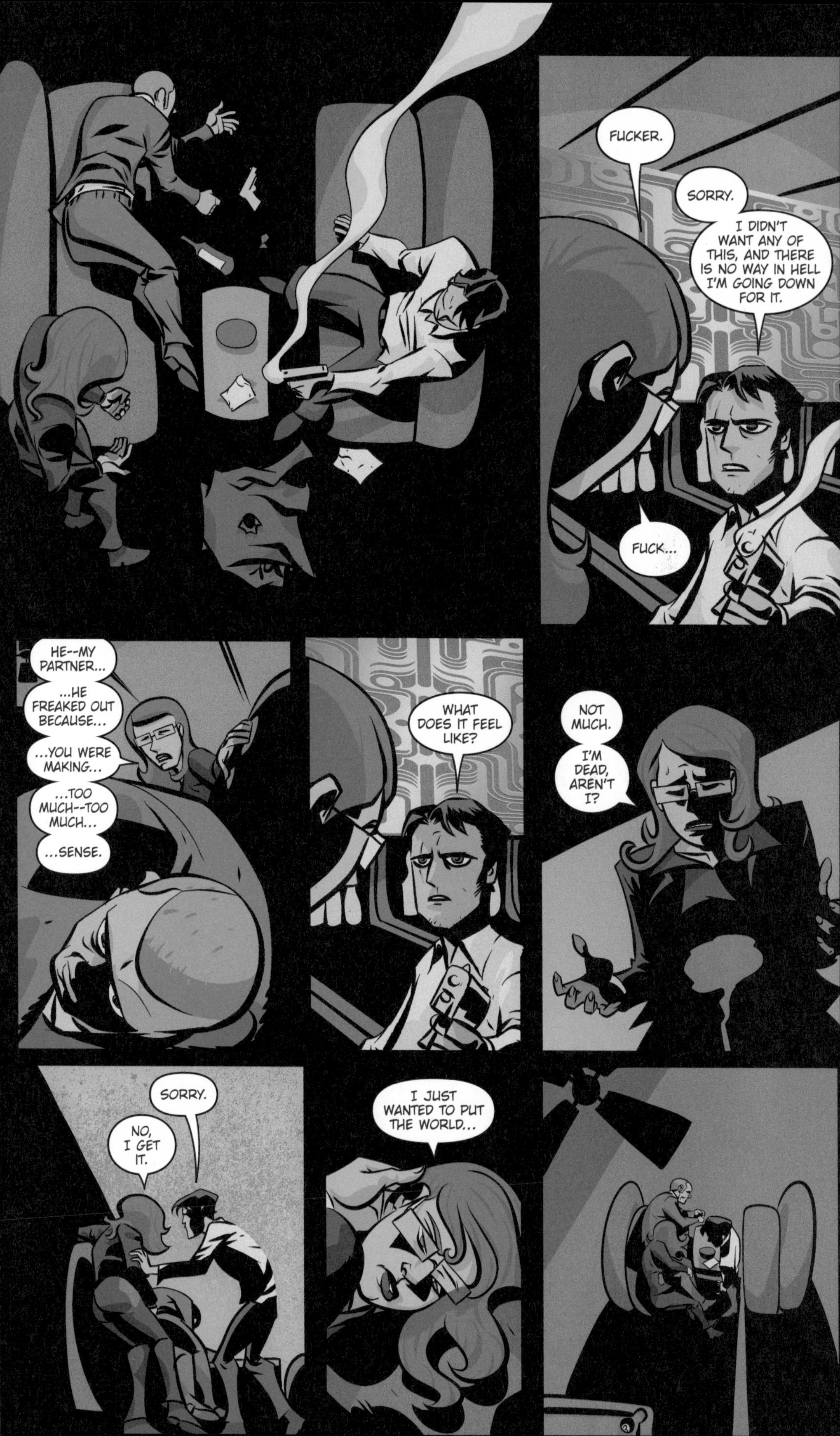
FUCKER.
SORRY.
I DIDN'T WANT ANY OF THIS, AND THERE IS NO WAY IN HELL I'M GOING DOWN FOR IT.
FUCK...
HE--MY PARTNER...
...HE FREAKED OUT BECAUSE...
...YOU WERE MAKING...
...TOO MUCH--TOO MUCH...
...SENSE.
WHAT DOES IT FEEL LIKE?
NOT MUCH.
I'M DEAD, AREN'T I?
SORRY.
NO, I GET IT.
I JUST WANTED TO PUT THE WORLD...

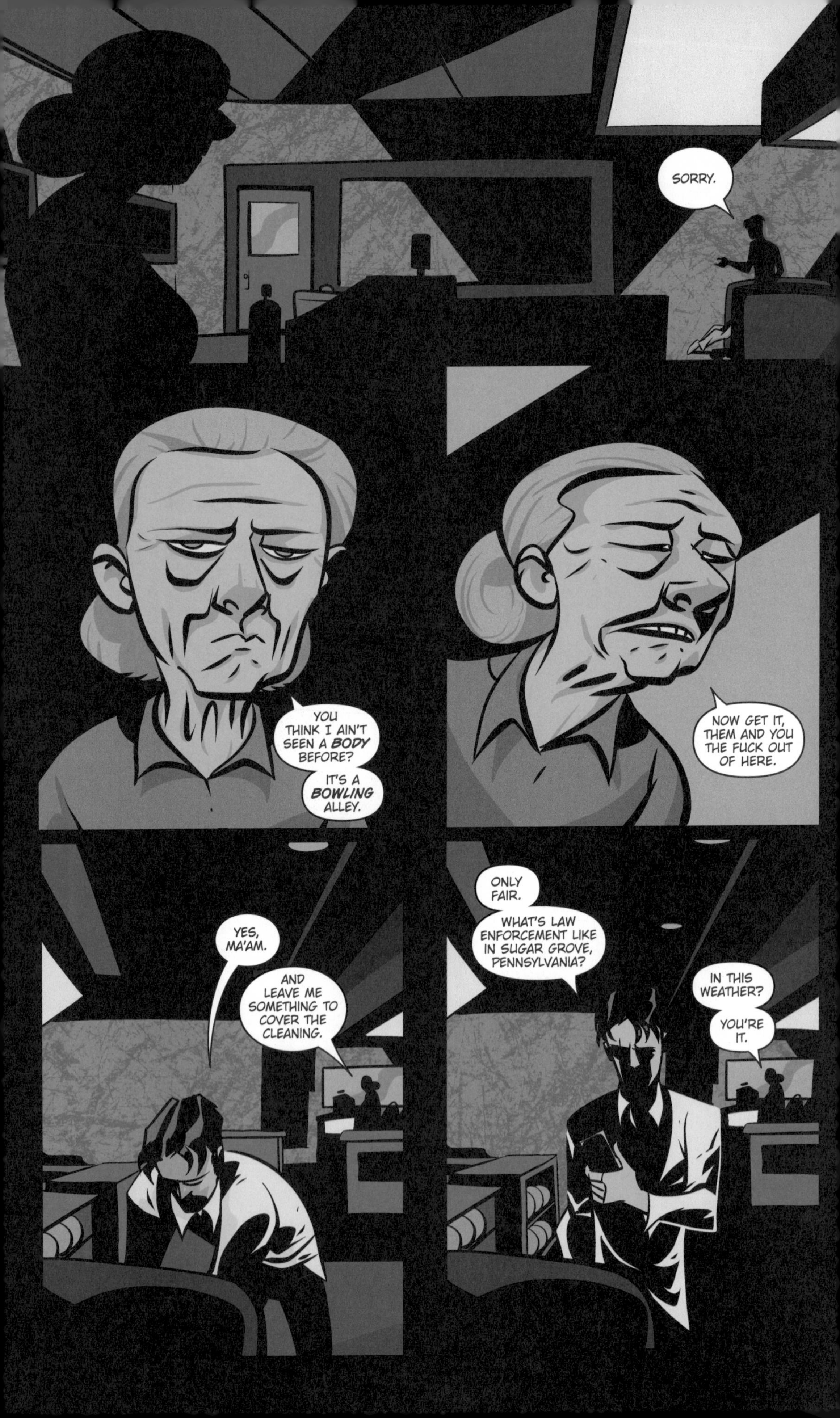
SORRY.
YOU THINK I AIN'T SEEN A BODY BEFORE?
IT'S A BOWLING ALLEY.
NOW GET IT, THEM AND YOU THE FUCK OUT OF HERE.
YES, MA'AM.
AND LEAVE ME SOMETHING TO COVER THE CLEANING.
ONLY FAIR.
WHAT'S LAW ENFORCEMENT LIKE IN SUGAR GROVE, PENNSYLVANIA?
IN THIS WEATHER?
YOU'RE IT.

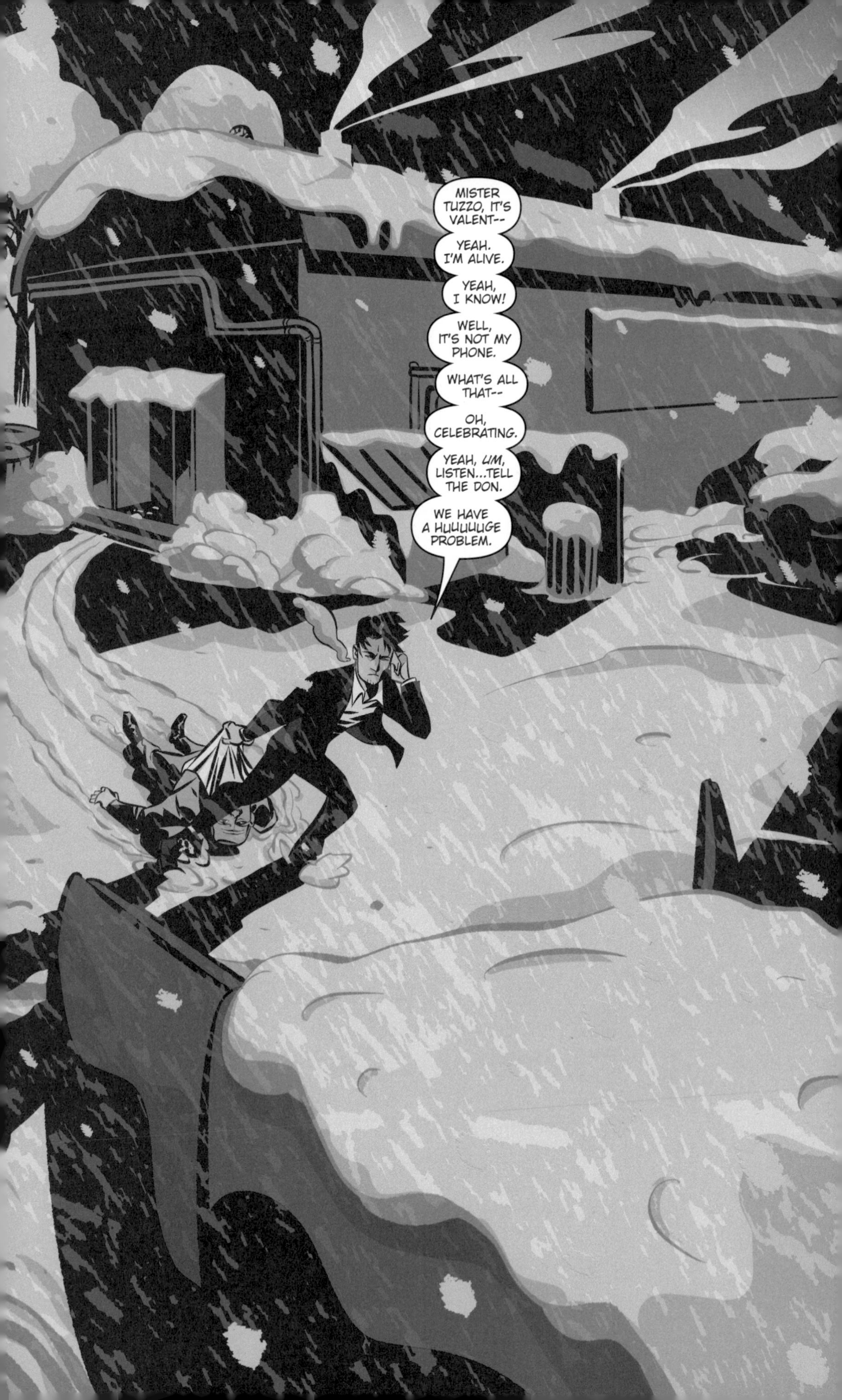
MISTER TUZZO, IT'S VALENT--
YEAH. I'M ALIVE.
YEAH, I KNOW!
WELL, IT'S NOT MY PHONE.
WHAT'S ALL THAT--
OH, CELEBRATING.
YEAH, *UM*, LISTEN...TELL THE DON.
WE HAVE A HUUUUUGE PROBLEM.

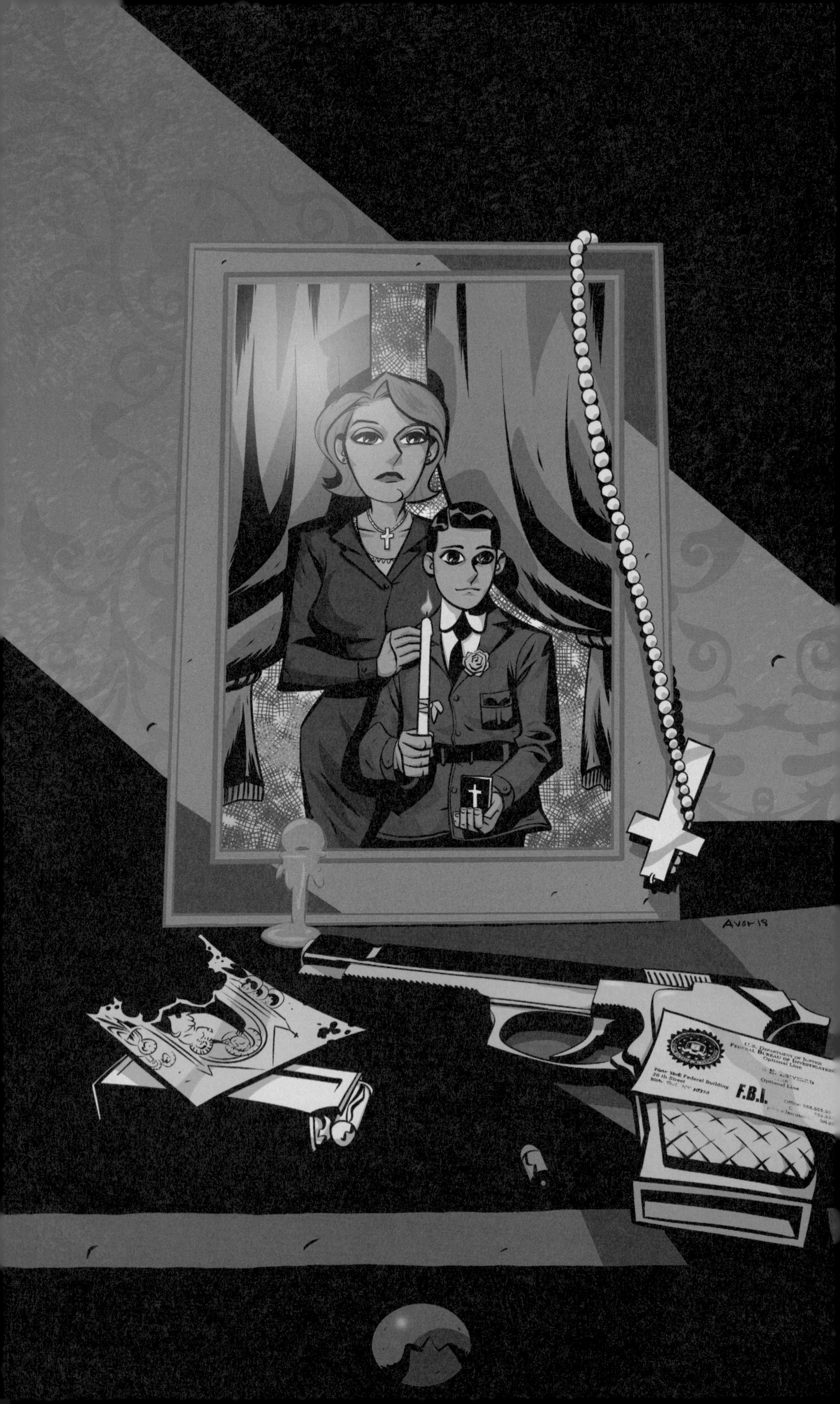

AVON 18
U.S. Department of Justice
Federal Bureau of Investigation
Optional Line
Optional Line
New York Federal Building
26 th Street
F.B.I.

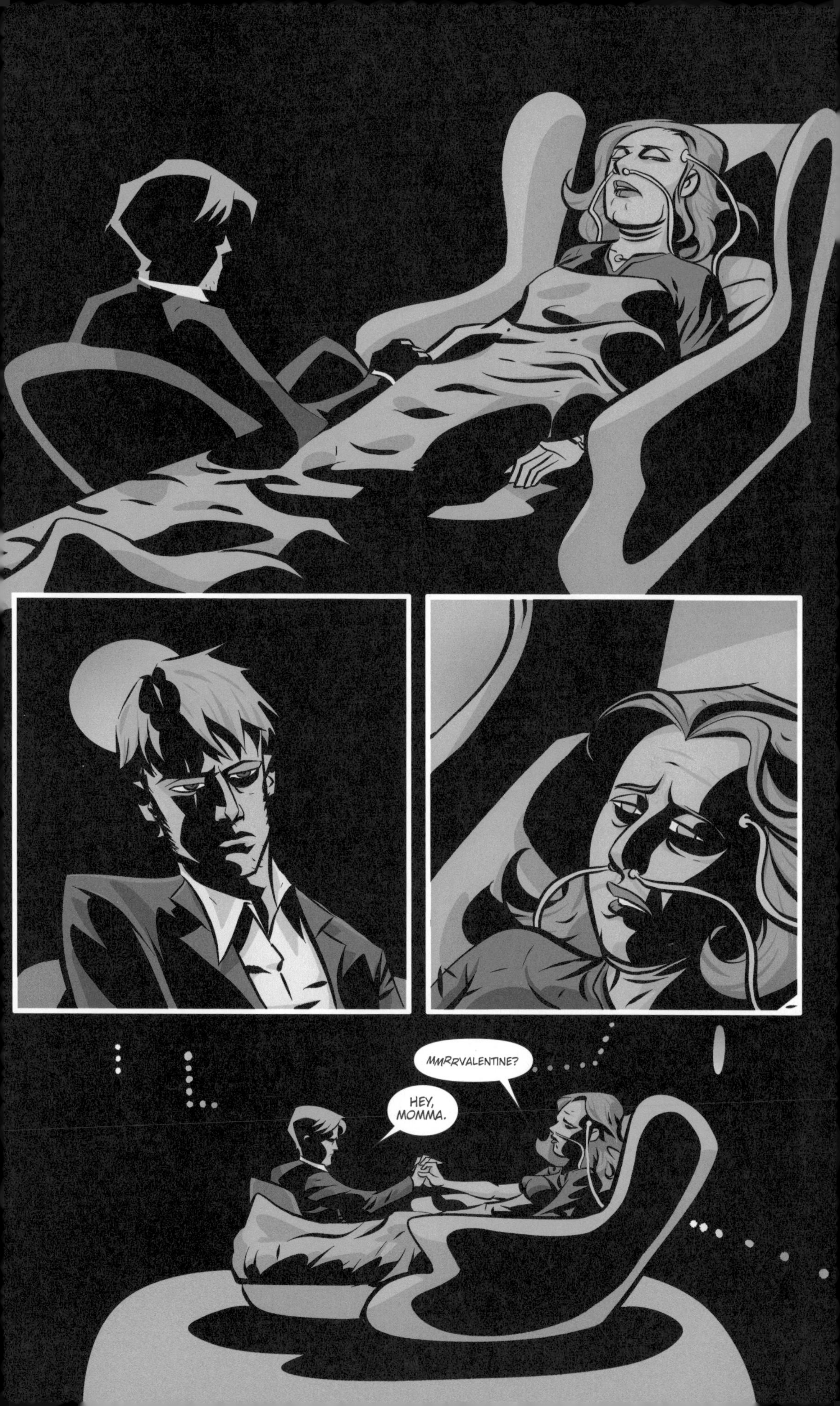
MMRRVALENTINE?
HEY, MOMMA.

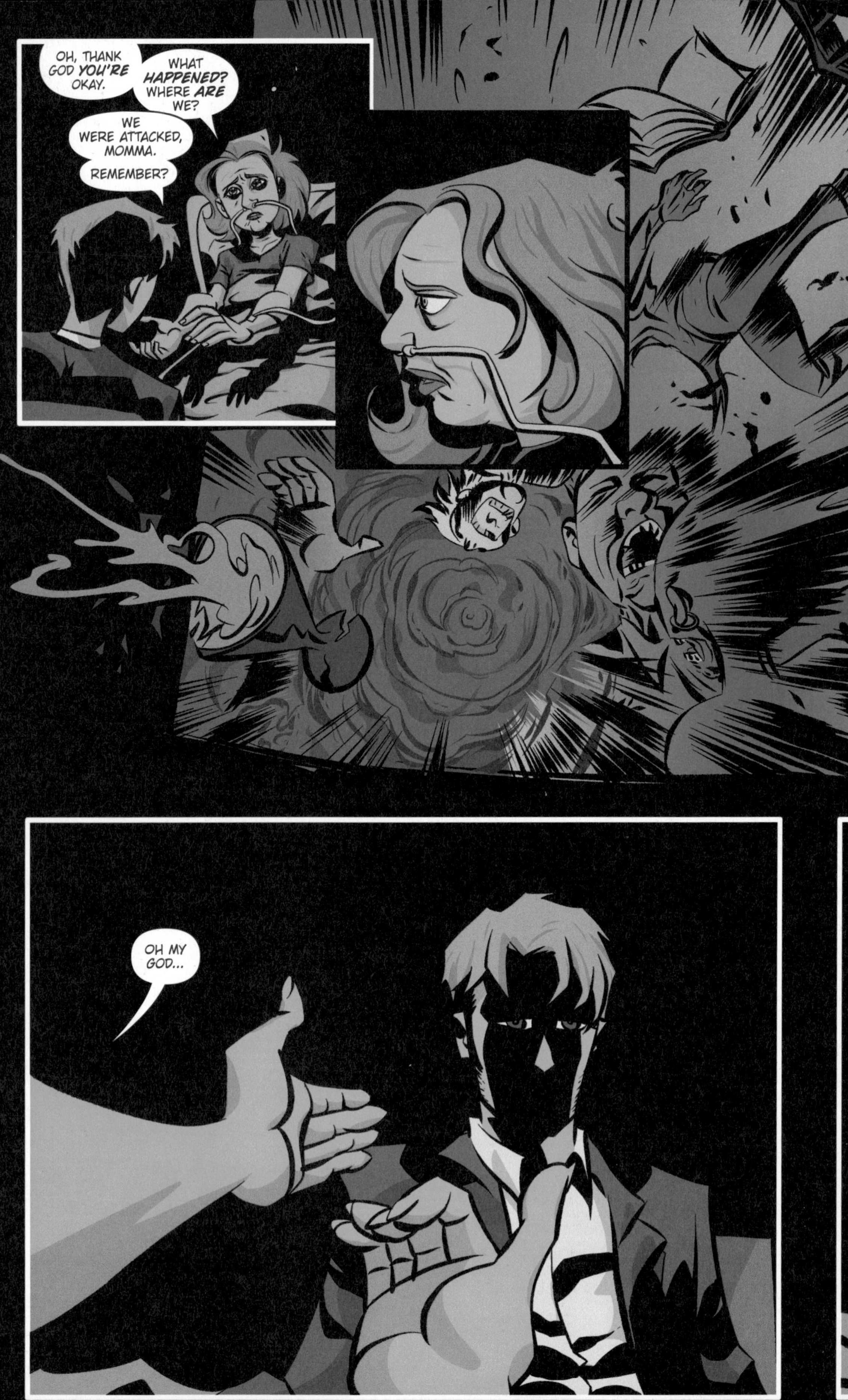
OH, THANK GOD **YOU'RE** OKAY.
WHAT **HAPPENED?** WHERE **ARE** WE?
WE WERE ATTACKED, MOMMA.
REMEMBER?
OH MY GOD...

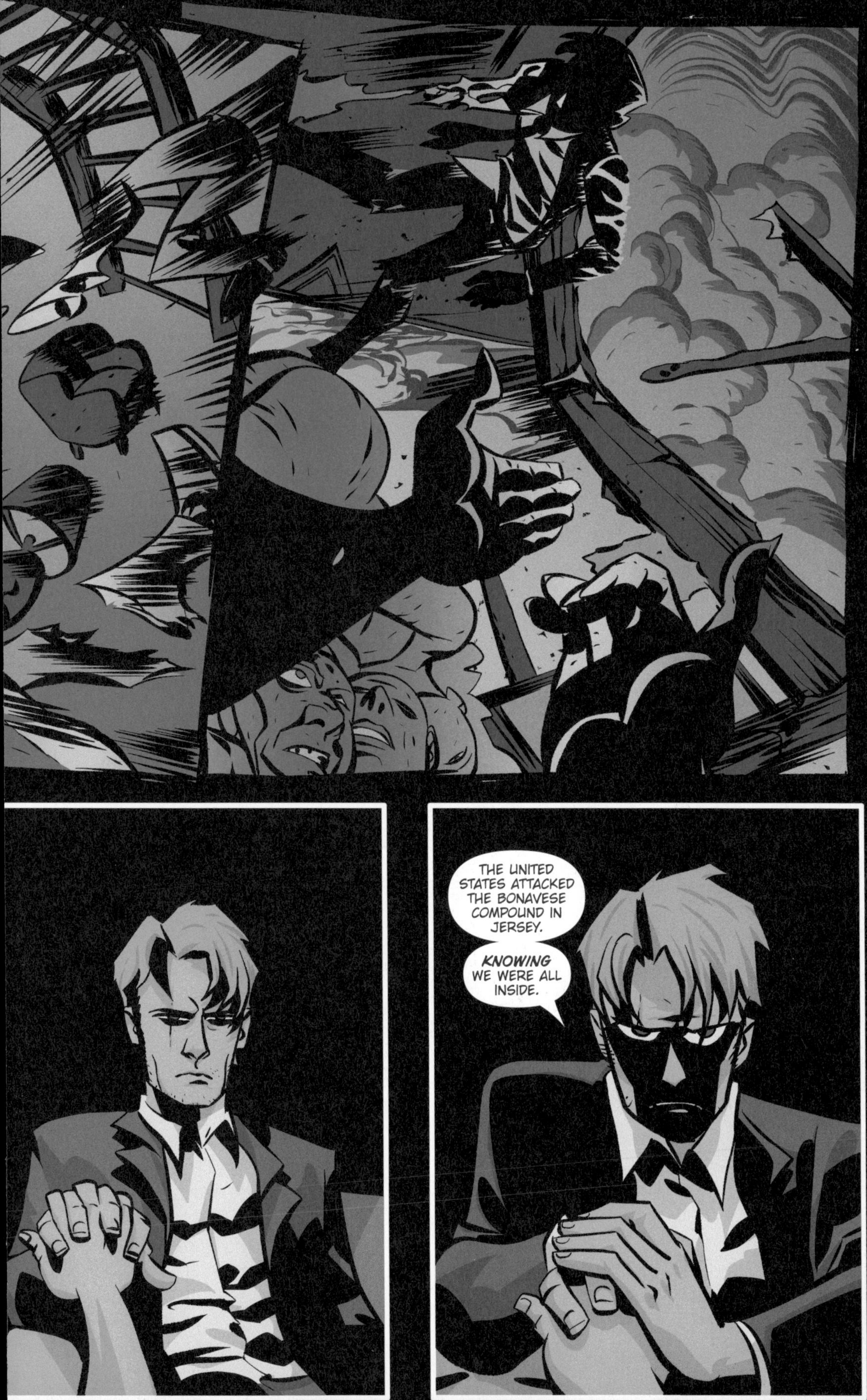
THE UNITED STATES ATTACKED THE BONAVESE COMPOUND IN JERSEY.
KNOWING WE WERE ALL INSIDE.

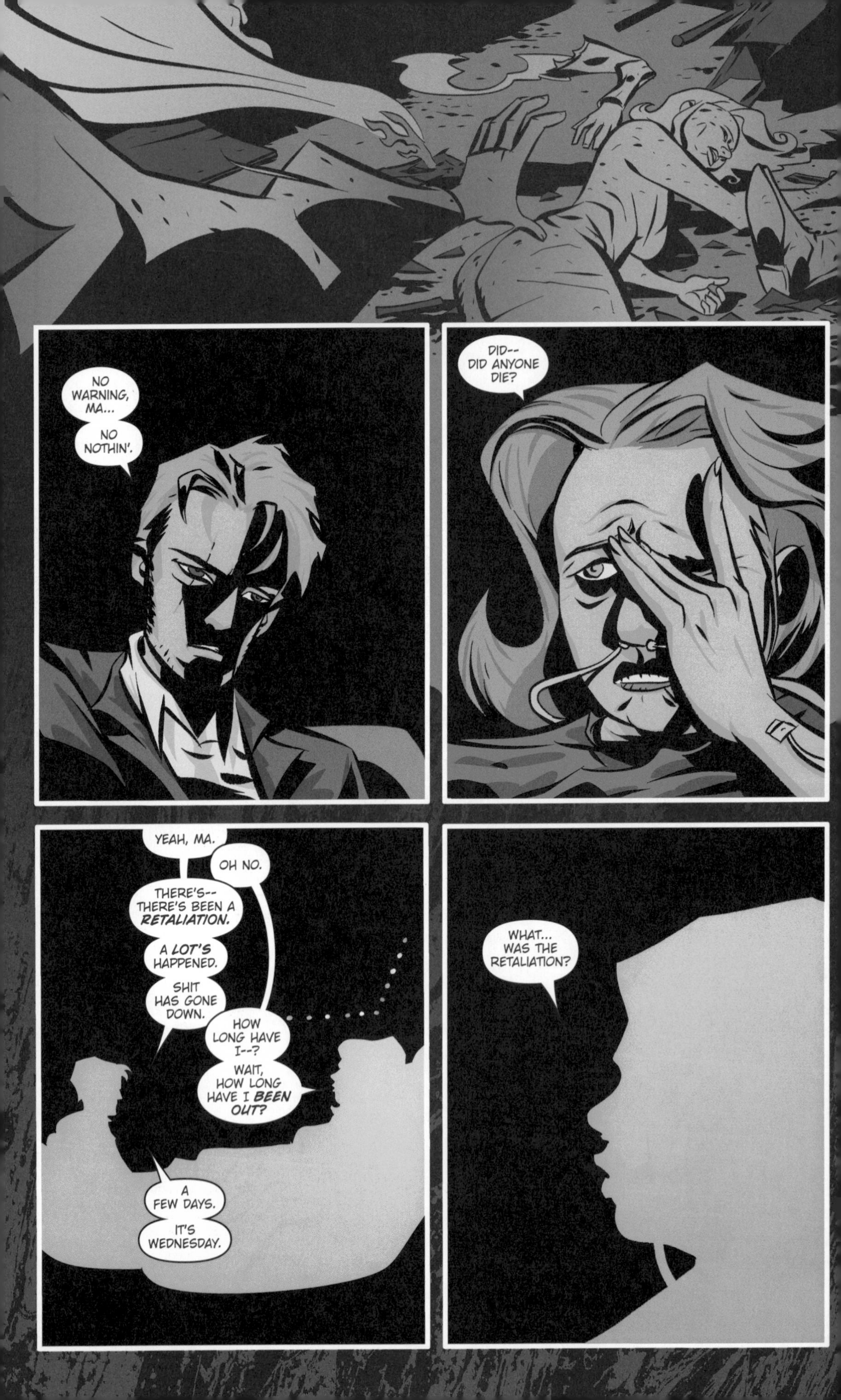
NO WARNING, MA...
NO NOTHIN'.
DID-- DID ANYONE DIE?
YEAH, MA.
OH NO.
THERE'S-- THERE'S BEEN A RETALIATION.
A LOT'S HAPPENED.
SHIT HAS GONE DOWN.
HOW LONG HAVE I--?
WAIT, HOW LONG HAVE I BEEN OUT?
A FEW DAYS.
IT'S WEDNESDAY.
WHAT... WAS THE RETALIATION?

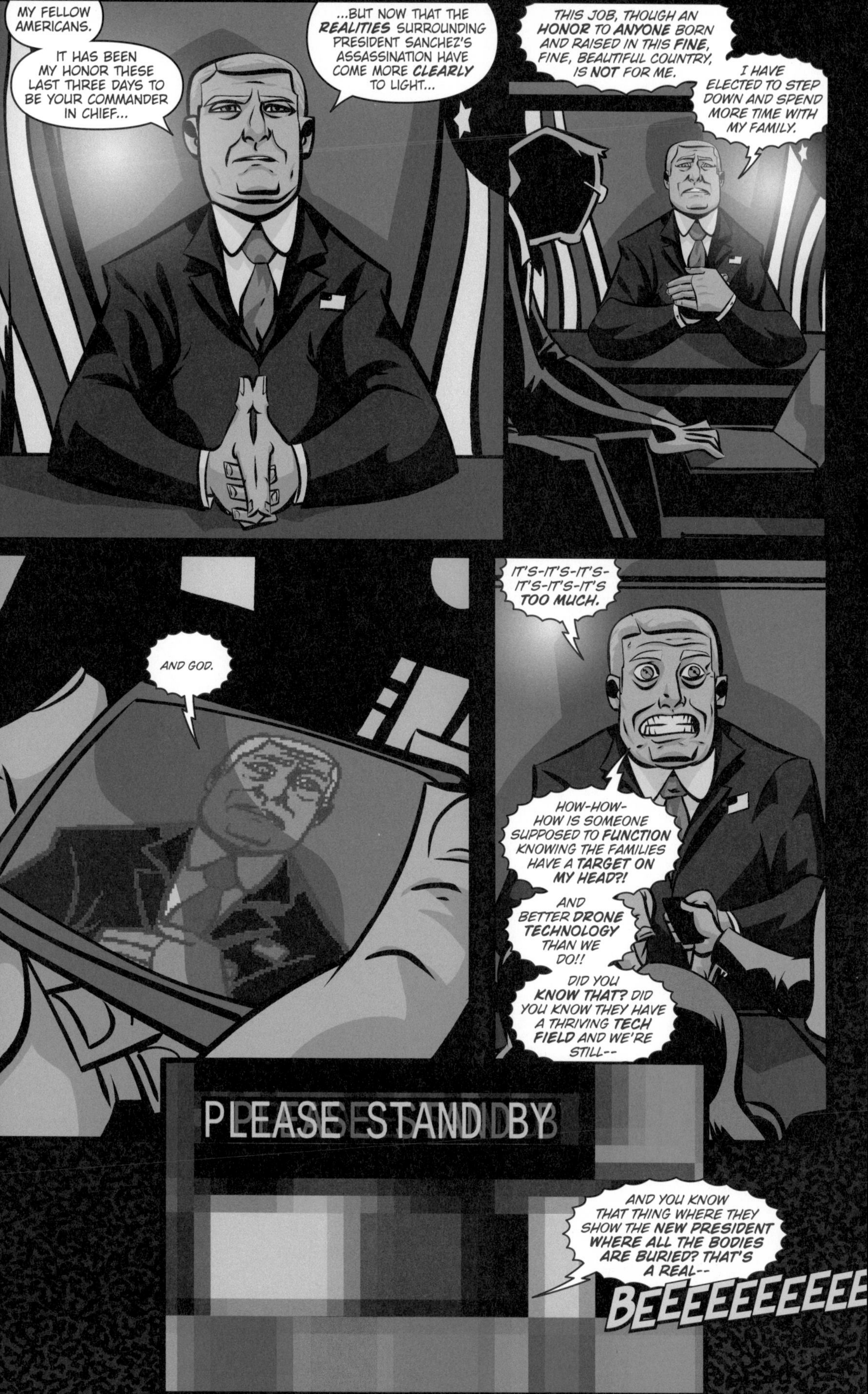

MY FELLOW AMERICANS.
IT HAS BEEN MY HONOR THESE LAST THREE DAYS TO BE YOUR COMMANDER IN CHIEF...
...BUT NOW THAT THE REALITIES SURROUNDING PRESIDENT SANCHEZ'S ASSASSINATION HAVE COME MORE CLEARLY TO LIGHT...
THIS JOB, THOUGH AN HONOR TO ANYONE BORN AND RAISED IN THIS FINE, FINE, BEAUTIFUL COUNTRY, IS NOT FOR ME.
I HAVE ELECTED TO STEP DOWN AND SPEND MORE TIME WITH MY FAMILY.
AND GOD.
IT'S-IT'S-IT'S-IT'S-IT'S-IT'S TOO MUCH.
HOW-HOW-HOW IS SOMEONE SUPPOSED TO FUNCTION KNOWING THE FAMILIES HAVE A TARGET ON MY HEAD?!
AND BETTER DRONE TECHNOLOGY THAN WE DO!!
DID YOU KNOW THAT? DID YOU KNOW THEY HAVE A THRIVING TECH FIELD AND WE'RE STILL--
PLEASE STAND BY
AND YOU KNOW THAT THING WHERE THEY SHOW THE NEW PRESIDENT WHERE ALL THE BODIES ARE BURIED? THAT'S A REAL--
BEEEEEEEEEE

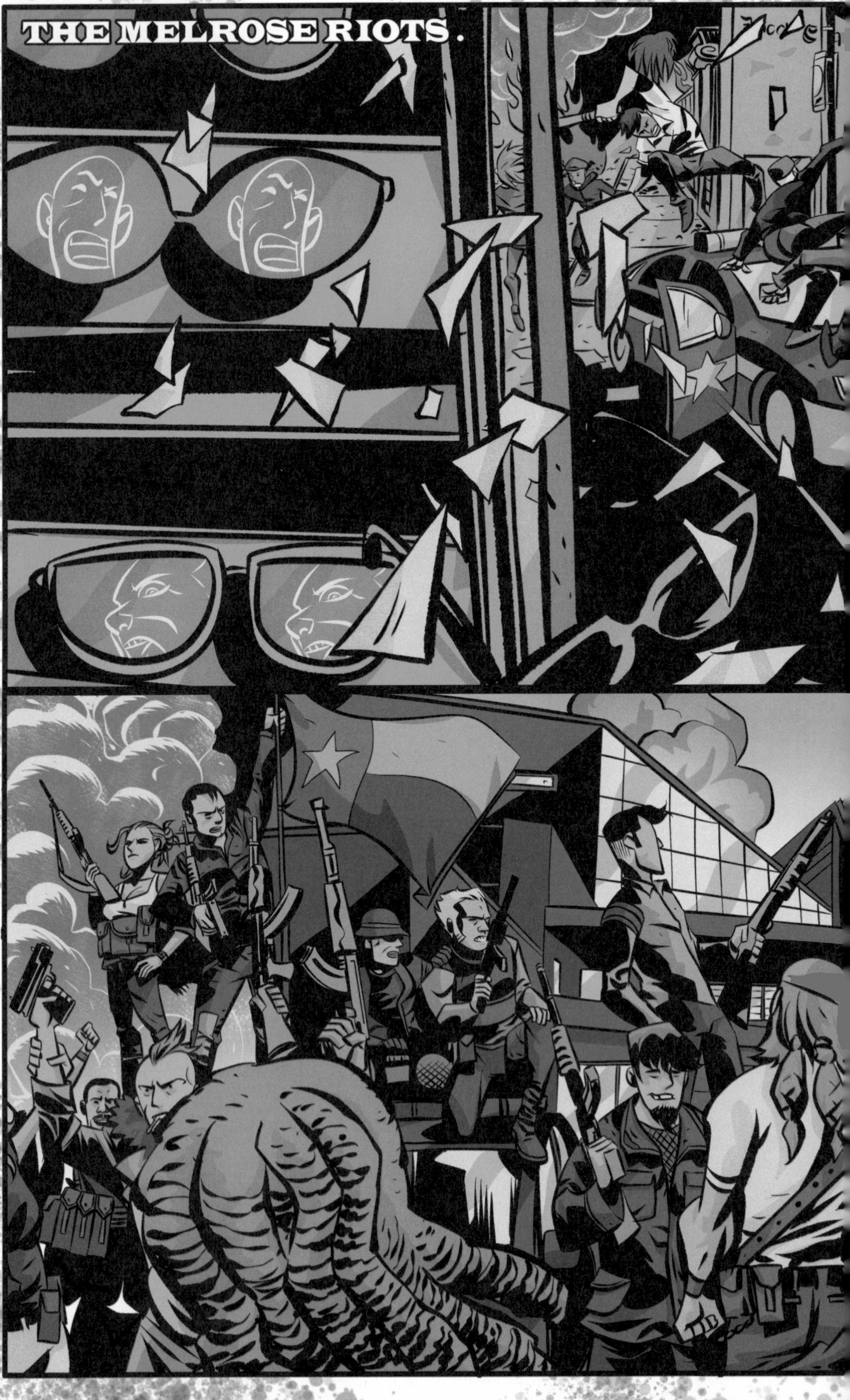
THE MELROSE RIOTS.

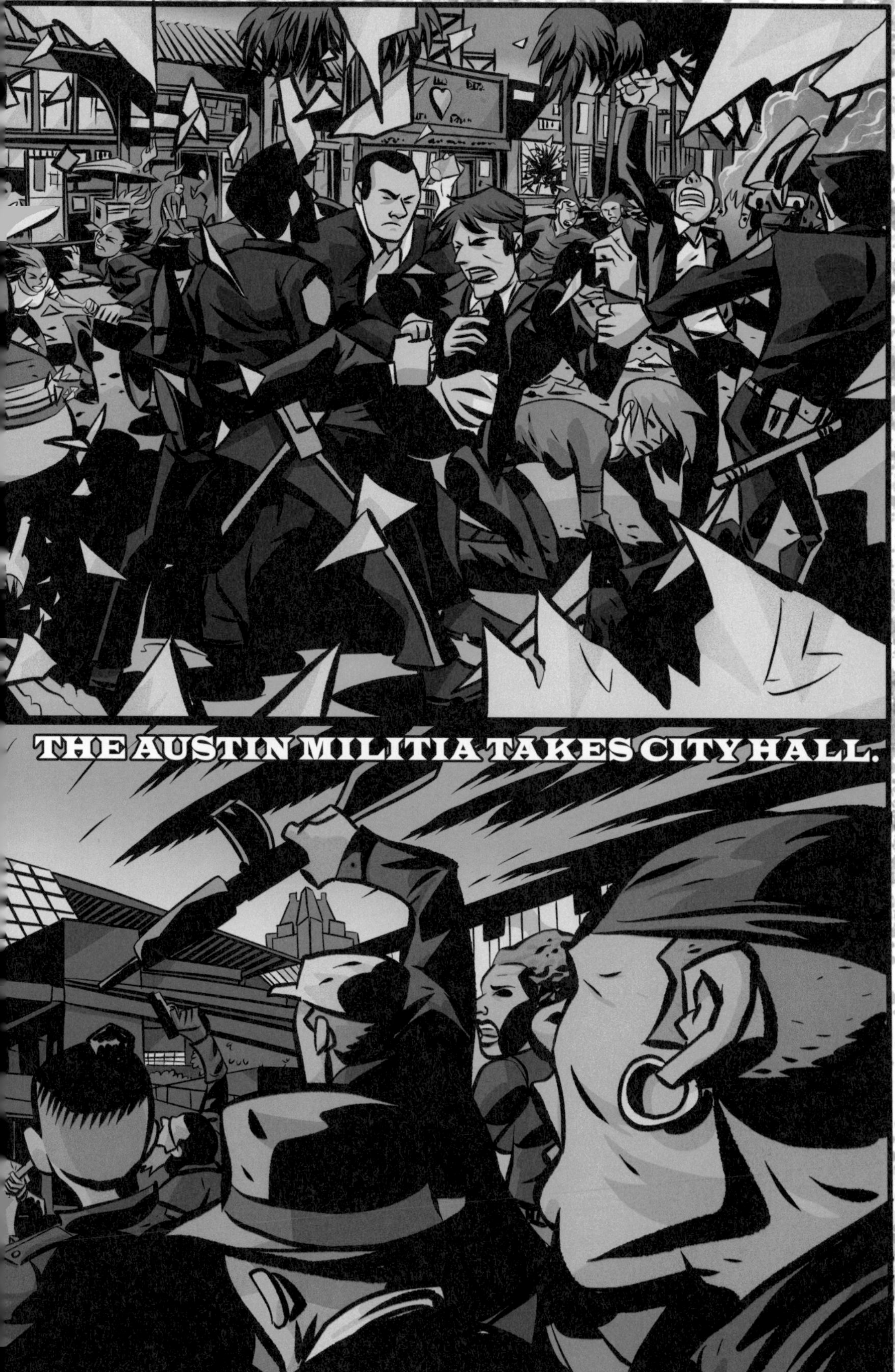
THE AUSTIN MILITIA TAKES CITY HALL.

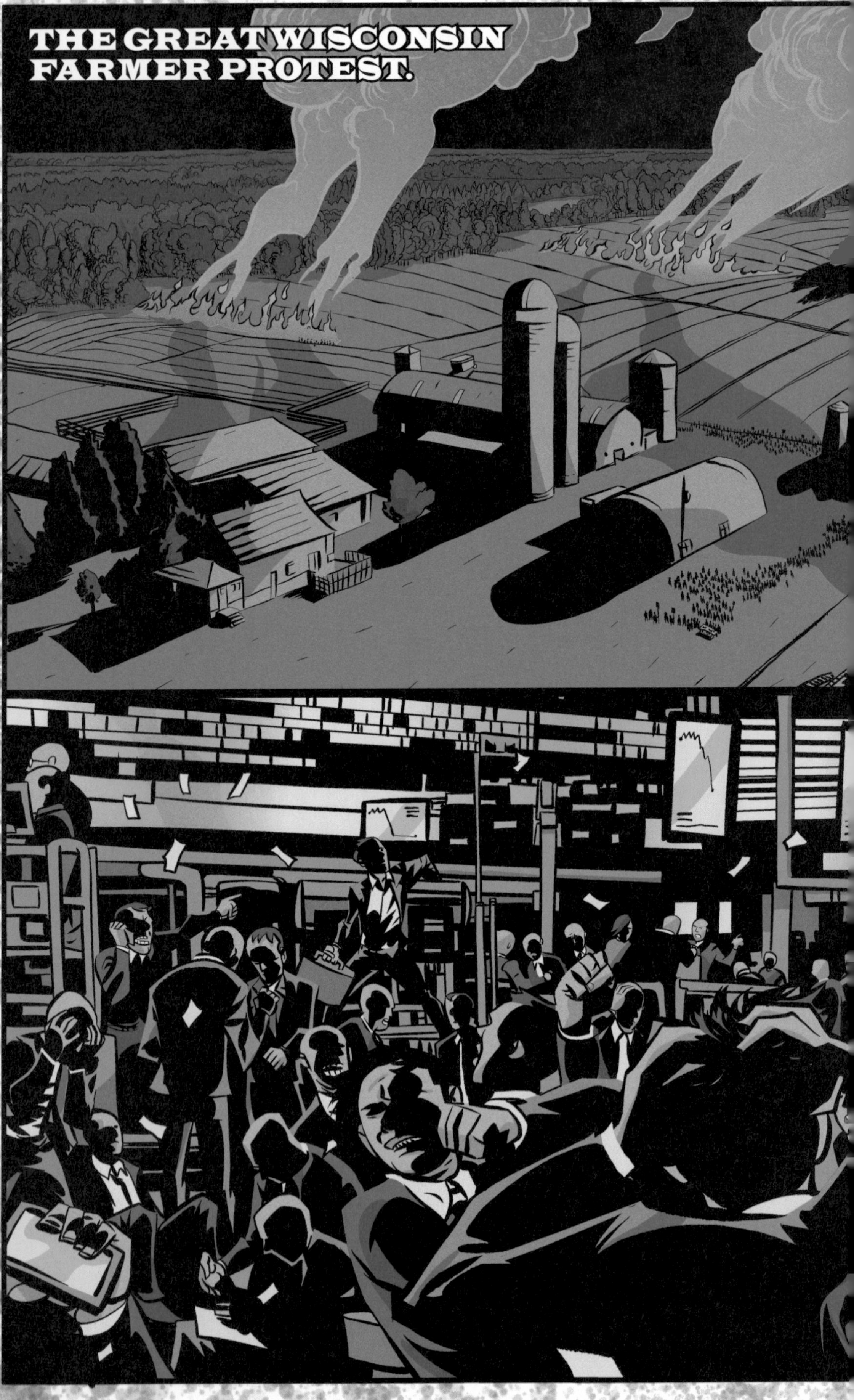
THE GREAT WISCONSIN FARMER PROTEST.

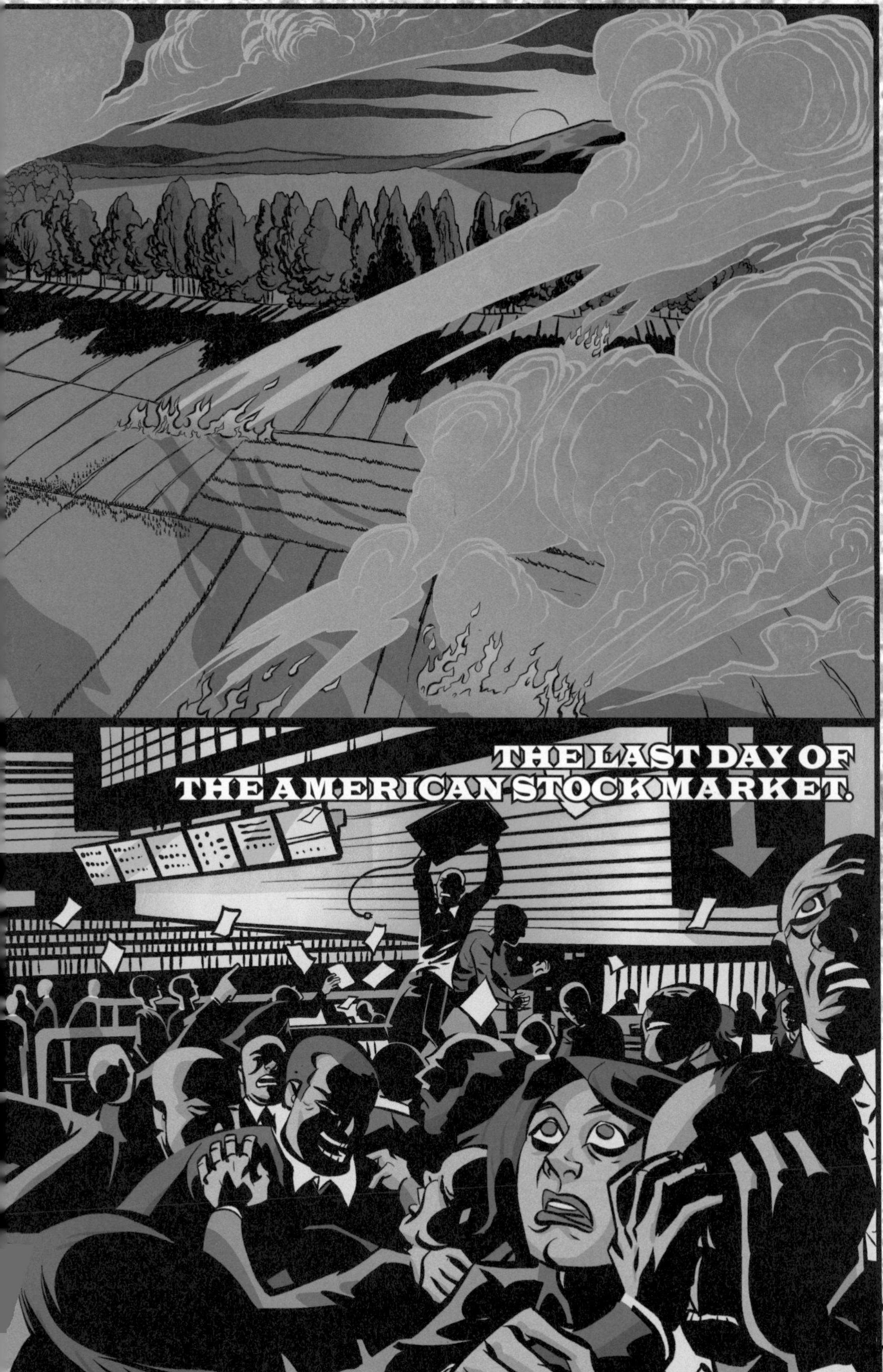
THE LAST DAY OF
THE AMERICAN STOCK MARKET.

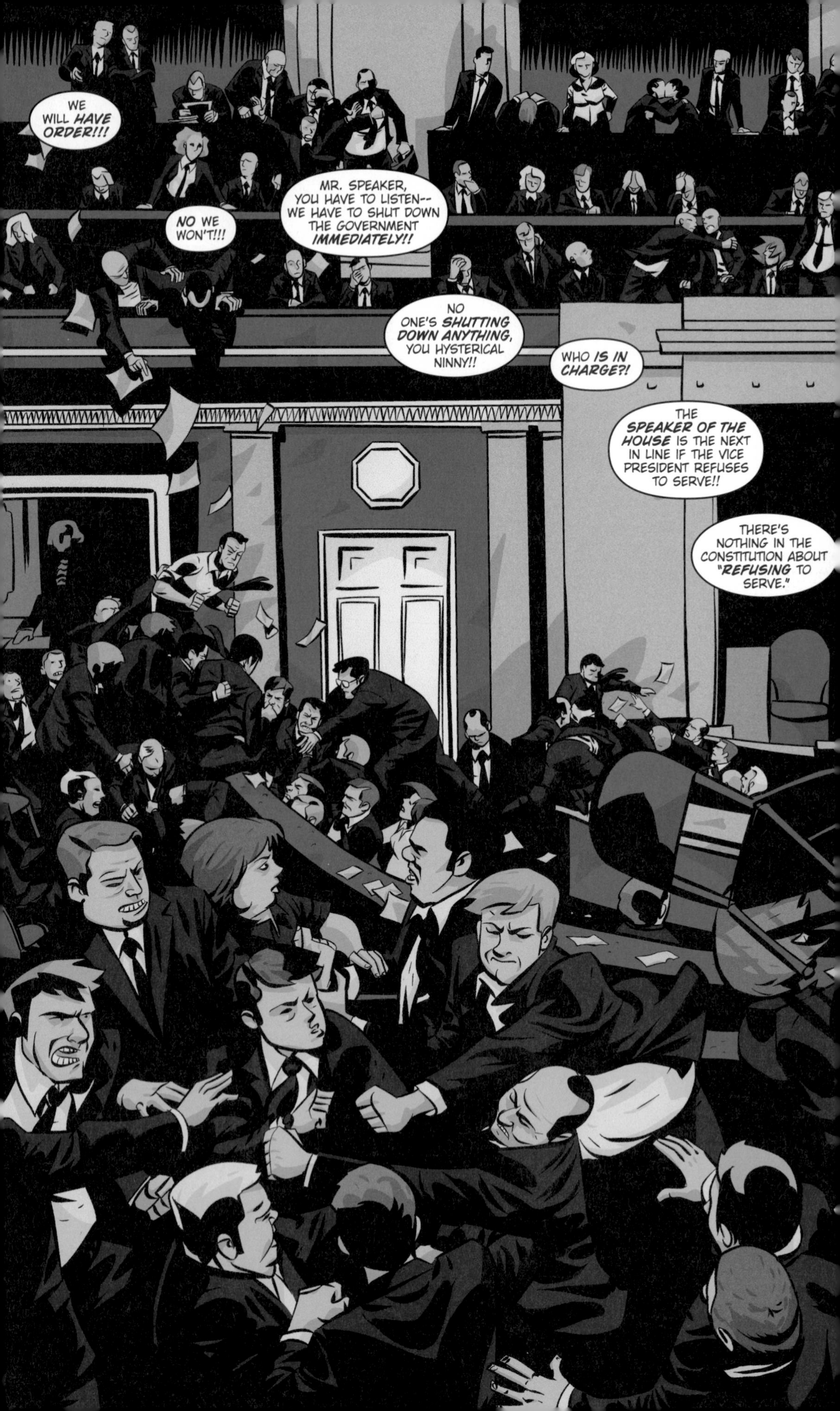

WE WILL HAVE ORDER!!!
NO WE WON'T!!!
MR. SPEAKER, YOU HAVE TO LISTEN-- WE HAVE TO SHUT DOWN THE GOVERNMENT IMMEDIATELY!!
NO ONE'S SHUTTING DOWN ANYTHING, YOU HYSTERICAL NINNY!!
WHO IS IN CHARGE?!
THE SPEAKER OF THE HOUSE IS THE NEXT IN LINE IF THE VICE PRESIDENT REFUSES TO SERVE!!
THERE'S NOTHING IN THE CONSTITUTION ABOUT "REFUSING" TO SERVE."

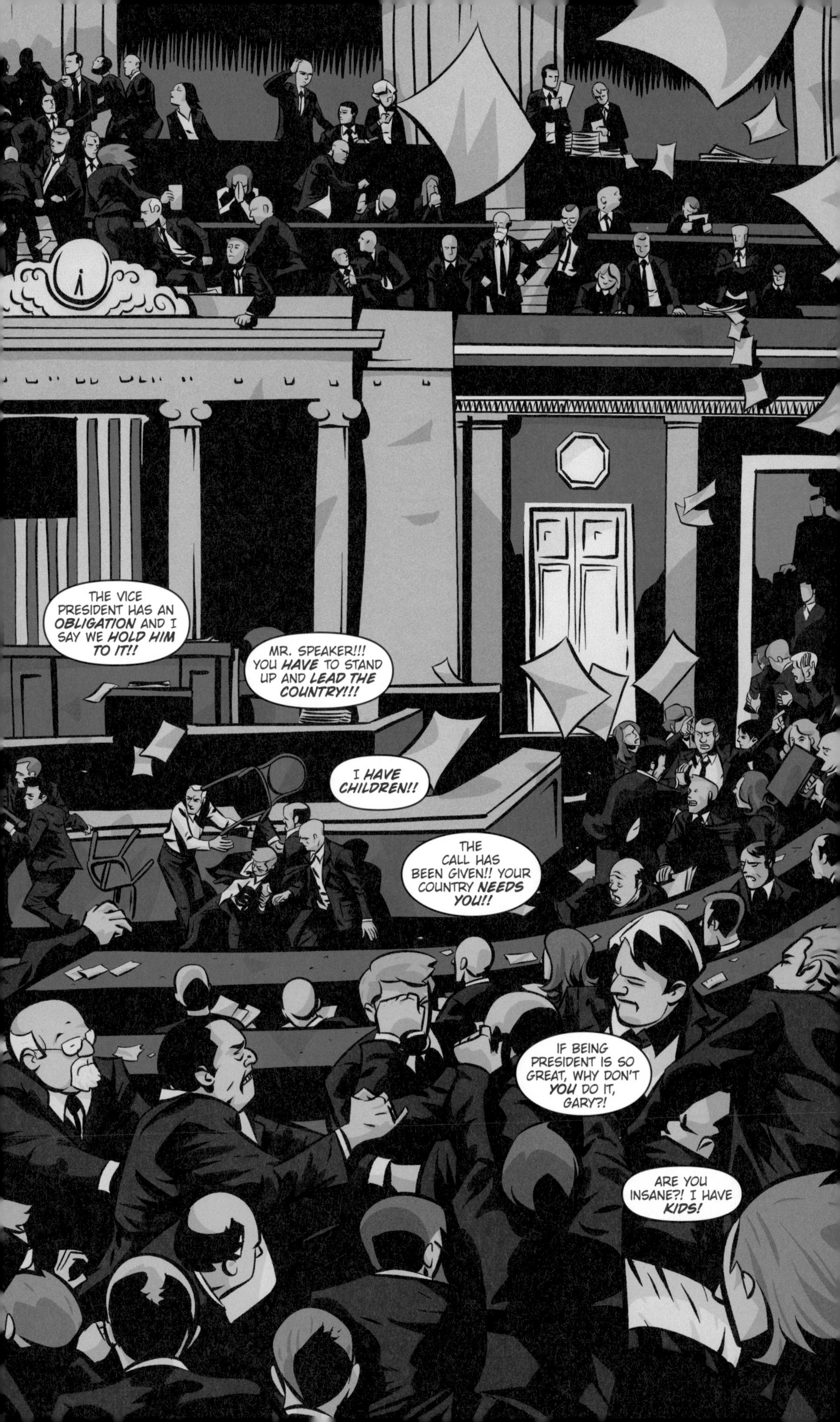
THE VICE PRESIDENT HAS AN OBLIGATION AND I SAY WE HOLD HIM TO IT!!
MR. SPEAKER!!! YOU HAVE TO STAND UP AND LEAD THE COUNTRY!!!
I HAVE CHILDREN!!
THE CALL HAS BEEN GIVEN!! YOUR COUNTRY NEEDS YOU!!
IF BEING PRESIDENT IS SO GREAT, WHY DON'T YOU DO IT, GARY?!
ARE YOU INSANE?! I HAVE KIDS!

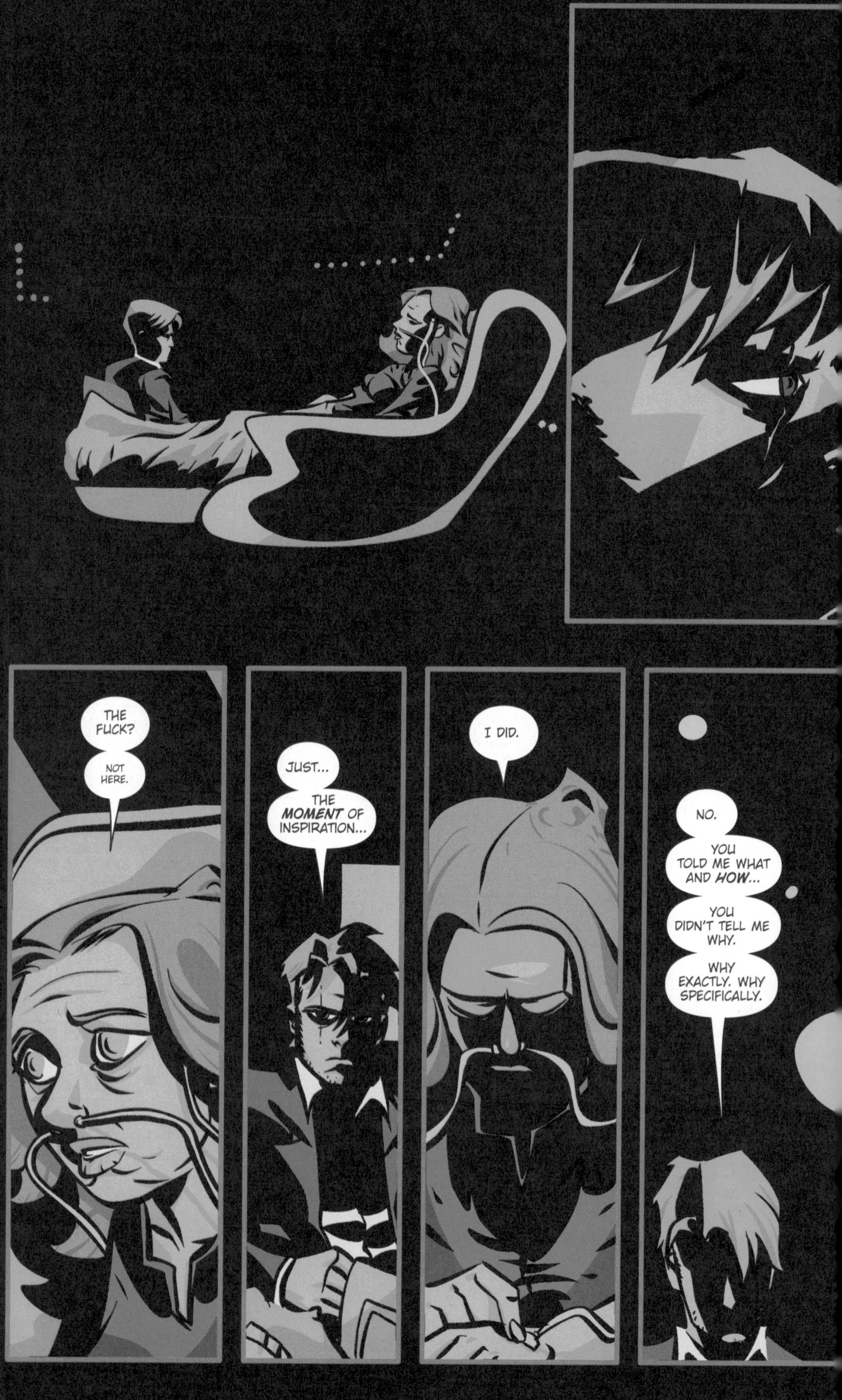
THE FUCK?
NOT HERE.
JUST...
THE *MOMENT* OF INSPIRATION...
I DID.
NO.
YOU TOLD ME WHAT AND *HOW*...
YOU DIDN'T TELL ME WHY.
WHY EXACTLY. WHY SPECIFICALLY.

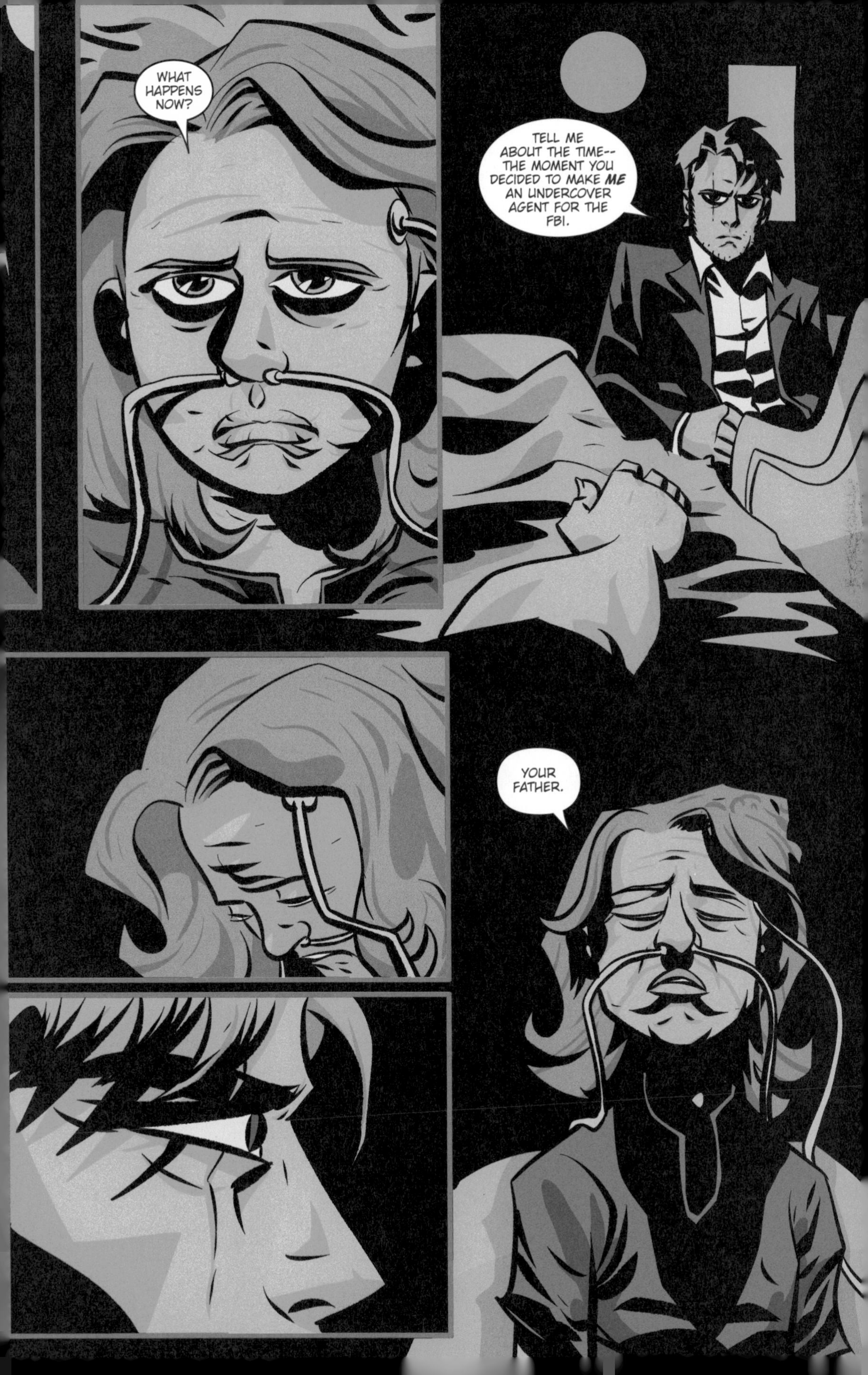
WHAT HAPPENS NOW?
TELL ME ABOUT THE TIME-- THE MOMENT YOU DECIDED TO MAKE **ME** AN UNDERCOVER AGENT FOR THE FBI.
YOUR FATHER.

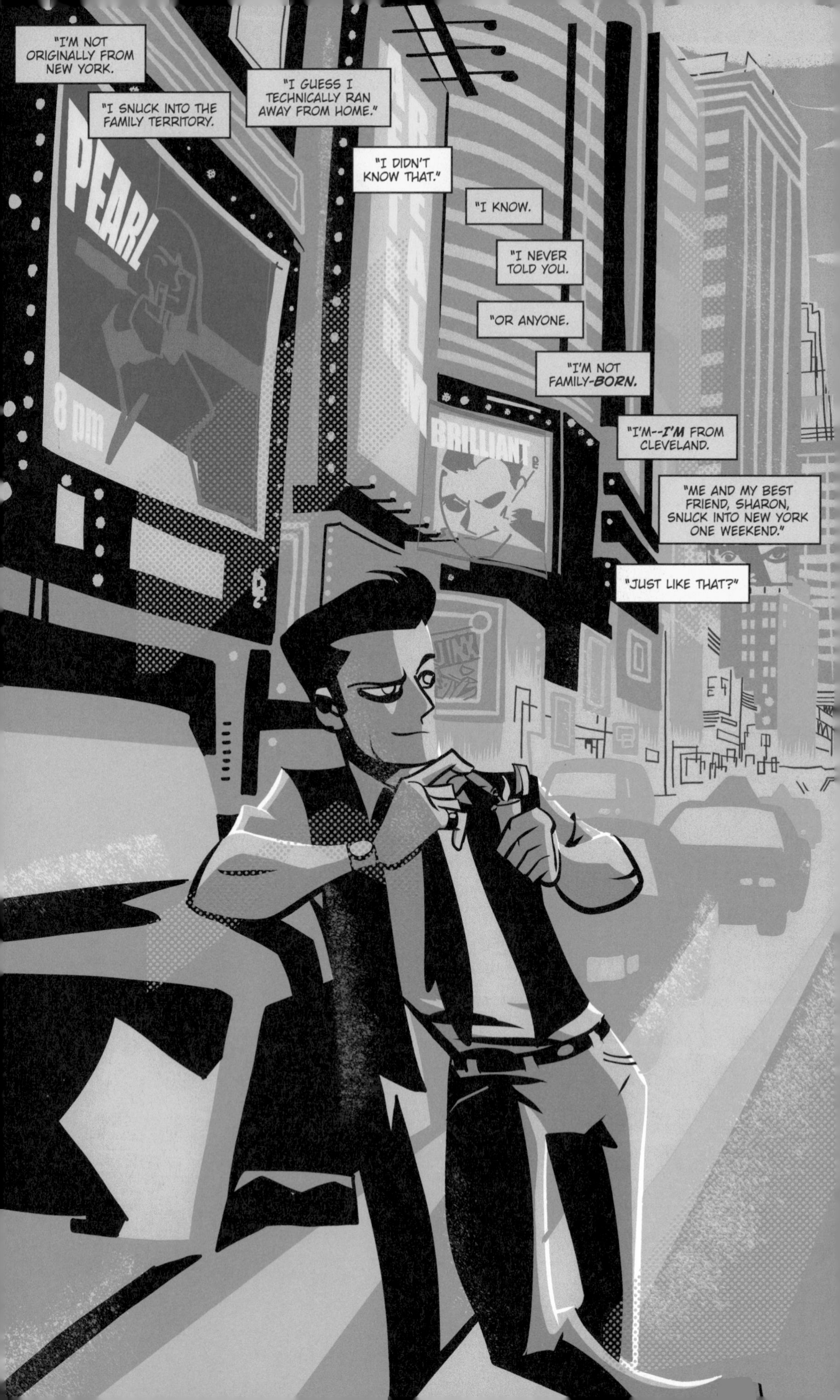
"I'M NOT ORIGINALLY FROM NEW YORK.
"I SNUCK INTO THE FAMILY TERRITORY.
"I GUESS I TECHNICALLY RAN AWAY FROM HOME."
"I DIDN'T KNOW THAT."
"I KNOW.
"I NEVER TOLD YOU.
"OR ANYONE.
"I'M NOT FAMILY-**BORN.**
"I'M--**I'M** FROM CLEVELAND.
"ME AND MY BEST FRIEND, SHARON, SNUCK INTO NEW YORK ONE WEEKEND."
"JUST LIKE THAT?"
PEARL
8 pm
BRILLIANT

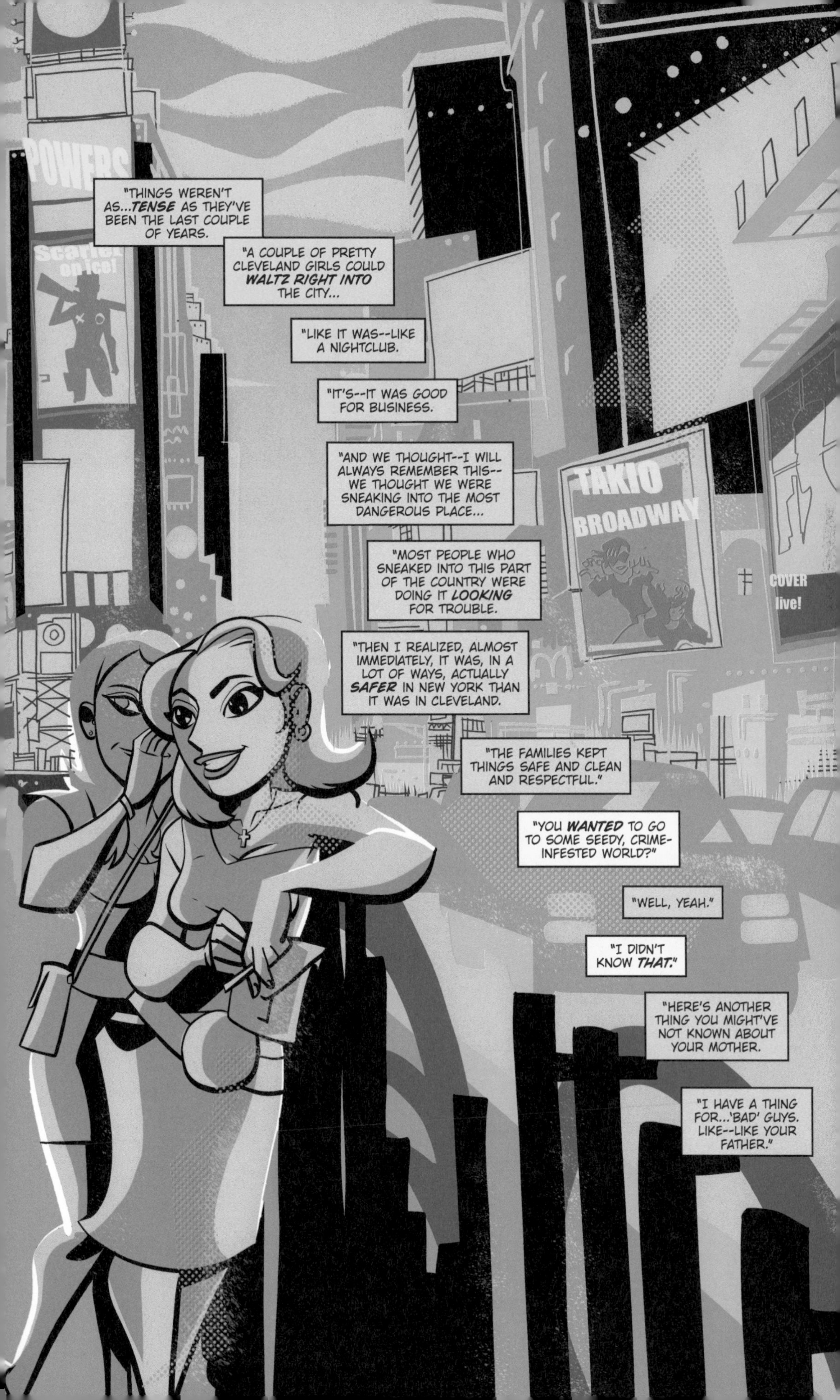
POWERS
"THINGS WEREN'T AS...TENSE AS THEY'VE BEEN THE LAST COUPLE OF YEARS.
"A COUPLE OF PRETTY CLEVELAND GIRLS COULD WALTZ RIGHT INTO THE CITY...
"LIKE IT WAS--LIKE A NIGHTCLUB.
"IT'S--IT WAS GOOD FOR BUSINESS.
"AND WE THOUGHT--I WILL ALWAYS REMEMBER THIS--WE THOUGHT WE WERE SNEAKING INTO THE MOST DANGEROUS PLACE...
TAKIO
BROADWAY
"MOST PEOPLE WHO SNEAKED INTO THIS PART OF THE COUNTRY WERE DOING IT LOOKING FOR TROUBLE.
COVER
live!
"THEN I REALIZED, ALMOST IMMEDIATELY, IT WAS, IN A LOT OF WAYS, ACTUALLY SAFER IN NEW YORK THAN IT WAS IN CLEVELAND.
"THE FAMILIES KEPT THINGS SAFE AND CLEAN AND RESPECTFUL."
"YOU WANTED TO GO TO SOME SEEDY, CRIME-INFESTED WORLD?"
"WELL, YEAH."
"I DIDN'T KNOW THAT."
"HERE'S ANOTHER THING YOU MIGHT'VE NOT KNOWN ABOUT YOUR MOTHER.
"I HAVE A THING FOR...'BAD' GUYS. LIKE--LIKE YOUR FATHER."

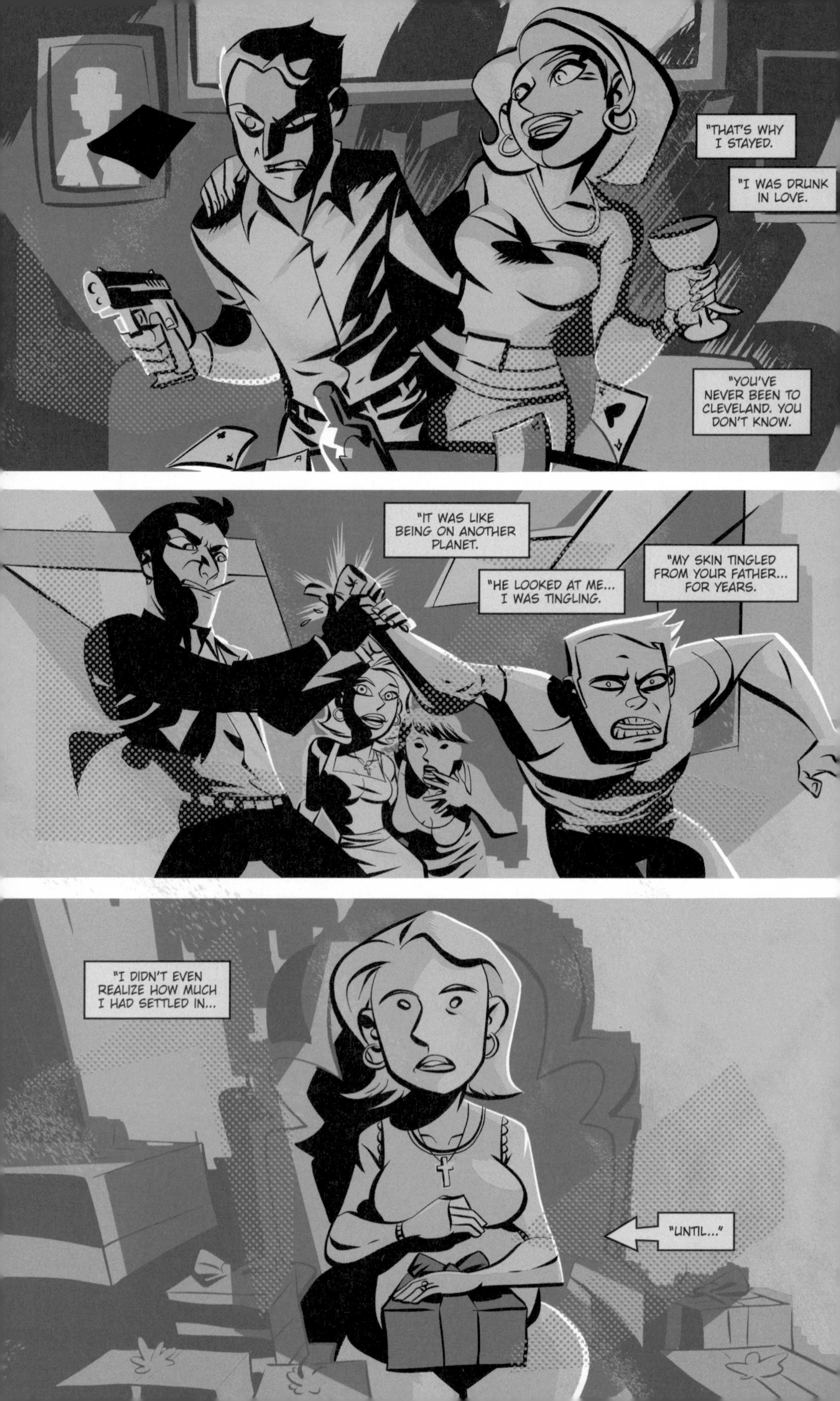
"THAT'S WHY I STAYED.
"I WAS DRUNK IN LOVE.
"YOU'VE NEVER BEEN TO CLEVELAND. YOU DON'T KNOW.
"IT WAS LIKE BEING ON ANOTHER PLANET.
"HE LOOKED AT ME... I WAS TINGLING.
"MY SKIN TINGLED FROM YOUR FATHER... FOR YEARS.
"I DIDN'T EVEN REALIZE HOW MUCH I HAD SETTLED IN...
"UNTIL..."

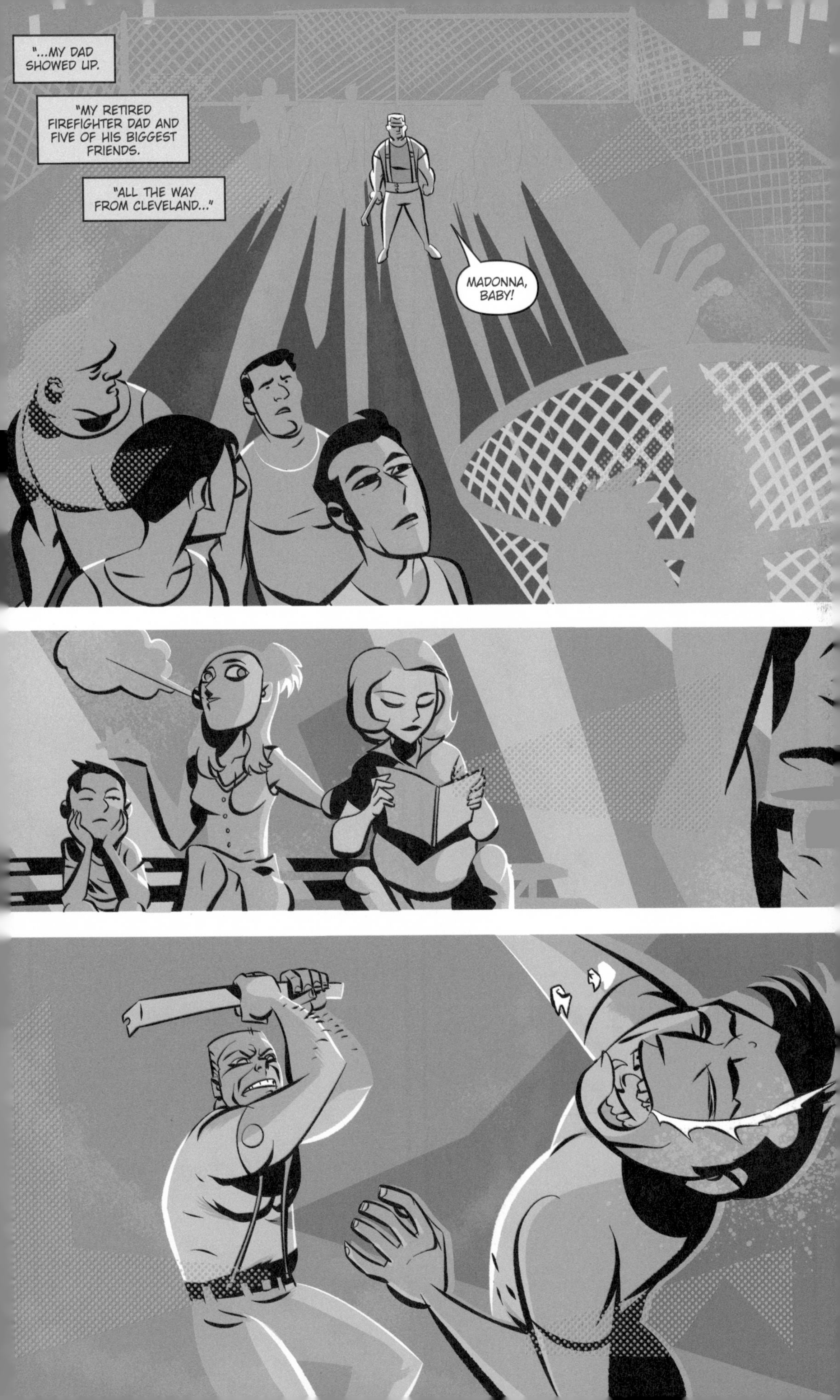
"...MY DAD SHOWED UP.
"MY RETIRED FIREFIGHTER DAD AND FIVE OF HIS BIGGEST FRIENDS.
"ALL THE WAY FROM CLEVELAND..."
MADONNA, BABY!

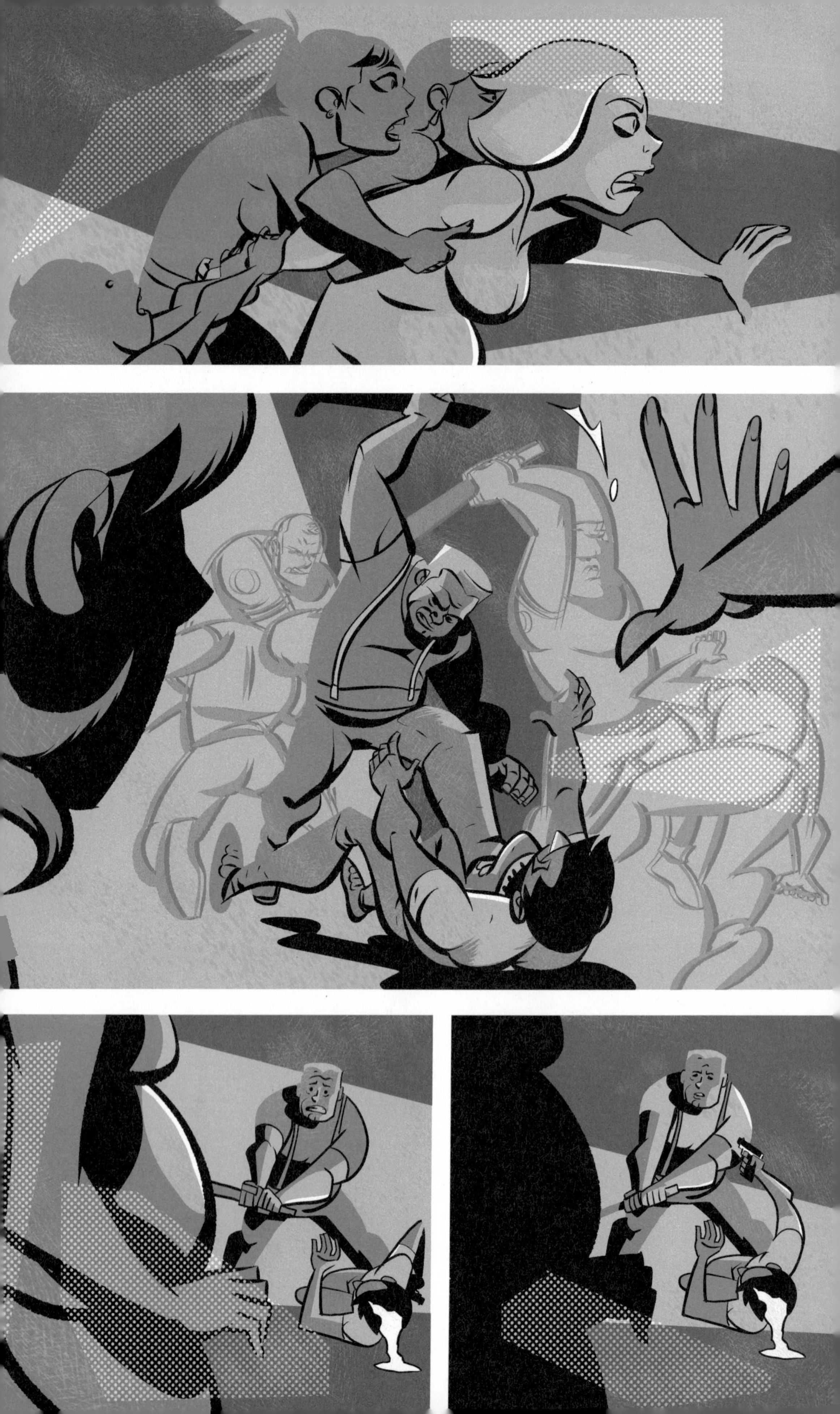

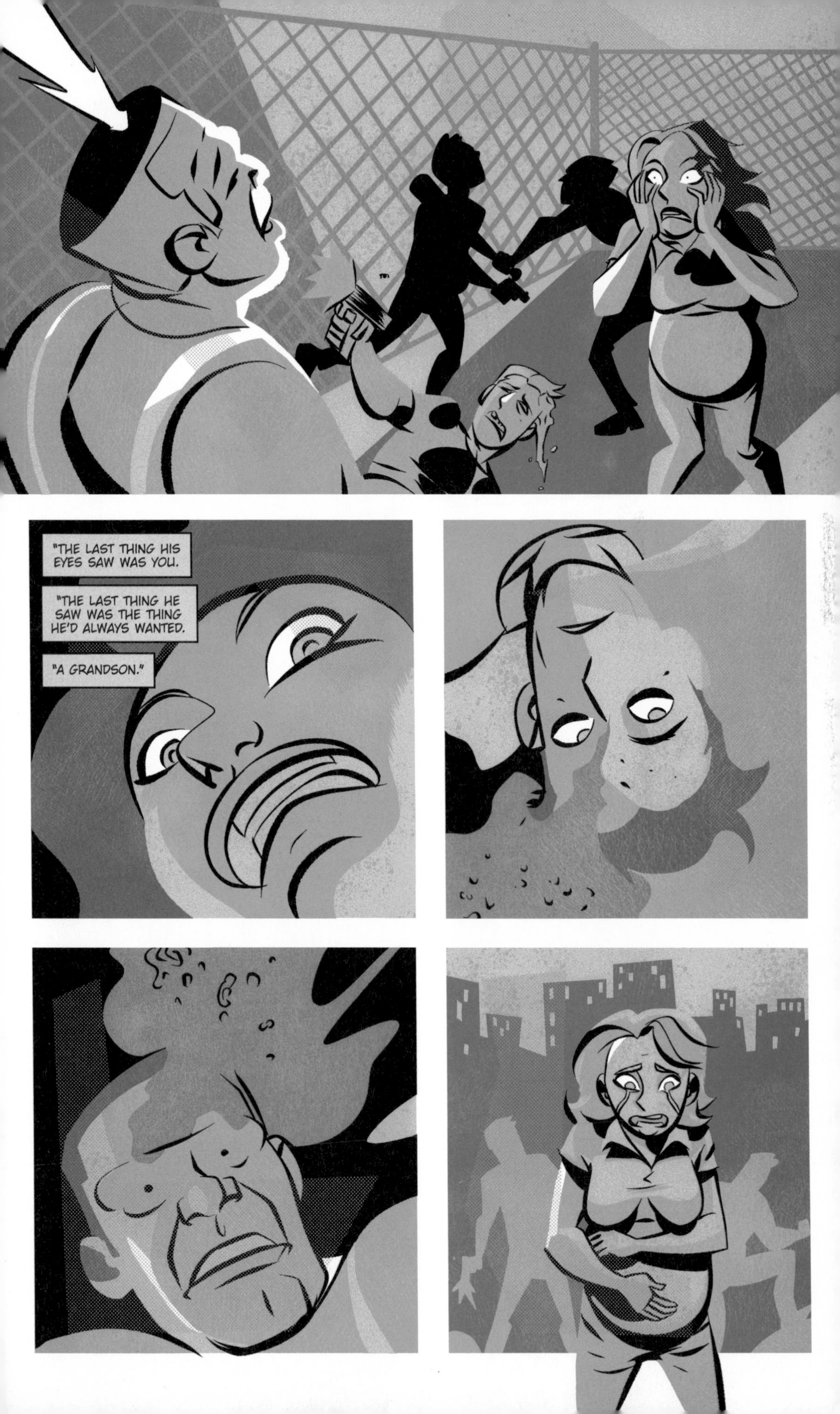
"THE LAST THING HIS EYES SAW WAS YOU.
"THE LAST THING HE SAW WAS THE THING HE'D ALWAYS WANTED.
"A GRANDSON."

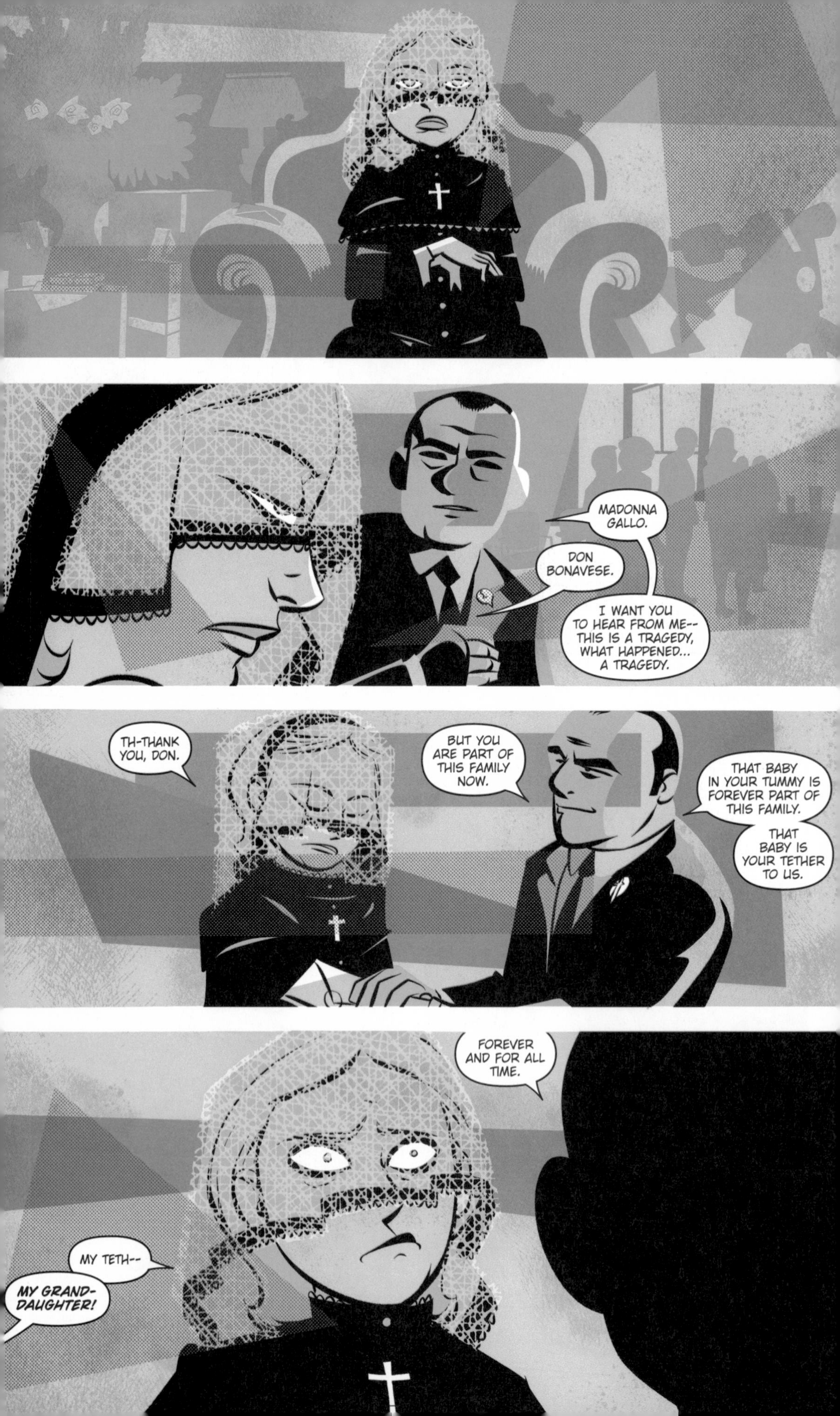
MADONNA GALLO.
DON BONAVESE.
I WANT YOU TO HEAR FROM ME-- THIS IS A TRAGEDY, WHAT HAPPENED... A TRAGEDY.
TH-THANK YOU, DON.
BUT YOU ARE PART OF THIS FAMILY NOW.
THAT BABY IN YOUR TUMMY IS FOREVER PART OF THIS FAMILY.
THAT BABY IS YOUR TETHER TO US.
FOREVER AND FOR ALL TIME.
MY TETH--
MY GRAND-DAUGHTER!

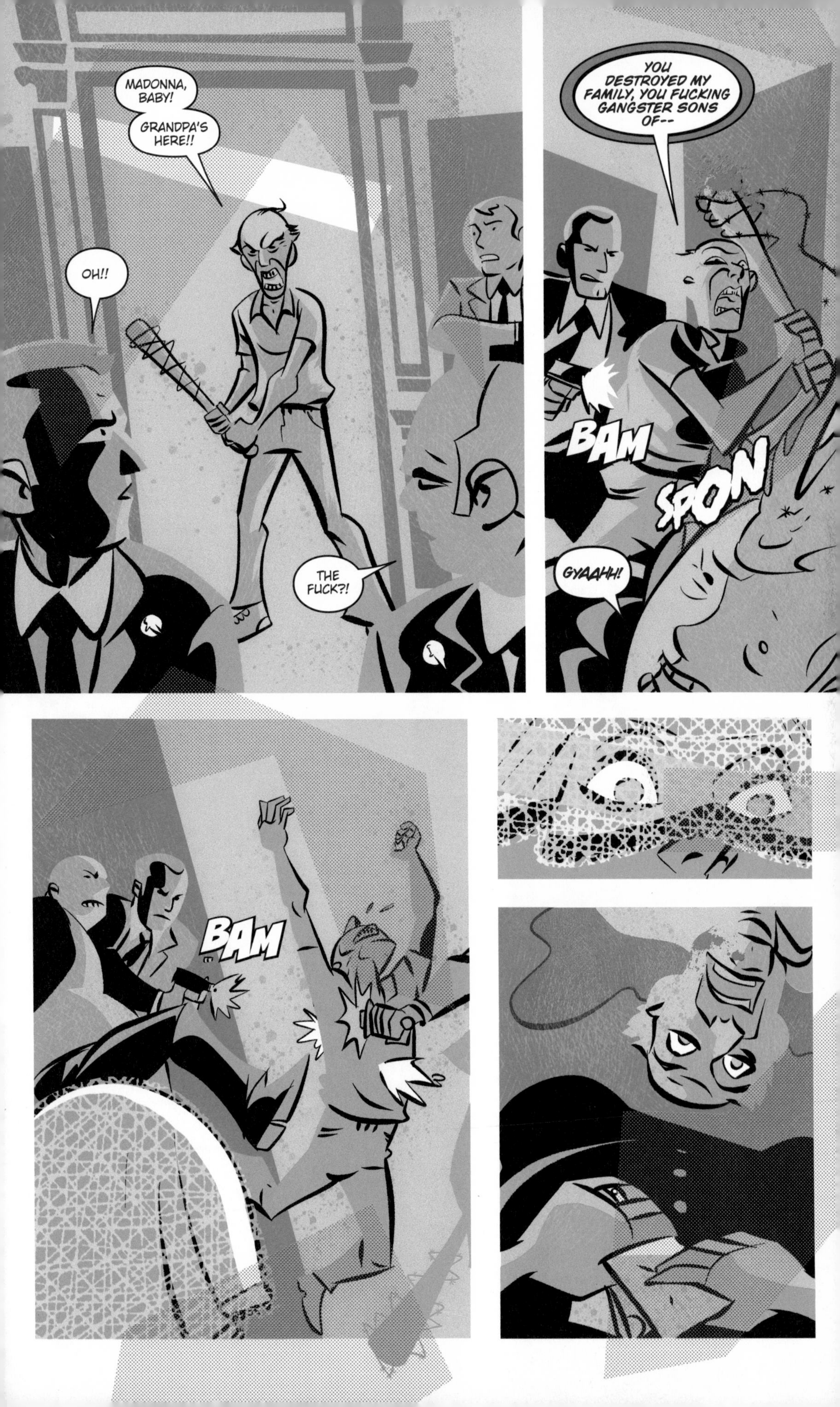

MADONNA, BABY!
GRANDPA'S HERE!!
OH!!
THE FUCK?!
YOU DESTROYED MY FAMILY, YOU FUCKING GANGSTER SONS OF--
BAM
SPON
GYAAHH!
BAM

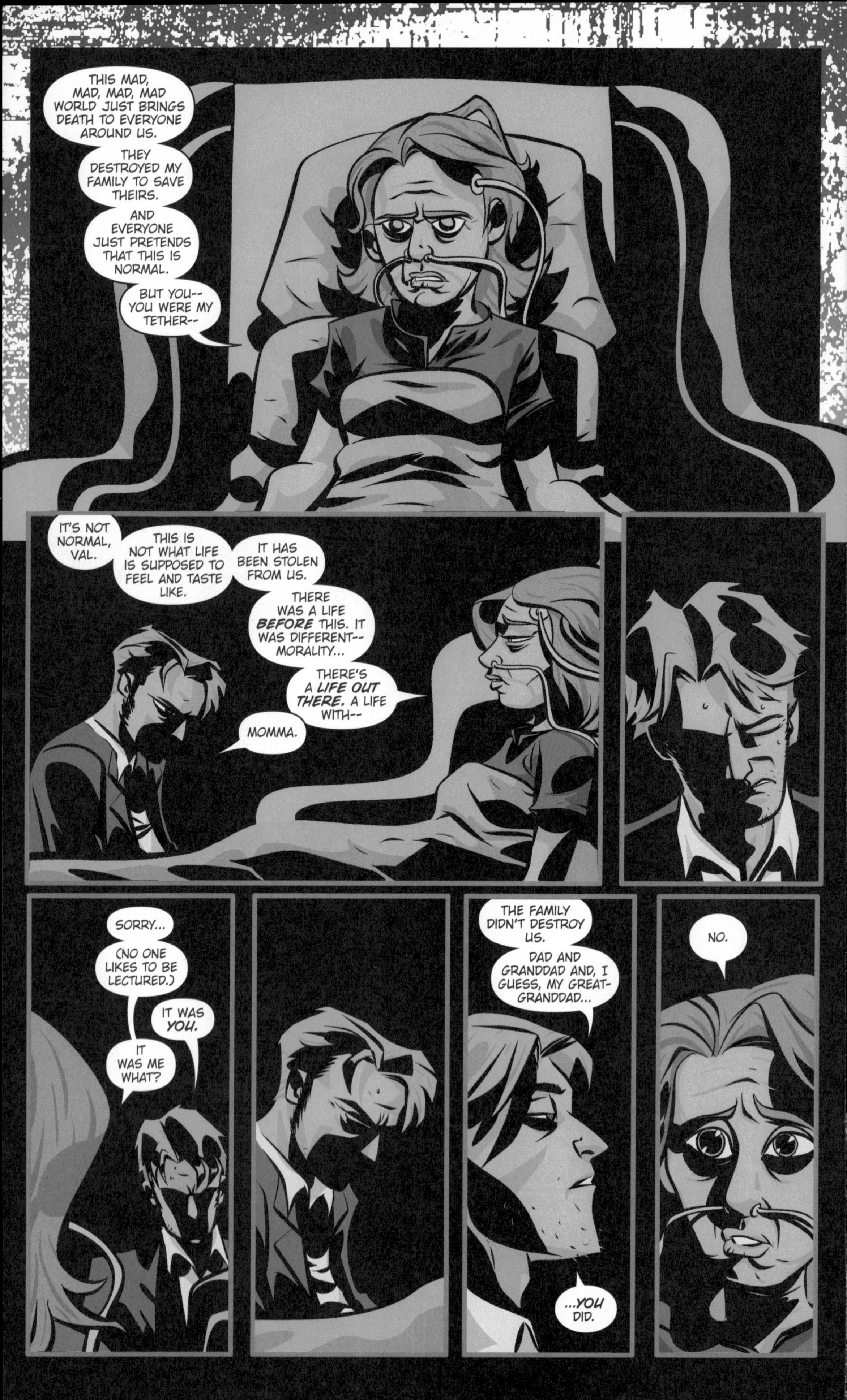
THIS MAD, MAD, MAD, MAD WORLD JUST BRINGS DEATH TO EVERYONE AROUND US.
THEY DESTROYED MY FAMILY TO SAVE THEIRS.
AND EVERYONE JUST PRETENDS THAT THIS IS NORMAL.
BUT YOU-- YOU WERE MY TETHER--
IT'S NOT NORMAL, VAL.
THIS IS NOT WHAT LIFE IS SUPPOSED TO FEEL AND TASTE LIKE.
IT HAS BEEN STOLEN FROM US.
THERE WAS A LIFE ***BEFORE*** THIS. IT WAS DIFFERENT-- MORALITY...
THERE'S A ***LIFE OUT THERE.*** A LIFE WITH--
MOMMA.
SORRY...
(NO ONE LIKES TO BE LECTURED.)
IT WAS ***YOU.***
IT WAS ME WHAT?
THE FAMILY DIDN'T DESTROY US.
DAD AND GRANDDAD AND, I GUESS, MY GREAT-GRANDDAD...
...***YOU*** DID.
NO.

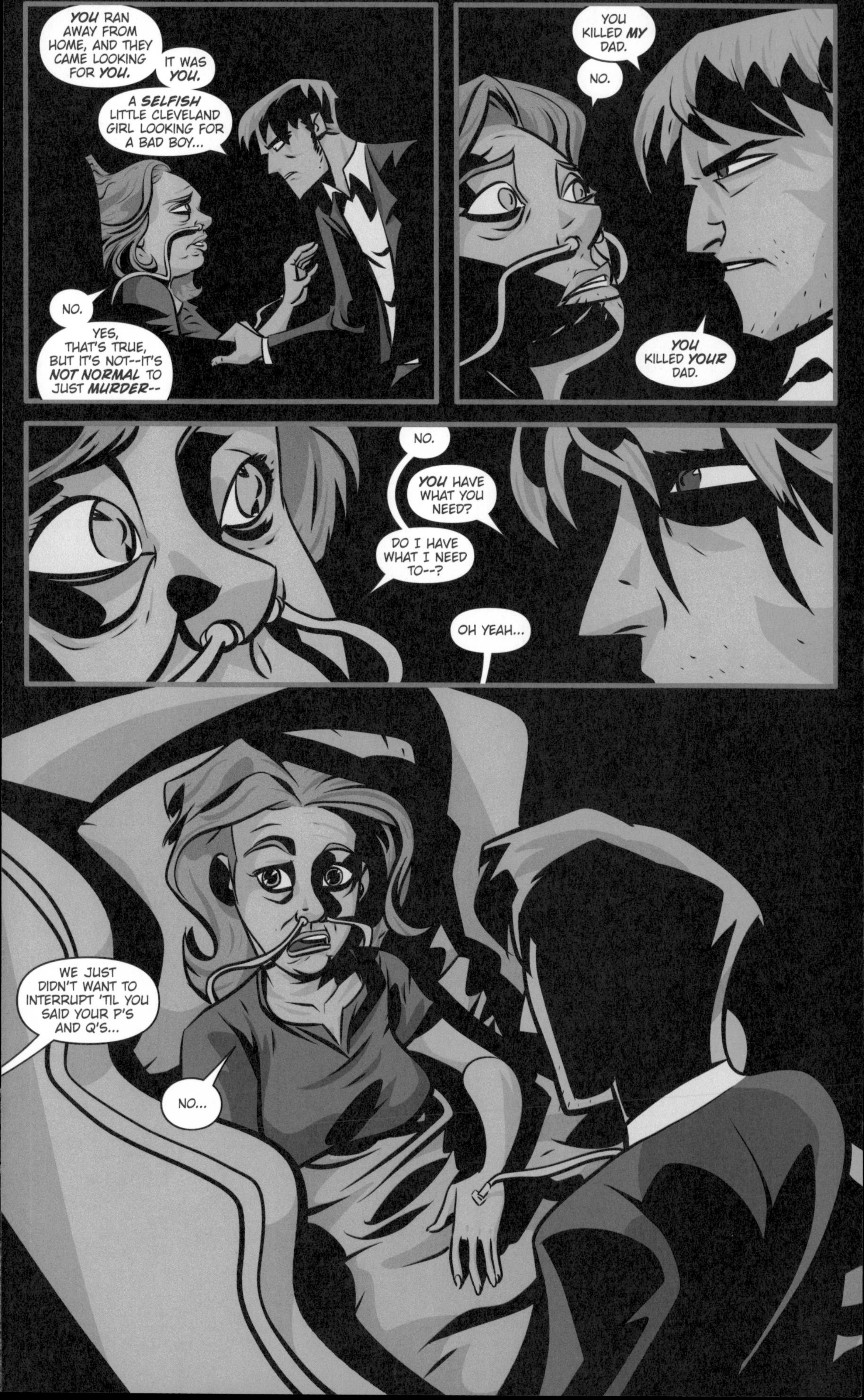
YOU RAN AWAY FROM HOME, AND THEY CAME LOOKING FOR YOU.
IT WAS YOU.
A SELFISH LITTLE CLEVELAND GIRL LOOKING FOR A BAD BOY...
NO.
YES, THAT'S TRUE, BUT IT'S NOT--IT'S NOT NORMAL TO JUST MURDER--
YOU KILLED MY DAD.
NO.
YOU KILLED YOUR DAD.
NO.
YOU HAVE WHAT YOU NEED?
DO I HAVE WHAT I NEED TO--?
OH YEAH...
WE JUST DIDN'T WANT TO INTERRUPT 'TIL YOU SAID YOUR P'S AND Q'S...
NO...

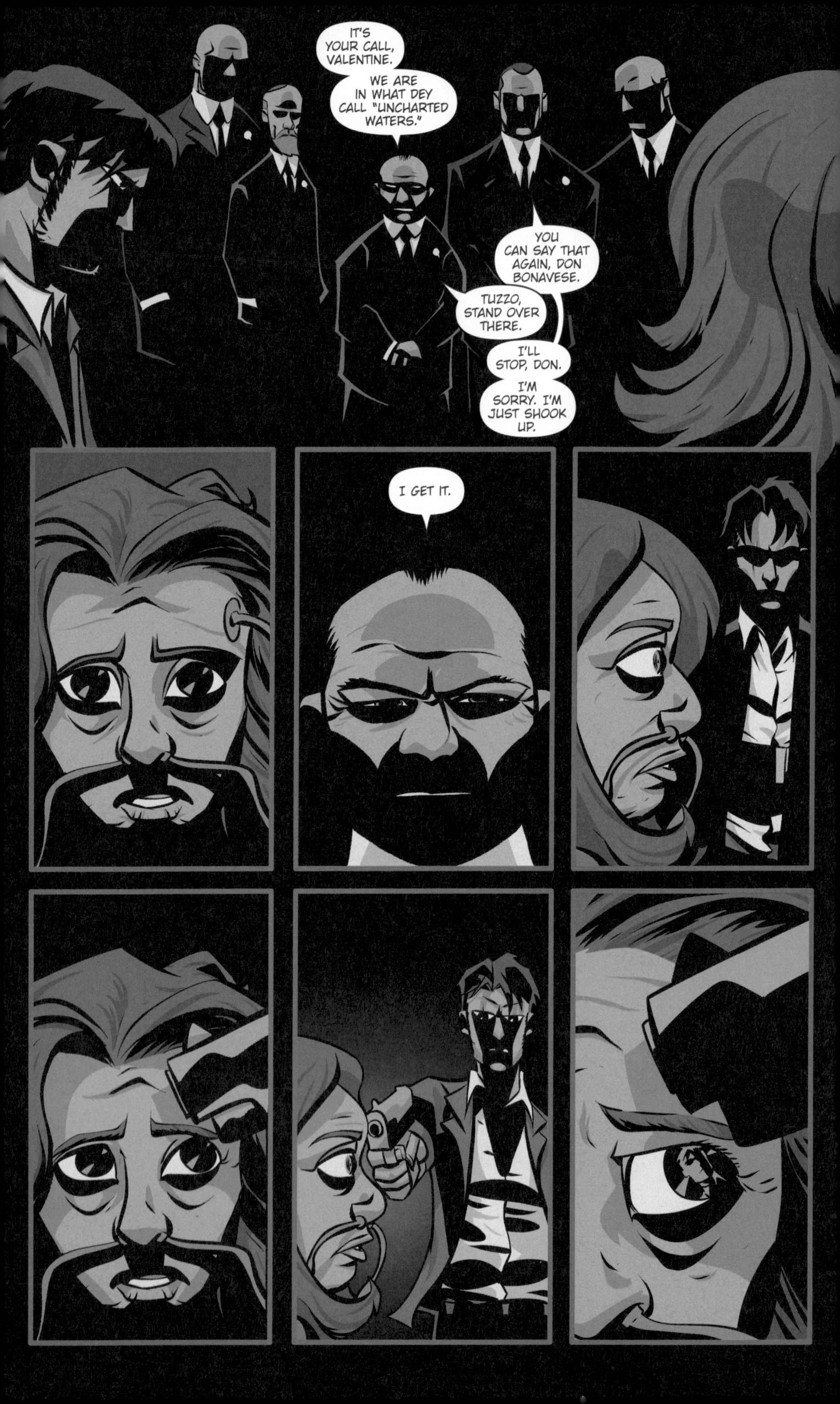
IT'S YOUR CALL, VALENTINE.
WE ARE IN WHAT DEY CALL "UNCHARTED WATERS."
YOU CAN SAY THAT AGAIN, DON BONAVESE.
TUZZO, STAND OVER THERE.
I'LL STOP, DON.
I'M SORRY. I'M JUST SHOOK UP.
I GET IT.

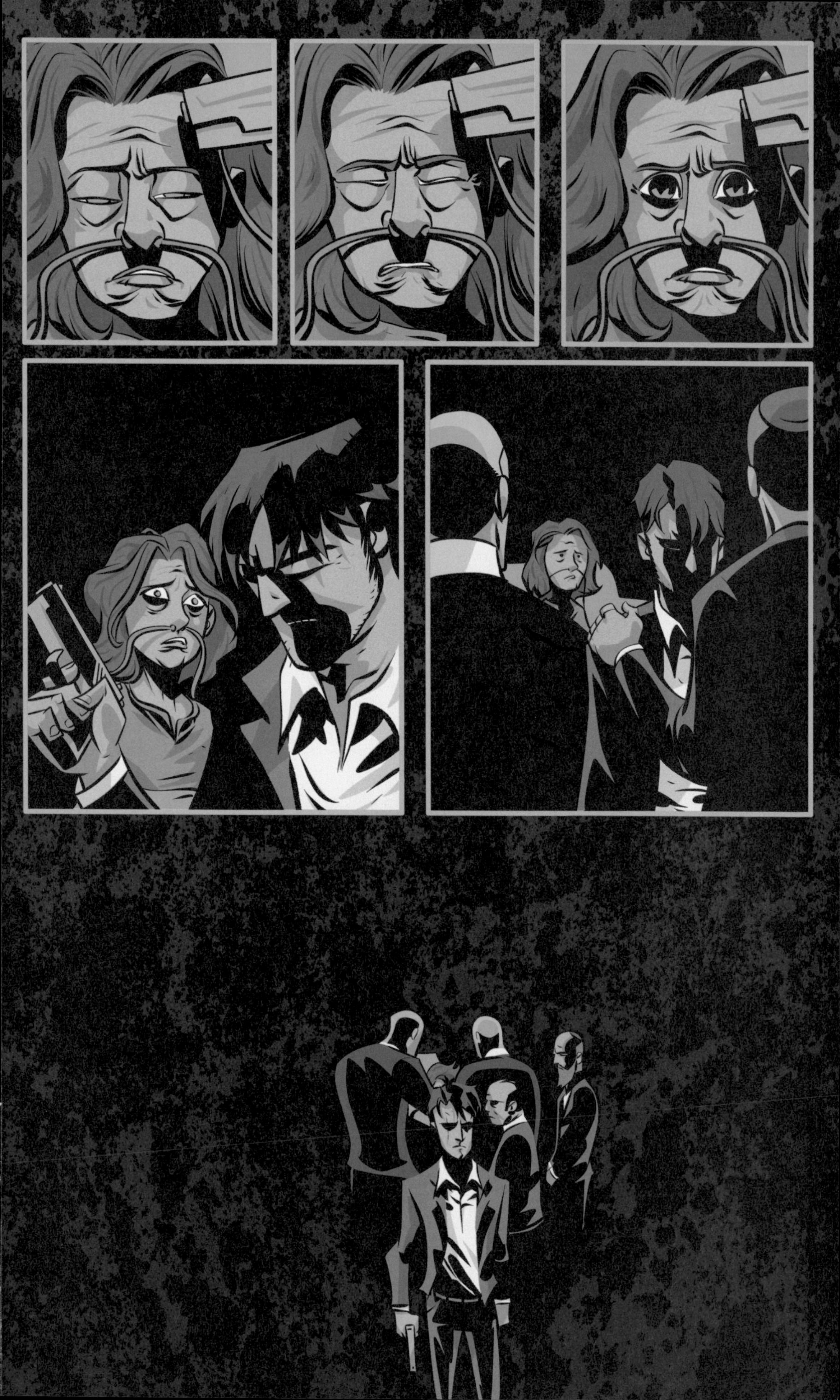

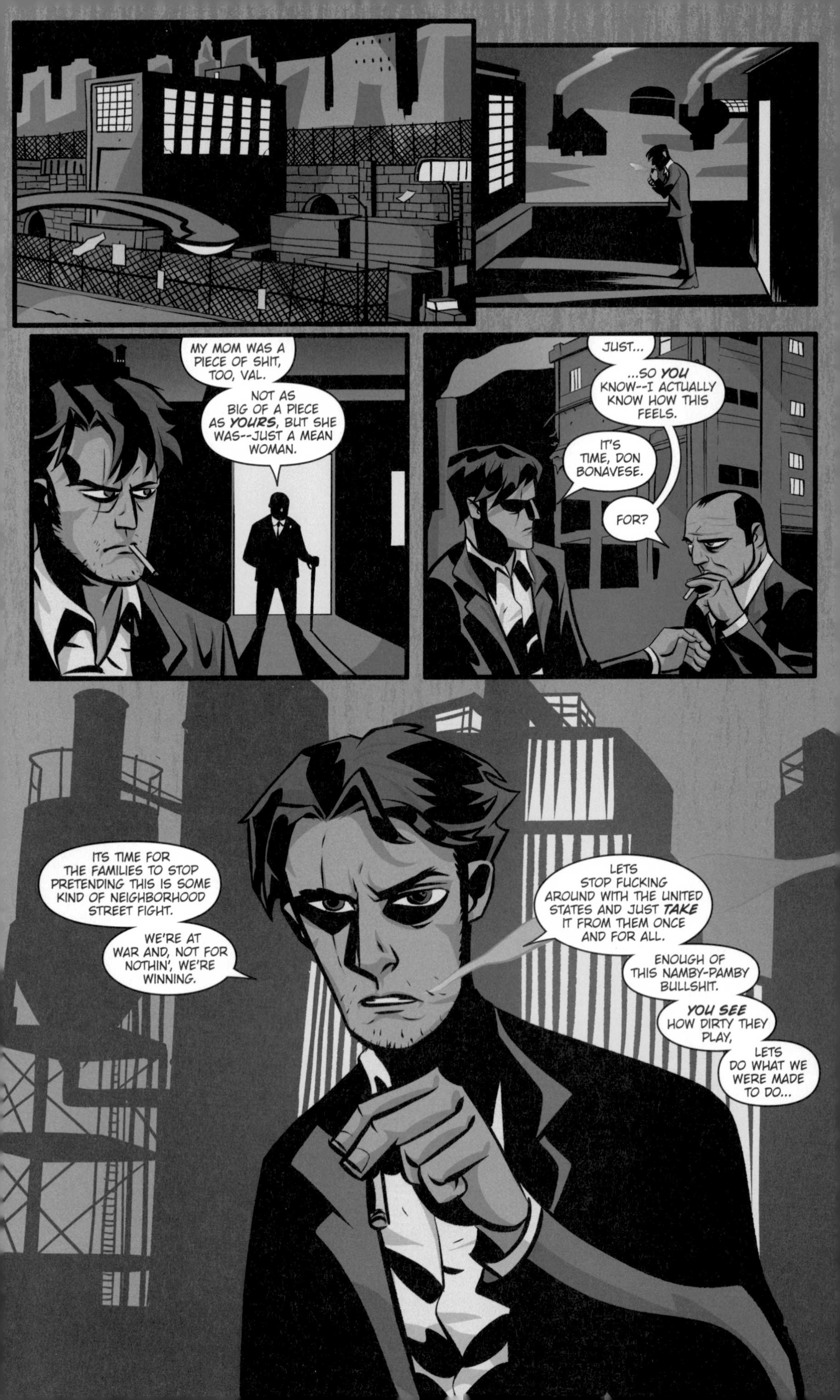
MY MOM WAS A PIECE OF SHIT, TOO, VAL.
NOT AS BIG OF A PIECE AS YOURS, BUT SHE WAS--JUST A MEAN WOMAN.
JUST...
...SO YOU KNOW--I ACTUALLY KNOW HOW THIS FEELS.
IT'S TIME, DON BONAVESE.
FOR?
ITS TIME FOR THE FAMILIES TO STOP PRETENDING THIS IS SOME KIND OF NEIGHBORHOOD STREET FIGHT.
WE'RE AT WAR AND, NOT FOR NOTHIN', WE'RE WINNING.
LETS STOP FUCKING AROUND WITH THE UNITED STATES AND JUST TAKE IT FROM THEM ONCE AND FOR ALL.
ENOUGH OF THIS NAMBY-PAMBY BULLSHIT.
YOU SEE HOW DIRTY THEY PLAY,
LETS DO WHAT WE WERE MADE TO DO...

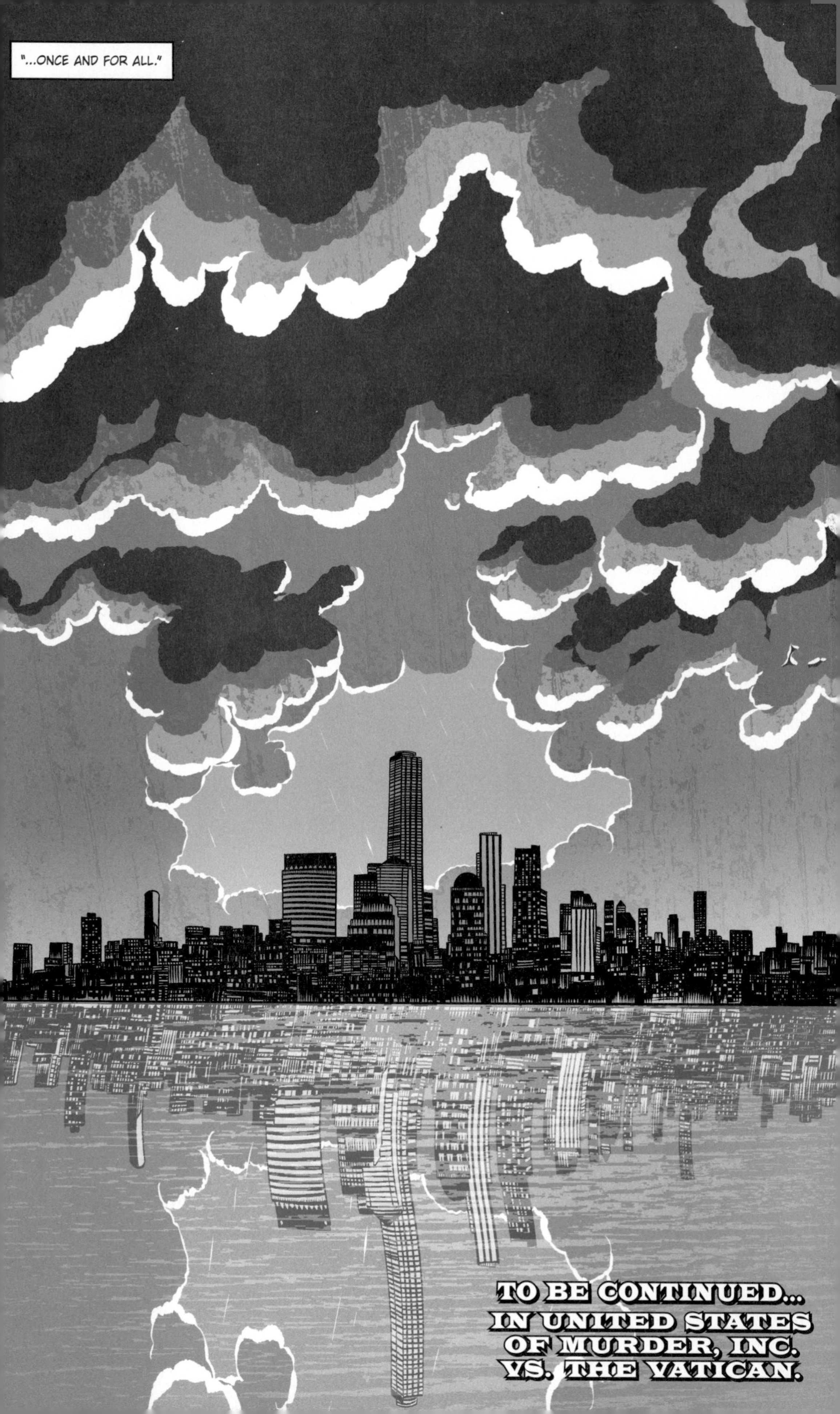
"...ONCE AND FOR ALL."
TO BE CONTINUED... IN UNITED STATES OF MURDER, INC. VS. THE VATICAN.

MICHAEL AVON OEMING sketchbook

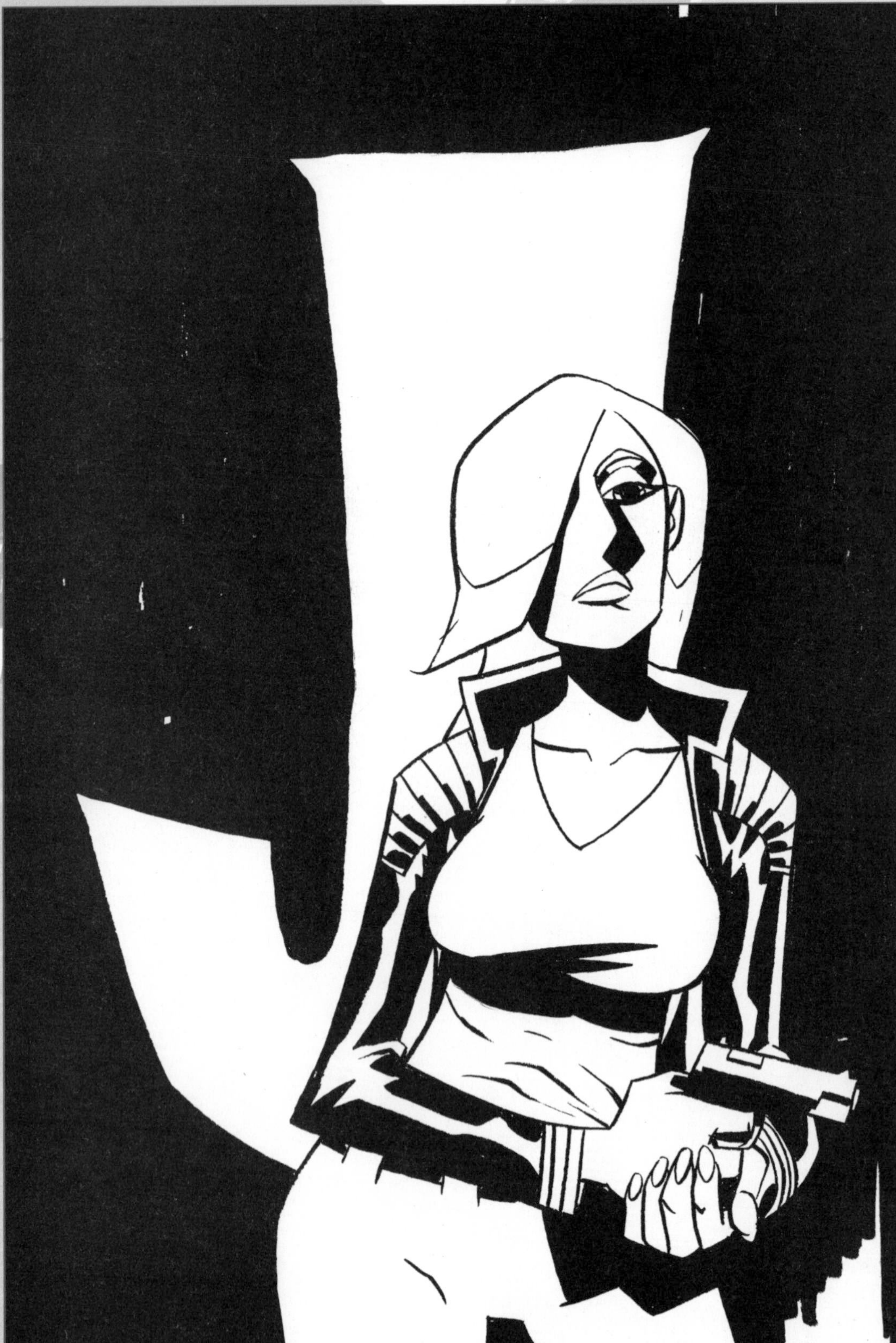
AVO 18

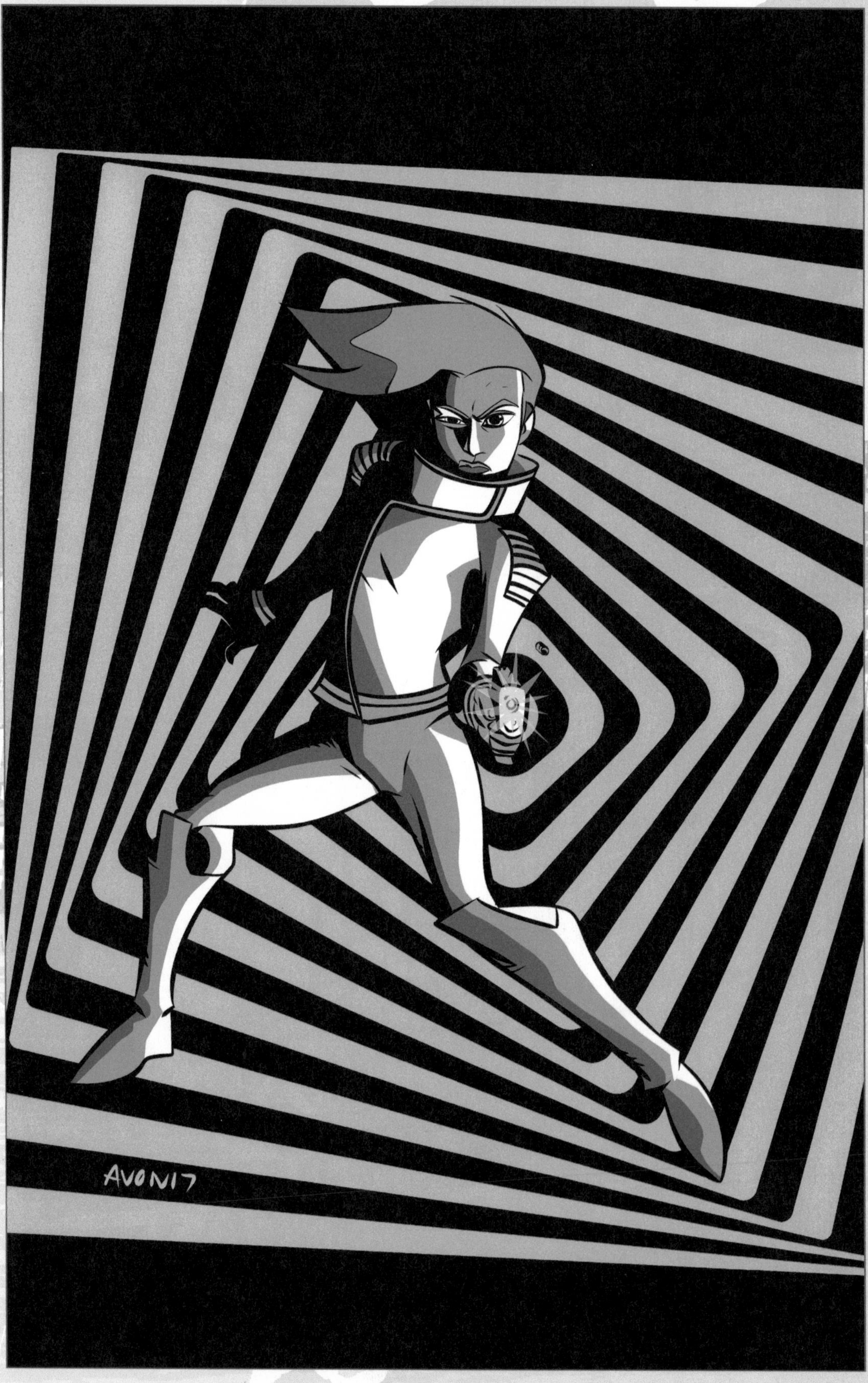
AVON17

Jagger sketch and promotional art.

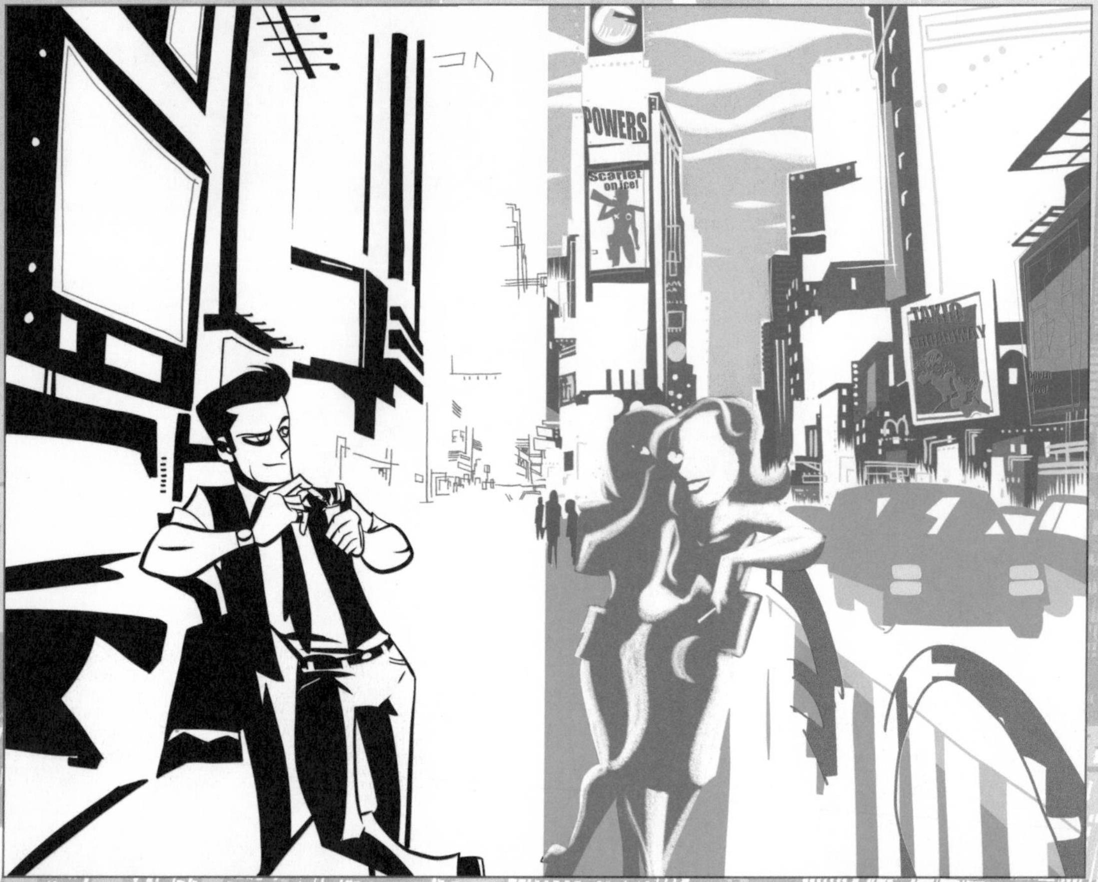
POWERS
Scarlet on ice!

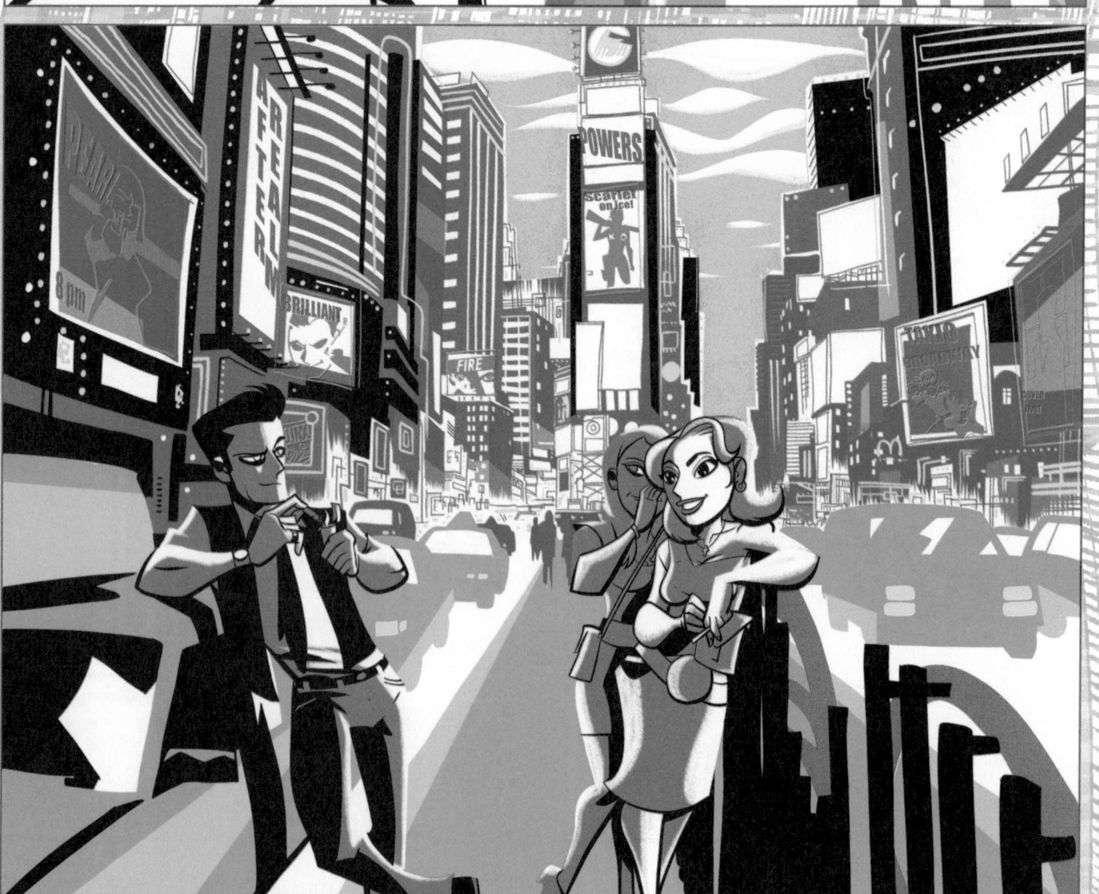
PEARL
8 pm
AFTER
REALM
BRILLIANT
FIRE
POWERS
Scarlet on ice!

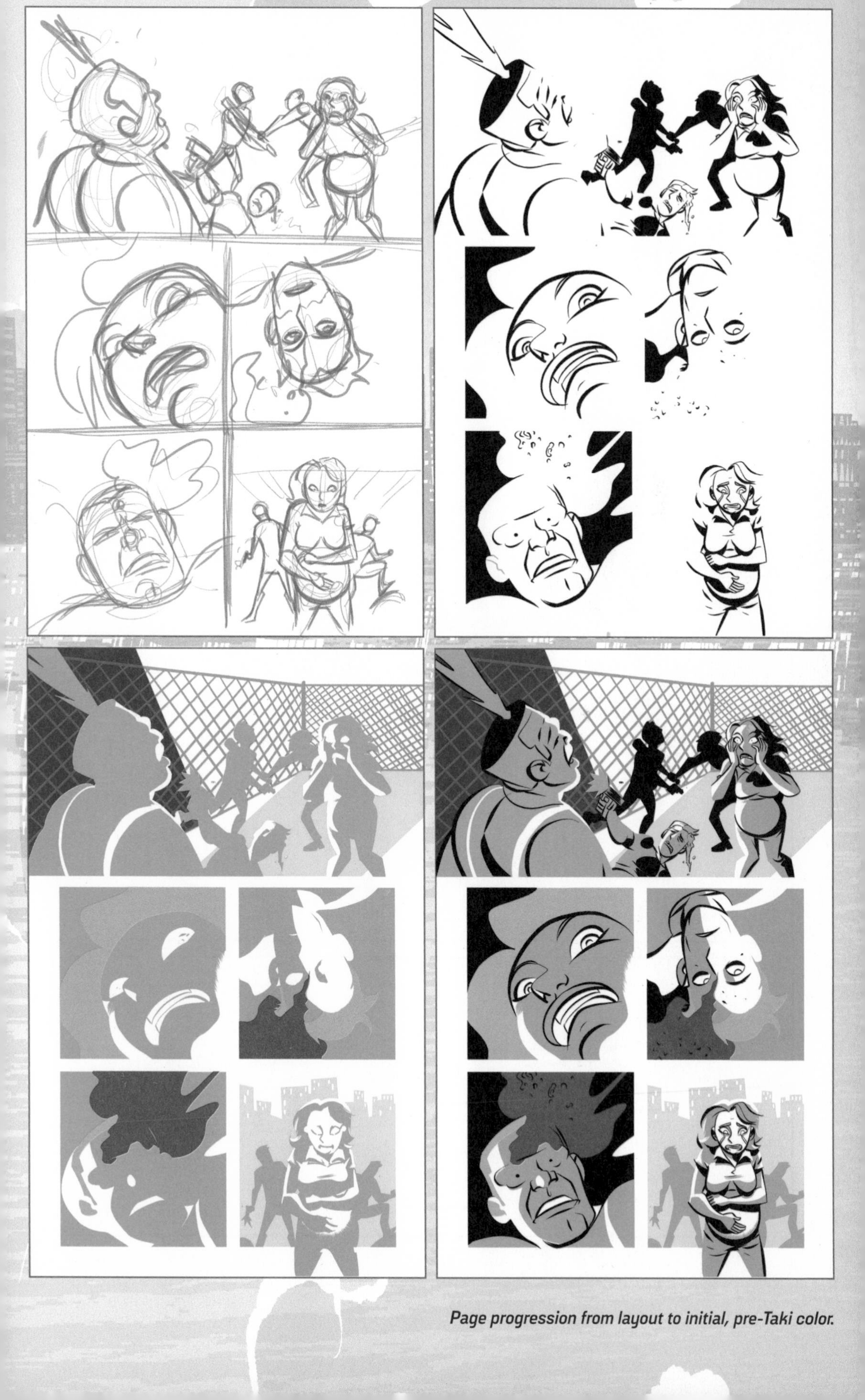

Page progression from layout to initial, pre-Taki color.

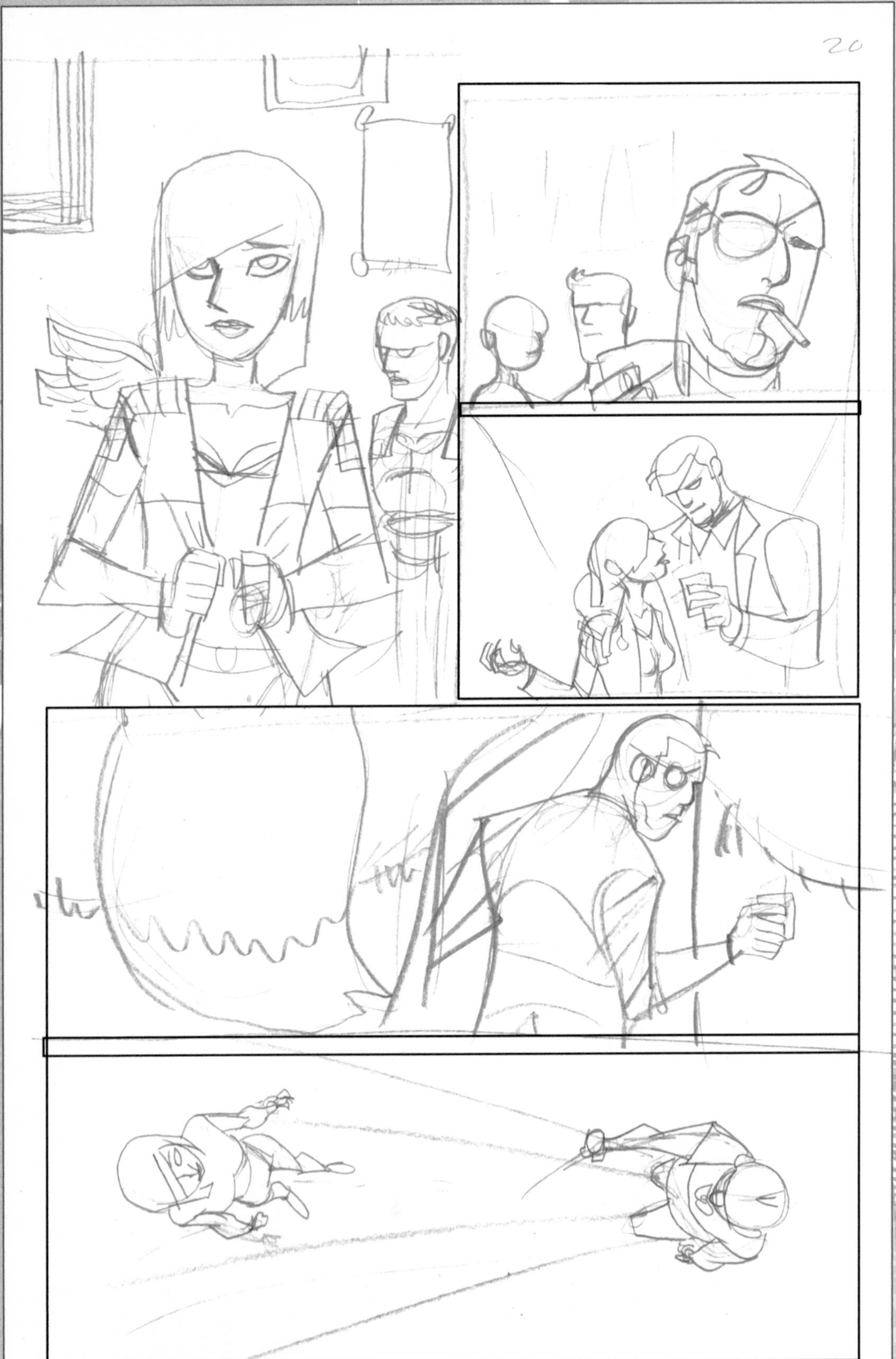
20

Page layout from issue #1.

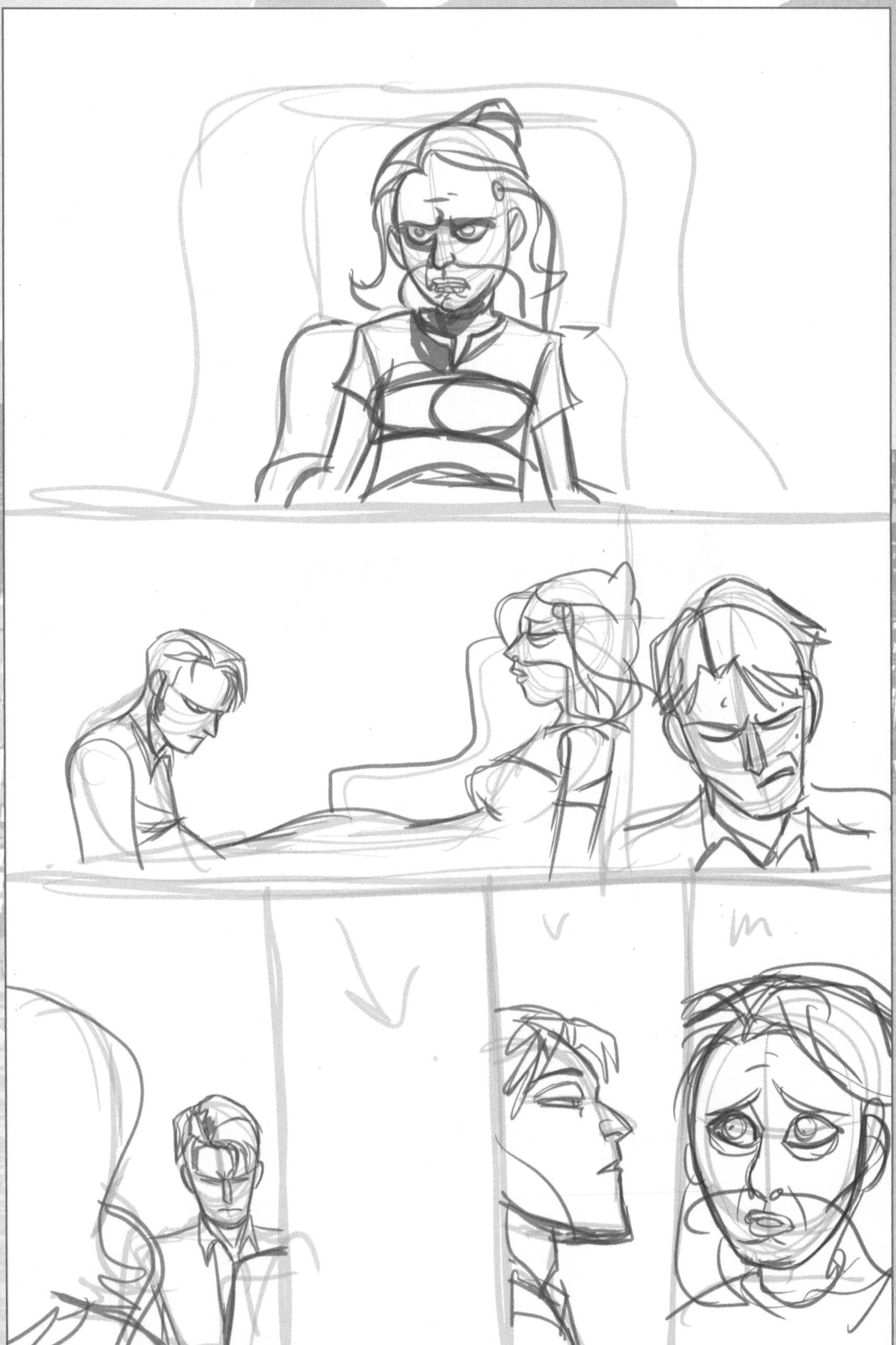

Page layout from issue #6.

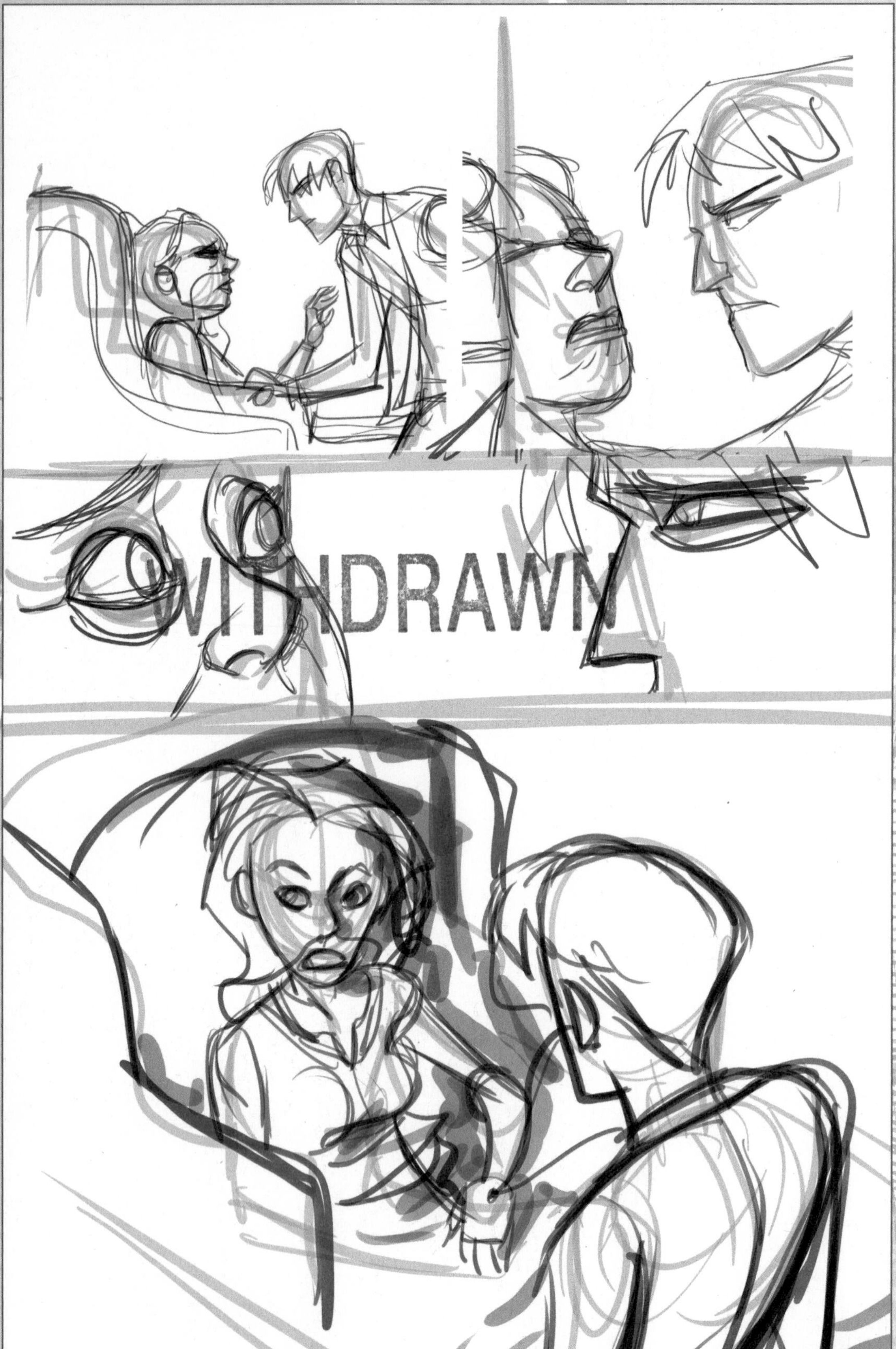

Page layout from issue #6.